JAMES P. COYNE

AIRPOWER In the GULF

An Air Force Association Book

Aerospace Education Foundation
1501 Lee Highway, Arlington, Virginia 22209-1198

James P. Coyne is a veteran fighter pilot. After retiring from the US Air Force as a colonel in 1984, he was a senior editor for Air Force Magazine and later became editor in chief of *Signal* Magazine. His previous book, *Strike Eagles*, was published by Avon in 1990.

Senior Research Associate: Col. T. C. Skanchy, USAF, Ret.

Maps, charts, design, production, and additional research
by the Air Force Association Gulf War Project team.

ISBN 0-9608492-1-1

Contents

Foreword

The Persian Gulf War of 1991 was barely two weeks old when the Air Force Association and the Aerospace Education Foundation committed themselves to the resources and effort required for this book. Iraq had not yet fled the field, but the outstanding performance of the US armed forces and their coalition partners was already apparent. Airpower had been strikingly impressive from the start.

It was a tremendous story. We wanted it to be told properly, and by people who understood it. Accordingly, we found James P. Coyne, a veteran fighter pilot and author, to write that story and organized a Gulf War Project team from our own staff to assist him.

This book is the result of that effort. Thousands of Air Force Association members helped make it possible with their contributions. We are also grateful to the many airmen of all grades who shared their experiences with us. Their recollections make *Airpower in the Gulf* more than a cold recital of facts and figures.

As the title indicates, our book is mostly about airpower. That is the particular part of the story we set out to tell. At the same time, we wish to express our highest regard for those who served at sea and on the ground. We hope that the account presented here does justice to the men and women of all services and from all of the coalition nations whose bravery and achievements led to victory in the Gulf.

O. R. Crawford
President
Air Force Association

Gerald V. Hasler
President
Aerospace Education Foundation

To Those Who Didn't Come Back.

US Airpower at a Glance

A-6E Intruder. Navy medium-attack fighter, in service for almost thirty years.

A-10 Thunderbolt II. USAF attack aircraft, specializing in antiarmor and close air support missions.

AH-1 Sea Cobra. Marine Corps attack helicopter.

AH-64 Apache. Army's primary attack helicopter.

AV-8B Harrier. Marine Corps jump jet.

B-52 Stratofortress. USAF heavy bomber, operational since the 1950s.

C-5A/B Galaxy. USAF's largest airlifter, able to carry outsize cargo such as tanks.

C-130 Hercules. USAF in-theater airlifter, but this rugged turboprop has many variants: the **AC-130** gunship, the **MC-130** special operations aircraft, the **EC-130H** communications jammer, the **EC 130E** airborne command and control and psychological operations aircraft, and the **HC-130** aerial refueling aircraft.

C-141 StarLifter. USAF long-range airlifter, carries oversize but not outsize cargo.

E-2C Hawkeye. Navy airborne early warning aircraft.

E-3 Airborne Warning and Control System (AWACS). Radar in rotating dome on top looks deep into enemy airspace, enables USAF to manage the air battle.

E-8A Joint STARS. USAF deep-looking radar aircraft for surveillance and control of the ground battle.

EA-6B Prowler. Navy electronic warfare and tactical jamming aircraft.

F-4G Wild Weasel. Hunts and destroys enemy radars and antiaircraft defenses.

F-14 Tomcat. Navy's premier fleet defense interceptor.

F-15 Eagle. USAF's top air-superiority fighter. **F-15E** variant equipped for deep interdiction at night and in bad weather.

F-16 Fighting Falcon. Multirole USAF fighter, used mostly for ground attack, but also quite good in air-to-air role.

F-111 "Aardvark." Low-flying, swing-wing USAF deep interdiction fighter. Aging, but still very effective. The **EF-111 Raven** variant is an electronic jammer.

F-117. USAF Stealth fighter, operational since 1985, but existence not revealed officially until 1988.

F/A-18 Hornet. Multirole Navy and Marine Corps strike fighter.

HH-3E Jolly Green Giant. USAF rescue helicopter.

KC-10 Extender. Dual-role USAF cargo/tanker aircraft.

KC-135 Stratotanker. USAF aerial refueling aircraft.

MH-53J Pave Low. USAF special operations helicopter.

MH-60G Pave Hawk. USAF rescue helicopter.

RC-135 Rivet Joint. Shadowy USAF electronic surveillance aircraft.

RF-4. Unarmed USAF multisensor reconnaissance aircraft.

TR-1/U-2. USAF high-altitude surveillance aircraft. Structurally identical, but with some internal variations, mostly in electronics. TR-1 is newer.

Source: *Air Force Magazine.*

A Guide to Acronyms

AAA Antiaircraft artillery

ABCCC Airborne Battlefield Command and Control Center

AFLC Air Force Logistics Command

AFRES Air Force Reserve

AFB Air Force Base

ANG Air National Guard

AOR (CENTCOM's) Area of Responsibility

ARCENT CENTCOM's Army component

ATO Air tasking order

AWACS Airborne Warning and Control System

BDA Bomb-damage assessment

C3 Command, Control, and Communications

CAFMS Computer-aided force management system

CAS Close air support

CBU Cluster bomb unit

CENTAF CENTCOM's Air Force component

CENTCOM US Central Command

CINC Commander in Chief

CRAF Civil Reserve Air Fleet

DOD Department of Defense

ECM Electronic countermeasures

FLIR Forward-looking infrared

GPS Navstar Global Positioning System

HARM High-Speed Antiradiation Missile

HUD Head-up display

IADS Integrated Air Defense System

IFF Identification, Friend or Foe

INS Inertial navigation system

IR Infrared

JCS Joint Chiefs of Staff

JTF Joint task force

KTO Kuwait theater of operations

LANTIRN Low-Altitude Navigation and Targeting Infrared for Night system

LGB Laser-guided bomb

MAC Military Airlift Command

MARCENT CENTCOM's Marine component

MFD Multifunction display

MRE Meal, Ready to Eat

NAVCENT CENTCOM's Navy component

PGM Precision-guided munition

RAM Radar-absorbent material

RCS Radar cross section

RPV Remotely piloted vehicle

SAC Strategic Air Command

SAM Surface-to-air missile

SAR Synthetic aperture radar; also search and rescue

SEAD Suppression of enemy air defenses

TAC Tactical Air Command

TEL Transporter erector launcher

TFR Terrain-following radar

TFW Tactical Fighter Wing (G=Group; S=Squadron)

TLAM Tomahawk land attack missile

TOT Time on target

TRW Tactical Reconnaissance Wing (G=Group; S=Squadron)

USAF US Air Force

USAFE US Air Forces in Europe

WSO Weapon system officer

The armed forces use acronyms by the thousands. Unfortunately, it is almost impossible to write—or read—above the superficial level about military operations without reference to acronyms and abbreviations, because that is how the armed forces refer to numerous weapons, functions, and organizations. This list should see you through *Airpower in the Gulf*. It should also be of help in your further reading.

A Word From the Air Boss

When I think of the Gulf War, I think first of the fear, the death, and the destruction. Those who talk of Operation Desert Storm as if it were some kind of sporting event are sadly wrong. Those who saw it as an antiseptic technology demonstration are wrong, too.

The technology worked superbly. The doctrine and planning were right on the mark. But it is the people—the aircrews, the combat troops, and all the support people giving 101 percent effort—that I remember most.

Between August 1990 and March 1991, the armed forces of the allied coalition did much to change the conventional thinking about how to prepare for and fight a war. We will be reflecting for a long time on the lessons learned.

It was, of course, gratifying to me that airpower played such a significant role in the outcome. I am proud of what the US Air Force accomplished, but I want to add quickly that I am also proud of the airmen from the Navy, Marine Corps, Army, and the coalition forces.

Their story is one of bravery and achievement. Those who say the task was easy or risk-free simply do not know what they are talking about.

Of all the books I've seen on the Gulf War, this one is the best and most detailed account so far of what happened in the air campaign and how it looked and felt to the airmen in the skies over Iraq.

Lt. Gen. Charles A. Horner
Joint Forces Air Component Commander

Forecast at Camp David

On the eve of the Persian Gulf War, President Bush summoned the Joint Chiefs of Staff to Camp David to hear their views on how it would go. The Air Force's Gen. Merrill A. McPeak "told me exactly what to expect from airpower" and was so upbeat about it that the President suspected him of overstating his case, Mr. Bush recalled later.

As it turned out, "General McPeak, like the rest of the Air Force, was right on target.... Lesson number one from the Gulf War is the value of airpower," the President declared.

From James W. Canan, "Lesson Number One,"
AIR FORCE Magazine, October 1991.

1. Airpower Opens the War

A shadowy F-117A refuels from an aerial tanker. As H-hour approached, these stealthy fighters slipped unseen through the darkness to strike Saddam's military stronghold.

Minutes before H-hour, helicopters and Stealth fighters slashed open a gap in the Iraqi defenses.

The moon had set. Layers of clouds swirled over much of Saudi Arabia and northward into Iraq. It was Jan. 17, 1991, and the Gulf War was about to begin. H-hour was 3 a.m., Baghdad time.

The execute order for Operation Desert Storm had gone out to the coalition air forces. The first two days of the war had been planned in detail. A massive air tasking order (ATO) specified exactly what each aircraft in the allied strike force would do.

In the early hours of January 17, the coalition would send 668 US, British, French, and Saudi Arabian aircraft, flying blacked out, streaking into Iraq to take Saddam Hussein and his armed forces by surprise.[1]

After midnight, Lt. Gen. Charles A. Horner—commander of Central Command Air Forces and "air boss" for the coalition—his Director of Operations, Maj. Gen. John A. Corder, and Brig. Gen. Buster C. Glosson, Director of Campaign Plans, gathered in the Tactical Air Control Center in the basement of the Royal Saudi Air Force Headquarters building in downtown Riyadh.

They had high confidence in the plan and the strike force, but they somberly contemplated how many coalition aircraft and crews might be lost by morning.

"I knew our people could execute the plan," Horner said. "But I also knew the probability was very high that we might lose several of them before it was over. It was tough to deal with that."[2]

Jet engines were already spooling up on the ramp at Riyadh Royal Saudi Air Base, less than two miles away. H-hour drew closer. From air bases across the Arabian peninsula and from carriers in the Red Sea and the Persian Gulf, pilots launched into the night and formed up in the air, well beyond the limits of Iraqi radar coverage.

Halfway around the world, US officers in the Pentagon awaited word that the war had begun. At H-hour, it would be 7 p.m., January 16, in Washington.

Up From Khamis Mushait

Deep in Saudi Arabia, at an air base called Khamis Mushait, high in the coastal mountains near the Red Sea, Air Force Maj. Gregory A. Feest scanned the cockpit displays of his F-117 Stealth fighter.

Khamis Mushait was the operating location for the 37th Tactical Fighter Wing, which had deployed to the Gulf from its secluded base at Tonopah, Nev. It was the only wing in the US Air Force that had the shadowy F-117 "Black Jet." In fact, the Air Force had not admitted the fighter existed until 1988. Feest was in the wing's 415th Tactical Fighter Squadron.

Satisfied all systems were "in the green," he pushed the throttles on his left console forward to their stops, released the brakes, and felt the airplane lunge forward. As runway lights flashed by on either side of the cockpit, Feest pulled back on the control stick and lifted his craft into the air.

Suddenly, he was alone in the night, with only the scattered lights of villages in the mountains and desert visible below him. Feest's radios were switched on but soundless. The strike force was keeping strict radio silence, well aware that Iraqi air de-

[1] "Reaching Globally, Reaching Powerfully: the United States Air Force in the Gulf War," USAF white paper, September 1991.

[2] Lt. Gen. Charles A. Horner, interview, Jan. 3, 1992.

USAF Photo by SSgt. Scott P. Stewart

fense centers were listening for any hint of the start of the attack.

Behind Feest, nine other pilots lifted their F-117s at precisely-timed intervals. One of them, Feest's wingman, would join up and fly with him to their tanker on the Nighthawk refueling track, which ran most of the length of Saudi Arabia.

After refueling, each would drop off the tanker at the north end of the track, not far from the Iraqi border, and fly alone to his assigned targets. With luck, they would get through unscathed and rejoin as they crossed the border on the way home.

The Longest Mission

The F-117s were not alone. Also bearing down on Iraq were seven heavy B-52G bombers. They covered the greatest distance of any combat aircraft that night and had been the first to launch for the war.

They had taken off from Barksdale AFB, La., at 6:35 a.m., Central Standard Time, January 16, nearly twelve hours before H-hour.

These bombers, part of Strategic Air Command's 2d Bombardment Wing, carried conventionally-armed air-launched cruise missiles, targeted against communications and power facilities deep inside Iraq.

The round-trip flight for the B-52s would last for more than thirty-five hours. It was the longest air combat mission in history and the first time the conventional ALCMs had been employed.[3]

Also in the air was the opening salvo of Tomahawk Land Attack Missiles (TLAMs), launched by US Navy vessels in the Red Sea and the Arabian Gulf. They cruised at some 450 knots and had about 700 miles to go.

The first TLAM, fired from the Red Sea by the cruiser *San Jacinto* at 1:30 a.m., would strike Baghdad about ninety minutes later, shortly after H-hour. Once *San Jacinto*'s TLAM was on its way, the USS *Bunker Hill* in the Persian Gulf and then the battleships USS *Wisconsin* and USS *Missouri* opened fire.

Opening the Gap

Greg Feest would have the distinction of dropping the first bomb in Operation Desert Storm. In December 1989, in the F-117's combat debut, Feest had dropped the first bomb during the Panama contingency, and in August 1990, he flew the lead fighter as the F-117s deployed from Tonopah to Khamis Mushait.[4]

Feest and the other aircrews of the strike force rendezvoused for aerial refueling with 160 KC-135 Stratotankers and KC-10 Extenders.[5] Each tanker was stacked 500 feet below the one ahead of it, along carefully-defined tanker tracks over Saudi Arabia.

Plowing through cloudbanks, the strike aircraft took turns on the refueling booms, topped off their tanks, and swung to attack headings.

Horner's huge strike force was controlled by three flying command posts, E-3 Airborne Warning and Control System (AWACS) aircraft. Radar beams from AWACS, orbiting near the Iraqi border, stabbed hundreds of miles into Iraqi airspace. Two Navy E-2C Hawkeyes, one over the Persian Gulf and the other above western Saudi Arabia, provided additional radar coverage.

A big RC-135 Rivet Joint aircraft eavesdropped electronically, pinpointing any Iraqi communicators or radar operators who were transmitting.

Unmanned aerial vehicles—drones launched by the Air Force, Army, and Navy—were poised to cruise through the attack areas at low altitude, confusing the air defenses and picking up data on enemy concentrations and emplacements.

Flying high above the battle area, at altitudes of more than 60,000 feet, U-2 and TR-1 long-range reconnaissance aircraft employed a variety of sensors to track the battle.[6]

The opening attack took place not in Baghdad but far to the southwest. There, the F-117s teamed up with Air Force and Army helicopters to slash open a gap in the western Iraqi air defenses.

At 2:39 a.m., twenty-one minutes before H-hour, Task Force Normandy, with Air Force MH-53 Pave Lows and Army AH-64 Apaches, knocked out two Iraqi radar sites just inside the border. The Apaches

[3] Pete Williams, Pentagon news conference, Jan. 16, 1992.

[4] Maj. Gregory A. Feest, interview, Dec. 17, 1991.

[5] Lt. Col. David A. Deptula, interview, June 27, 1991.

[6] Col. Thomas J. Keck, interview, July 17, 1991.

employed Hellfire missiles to wipe out control vans and support equipment.

Feest's target was an interceptor operations center about fifty miles inside Iraq. That IOC was a key link between border radar sites and the air defense headquarters in Baghdad.

"We had practiced a lot, and we had become very good at finding a target and hitting it exactly on time, within one second," Feest said.[7]

"This was a little different than practice, though, because I knew they were going to be shooting back at me. So, as I came to my first IP,[8] I was kind of apprehensive.

"It was a very difficult target, well hidden and camouflaged. The most difficult part of the mission was finding the IOC, which was housed in a hardened bunker at a town named Nukhayb."

Before takeoff, Feest had entered the exact latitude and longitude of each checkpoint along his route, as well as the position of the target, in the inertial navigation system.

Fence Check

Flying across the border, he performed a "fence check," a last detailed check of the aircraft. From here on, events would unfold rapidly. Feest made sure that all his external lights were off because, sometimes, under the stress of combat, the most obvious things are left undone. A single wingtip light, visible to enemy gunners, could mean disaster.

Inside the cockpit, the only light came from the dimly glowing multifunction displays arrayed before him. Using switches on the throttles and pushing actuator buttons near the video displays, he could call up target information on one MFD while keeping aircraft status information like airspeed, attitude, and altitude on another.

Still another display showed Feest information his sensors were gathering on the enemy's radar system. He could call up almost any combination of data he wanted.

He selected the next checkpoint on the inertial navigation system and checked the latitude and longitude readout. The autopilot turned the aircraft.

Feest changed his heading frequently, as all F-117 pilots do, to complicate target tracking by an enemy radar that might get some slight return from the stealthy aircraft. On-board sensors told Feest where the probing radars were, and he flew a course to avoid them.

To complete the fence check, he compared the amount of fuel remaining with the level the precomputation said he should have and made sure his warning and caution lights were out.

Feest was riveted on his displays, hearing only the hum in the cockpit as he sped through the night. He prepared to drop the first of two laser-guided, 2,000-pound bombs, designed to penetrate deep into enemy bunkers before detonating. These special bombs, were carried in the Gulf War by the F-117s and F-111s.[9]

He punched up the armament display on an MFD. It told him that both bombs were operative and that the release system was ready. Feest armed his weapons and switched the armament system to "weapons armed, off safe" to prevent inadvertent release.

As he approached Nukhayb, Feest switched his computer system from the "Nav" mode to "Weapons Delivery." He turned to a new heading over the pre-IP (pre-initial point), then passed over the IP.

He called up the target position on the inertial navigation system and watched as aiming cross hairs positioned themselves over the computed position of the target. He was now looking at the infrared picture on one of the MFDs. The infrared sensors gather heat emanations from the ground and an MFD displays their image, which looks much like a black-and-white television picture.

On the Target Run

Feest's pulse rate was up, and he was breathing fast and heavily. He set the autopilot to hold steady on the target run. He checked the MFDs to ensure that his altitude, heading, and airspeed were correct for this delivery, checked his armament

[7] Feest interview.

[8] Initial point, navigational coordinates for first leg of mission; next IP will be start of bomb run.

[9] There were slight differences in these improved laser-guided bombs. Those carried by the F-117s were designated GBU-27s, and those carried by the F-111s were GBU-24s.

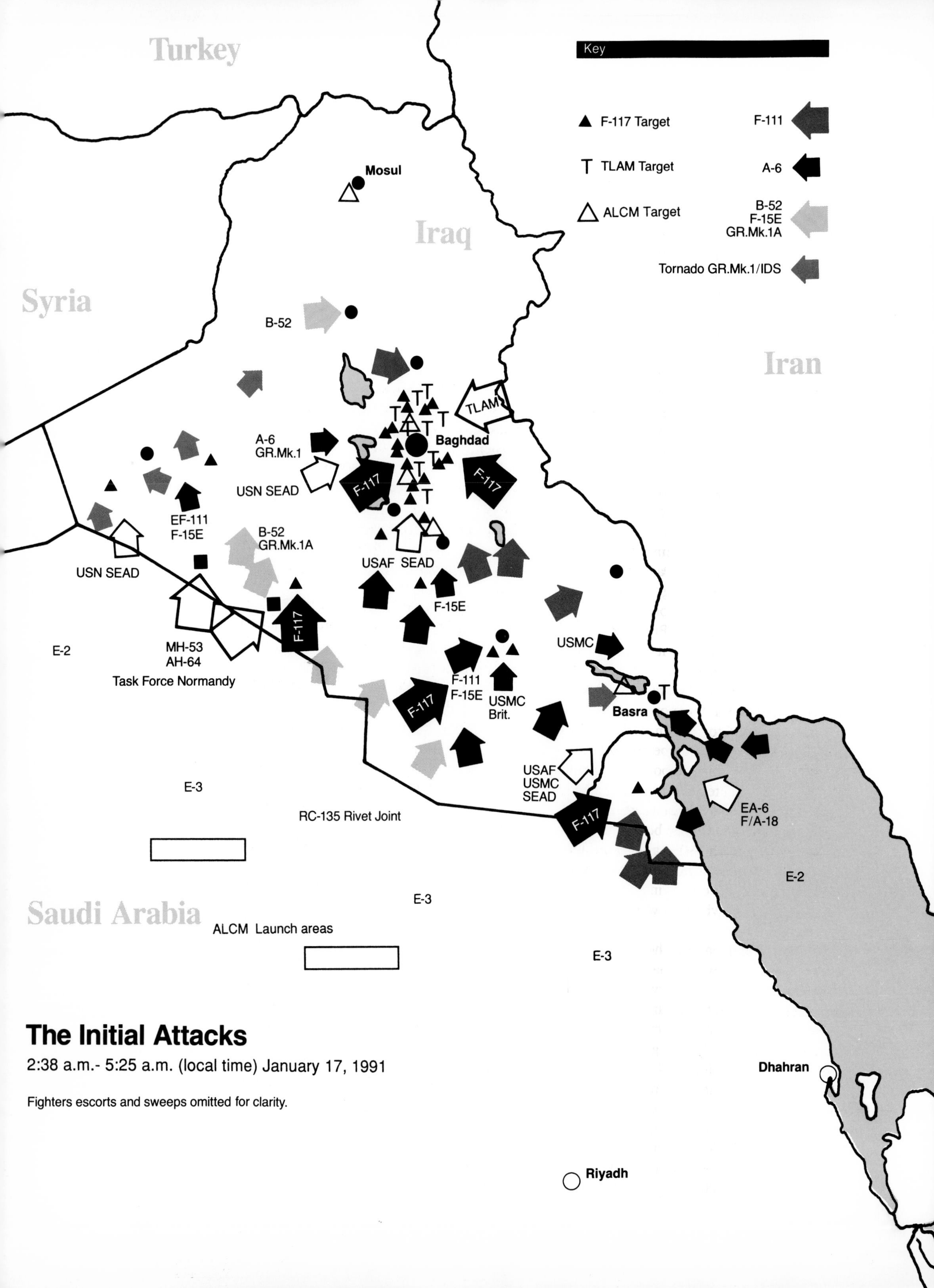

The Initial Attacks

2:38 a.m.- 5:25 a.m. (local time) January 17, 1991

Fighters escorts and sweeps omitted for clarity.

system one more time, and then flipped the master arm switch to "arm."

Outside, all was dark except for a few lights in the town. The F-117's infrared sensors, however, picked out buildings, dry watercourses, and an unpaved road. Feest could see these in stark clarity on his MFD. He had studied his target intently beforehand, so he knew exactly where the bunker was in relation to the sparse terrain features. He compared what he saw on the MFD with an aerial photo strapped to his legboard. As he flew closer, he could see the outline of the bunker and some of its support structures for positive target identification.

Feest moved the fingertip target designator (TD) button mounted on one of the throttles, slewing the cross hairs until they were precisely over the aimpoint, which is called the "designated mean point of impact" (DMPI). Depending on size, hardness, and other considerations, a target may have more than one DMPI. In this case, though, the single aimpoint was the center of the top of the bunker.

By depressing and then releasing the TD button, Feest told the computer exactly where he wanted to aim. Immediately, the F-117's laser designator began to shoot a continuous, invisible, pinpoint beam at the DMPI. The reflected laser energy, bouncing back from the target to the aircraft, provided guidance for the bomb.

Symbology on the MFD and on the head-up display (HUD)[10] cued Feest to fly left or right to correct for crosswinds. More symbology told him when he was in range of the target.

Once he had passed the "max range" point, the bomb would have enough energy, imparted by the forward motion of the F-117, to arc into the target. Pilots refer to such a shot as "putting it into the basket."

Feest saw the "in range" symbology, checked his position and the target, decided he agreed with the computer's logic, and depressed the red button on the top of his control stick. The weapons bay doors snapped open, and he heard the *"clunk!"* as the huge bomb released from its shackles in the weapons bay. The doors snapped closed.

Watching It Hit

As the weapon dropped away, its nose sensor homed on the reflected laser beam and sent signals to the guidance system, which moved vanes on the side of the bomb to control the arc of flight.

Feest watched the IR display intently. The plunging bomb appeared at the bottom of the display just before it hit.

"I saw the bomb go in," he said. "I saw it penetrate. Then the explosion came out the hole the bomb had made, and then the doors blew off the bunker. I knew I had knocked out the target."

Then, Feest said, the reality of war hit home: "I turned toward my next target. I looked back and that was the first time I had ever seen anyone shooting at me. They had started shooting as soon as my bomb went off. I thought, 'Boy, I'm glad I am through there and don't have to fly through that.'"

But Feest's night wasn't over. The airspace over Baghdad and western Iraq turned into a beehive of flak when the Apaches hit the radar sites.

Feest's first bomb struck at H minus nine minutes. His next attack, at an airfield in the extreme west of Iraq, would fall some ten minutes after H-hour.

"I looked out in front of me and I was heading out to western Iraq now, and I saw what everybody at home saw on television," he said.

"It was the same as downtown Baghdad. Tracers, flashes, flak all over the place. And that was scary and I knew I had to go into that to drop my second bomb.

"The whole country came alive then. It was, apparently, all barrage fire. It was probably twenty minutes later that I was going to hit my next target, a couple of hundred miles away. Looking out and seeing what was in the target area was scary. I had to go into that stuff."

Feest wondered about his chances of surviving the mission. "I didn't think I was going to make it through there because the barrage fire was so intense," he said. "I saw SAMs in front of me and behind me. They flew right through my altitude. Luckily, they didn't track me.

[10] Transparent panel between pilot and windscreen; information about flight, navigation, attack, etc., superimposed on it.

"I just concentrated on finding my target. I found it and tracked it, just like the first time. I hit it, came off, and turned back south toward Saudi Arabia. Stuff was going off above me and below me.

"Flying that first night, after seeing what we had to fly through, we all thought we would probably never make it home. Even though it was barrage fire, there was so much of it, I just knew I'd get the golden BB, the one with my name on it.

"My wingman, flying about a minute behind me, had to hit another target. I knew he had to fly through the same sort of stuff. I didn't think he could make it. For both of us to make it would require too much luck, I was sure. But we all made it home okay."

The opening attack by the helicopters and the F-117s had blown a gap in the Iraqi air defenses, but it had also alerted the enemy that the air war had begun. Through the breach, nonstealthy Air Force F-15Es, equipped with Low-Altitude Navigation and Targeting Infrared for Night (LANTIRN) pods, streaked into western Iraq at near supersonic speed, on the deck, to strike fixed Scud sites.

On the Leading Edge

On the leading edge, flying far ahead of the main strike force, the ten F-117s from Khamis Mushait knocked out command and control centers and key air defense points. Most of these targets were in Baghdad. (In the next twenty-four hours, another thirty-two F-117 sorties would be flown against forty more targets in Iraq.)

Minutes earlier, when Feest and the helicopters knocked out air defenses to the southwest, the batteries in Baghdad had filled the night sky with hot metal, not because the city was under attack but as a reaction to the helicopter attacks more than 200 miles away. Ironically, the batteries fell silent again just before H-hour as the F-117s were starting their bomb runs on Baghdad. The incoming Stealth fighters had not been detected or tracked.

"The city was lighted up, with cars in the streets," said Col. Klaus J. Klause, 37th TFW Deputy Commander for Operations.[11] The Iraqis believed that the initial attacks on Baghdad were over. In fact, they were about to begin.

[11] Stewart M. Powell, "Voices From the War," *Air Force Magazine*, April 1991.

Only the F-117s were stealthy enough to penetrate the central Baghdad air defenses without a supporting force of aircraft to suppress antiaircraft defenses. Furthermore, the superb accuracy of the F-117 weapon delivery systems reduced the probability of harm to civilians or collateral damage to nonmilitary structures adjacent to targets. Stealth and accuracy were the reasons why the F-117s were the only attack aircraft to strike targets in central Baghdad throughout the war.

Before enemy radars were knocked out or jammed, the F-117s blinded the Iraqi air defense command and crippled the central nodes of a system that could not operate effectively without centralized control.

When the first bombs fell on Baghdad, the Iraqi air defenses opened up again, full bore. Millions of viewers around the world saw the awesome display on television. Streams of deadly red tracers and hundreds of SAMs rose up in a blind barrage.

"They were sending up antiaircraft fire," Klause said. "We could see the lights of their flak twinkling all over the place."

The Main Attack

At H-hour, a Stealth pilot positioned his cross hairs on the Iraqi International Telecommunications Centre in downtown Baghdad. (The actual name of this facility was too long to fit on the handwritten copy of the master attack plan, so the operations staff dubbed it the "AT&T Building," as shorthand of convenience and the name stuck.)

In Riyadh, Horner had sent Maj. "Buck" Rogers, a member of his staff, to his office to listen to ABC and CNN, which were broadcasting live from Baghdad. CNN correspondent Bernard Shaw said to his colleague, Peter Arnett, "We have not heard any jet planes yet, Peter."

Arnett told the listening audience, "Now the sirens are sounding for the first time. The Iraqis have informed us...."

The transmission stopped abruptly. The first bomb had penetrated the telecommunications building and exploded. Saddam's

The First Day in Baghdad

During the first twenty-four hours of the war, coalition aircraft struck critical targets in Saddam's capital and elsewhere. Weeks of fighting remained, but the initial attack was so overwhelming that Iraq was unable to mount a coherent military response thereafter. First day targets in Baghdad are numbered on the map.

1. Directorate of Military Intelligence
2, 5, 8, 13, 34. Telephone switching station
3. Ministry of Defense national computer complex
4. Electrical transfer station
6. Ministry of Defense headquarters
7. Ashudad highway bridge
9. Railroad yard
10. Muthena airfield (military section)
11. Air Force headquarters
12. Iraqi Intelligence Service
14. Secret Police complex
15. Army storage depot
16. Republican Guard headquarters
17. New Presidential Palace
18. Electrical power station
19. SRBM assembly factory (Scud)
20. Baath party headquarters
21. Government conference center
22. Ministry of Industry and Military Production
23. Ministry of Propaganda
24. TV transmitter
25, 31. Communications relay station
26. Jumhuriya highway bridge
27. Government Control Center South
28. Karada highway bridge (14th July bridge)
29. Presidential Palace command center
30. Presidential Palace command bunker
32. Secret Police headquarters
33. Iraqi Intelligence Service regional headquarters
35. National Air Defense Operations Center
36. Ad Dawrah oil refinery
37. Electrical powerplant

central communications system was off the air.

Rogers relayed word that CNN was off the air. Horner and his staff were elated. The first bomb-damage assessment of the war had been delivered by network television. The target had been knocked out.[12]

F-117 pilots decline to give specifics on targets they bombed in Baghdad. However, one pilot (who did not fly over Baghdad on the first night but who later attacked targets in the city) described a typical attack.

"Your weapons are armed and ready to go," said Maj. Robert D. Eskridge. "You make sure your system is in the weapons delivery mode. You check it and, thirty seconds later, you check it again.

"When you're still several miles out, the city is an indistinct collection of infrared splotches. With a fingertip you slew your cross hairs over the general location of your target, which might be the northeast quadrant of the city. As you approach the IP, you can see the city much more distinctly on your MFD, just like a black-and-white photograph.

"Getting closer, you can see major boulevards and the river on the MFD. You know your target, let's say it's a command bunker, is east of the river and north of a main boulevard. You refine the cross hairs positioning."

The aiming becomes very precise, Eskridge emphasized. "You are fixated on the MFD. You know stuff is coming up indiscriminately, bursting around you, but you have to ignore it and concentrate on that target. Your flight path takes you closer and closer.

"The image is now larger and very distinct. Now you can see cross streets. You check the photo strapped on your legboard. You know the bunker is, say, four streets to the north of the last major boulevard. You also know it's three blocks east of the river. You refine the cross hairs position some more.

"Closer. Now you can see separate buildings. You know the bunker is in the backyard of the third building from the corner, on the north side of the street. You can see the building. You can see the backyard. You can see the bunker. You can see the bunker air shaft.

"You make one final adjustment to the cross hairs, and you depress the TD button. The laser designator starts to do its thing, which is pinpoint the exact spot you want the bomb to hit.

"You fly the aircraft and follow the symbology to correct for drift. You wait for the indicators to tell you that you're inside 'max range.'

"Then, when you're sure you're within the parameters to drop the bomb in the basket, you depress the pickle button[13] on the stick. The bomb releases. As it plunges toward the target, you make sure those cross hairs stay centered on the aimpoint, the DMPI.

"After what seems like a long time, but is really just seconds, you see the bomb flash into view, homing on that laser reflection. It penetrates exactly where you aimed it. You see smoke billow out of the hole. Probably, the doors fly off the bunker.

"Then, you roll into your preplanned turn and get out of there as fast as you can. One thing is certain. Nobody has ever been able to egress a target fast enough. Nobody. Ever."[14]

The Force Comes In

As the F-117 took out the Baghdad telecommunications center, the nonstealthy part of the strike force, less than thirty minutes away, penetrated Iraq from positions beyond the air defense radar coverage.

On that first night, as the F-117s banked steeply away from their targets, Air Force F-15 Eagles and Navy F-14 Tomcats sped toward their combat air patrol positions over Iraq. There, they orbited with their look-down/shoot-down missile systems, ready to destroy Iraqi interceptors. Unseen, the lead F-117s flew swiftly beneath them, and headed back to their mountaintop base in Saudi Arabia.

The strike force, timed to attack dozens of targets simultaneously, moved in. Air Force F-15Es, F-16s, F-111s, B-52s, and more F-117s—as well as British and Saudi Tornados, Kuwaiti A-4s, Navy A-6s, and

[12] USAF white paper, September 1991.

[13] Weapon release switch.

[14] Maj. Robert D. Eskridge, interview, Dec. 20, 1991.

Navy and Marine F/A-18s—swept into Iraq and Kuwait from the east, south, and west. The barrage of TLAMs from the US Navy continued.

The attack aircraft were supported by Air Force EF-111 Raven electronic jammers, Navy EA6B Prowlers, Air Force F-4G Wild Weasel radar suppression aircraft, and Navy F/A-18s and EA-6Bs.[15]

Altogether, between 2:38 a.m. and 5:25 a.m., Baghdad time, almost 400 coalition "shooter" aircraft attacked more than 100 targets across Iraq and Kuwait. Targets included air defense sites, command, control, and communications facilities, airfields, Scud storage and launch points, troop concentrations, chemical, biological, and nuclear factories and storage sites, and fortifications, as well as antiaircraft and SAM control nodes and batteries.[16]

Aircrews in the large strike force, flying with lights out, exercised extraordinary discipline and precision to avoid midair collisions. Bad weather over Saudi Arabia was an unexpected problem, but coalition airmen got some good breaks, too.

In briefings to President Bush and US military leaders, Glosson had said he did not expect more than twenty to thirty Iraqi fighters to be airborne at once. In fact, not more than twenty got into the air at once.

By the end of the first day, eight Iraqi fighters had been shot down, six by the US Air Force and two by the Navy.[17] One coalition aircraft, a US Navy F/A-18, was destroyed by a SAM, and the pilot was killed.

Horner and his people left the TACC sometime after sunrise. The night, including the bombing results and the coalition's light losses, had gone better than expected.

Saddam's central control of his air defense system was fatally damaged, forcing the Iraqi defenders to depend on barrage antiaircraft fire and uncontrolled missile launches.

As Gen. Merrill A. McPeak, Air Force Chief of Staff, would say later, "it was a very heavy attack, very precisely delivered. In my judgment, the Iraqi air force never recovered from this opening attack. We took the initiative at the beginning, and we held it throughout the war."[18]

BDA would eventually confirm in detail that the first night of the air war was a sweeping success, but the general results were clear within hours. Horner had begun to orchestrate the most impressive air campaign in history. ■

[15] "The United States Navy in Desert Shield/Desert Storm," Department of the Navy, May 15, 1991.

[16] USAF white paper, September 1991.

[17] Gen. H. Norman Schwarzkopf, CENTCOM news conference, Jan. 18, 1991.

[18] Gen. Merrill A. McPeak, Pentagon news conference, March 15, 1991.

2. Saddam Triggers a Crisis

At the time of the invasion, Lt. Gen. Charles A. Horner commanded the CENTCOM air component. His responsibility widened as he became "air boss" of Operation Desert Storm.

Kuwait was a pushover, but the self-styled general had miscalculated the US reaction.

In the spring of 1990, Saddam Hussein was primed to take over the Middle East, locus of the world's most valuable oil reserves and, geographically, one of the most strategic areas on earth.

Saddam cultivated the image of a military leader, but he was, in fact, abysmally ignorant of strategy and tactics. He was a political ruffian who had been made a general after receiving an honorary degree from Iraq's military college in 1970.[1]

He was born in 1937 in a hardscrabble village near the town of Takrit, north of Baghdad and not far from the site of ancient Babylon. Iraq had gained its independence with the end of the British mandate in 1932, and the nation was still a hotbed of political unrest.

Saddam, abused by a tyrannical stepfather, grew up tough. At age ten, he moved to Baghdad to live with his uncle, a political activist. Before he was twenty, he joined the Baath party and soon distinguished himself as a willing gunman on partisan hit squads. One of his victims was his own brother-in-law.[2]

The writings of Iraqi nationalist Sami Shaukat are said to have been an early influence on Saddam. Shaukat's aggressive intensity is illustrated by this line from *These Are Our Aims* (1932): "The nation that does not excel in the art of death with iron and fire will die under the horse's hooves and under the boots of foreign soldiers." [3]

Saddam did not use his family name (al-Majid), preferring to call himself Saddam Hussein al-Takriti (meaning "from the town of Takrit").[4] That emphasized a connection with Saladin, the great Muslim leader from Takrit who drove the Crusaders out of Jerusalem in 1187. Ironically, Saladin was a Kurd, and Saddam persecuted the Kurdish minority in Iraq ruthlessly.

Another of Saddam's heroes was Nebuchadnezzar, the king of Babylon who conquered Jerusalem in 507 B.C. and brought vast numbers of Jews to Babylon in captivity.

When the Baath party seized power in 1963, Saddam became a leader in the government and was named chief of security. Within a year, the Baathists were overthrown and their leaders, including Saddam, were jailed. When they returned to power in a 1968 coup, Saddam was one of the troika that headed the government. He was again chief of security, heading an organization that conducted assassinations and looked for "subversives" among the citizenry.

In 1979, Saddam purged both the party and the government and took control himself. The Iraqi armed forces were always a central element in his thinking, but following the Baathist tradition, he put far more emphasis on political loyalty than on military competence.

The Iran-Iraq War

Through the 1970s and 1980s, Saddam used money from oil sales to purchase huge stores of Soviet-made weapons. He also bought French fighter aircraft.

Saddam invaded Iran in 1980, setting off a costly eight-year war of attrition with

[1] Anthony H. Cordesman and Abraham R. Wagner. *The Lessons of Modern War: the Iran-Iraq War*. Westview Press, 1990.

[2] Judith Miller and Laurie Mylroie, "The Rise of Saddam Hussein," in Sifry and Cerf, ed., *The Gulf War Reader*, 1991.

[3] Simon Henderson. *Instant Empire: Saddam Hussein's Ambition for Iraq*. Mercury House, 1991.

[4] Henderson.

Photo by J. Witt/Sipa Press

hundreds of thousands of casualties. US sympathies tilted toward Iraq. American officials recognized that Saddam was a ruthless character, but still perceived him more favorably than they did the Ayatollah Khomeni in Iran.[5]

Both Iran and Iraq targeted each other's cities with Scud missiles, marking Saddam's first use of the weapon he would employ with psychological effect in the Gulf War of 1991. Iraq also used poison gas at least two times against Iran.

In 1986, Saddam's motley army suffered a disastrous defeat when Iranian forces punched deep into Iraq at the battle of Al Faw. Iran was too exhausted to exploit that victory, however, so the conflict stagnated.

Considering how poorly they performed, Saddam and his armed forces were fortunate to emerge as well as they did from the war with Iran. They never demonstrated a grasp of strategy, failed to concentrate or coordinate their use of force, and were often amateurishly unrealistic in their expectations.

On the first day of the war, the Iraqis sent almost every fighter and bomber they could get into the air against Iranian air force and army bases. The attacks were ineffective, and the next day, the Iranian air force flew 100 sorties against Iraq. The Iranians were not very effective either, but their counterattack was a shock to the Iraqis.

Although Saddam still had three or four times as many combat aircraft as Iran did, he immediately dispersed them to bases in neighboring countries and in the western part of Iraq. He eventually brought them back, but thereafter generally held his air units out of battle as a reserve for the ultimate defense of the nation and the Iraqi forces.[6]

It was in several respects a preview of the flight of the Iraqi air force to Iran in the Gulf War of 1991.

After the conflict with Iran, Saddam began to rebuild his shattered capability around the Republican Guard, which had originally been his small and loyal palace security force. He developed it into an elite force of more than 100,000 men, led by the best officers in the army and supplied with modern Soviet equipment and training. Other military forces, the popular guard and regular army, were intensively trained and were well equipped for unit fighting.

By 1988, Saddam had more than 1,000,000 troops. In April, he sent his new tanks, artillery, helicopters, and infantry back into battle with Iran. They fought for five months, won every battle, and shouldered into Iranian territory before the war ended in a truce.

Iraq's armed forces, newly blooded and newly successful, gave Saddam renewed confidence. By the summer of 1990, he had the world's fourth largest army and the world's sixth largest air force.

The burden of his military budget was $721 a year per Iraqi citizen in a nation where the average annual income was $1,950.[7]

Ominously, Saddam was stockpiling poison gas and the means to deliver it. He developed the technology to build nuclear weapons. And, remembering the terror induced among the Iranian people by the Scud missiles, he continued to buy and build them. By the time of the Gulf War, US intelligence estimated that he had about 1,200 Scuds and Scud derivatives.

He believed he could unite the Arabs by first conquering some Arab states and then persuading the others to join him in a Pan-Arab union. History, he believed, made Iraq the logical country to head such a union and him the man to lead it.

The United States and other nations, including Saddam's Arab neighbors, watched this military buildup with concern. It had the clear look of a force meant for offensive purposes.

Warnings Ignored

Some Pentagon officials pointed to the potential threat posed by Iraq, but few Americans heard or believed the warning. With the Soviet military empire collapsing, the dominant defense issue in the United States was how to reduce the armed forces and allocate the peace dividend. Critics jeered that the Pentagon no longer faced any challenge except justifying its own continued existence.

[5] Paul K. Davis and John Arquilla, "Deterring or Coercing Opponents in Crisis," RAND, 1991.

[6] Cordesman and Wagner.

[7] USAF white paper, September 1991.

In Israel, however, Saddam's actions were not taken so lightly. It was the Israelis who had launched a daring air attack that wiped out Iraq's most advanced nuclear development site in 1981. Saddam was infuriated but did not retaliate because he believed the United States would support Israel, and in 1981, he did not feel strong enough for that match up.

Although the United States had declared the Persian Gulf region vital to its national interests since the Carter Administration, it maintained no large military presence in the area.

Military responsibility for contingencies in the Middle East, Southwest Asia, and Northeast Africa is assigned to US Central Command, headquartered at MacDill AFB, Fla. The organization traces its lineage from Strike Command, formed at MacDill in 1962. It evolved into US Readiness Command (1972) and then the Rapid Deployment Joint Task Force (1980) before emerging as Central Command in 1983.

CENTCOM has no forces of its own. In peacetime, the headquarters is staffed by a cadre of some 700 people from the Army, Navy, Air Force, and Marine Corps. In wartime, the individual services augment CENTCOM with troops, weapons, and equipment.

As part of its responsibility to CENTCOM, the US Air Force had stored more than $1 billion worth of fuel, ammunition, and equipment in Oman. Still other materiel was prepositioned on ships. For its part, Saudi Arabia built dozens of airfields and related installations for the use of forces that could deploy there in times of emergency.[8]

In 1990, the Commander in Chief of Central Command (CINCCENT) was Army Gen. H. Norman Schwarzkopf. His air component—US Central Command Air Forces (CENTAF)—was commanded by Lt. Gen. Charles A. Horner, USAF, who was also commander of 9th Air Force at Shaw AFB, S.C.

Schwarzkopf and Horner watched as Saddam positioned forces to move against his first target, Kuwait. The US could not move forces into the region for diplomatic reasons. In any case, the two US generals did not believe it was possible to keep the militarily superior Iraqi forces from overrunning Kuwait in a few days. Moreover, it would take weeks or months to deploy forces strong enough to drive Saddam out of Kuwait once he had taken it.[9]

The real worry was that he would then invade Saudi Arabia, which was no match for his armed forces either. If Saddam took Saudi Arabia, he would control more than half of the world's oil. Horner was acutely aware that the best way, perhaps the only way, to deter Iraq from attacking Saudi Arabia was the rapid deployment of US Air Force fighters, bombers, tankers, and reconnaissance aircraft to the kingdom.

If Saddam invaded Kuwait, Horner's job would be to get airpower into Saudi Arabia in the first few hours and then be prepared to hold out until ground and naval forces could arrive. In any event, Horner knew, Saudi Arabia's King Fahd would have to grant permission for any forces to be lodged on Saudi soil. Political realities in the Arab world, however, made it difficult for him to invite such forces until hostilities began or circumstances were demonstrably dire.

Iraq had threatened Kuwait before, during the Lebanon crisis in 1958, and again in 1961. Annexing Kuwait by force would provide seaports, which Iraq lacked with the boundaries drawn under the British Mandate. Saddam furthermore repudiated the earlier settlement of an ancient border dispute.

Kuwait held vast oil reserves, including part of the Rumalia field, which extended from Iraq across the border under Kuwait. Saddam needed Kuwait's wealth to help make his payments on more than $40 billion in debts from the Iran-Iraq war. He was nettled that while most of the Arab nations that loaned him money to fight Iran had forgiven the debt, Kuwait still demanded repayment.

On July 17, he made a televised speech in which he threatened to attack unless Kuwait agreed to settle the old boundary dispute and lower its oil production, which he hoped would drive up the price of oil on the world market. He also accused Kuwait

[8] USAF white paper, September 1991.

[9] Horner, interview, May 30, 1991.

of slant drilling under the border into Iraq's area of the Rumalia field and demanded it be stopped.

The "Internal Look" Rehearsal

At about the time Saddam was speaking, Schwarzkopf and Horner quietly kicked off a computer-based command post exercise, *Internal Look*, at Eglin AFB, Fla. The scenario of the two-week exercise was the invasion of Kuwait and Saudi Arabia by "a nation from the north." No military forces were actually used during the exercise, but it provided valuable experience for commanders and excellent information on the flow, reception, and beddown of US air and ground forces in Saudi Arabia.

Schwarzkopf took the time to receive a courtesy call from US Air Force then-Brig. Gen. Buster C. Glosson, who was on his way to an assignment as Deputy Commander, Joint Task Force Middle East. Schwarzkopf told Glosson to be ready to take part in *Ivory Justice*, a joint exercise in which fighters from the United Arab Emirates would practice refueling operations with US KC-135 tankers. AWACS aircraft would be involved.

On July 21, Schwarzkopf directed Glosson to take command of exercise *Ivory Justice*.[10] The United States and the United Arab Emirates issued a joint announcement July 24. They said *Ivory Justice* was an exercise, not training. Saddam summoned the US Ambassador to Iraq, April Glaspie, and told her he interpreted the exercise as US support for Kuwait. He expressed surprise at the openness of the support, but he also stated he would not invade Kuwait.

The next day, Kuwait acquiesced to Iraq's demand for reduced oil production. On July 30, the CIA reported 100,000 Iraqi troops and more than 300 tanks massed on the Kuwait border. The same day, Kuwaiti and Iraqi negotiators met in Jiddah, Saudi Arabia, with Saudi arbitrators. The talks failed. Nevertheless, Saddam assured President Hosni Mubarak of Egypt and King Fahd of Saudi Arabia that he was not going to attack Kuwait.

Three days later, at 1 a.m. local time, August 2, Iraq invaded Kuwait.

The Kuwaiti royal family and key government officials barely had time to escape before the invading Iraqis were at the gates of Kuwait City. Kuwaiti ground forces were overwhelmed. Several Kuwaiti Air Force fighters employed their weaponry against the invaders and then escaped to neighboring countries.

The CENTCOM staff at MacDill spent August 3 polishing a standard concept for an air campaign designed to keep Saddam's forces at bay and eventually drive them from Kuwait. That evening, Schwarzkopf and Horner put finishing touches on the plan, then flew to Washington and checked into visitors' quarters at Fort Myer, Va., near the Pentagon, around 3 a.m., August 4.[11]

After a couple of hours sleep, they met with Dick Cheney, the Secretary of Defense, and Gen. Colin Powell, Chairman of the Joint Chiefs of Staff. The four of them flew to Camp David, where Schwarzkopf and Horner presented the concept in a briefing. President Bush dispatched Cheney, Schwarzkopf, and Horner to Saudi Arabia to meet with King Fahd.

In Saudi Arabia on August 6, the king listened intently as they proposed "Operation Desert Shield," which eventually would deploy 250,000 American soldiers, sailors, and airmen to the Persian Gulf in less than three months. King Fahd agreed.[12]

Secretary Cheney and General Schwarzkopf returned to the United States. General Horner, now designated "CINCCENT Forward," remained in Riyadh, Saudi Arabia, to receive and command Desert Shield forces. General Glosson came over from the United Arab Emirates August 22 to be Director of Campaign Plans and, later, commander of the 14th Air Division as well.

Back in Washington, Schwarzkopf made one of the fateful decisions of the Gulf crisis. Having weighed the August 3 plan against his requirements, he asked the Air Force to develop a *strategic* air campaign as well. *[See Chapter 4 , "Plan of Attack," p. 43.]*

First Eagles Arrive

At 9 a.m. GMT, August 8, an Air Force

[10] Maj. Gen. Buster C. Glosson, interview, May 28, 1991.

[11] Lt. Gen. Charles A. Horner, interview, May 30, 1991.

[12] Horner interview.

C-141 carrying an airlift control element touched down in Dhahran. Close behind it were F-15 Eagles from the 1st Tactical Fighter Wing, Langley AFB, Va.

Along with them came US E-3 Airborne Warning and Control System (AWACS) aircraft, adding their deep-look radar coverage to augment the Saudi AWACS that had been orbiting since the crisis began. Later the same day, the first elements of the 82d Airborne Division from Fort Bragg, N.C., arrived. General Horner put his air force units on immediate alert.

In less than a week, five more fighter squadrons were operating in Saudi Arabia and around the Gulf. Horner and his colleagues put together a detailed operational plan for the air defense of Saudi Arabia.

At first, Saddam Hussein's forces were concentrated around Kuwait City and the oil fields to the east, stripping and looting the cities and towns. Iraqi combat engineers fortified the Saudi-Kuwaiti border, laid minefields, mounded up huge berms, and bulldozed miles of trenches that they filled with oil to be set afire if coalition troops advanced. They cut miles of troop trenches and built underground command bunkers. The tanks dug in.

US intelligence estimated that Saddam had more than 150,000 troops, including large elements of the crack Republican Guard, in and around Kuwait. He announced that Iraq was annexing Kuwait as its nineteenth province. It was apparent he would stay in Kuwait unless driven out.

By August 21, the US Air Force had a wider variety of aircraft on the scene: more F-15s for air superiority, dual-role F-15Es, equipped for long-range interdiction at night and in bad weather, F-16 multirole fighters, F-4G "Wild Weasels" for suppression of enemy radar, E-3 AWACS for airborne command and control, squat A-10 "Warthogs" for attacking tanks, RC-135 reconnaissance aircraft, KC-135 and KC-10

Long Reach to the Gulf

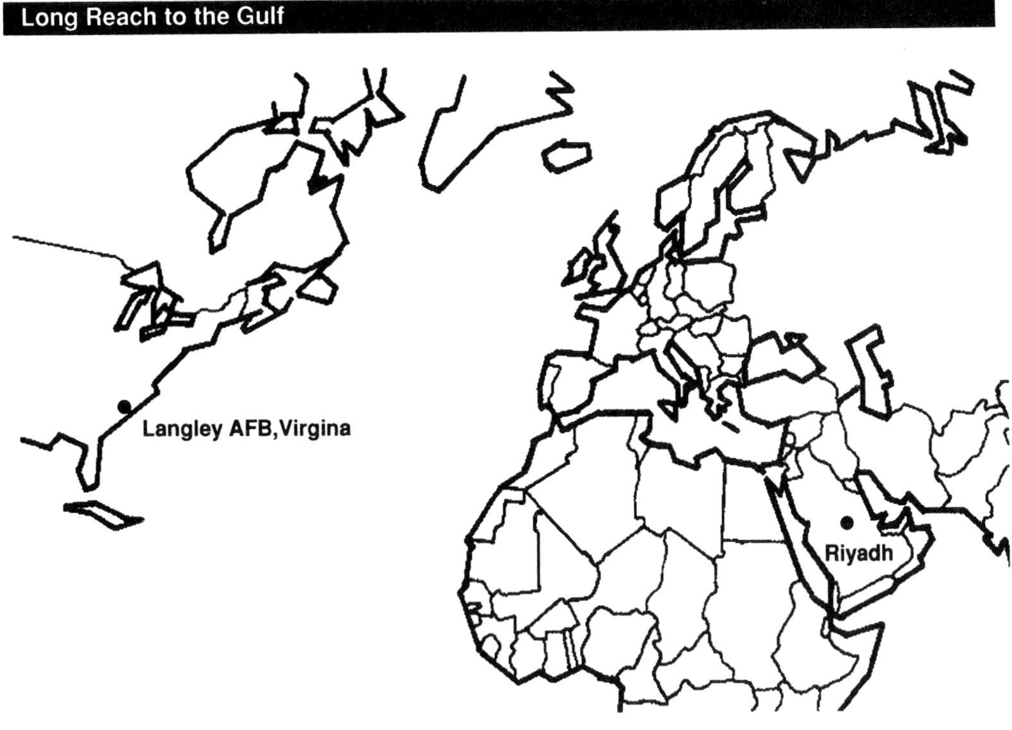

F-15s Depart
5:20 p.m., August 7,1991, Langley time
(12:20 a.m., August 8, 1991, Riyadh time)

F-15s Arrive
7:20 a.m., August 8,1991, Langley time
(2:20 p.m., August 8, 1991, Riyadh time)

tankers, and C-130 Hercules transports. Also present were the F-117 Stealth fighters, which would make their mark in history during this campaign. Army Patriot and Stinger missiles had arrived to strengthen the air defenses.

Most of the aircraft were operating from the deployment airfields Saudi Arabia had built, and they were using ammunition, equipment, and supplies from the US Air Force's $1 billion cache of prepositioned materiel.

Secretary Cheney announced August 21 that Saudi Arabia was defended strongly enough to prevent an Iraqi invasion. Airpower had deterred a ground attack. At the end of the month, President Bush asked other nations to contribute funds, manpower, and equipment to make Desert Shield an international coalition effort.

Events took a bizarre turn September 17 when Secretary Cheney summarily fired Gen. Michael J. Dugan, the Air Force's popular Chief of Staff. The previous day,

[13] Rick Atkinson, "US to Rely on Air Strikes if War Erupts," Washington *Post*, Sept. 16, 1990.

[14] Secretary Dick Cheney, Pentagon news conference, Sept. 17, 1990.

[15] Gen. H.T. Johnson, interview, Oct. 23, 1991.

United Nations Security Council Resolutions

Aug. 2	**660.** Condemned invasion. Demanded withdrawal. Adopted 14-0-1, Yemen abstaining.
Aug. 6	**661.** Imposed a trade and financial embargo. Established special sanctions committee. Called on UN members to protect Kuwaiti assets. Adopted 13-0-2, Cuba and Yemen abstaining.
Aug. 9	**662.** Declared Iraq's annexation of Kuwait null and void. Adopted unaimously.
Aug. 18	**664.** Demanded immediate release of foreigners from Kuwait and Iraq. Insisted Iraq rescind its order closing diplomatic missions in Kuwait. Adopted unanimously.
Aug. 25	**665.** Called on UN members cooperating with Kuwait to enforce sanctions by inspecting and verifying cargoes and destinations. Adopted 13-0-2, Cuba and Yemen abstaining.
Sept. 13	**666.** Reaffirmed Iraqi responsibility for safety of foreign nationals. Specified guidelines for delivery of food and medical supplies. Adopted 13-2, Cuba and Yemen against.
Sept. 16	**667.** Condemned Iraqi aggression against diplomats. Demanded immediate release of foreign nationals. Adopted unanimously.
Sept. 24	**669.** Emphasized only special sanctions committee could authorize food and aid shipments to Iraq or Kuwait. Adopted unanimously.
Sept. 25	**670.** Expanded embargo to include air traffic. Called on UN members to detain Iraqi ships used to break the embargo. Adopted 14-1, Cuba against.
Oct. 29	**674.** Demanded Iraq stop mistreating Kuwaitis and foreign nationals. Reminded Iraq of liability for damages. Adopted 13-0-2, Cuba and Yemen abstaining.
Nov. 28	**677.** Condemned Iraq's attempts to change Kuwait's demographic composition (removal of Kuwaitis and other nationalities) and Iraq's destruction of Kuwaiti civil records. Adopted unanimously.
Nov. 29	**678.** Authorized UN members to use "all means necessary" to enforce previous resolutions, if Iraq does not leave Kuwait by January 15, 1991. Adopted 12-2-1, Cuba and Yemen against, China abstaining.
Mar. 2	**686.** Demanded Iraq cease hostile action, return all POWs and detainees, rescind annexation, accept liability, return Kuwaiti property, and disclose locations of land and sea mines. Adopted 11-1-3, Cuba against, Yemen, China, and India abstaining.

Source: Department of Defense.

Cheney had been infuriated by a front-page article in the Washington *Post* that reported that Dugan had declared airpower to be "the only effective option to force Iraqi forces from Kuwait if war erupts."[13] Dugan confirmed to Cheney that he had made the statements, including a general discussion of possible targets and tactics, attributed to him by the article.

Cheney said he fired Dugan for "lack of judgment," "wide-ranging speculation," "demeaning the contributions of other services," and discussing "the substance of operational matters."[14] Within the Air Force, however, Cheney's actions were widely interpreted as yet another put-down of military airpower, which had been under continuing assault by armchair critics as "not decisive" in war. *[See "The Airpower Controversy," p. 40.]*

The Air Force regrouped under its new Chief, Gen. Merrill A. McPeak, and moved forward. After the Gulf War was concluded, many who reread Dugan's statements from September 1990 remarked on how accurately he had predicted what was about to happen.

In late October, Iraqi troops were still pouring into Kuwait. With almost 240,000 US personnel in the Gulf region, General Schwarzkopf weighed the odds and told the President he would need at least 200,000 more troops to drive Saddam out. On November 8, the President announced that he had authorized the force Schwarzkopf requested. Horner also asked for—and got—reinforcements, almost a doubling of the air forces under his control.

The Forces Square Off

By mid-January, just before Desert Storm began, the coalition forces had 2,614 aircraft in the Persian Gulf Area of Operations. Of these, 1,990 were American. Of the American aircraft, 1,540 were land-based and 450 were aboard six Navy carriers. More than three quarters of the American aircraft were fighter and attack aircraft. Joining the Americans were the air, ground, and naval forces of thirty-eight other nations, including eight Arab nations. Egyptian and Saudi Arabian leaders were especially motivated to fight alongside the Americans since Saddam Hussein had lied to them about his invasion plans.

US airlift moved more than 300,000 tons of cargo and 209,000 troops to the Gulf. It was the largest airlift in history, surpassing the Berlin airlift in deliveries in only six weeks.[15]

Arrayed against the coalition forces, Saddam had 900,000 battle-toughened

Iraq's Major Military Lineup

5,530 Main Battle Tanks	Soviet: 1,500 T-54/55 and M-77; 1,500 T-62; 1,000 T-72 Chinese: 1,500 T-59/69 British: 30 Chieftain
100 Light Tanks	Soviet PT-76
1,500 Infantry Fighting Vehicles	Soviet BMP
6,000 Armored Personnel Carriers	Including Soviet BTR-50/60/152 and MTLB; US M113A1/A2; French, Brazilian, Czech, and Chinese vechicles
500 Self-Propelled Artillery	Including Soviet 2S-1 (122-mm) and 2S3 (152-mm); US M109; and French AUF-1 GCT (155-mm)
3,000 Towed Artillery	Including Soviet and Yugoslav 105-mm, 122-mm, 130-mm, 152-mm weapons; US M114 (155-mm)
200 Multiple Rocket Launchers	Including Soviet, Brazilian, and Iraqi weapons in various sizes
1,800 Surface-to-surface missile launchers	Soviet: 50 FROG-7, 32 Scud-B (fixed) 36 plus Scud-B (mobile); 500 plus Scud-B missiles
159 Attack Helicopters	Soviet: 40 Mi-24; Spanish: 56 Bo-105; French: 20 SA-342, 30 SA-316, 13 SA-321
360 Attack Fighters	Soviet: 90 MiG-23, 30 Su-7, 70 Su-20, 60 Su-25; French: 64 Mirage EQ5/200; Chinese: 30 J-6, 16 Su-24
275 Air-Superiority Fighters	Soviet: 25 MiG-25, 150 MiG-21, 30 MiG-29; Chinese: 40 J-7; French: 30 Mirage F1EQ

There are variations among the unclassified estimates of major weapon systems in the Iraqi military inventory at the start of the Gulf War. This accounting, based on data compiled by* Congressional Quarterly, *illustrates the scope and caliber of the equipment with which Saddam approached the conflict and from where it came.

Source: Congressional Quarterly. *The Middle East.* 7th Edition, 1991.

troops in Iraq and Kuwait. They were equipped with modern weaponry, including 5,700 tanks, 5,000 armored vehicles, and 5,000 support vehicles. They had more than 3,700 artillery pieces and large numbers of multiple rocket launchers. Iraqi combat engineers were highly regarded. Iraq possessed high-quality, redundant command, control, and communications facilities and many dispersed switching stations as well as command posts and bunkers that were considered bomb proof.

Saddam had 750 fighter, bomber, and armed trainer aircraft and 200 support aircraft. In his inventory were the MiG-27 Flogger strike fighter, the MiG-25 Foxbat interceptor, the MiG-23 Flogger fighter-bomber, the MiG-21 Fishbed fighter, the Su-25 Frogfoot ground attack airplane, the Su-24 Fencer strike aircraft, the Su-17 Fitter fighter-bomber, and the Tu-16 Badger and Tu-22 Blinder bombers. His French Mirage F1 fighters were particularly good, but the best tactical airplane in his fleet was probably the MiG-29 interceptor.

While many of these aircraft were old and of limited military value, some of them were modern and very capable.

The Iraqi air force operated from twenty-four main operating bases and thirty dispersal fields, with extensive, nuclear-hardened shelters and multiple taxiways to multiple runways. Many of the pilots were veterans of the war with Iran. They were equipped to employ a large variety of Soviet and European air-to-air missiles, bombs, and smart weapons—including laser-guided munitions.

For air defense, Iraq followed the Soviet model, with strongly redundant nets and layers with radars, and command and control centers that were hardened and buried. The system could employ and control surface-to-air missiles, interceptors, and antiaircraft guns.

Saddam possessed more than 16,000 radar-guided and heat-seeking SAMs, ranging from Vietnam-era SA-2s and eight other older types through the SA-16 and the Franco-German Roland missile. He also had 7,000 antiaircraft guns. The defenses of Baghdad were denser than the most heavily defended targets in eastern Europe at the height of the cold war.

And, of course, Saddam possessed more than 1,000 Scuds, with numerous launch sites near the Jordanian border. Israel was well within range.

By January 1991, the Iraqi and coalition forces were arrayed against each other, the Iraqis dug in to defend and counterattack, and the coalition forces poised to attack.

With more than 500,000 American and coalition troops deployed, President Bush issued an ultimatum to Saddam Hussein: begin to withdraw from Kuwait by January 15, or else.

Saddam didn't budge. The buildup phase of the war was over.

Coalition air forces attacked in strength early on the morning of January 17. Desert Storm had begun. ■

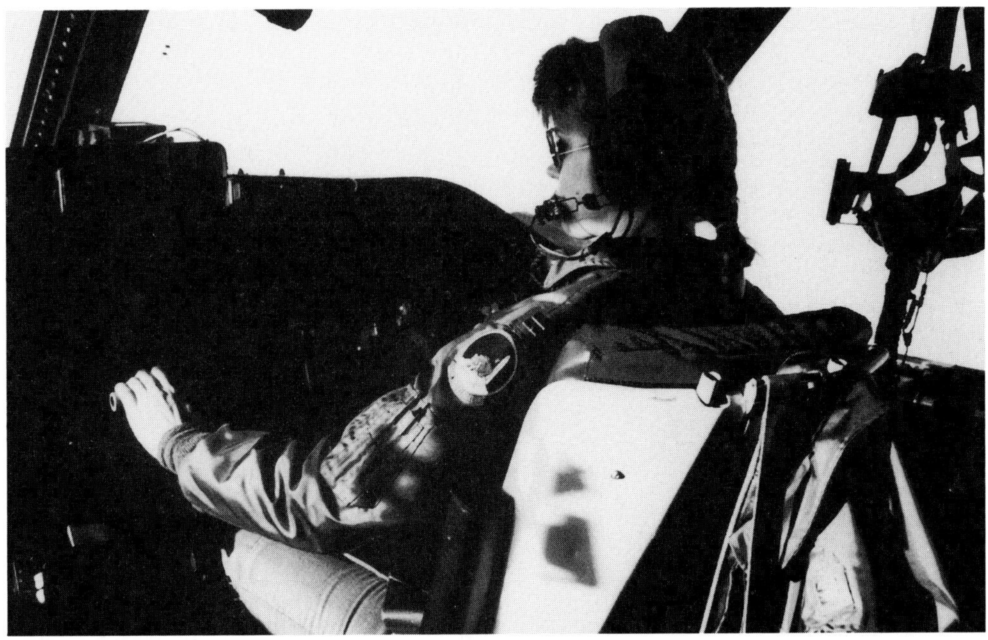

Photo by Robert F. Dorr

Capt. Karen Morgan, an Air Force Reservist, normally flies for Federal Express. During Operation Desert Shield/Desert Storm, she logged her air time in a C-141B of the 459th Military Airlift Wing, Andrews AFB, Md. The 459th was an early part of the "Aluminum Bridge." In fact, a Reserve crew from that wing flew the first US aircraft to land in Saudi Arabia after the crisis began.

F-15s from the 1st TFW, Langley AFB, Va., landed in Saudi Arabia at 2:20 p.m., local time, August 8. More combat forces would joint them soon, but those arriving first were acutely aware of their vulnerability to a much larger hostile force across the border.

Turkey
Incirlik
Mediterranean Sea
Syria
Tehran
Tigris R.
Euphrates R.
Iran
Baghdad
Tel Aviv
Iraq
Israel
Cairo West
Jordan
Basra
Kuwait City
Tabuk
Egypt
King Khalid Military City
Khafji
King Fahd IAP
Dhahran
Shaikh Isa
King Khalid IAP
Riyadh
Al Kharj
USS America
USS Saratoga
USS John F. Kennedy
Jiddah
Taif
Saudi Arabia
Red Sea
Khamis Mushait
Yemen

The Kuwait Theater of Operations

USS *Midway*
USS *Ranger*
USS *Theodore Roosevelt*

Minhad
ubai
Sharjah
Al Ain
Gulf of Oman
Bateen
hafra
Seeb
Oman
Masirah
umrait
Arabian Sea

Where the USAF Was

Saudi Arabia

Al Kharj
F-15C
F-15E
F-16A
C-130

Dhahran
F-15C

Riyadh
KC-135
E-3
RC-135
C-21
EC-130E ABCCC
E-8

King Khalid IAP
KC-135A
KC-135R
EC-135L

King Fahd IAP
A-10
OA-10
AC-130H
EC-130
C-130
C-130 (JACC-CP)
MC-130
HC-130
MH-53
MH-60

Tabuk
F-15C

Khamis Mushait
F-117

Taif
F-111F
EF-111
U-2
TR-1

Jiddah
KC-135E
KC-135A
KC-10
B-52

Oman

Masirah
C-130
KC-135

Seeb
KC-135R
KC-10

Thumrait
C-130

Al Minhad
F-16C

Sharjah
C-130

United Arab Emirates

Bateen
C-130
EC-130

Al Ain
C-130

Al Dhafra
F-16C
KC-135

Dubai
KC-135E

Abu Dhabi
KC-135E

Qatar

Doha
F-16

Turkey

Incirlik AB
F-111E
F-15C
F-16C
KC-135A
F-4G
EF-111
HC-130
E-3
EC-130
RF-4C

Egypt

Cairo West
KC-135E

Spain

Moron AB
B-52G

Diego Garcia

B-52G
KC-135R
KC-10

Bahrain

Shaikh Isa
F-4G
RF-4C

3. A Line in the Sand

Sgt. Harland McCallum, assistant crew chief with the 963d Aircraft Maintenance Unit, surveys the flight line before the takeoff of an E-3 AWACS in Saudi Arabia.

USAF Photo by TSgt. Hans Deffner

During the five months of Desert Shield, the coalition deploys and prepares for war.

Long before Saddam Hussein's invasion of Kuwait, Gen. Colin Powell, Chairman of the Joint Chiefs of Staff, Gen. H. Norman Schwarzkopf, Commander in Chief of US Central Command, and Lt. Gen. Charles A. Horner, commander of CENTCOM air forces, were watching the Iraqi dictator's moves with grave concern.

When Schwarzkopf had first come to CENTCOM, Horner recalls, "we talked about what kind of military planning we should be looking at. Before, we had focused on a Russian invasion of Iran. That was in the early 1980s.

"General Schwarzkopf said, 'That's just not going to happen. They have internal problems that will preclude them from attacking Iran. So what we need to do is look at other situations where our country may call upon us to function.'

"The obvious potential," Horner said, "was this huge military power called Iraq causing problems for Kuwait and Saudi Arabia. We went back and studied the problem. [Around March 1990] I went back to General Schwarzkopf and gave him a long briefing that I had coordinated with the Army, with Lt. Gen. John Yeosock [commander of CENTCOM Army forces].

"We looked at what kind of things would be important from an air standpoint if we were going to be in a conflict in this part of the world. At that time, we talked about Patriots defending against Scuds. We talked about how we could provide close air support to the Army in a very fluid desert maneuver battle. We talked about chemical weapons and how we could counter chemical weapons.

"Also during that time," Horner emphasized, "we talked about attacking [Saddam's] war-making potential—strategic targeting, if you want to call it that."[1]

Across the Potomac River from the Pentagon, the State Department in the summer of 1990 had just completed a year-long review of policy toward Iraq and concluded that the US should support Saddam as a regional counterbalance to the fundamentalist regime in Iran.

Until shortly before Saddam attacked, CIA analysts believed that Iraq was exhausted after its eight-year war with Iran and would now turn away from war to concentrate on oil production and economic recovery. Then, on July 20, the CIA reported 30,000 Iraqi troops deployed along the Kuwait border.[2]

On July 30, CIA analysts reported that Saddam's forces on the Kuwaiti border had grown to 100,000 troops and more than 300 tanks. In Washington, on August 1, the afternoon before the attack, Mohamed al-Mashat, the Iraqi ambassador, informed the State Department that Iraq was merely moving its armed forces around within its own borders.

That evening, the CIA concluded an attack was imminent. At 1 a.m., Kuwait time, on August 2, Saddam struck and quickly rolled over the Kuwaiti defenses.

Saddam Signals More Action

As soon as Saddam had overrun Kuwait, he began to redeploy his forces for another move. Within a matter of hours, he had positioned troops a few miles from the Ku-

[1] Richard Mackenzie, "A Conversation With Chuck Horner," *Air Force Magazine*, June 1991.

[2] James Blackwell, *Thunder in the Desert*, Bantam, 1991.

waiti border with Saudi Arabia. From all indications, he was preparing for a further thrust down the Arabian peninsula, this time into another oil-rich nation. Saudi ground forces totaled less than 70,000 men. They could not stand against Saddam's overwhelming numbers.

In the White House, National Security Advisor Brent Scowcroft had advised President Bush of the invasion early on the morning of August 2. Before breakfast, Bush signed executive orders freezing Kuwaiti and Iraqi assets in the US and prohibiting trade with the two countries.

Working through envoys from the State Department and in the United Nations, he set in motion diplomatic machinery to encourage other nations to follow suit. The UN passed a resolution condemning the Iraqi attack. In Moscow, Secretary of State James Baker and Soviet Foreign Minister Eduard Shevardnadze jointly called for Iraq to withdraw from Kuwait. Algeria, Egypt, Morocco, and the Arab League also called for Iraqi withdrawal.

After a short National Security Council meeting at the White House in the morning, the President ordered the Navy to move aircraft carriers toward the Middle East. The *Eisenhower* steamed from the Mediterranean to the Red Sea, and the *Independence* moved across the Indian Ocean toward the northern Arabian Sea. The President knew his most responsive forces were in the US Air Force, but he could not send them to Saudi Arabia without an invitation from King Fahd.

In Aspen, Colo., to make a speech, President Bush conferred with Margaret Thatcher, Prime Minister of Great Britain. She advised him to stand firm and promised the British would send forces if American forces were deployed to the battle area.

Bush spoke to King Fahd by telephone from Aspen and offered military support. The king avoided a definite answer. He was worried that US forces might not stay long enough to do the job if the conflict turned out to be a long one, and, conversely, that the US forces might be reluctant to leave immediately when it was over. The king also wanted assurance that the US would sell Saudi Arabia high-tech weaponry in the future.[3]

On August 3, Bush convened another NSC meeting to discuss options. Secretary Cheney brought Schwarzkopf along. The CENTCOM commander presented a plan to send more than 150,000 US troops, 500 aircraft, several carriers, and supporting ships to the Persian Gulf. It would be the largest force to be deployed by the US since Vietnam. For the first time, some sense of the magnitude of the operation had been expressed.

When the NSC meeting ended, the President directed Cheney and General Powell to brief the scope of the situation in detail to Prince Bandar bin Sultan, nephew of King Fahd and Saudi Ambassador to Washington. Prince Bandar was impressed. After a call to King Fahd, Bandar assured Cheney that an invitation to deploy US forces to Saudi Arabia would be forthcoming.

The next day, however, Egyptian President Mubarak informed President Bush that King Fahd had decided *not* to accept the deployment. The President called King Fahd and proposed sending Cheney to give him a detailed briefing. The king thought about it for several hours, then agreed.

Conferring in Riyadh with King Fahd and his advisors, Cheney and Schwarzkopf described the deployment plans and shared the latest intelligence reports. They suggested that the Saudis shut down the Iraqi oil pipeline stretching south from Basra and then west across the Arabian Peninsula.

While the Saudis were deliberating, Bush ordered two squadrons of F-15s to prepare to go to the Gulf and sent long-range B-52s from the United States to Diego Garcia, the island base in the Indian Ocean. The B-52s would be employed against the Iraqis if they moved on Saudi oil fields before US ground troops were in position to defend them. Maritime prepositioning ships, carrying tanks, equipment, and supplies for a complete Marine Amphibious Brigade, were ordered out of Guam and Diego Garcia and toward Saudi Arabia.

[3] Otto Frederick, ed. *Desert Storm.* Little, Brown, 1991.

Late in the day, King Fahd told Cheney he would allow US and coalition troops on Saudi soil if President Bush promised not to launch the war without the king's approval and to withdraw all troops when the war was over. Cheney telephoned the President and got his agreement.

Operation Desert Shield—the five-month preliminary to the Gulf War—was under way.

Not Like Vietnam

President Bush was determined to avoid the mistakes of Vietnam. That meant committing adequate forces and firepower to get the job done. Furthermore, Bush intended that the field commanders would command. That was radically different from the Vietnam War, which had been micromanaged, politically and strategically, from Washington.

As Secretary Cheney would explain later, the swift, strong military reaction in Operation Desert Shield represented "the Don't Screw Around school of military strategy."[4]

The first US aircraft to land in Saudi Arabia in the Desert Shield deployment were a Military Airlift Command C-141 carrying the Airlift Control Element (ALCE), F-15s from the 1st Tactical Fighter Wing at Langley AFB, Va., and KC-10 refueling aircraft from Barksdale AFB, La. The first soldiers were 2,300 troops from the 82d Airborne Division at Fort Bragg, N.C. Arriving along with the airborne on August 8 were several AWACS aircraft, more tankers, and transports and support elements from MAC.

The American presence would soon swell to epic proportions, but the first arrivals found themselves in rather stark circumstances. "There was nobody between us and them—*nobody*," said Sgt. Fred Dunning of Richmond, Va., an aircraft mechanic. "I can't speak for others, but I know I was kind of shaky."[5]

Horner, in charge until Schwarzkopf arrived, understood the feeling. "Every night before I go to bed, I have to say to myself, 'What if the attack comes tonight? What do we do?'"[6]

Horner also recalled that "when the A-10s from Myrtle Beach landed over at King Fahd [air base], the wing commander phoned me, and I asked, 'Sandy, how much gas do you have in those airplanes?' He said, 'about 5,000 pounds.' I said, 'you've got ammo in your guns, so you go on alert right now. Be prepared to launch and then recover in the United Arab Emirates, because you could be overrun in hours.' So in those initial days, we felt we were in danger of being pushed out of Saudi Arabia."[7]

The deploying forces were acutely aware of their vulnerability, and rumors fed on the uncertainty. Capt. John Carter, who arrived from Myrtle Beach AFB, S.C., in August, described the night that attack was said to be imminent at a point when "we had about an hour's worth of fuel in the jets, a full gun, and nobody stood between us and the Iraqi army.

"A mission planning team went in to glue maps together while the lucky ones (like me) tried to get some sleep for our 0330 show time. CAS [close air support] pilots are competent with maps and it did not take us long to realize that Iraqi tanks could be sitting in our compound before dawn.

"My roommates and I decided that the prudent Hog driver[8] should sleep in his desert BDUs[9] with his boots handy in case a short-notice tactical retreat became necessary. If we lived to see the morning, we had enough gas to fly a short perimeter defense mission and no way to refuel the jets."

The rumor turned out to be a false alarm, but anxieties continued, and there were differences in how deploying troops elected to make their individual preparations.

"When the next A-10 squadron arrived a few days later, the pilots showed up in the dining hall wearing their sidearms but minus their gas masks," Carter said. We shook our noggins, patted our gas masks, and realized they could not appreciate our sense of urgency."[10]

Interservice rivalries were forgotten. The Air Force was very glad when the Army got there to provide defense on the ground, and the Army was very pleased to have the Air Force holding Saddam's fighters at bay.

[4] James W. Canan, "A Line in the Sand," *Air Force Magazine*, November 1990.

[5] Stewart M. Powell, "Desert Duty," *Air Force Magazine*, February 1991.

[6] Powell, "Desert Duty."

[7] Horner interview, May 30, 1991.

[8] A-10 pilot.

[9] Battle dress uniform.

[10] Capt. John Carter, 511th TFS, written statement, May 1991.

Airmen sweltered in heat that reached 130 degrees at midday and pounded pegs into rock-hard sand to create "Bedrock City," a billeting area of tents for 1,100 persons located near a flight line.[11] Despite the preparations made by the Saudis, the environment was austere.

About nine percent of the US personnel deploying to the Gulf were in Civil Engineering and Services. In one instance, they built a base from the ground up in forty days.

In the meantime, President Bush continued his efforts to build a coalition. At the urging of US Ambassador Thomas Pickering, the UN Security Council imposed a trade embargo on Iraq August 6.

Secretary Baker traveled to Turkey. Turkey earned more than $300 million a year in oil pipeline fees from Iraq and obtained half its oil from Iraq, which was also a major trading partner. Baker asked the Turks to shut down the pipeline, join in the trade sanctions, and allow major NATO air forces to be added to those already in place at Incirlik, near the border with Syria.

The Turks estimated they would lose about $2.5 billion annually by those actions. At Baker's suggestion, the Emir of Kuwait offered to compensate the Turks for the full amount of their estimated losses. Turkish President Turgut Ozal agreed to Baker's requests. Analysts later estimated the beefed-up forces at Incirlik caused Saddam to keep more than 100,000 troops in northern Iraq.[12]

Bush, Baker, and other high-level officials worked the telephones. Over the next three weeks, the President called some sixty foreign leaders. He urged Japan, Germany, and wealthy Arab states to provide fast assistance to Turkey, Egypt, and Jordan, countries hard hit by the trade embargo. He asked other oil producing countries to increase their production to replace the lost output from Iraq and Kuwait.

After Bush promised to forgive Egypt's $6.7 billion military debt, President Mubarak agreed to send 5,000 troops to join the coalition. Bush even convinced Syrian President Hafez Assad to join the coalition, an action for which Syria was paid some $3 billion by Gulf oil states.

Members of Congress joined the President in soliciting help. Germany and Japan, which said they could not provide military forces because of constitutional constraints, came through with pledges of $5.5 billion and $9 billion, respectively, after the House of Representatives voted to withdraw the 50,000 troops the US has stationed in Japan. (The bill was never considered by the Senate and did not become law.)

On August 9, the UN passed a resolution rejecting Iraq's annexation of Kuwait. On August 10, the NATO Ministers in Brussels stated "strong support" for the US deployments and endorsed actions by NATO member nations, including France and Great Britain, which promised to send naval forces, and Italy, Spain, and Portugal, which offered the coalition use of their air bases.

[11] Powell, "Desert Duty."

[12] Frederick, *Desert Storm.*

The USAF Fighter Buildup

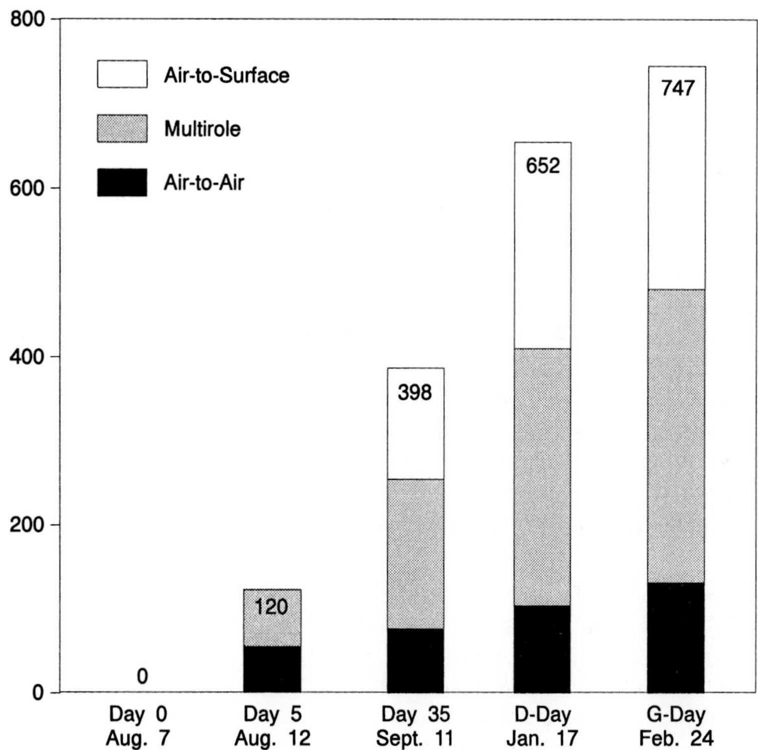

Eventually, the coalition would put 2,790 fixed-wing aircraft of all types—half of them from the US Air Force—into the war zone. Of these, 747 would be USAF fighters, the equivalent of 10.4 tactical wings.

Source: Air Force briefing, March 21, 1991.

The Aluminum Bridge
Cumulative Passengers and Tons of Cargo Airlifted

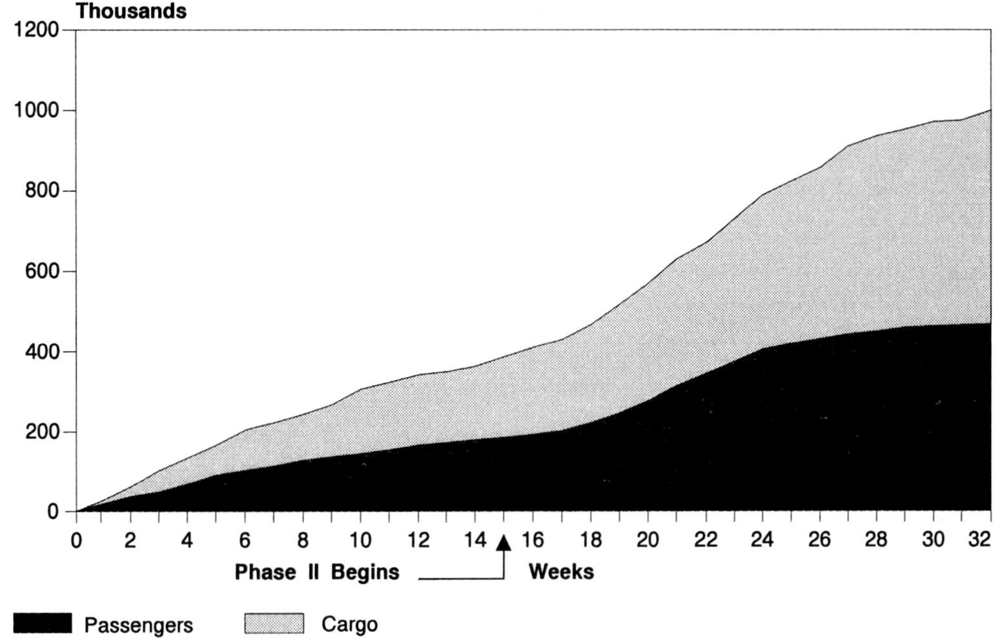

Source: Military Airlift Command; excluding C-130, MAC Mission Support.

[13] "Air Force Performance in Desert Storm," USAF white paper, April 1991.

On the same day, at an emergency Arab summit, the Arab League voted to send a pan-Arab force to defend Saudi Arabia.

By mid-August, American forces and the forces of other nations were pouring into Saudi Arabia. The remainder of the 82d Airborne was coming by air, and the 24th Mechanized Infantry Division from Ft. Stewart, Ga., was en route aboard the USNS *Capella*, a Navy fast sealift ship. The hospital ships USS *Comfort* and USS *Mercy* were activated. Australia and Canada announced they were sending war ships to the Gulf.

The first Egyptian and Moroccan troops arrived August 11. On August 12, the I Marine Expeditionary Force left Camp Pendleton, Calif., and the 101st Airborne Division, Fort Campbell, Ky., moved toward embarkation points. The deployment of the 101st was illustrative of the logistics required by Desert Shield. It took 1,174 trucks from twenty-seven carriers five days to move the division from Fort Campbell to the port at Jacksonville, Fla.

Coalition Forces Pour In

The coalition forces came and kept coming. Thirty-eight hours after the notice to deploy, US F-15s were flying defensive patrols along the Iraqi border. Within thirty-five days, the coalition air forces had a fighter force in the Gulf that equaled Iraq's fighter capability.[13]

On August 14, King Hussein of Jordan met with Saddam and later reported to President Bush that Iraq was determined to fight. Saddam informed Iran he would return territory and prisoners taken during the eight-year war. By August 16, Saddam had more than 160,000 troops and 1,000 tanks in Kuwait. He threatened to intern 4,000 Britons and 2,000 Americans still living in Iraq. The next day, the Speaker of the Iraqi Parliament announced the Britons and Americans would be held as "human shields."

Saddam offered to release the detainees if President Bush guaranteed in writing to withdraw US forces and end the economic embargo. Bush replied that Iraqi treatment of the hostages was "unacceptable and an

The Desert Shield Deployment Begins
The Airlift in August 1990

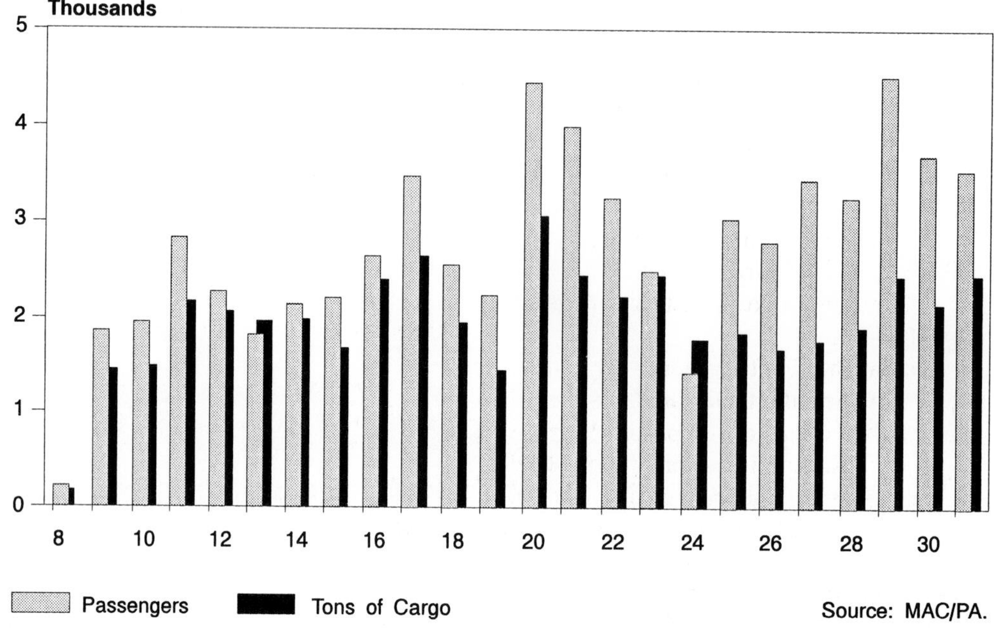

Source: MAC/PA.

offense against all norms of international behavior."

Military Airlift Command people and aircraft were working overtime everywhere. The Air National Guard and Air Force Reserve had been asked for volunteers as soon as the Iraqi invasion began. Almost overnight, more than 6,000 volunteers were on active duty, most of them augmenting MAC.

On August 17, Gen. H. T. Johnson, Commander in Chief of US Transportation Command and Military Airlift Command, activated Stage I of the Civil Reserve Air Fleet. This was the first time in its thirty-eight year history that the CRAF had been activated. Under Stage I, sixteen civilian airlines provided eighteen long-range international passenger aircraft to carry troops and twenty long-range cargo aircraft with specially reinforced floors to carry military equipment. Along with enough crew members to fly them around the clock, they joined the airlift effort.

Fully ninety-four percent of the C-5s in the Military Airlift Command fleet and most of the C-141s were required for missions into the Gulf. The C-141s, which normally flew about five hours a day in peacetime, were now averaging fourteen to fifteen hours in the air per day.[14]

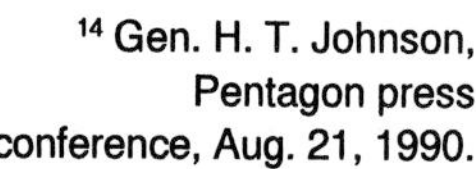
[14] Gen. H. T. Johnson, Pentagon press conference, Aug. 21, 1990.

Elements of the Airlift

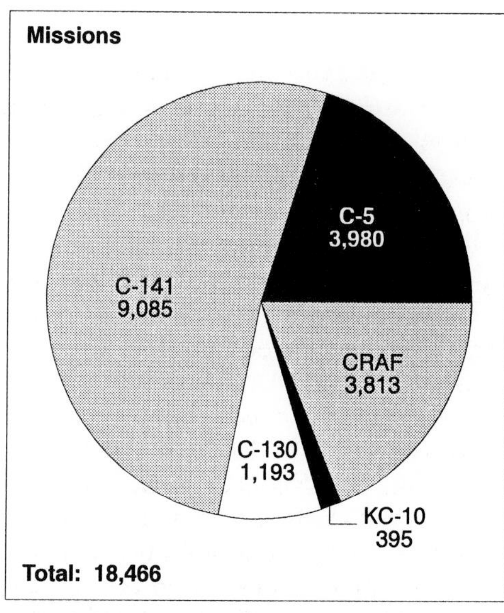

The C-141 was the workhorse of the intertheater airlift into the Gulf during Desert Shield and Desert Storm. The Civil Reserve Air Fleet carried the majority of the personnel.

Source: Department of Defense.

The airlift was an "aluminum bridge" to the Gulf. Grueling as it was, General Johnson provided a reminder that it could have been much harder. "We're fortunate we didn't have to fight our way in," he said.[15]

Some eighty-five percent of the equipment for Operations Desert Shield and Desert Storm was transported by ship, but the majority of people were transported by airlift. In August alone, MAC flew more than 2,000 missions hauling more than 106 million pounds of cargo and carrying more than 72,000 people over distances exceeding 7,000 miles.

Running the airlift was not simply a matter of matching the total number of transports to the volume of troops and cargo to be carried. The configuration of the CRAF airliners—the size and location of the doors, for example—made them useful mainly for transporting troops. The C-141 StarLifter was the workhorse of the airlift, but it cannot handle either oversize (very large) or outsize (extremely large) cargo, such as Abrams tanks. During the early deployments, sixty percent of the air cargo was oversize, and twenty-five percent was outsize,[16] which put a heavy burden on MAC's big lifters.

The Call-up

President Bush signed an executive order August 22 authorizing the call-up of Selected Reservists for ninety days of active duty. (The authorization would be widened and the length of tour extended by subsequent actions.) Indeed, many Guardsmen and Reservists were called and did serve in the Gulf War—but many of them had already volunteered before the order was issued.

Massive US and coalition deployments continued, but President Bush knew he had enough military might in the Gulf region to deter an attack by Saddam. The question now was whether to wait for the economic sanctions to work or to go to war. In September, Bush met with Mikhail Gorbachev in Helsinki, Finland. The Soviet leader stated he supported the US position that Saddam must pull out of Kuwait immediately.

The sanctions were having some effect, cutting off ninety percent of Saddam's trade, but it did not appear that they would be enough to force him to leave Kuwait. He would have to be driven out.

As the American presence grew, so did Saddam's. By the end of October, the coalition had 275,000 troops—about 210,000 of them Americans—in the region.

Saddam, however, had increased his force in Kuwait to an estimated 430,000. He had massive reserves of military manpower re-

[15] Powell, "Desert Duty."

[16] *Conduct of the Persian Gulf Conflict: An Interim Report to Congress.* Department of Defense, July 1991.

Combat Aircraft of the Coalition Air Forces

Country	Type	Number of Aircraft
Bahrain	F-5E	12
Belgium	F-16	18 (to Turkey)
Canada	CF-18	30
France	SEPECAT Jaguar GR Mk 1 Mirage 2000C Mirage F1-C Mirage F1-CR	24 12 8 4
Germany	Alpha Jet, G91R	18 (to Turkey)
Italy	Tornado Alpha Jet, G91R	8 18 (to Turkey)
Kuwait	Mirage F1-K A-4KU	15 20
Netherlands	F-16	18 (to Turkey)
Oman	Jaguar, Hawker Hunter, and BAC-167 Strikemaster	50
Qatar	Mirage F1-C, Hawker Hunter, and Alpha Jet	19
Saudi Arabia	Tornado IDS F-5E/F F-15 RF-5E BAC-167 Strikemaster	48 53 69 10 36
United Arab Emirates	Mirage 2000Es, Mirage 5AD, Hawker Hunter, MB.339, and MB.326K	57 21
United Kingdom	Tornado GR Mk 1 Tornado GR Mk 1A SEPECAT Jaguar GR Mk 1 Buccaneers Tornado F-3	42 6 12 12 18

Sources: *Air Force Magazine;* Department of Defense; *Aviation Week & Space Technology*; World Defense Almanac.

maining. With full mobilization, he could raise his force to two million—fully seventy-five percent of all Iraqi men between the ages of eighteen and thirty-four.[17]

Along the border, the forces watched and took each other's measure. Iraqi pilots raced their MiG-25s to the frontier, then turned back when US F-15s picked them up on radar.[18] Lt. Col. Laszlo Bakonyi of Austin, Tex., an AWACS mission commander, supplied an apt name for this tactic: "They just like to duke the border," he said.[19]

The flying activity during the Desert Shield buildup served another purpose. Day after day, the Iraqis saw the coalition air forces surge sorties, launch tankers, fly command and control orbits, and conduct air patrols along the border. They gradually became conditioned to this activity, and thus did not take it as unusual when the coalition marshalled its strike force and launched for the actual attack on January 17.[20]

The Force in the Desert

As in all wars, the troops quickly developed their own irreverent patois. In "Sandspeak," any Iraqi or Bedouin was "Bob," Saddam Hussein was "Sammy," the desert sun was "Big Red," and a "pogue" was anybody who got there after you did.[21]

"A seemingly simple trek to the shower or toilet involves a walk through deep, powdery sand. Once you finish a shower and trudge back to your tent through the blowing sand, you're ready for another shower," reported *The Vulture*, published by the 10th TFW.[22]

The Vulture, circulating from "somewhere in Eastern Saudi Arabia," thought ahead to the war's end and told the folks back home (who no doubt received at least a few copies of the ebullient newsletter) not to be surprised if a returning spouse:

"Goes over to the neighbors' house to take a shower with them.

"Does his laundry with the garden hose and a mop bucket.

"Calls all stores 'Abdul's,' 'Aubi's,' or 'Aukmaud's.'

"Puts all his luggage under his bed and lives out of it until he builds a dresser out of cardboard.

"Stops all buses and asks the driver if he is going to Tent City.

"Writes 'FREE' on all envelopes to be mailed.

"Asks every morning, 'How old is this newspaper?'

"Asks the neighbors if they got any mail."[23]

As Operation Desert Shield progressed, the deploying Air Force units and personnel spread out to more than two dozen bases in Saudi Arabia, Bahrain, Qatar, the United Arab Emirates, Oman, and Turkey and on Diego Garcia in the Indian Ocean.

Conditions were primitive at some of the locations, but airmen made the best of it. "Almost as quickly as the tent city was erected, it was transformed from a slum into a village with its own personality," the 52d TFW reported. "A town hall was established. Street names such as Harm's Way and Scud Row popped up.... Nearly every living facility on the entire base proudly displayed the American flag somewhere."[24]

Troops near the Iraqi border could tune in "Baghdad Bruce" or "Baghdad Betty," whose English-language broadcasts informed them that "When our dear leader's patience has ended, the sands of Arabia shall become your unmarked grave."

The effect on American GIs was not exactly what the propagandists intended. As one American said, "When you're feeling a little down, Iraq Radio really picks up your spirits."[25]

One newly-arrived unit, taking advantage of an opportunity to sleep in the first day in Saudi Arabia, was awakened by the loud wail of a siren. As the shaken troops grabbed for their gas masks, the siren ceased and the speakers picked up what one NCO termed "a bunch of Arabic."

What the GIs had interpreted as a chemical attack warning had been, in fact, the opening measures of the Islamic call to worship.[26]

The US troops in the desert were a combination of active duty, Guard, and Reserve forces. The mix shifted constantly, but at the time of the cease-fire, twenty-

[17] USAF white paper, April 1991.

[18] USAF white paper, September 1991.

[19] Powell, "Desert Duty."

[20] *Conduct of the Persian Gulf Conflict.*

[21] E.M. Flanagan, Jr., "Before the Battle," *Army*, November 1991.

[22] Capt. Sue Pfister, "A Day in the Life," *The Vulture*, Jan. 6, 1991.

[23] MSgt. Rick Rountree, "Don't Be Alarmed," *The Vulture*, Feb. 27, 1991.

[24] 52d TFW Unofficial History, Spangdahlem AB, Germany, 1991.

[25] Powell, "Desert Duty."

[26] Unpublished anecdotal records, 10th TFW.

two percent of the Air Force people in the Gulf would be Guardsmen or Reservists.

By the Pentagon's count for active duty forces on Jan. 6, 1991, a total of 13,387 single parents (1,054 of them Air Force) were in the Gulf theater.[27] Many single parents from the Guard and Reserve also deployed. Most of the single parents had planned against such a contingency and coped with the situation, but the plight of those who had not planned (and consequently faced separation from their children under harrowing circumstances) became a staple of television reports during the buildup.

Since 1972, the number of women on active duty in the armed forces had risen from 45,000 to 223,000, with a similar increase in the Reserve forces. By the time of the Gulf crisis, women made up eleven percent of the active forces and thirteen percent of the Guard and Reserve forces.

Not all of the US troops who deployed to the Gulf had come there from the United States. US European Command shifted from its traditional role as a *supported* command to become a *supporting* command for Desert Shield and Desert Storm.

With cold war tensions easing, EUCOM deployed one third of its combat forces to the Persian Gulf, Turkey, and Israel. All told, European Command would send about 90,000 troops to the Gulf.[28]

The average age of US troops deployed to the Gulf was twenty-eight, but there were some remarkable variations. Everybody on one Air Guard C-130 transport crew, for example, was older than fifty and their average age was fifty-four. Col. Winston Williams, the pilot, was a relative youngster at fifty-one. CMSgt. Howard Cottrell, fifty-eight, was a B-47 bomber crewman in Morocco in 1953, and the loadmaster, SMSgt. John Kephart, fifty-nine, had been in uniform since 1949 and was a mechanic in the Korean War. The crew had been together for many years, and took particular pride in serving in one more action.[29]

US Airpower Afloat

The Persian Gulf	The Red Sea
USS *Midway*	**USS *Kennedy***
F/A-18	F-14
A-6E	A-7
KA-6D	A-6E
E-2	KA-6D
EA-6B	E-2
SH-3	EA-6B
	S-3B
USS *Ranger*	SH-3
F-14	
A-6E	**USS *Saratoga***
KA-6D	F-14
E-2	F/A-18
EA-6B	A-6E
S-3	KA-6D
SH-3	E-2
	EA-6B
USS *Roosevelt*	S-3B
F-14	SH-3
F/A-18	
A-6E	**USS *America***
KA-6D	F-14
E-2	F/A-18
S-3B	A-6E
EA-6B	KA-6D
SH-3	E-2
	EA-6B

Women in the War

Women accounted for six percent of the US force in the Persian Gulf, lower than their overall representation in the services because they were restricted from assignment to direct combat positions.[30]

To the Saudis, the sight of women wearing Western clothing and driving vehicles was unsettling. To US military women, there in defense of Saudi Arabia and the Gulf region, the local reaction was galling. To avoid cultural clashes within the coalition, officials kept the troops isolated. On their infrequent trips to Riyadh marketplaces, women wore flowing robes atop their regular clothes.[31]

Many women flew helicopters and reconnaissance and refueling aircraft in the Gulf War. They also drove trucks, fixed airplanes, and performed other tough jobs. Women commanded units up to brigade size in combat support and combat service areas. Two were captured by the Iraqis as prisoners of war.[32]

Capt. Pollyanna A. Padden, a C-141 aircraft commander from the 437th Airlift Wing, Charleston AFB, S.C., was one of

[27] *Defense 91 Almanac*, Department of Defense, September-October 1991.

[28] Gen. John R. Galvin, Senate Armed Services Committee, March 7, 1991.

[29] Cmdr. Frank Evans, "Senior Aircrew Share Much More Than Memories," *Airman*, June 1991.

[30] Assistant Secretary of Defense Christopher Jehn, Senate Armed Services subcommittee, April 17, 1991.

[31] Powell, *"Desert Duty."*

[32] *Conduct of the Persian Gulf Conflict.*

the pilots who flew the "aluminum bridge" between the United States and the Gulf.

"I was gone twenty-three or twenty-four days a month, going and coming back," she said. "We would go six or seven days at a time, come back, get a change of clothes, pay some bills, and be out the door again within twenty hours from the time we came back."[33]

MAC set aside the regulation for crew rest, she said. "Normally when you go out on a mission, every three days you are off station, you get a twenty-four hour crew rest day. But during the war, MAC waived that. All you needed was twelve hours notification prior to a mission. If you were on alert, there was no prior notification.

"Probably the most frustrating and exhausting thing about the war was that you never knew when you were going to go, you never knew where you were going to be, and you never knew how long you'd be gone."

The aircraft stopped flying only long enough for a crew change, refueling, and offload or onload of cargo. "You would pick up cargo in the States and fly to Torrejon Air Base in Spain," she said. "Forty minutes out of Torrejon, you'd radio the command post that you were inbound. They would alert the next crew to get ready.

"You would land and go right to the billeting office and be assigned someplace to sleep. You'd probably pass the new crew on the way. The aircraft would be on the ground two hours, or less, and the new crew would fly it into Saudi Arabia and back to Europe.

"After twelve or fifteen hours rest, you would pick up a C-141 and fly it into the AOR.[34] Eight hours or so down, four hours or more turning around in Saudi, and then another eight or more back to Torrejon or Ramstein AB, Germany. From there, after crew rest, you might fly back to the States, or turn around and go back down range [into the war zone].

Padden was one of many women who flew the pipeline to and from the war zone. She never flew as a member of an all-woman crew. "We were each assigned to a crew as our turn came up," she said. On more than one occasion, she commanded a crew of three women and two men.

"Flying the wartime schedule was hard," she said. "Now that it's over, everything we do seems easy by comparison."

She described the camaraderie that developed in Saudi Arabia.

"Once, when we stayed overnight in the AOR and they put us in tents in King Khalid Military City, I got up really early in the morning and walked over to a communications center," she said. "Some of the communicators, the ones not working, were listening to the NCAA basketball finals on AFN [Armed Forces Network]. And I sat with those guys who had been there for six long months—you know, forever. We were far, far, away, but we could listen to basketball back home. It was a neat feeling to be there with them. All of us, together, in the war zone."

It was gratifying, Padden said, to be a part of the huge transportation effort. "I saw, over the length of the war, everybody I had ever known in C-141s," she said. "We could recognize each other's voices on the radio, all my classmates who were flying in MAC. It made me feel good about what we were doing, because it was so important. And it was what we were trained to do."

Buford, Boudreau, and Friends

As it turned out, the Iraqis never used their chemical weapons against the coalition, but the men and women on the Saudi side of the border, waiting for the war to start, could not know that yet. They sweated as they worked in protective gear and listened for sirens that would be set off by the machines that continuously analyzed the air content around the bases.

In some cases, they contrived low-technology backup systems for monitoring. One air base named its newspaper *Buford Talks*.[35] Buford was a local chicken, highly regarded by the airmen who saw him as the counterpart of the canaries that miners used to carry into the shaft for early warning of poisonous gases. The theory, for both the miners and the airmen, was that any dangerous chemicals in the air

[33] Capt. Pollyanna A. Padden, interview, Dec. 13, 1991.

[34] CENTCOM's Area of Responsibility.

[35] Frederick, *Desert Storm*.

would get the bird first and give them time to react.

(After the war, reporters asked Schwarzkopf to speculate on why the Iraqis did not use chemical weapons. "Number one," he said, "we destroyed their artillery. We went after their artillery big time. They had major desertions in their artillery, and that's how they would have delivered their chemical weapons. Either that or by air, and we all know what happened to the air."[36])

Buford the Chicken wasn't the only animal adopted locally by the troops. There was also Boudreau the Donkey, who "wandered in off the desert," according to MSgt. Steven M. Williams, deployed to King Fahd AB, Saudi Arabia, from RAF Alconbury in England.

Unlike Buford, Boudreau could not claim even a nominal function other than pet, but his contribution to morale seems to have been considerable, and his appetite for GI rations earned him at least passing notoriety.

"He really liked MREs, and especially chocolate covered cookies," Williams said. "We also fed him carrots, lettuce, and other healthy foods from the mess tent. Our outfit became famous at King Fahd for our donkey. Pretty soon, people began dropping by to see Boudreau and have their picture taken with him.

"We were really sad when we were told we'd have to let him go because of the threat of anthrax. Also, the bosses were afraid he'd become dependent on our kind of chow and after we left, Boudreau might not be able to care for himself. We were pretty heartbroken about it because we had gotten fond of him.

"We used some chocolate covered cookies to lure him into the back of a little pickup truck and took him out past the cement plant near the end of the runway. We let him go there."[37]

The Epicenter in Riyadh

The epicenter of the US presence was Riyadh, the Saudi capital. General Schwarzkopf had his CENTCOM headquarters and operations center in the Ministry of Defense, a city-block-square compound of modern masonry buildings. It did not look a great deal different from its peacetime appearance, except for the armored vehicles and guards every hundred feet or so along the sidewalk.

At Riyadh Air Base, the military runway was parallel to the civilian strip, which lay on the other side of a wide depression in the ground. The most notable feature of this wadi was the Patriot missile compound. The Patriot batteries stood above the depression, with camouflage netting above their radars.

Military airplanes, including row after row of C-130s, AWACS, and Joint STARs radar aircraft, and KC-135 tankers, filled the parking ramps. The apron on the military side grew daily as workmen poured fresh concrete as quickly as it could be manufactured.

In a small building somewhat back from the flight line, Col. Charles M. Pettijohn was in charge of solving problems and performing occasional miracles. As commander of ELF-One, the permanent Air Force unit

[36] Schwarzkopf, news briefing, Feb. 27, 1991.

[37] MSgt. Steven M. Williams, interview, Aug. 8, 1991.

The USAF Combination

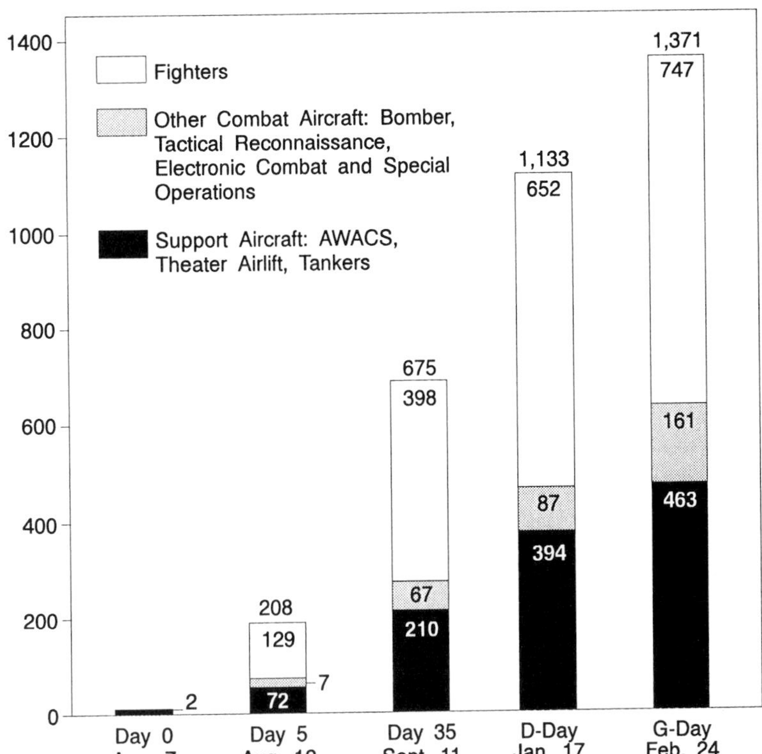

assigned to Riyadh, Pettijohn had seen his command grow from thirty-five people to thousands in a matter of weeks. Among other duties, it was Pettijohn's responsibility to find billeting for 16,000 troops.

CENTAF headquarters and operations centers were housed in the Royal Saudi Air Force compound. A children's playground nearby was soon occupied by trailers, vehicles, tents, and camouflage netting. This area, like many others in Riyadh, was festooned with satellite dishes, antennas, cables, wiring, and stacks of boxes in which military equipment had been delivered.

On the Home Front

On the US home front, defense industry and the services had shifted preparations into high gear, making the most of every day available to them before the fighting started. The armed forces, which had barely begun the twenty-five percent drawdown agreed to the past summer by Congress and the Administration, were generally well-equipped and well-supplied.

Since stocks of weapons and equipment had been built up considerably in the 1980s, industry would not be asked for new production of major items for the Gulf War. There was a need, however, to expedite what was already in the production pipeline, and the Pentagon found itself scrambling for some consumable and expendable products.

When Desert Shield began, for example, the Defense Department had *no* production base for desert boots. Sixty days later, four contractors were producing 136,000 desert boots (including the popular new Schwarzkopf model) a month. In August, three producers could supply three million Meals, Ready to Eat (MREs)—the standard field

[38] David J. Berteau, House Banking Subcommittee, June 4, 1991.

[39] Air Force Association. *Lifeline Adrift: The Defense Industrial Base in the 1990s. September 1991.*

[40] John T. Correll, "Let's Hear It For the Loggies," *Air Force Magazine*, August 1991.

[41] The 401st TFW Unofficial History of the Gulf War, Torrejon AB, Spain, 1991.

Airlift Within the Theater
Sorties Per Day

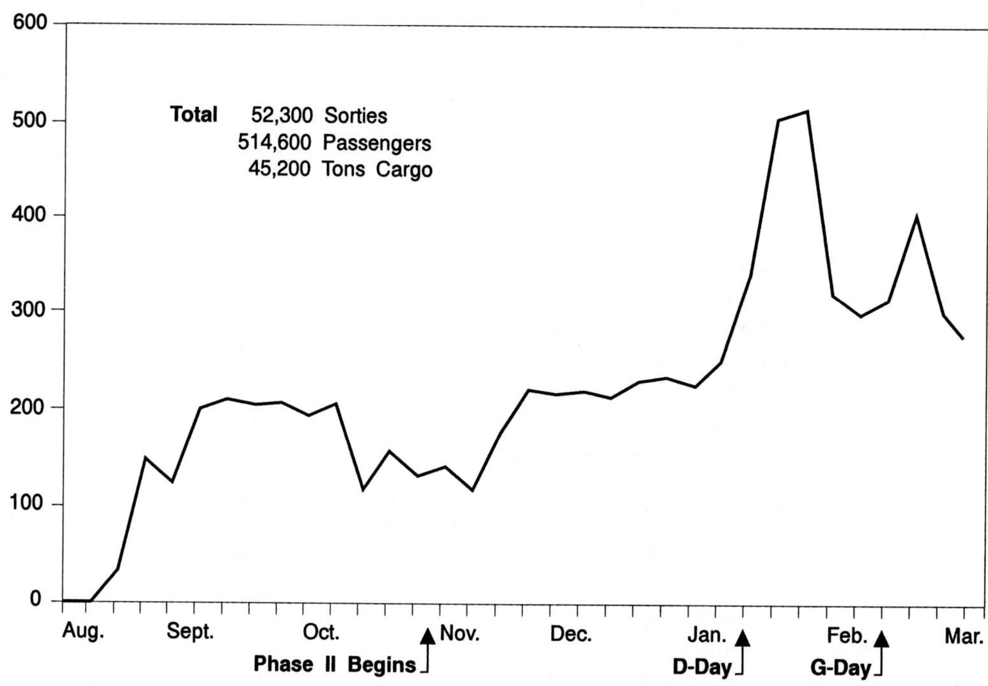

In addition to carrying passengers and cargo to the Gulf, the airlifters had a heavy schedule of missions within the combat theater. At one point while Schwarzkopf was moving his forces west in the "Hail Mary" redeployment, C-130s were landing at a rate of one every ten minutes.

Source: AF Briefing.

ration—a month. That quickly climbed to twenty-two producers and sixteen million MREs a month.[38]

Suppliers proved themselves willing to forget the formalities in the interest of supporting Desert Storm. When the Department of Defense needed shackles to secure M1 tanks for overseas movement, AM General provided them in three days without a page of government paperwork.[39]

Support commands pulled out the stops, too. Air Force Logistics Command accelerated the repair of some 80,000 critical parts and expedited the overhaul of seventy aircraft. Returning these aircraft to operation ahead of time gave the Air Force a cumulative 931 days of additional flying service.[40]

Sometimes those supporting the effort on the home front added a bit extra to send their regards to the force in the desert. "A special 5,400-pound present from General Electric made it through the supply system just in time for Christmas," the 401st TFW reported. "A needed F-16 engine came wrapped in plastic, decorated with paper Santas, reindeer, and candy canes. Small passport-size photos of GE workers were pasted below the 'Season's Greetings' inscription at one end of the engine."[41]

Plan to Double Forces

General Powell flew to Riyadh on October 21 to confer with Schwarzkopf and review his plans. Their consensus was that a doubling of US forces to at least 400,000 was required to provide a good chance of driving Saddam out of Kuwait with a minimum of US and coalition casualties. When Powell returned to Washington, Bush approved the plan. Because of weather considerations (it is usually bad in the Gulf region in the spring) and religious holidays in March, a January start date for an air war, followed by a ground attack, was agreed upon. That meant the forces would have to be doubled between November and mid-January.

The President realized he needed the United Nations, Congress, and the American people with him. He decided to go after UN concurrence first, reasoning that congressional approval would follow. The US held the rotating UN Security Council chairmanship in November; that was the best time to bring his proposal before the council.

On November 8, the President and Secretary of Defense announced that troop strength in the Gulf would be doubled and that deployments would continue "to ensure that if force is needed, adequate military strength will be available."

US Active-Duty Troops Deployed

As of February 15, 1991

Grade	Army	Navy	Marine Corps	Air Force	Total
E-1	3,074	4,341	292	10	7,690
E-2	12,588	9,772	4,119	622	27,101
E-3	40,092	17,794	26,433	6,437	90,756
E-4	75,364	21,459	17,483	14,758	129,064
E-5	47,878	16,940	8,615	12,113	85,546
E-6	24,847	11,678	4,475	5,239	46,239
E-7	12,989	4,852	2,466	2,774	23,081
E-8	3,405	1,441	1,063	551	6,460
E-9	849	620	315	200	1,984
W-1	1,059	----	78	----	1,137
W-2	2,632	345	387	----	3,364
W-3	1,364	106	137	----	1,607
W-4	578	120	73	----	771
O-1	3,063	820	443	213	4,539
O-2	4,880	2,026	1,611	1,304	9,821
O-3	7,446	3,360	2,033	4,256	17,095
O-4	2,942	1,841	755	1,269	6,807
O-5	1,232	831	356	625	3,044
O-6	360	314	102	191	967
O-7	25	9	11	4	49
O-8	9	7	6	4	26
O-9	5	3	1	1	10
O-10	1	----	----	----	1
Totals	**246,682**	**98,652**	**71,254**	**50,571**	**467,159**

Deployment figures changed constantly, but the Department of Defense says that these numbers are illustrative of the totals deployed. For data on Guard and Reserve deployments, see Chapter 11.

Source: Department of Defense.

The antiwar movement picked up steam. On Capitol Hill, some congressmen and senators, who had just begun a two-month recess, called for a special session to consider whether a declaration of war was needed.

Sen. Sam Nunn (D-Ga.), Chairman of the Senate Armed Services Committee, called his committee back to Washington for a special hearing. Adm. William Crowe and Air Force Gen. David Jones, both former chairmen of the Joint Chiefs of Staff, argued that the sanctions would work. So did former Defense Secretary James Schlesinger, former Secretary of State Cyrus Vance, and former National Security Advisor Zbigniew Brzezinski. Former Secretary of State Henry Kissinger, however, argued for the use of force.

Secretary Baker, Ambassador Thomas Pickering, and the President went to work on the UN vote. At a session of the Conference on Security and Cooperation in Europe meeting in Paris, they lined up thirty-three national leaders who agreed to support a resolution for the use of force in the Gulf. Baker traveled to Yemen and Latin America, among other places, soliciting support. On November 29, the Security Council voted 12-2 for Resolution 678, authorizing the use of force to expel Iraq from Kuwait if Iraqi forces were not withdrawn by January 15.

The President then invited the Iraqi Foreign Minister, Tariq Aziz, to Washington and offered to send Secretary Baker to Baghdad with a message for Saddam. In public statements, he hardened his position. Before, he had talked only of getting Saddam out of Kuwait. Now he spoke also of blunting Iraq's military prowess and eliminating its nuclear, biological, and chemical warfare capability.

Bush sent Baker to meet with Aziz in Geneva on January 9. At the meeting, Baker gave Aziz an explicitly-worded personal letter from Bush to Saddam. The ambassador refused to deliver it. The meeting failed. Baker then flew to Riyadh and got King Fahd's approval to start the air war.

On the Eve of War

As peace initiatives faltered, the pace of activity quickened at air bases in the desert. In late December, US fighters started flying round-the-clock combat air patrols to defend AWACS aircraft operating along the Iraqi-Saudi border.

The 36th TFW unit history recalls the adjustment required at that point by the "night guys," who got their turns to rest during the daytime: "Noise from tent city construction, generators, and flapping tent canvas, along with the lack of darkness in tents made sleeping tough. The use of ear plugs and creatively-designed eye covers made the change of lifestyle at least liveable."[42]

[42] *The Gulf War: the 36th TFW Story*. Bitburg AB, Germany, 1991.

On January 12, both houses of Congress approved the President's use of force if he deemed it necessary. On January 15, the President signed the National Security Directive authorizing the beginning of the war.

At the end of December, 132 US ships were enroute to Saudi Arabia and forty-four were returning to the United States. The Military Traffic Management Command had used nearly 16,000 rail cars and 28,000 trucks to deliver supplies and equipment to ports. The airlift—which at its peak had an airplane landing in the desert every eleven minutes—continued.

Three more carrier battle groups had been added, for a total of six in the Gulf. US troop strength in the region stood at 430,000. The coalition fielded 2,614 aircraft, of which 1,990 were American.

Saddam was soon to experience the massive might of American airpower. ■

USAF Photo by SSgt. F. Lee Corkran

SSgt. Karen Fulce and A1C Will Grant of the 401st TFW make sure an AIM-9 missile is secure on the wing of an F-16 fighter.

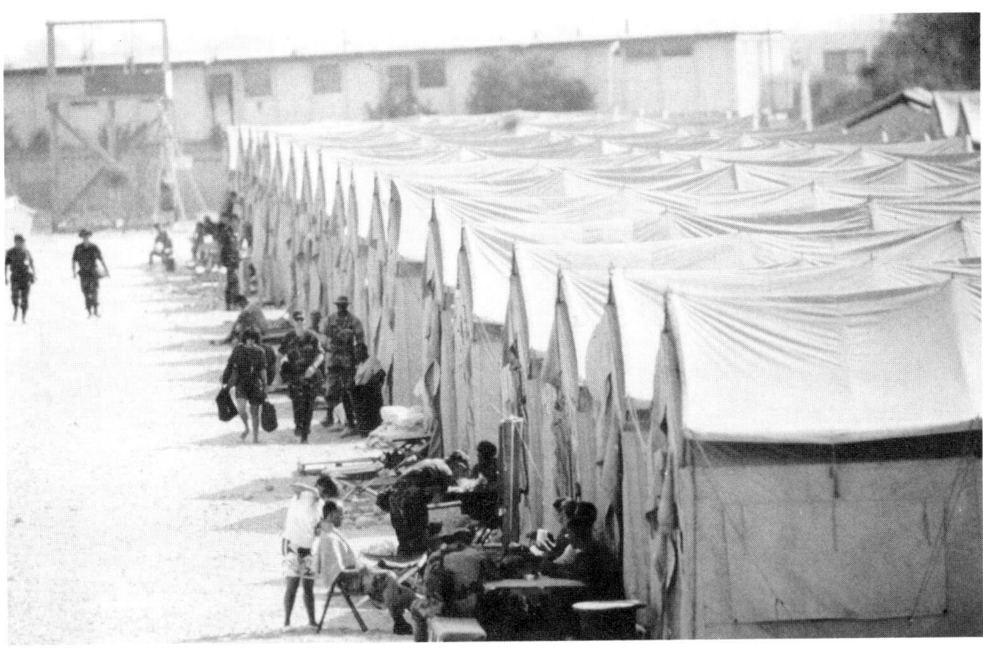

This tent city was one of many that US forces put up in the desert. Conditions were difficult, especially for those on duty at night and getting their sleep in the daytime, but the troops made the most of it, and the tent city soon developed into a village with its own personality.

The Airpower Controversy

For all of its dashing public image, the US Air Force entered the 1990s fighting off an assault on its fundamental concepts. A commentary by military reformer Jeffrey Record, for example, repeated an old allegation that airpower is not "decisive" in war and asked "Should we abolish the Air Force?"[1] Dr. Records's article, widely read and reprinted, distills the flavor of the attack, and will serve as a reference for those who want to examine the controversy in more detail.

The "not decisive" issue and related ones—such as the accusation that airpower had been "oversold"—had become popular fare for newspaper columnists and sideline critics. As US forces began deploying to the Gulf, David C. Morrison of the *National Journal* termed the Air Force's performance in three wars a "history of costly failure," and popular strategist Harry G. Summers warned against "the fanciful notion that a war can be won quickly and decisively by the use of airpower alone."[2]

The Air Force might have shrugged it off as media speculation except that it was gaining some attention and credibility on Capitol Hill.

In fact, the modern Air Force had not claimed a capability to win wars alone. That proposition, as well as the more extreme promises about the "decisiveness" of airpower, had been made mainly by Giulio Douhet, an Italian airman writing in the 1920s, who said flatly that future wars would be won and lost in the air.[3] (In hindsight, Douhet stands up better than his contemporaries who argued against airpower, but his predictions were excessive.)

Even the harshest critics acknowledged that military airpower is useful but held that it was inherently a supplement or an adjunct to the classic forms of military power, represented by the Army and the Navy.

Airmen had heard all these questions before. During World War II, allied bombing wrecked German war production capacity, tied up forces and weapons in air defense, interdicted the railroads, and cleaned the Luftwaffe out of the skies before D-Day, but still the critics wondered how much airpower had contributed. Only in an unusual instance, the dropping of the atomic bomb on Japan, had it been truly "decisive," they said.

The Air Force also found itself compared unfavorably with the US Navy, which was articulating a "maritime strategy" in which the Navy and Marine Corps were seen as the "military forces of choice" in times of national crisis.[4]

As the youngest of the services, having gained its independence from the Army in 1947, the Air Force is the only service that faces continuing challenges to justify its existence. It is not lost on airmen that nobody ever asks whether seapower or landpower is decisive alone, or wonders if the Army or the Navy should be abolished.

Beset with these criticisms—and seeking to position itself to meet requirements in a changing world, where it might be called upon to project power to faraway places without the benefit of established bases at the scene of crisis—the Air Force had begun to formulate new doctrines.[5] It presented its concept, called "Global Reach—Global Power" to the public and Congress in a white paper in 1990.[6] The critics sneered.

The Air Force went into the Gulf War with something to prove. ■

[1] Jeffrey Record, "Into the Wild Blue Yonder: Should We Abolish the Air Force?" Heritage Foundation *Policy Review*, Spring 1990.

[2] John T. Correll, "The Indictment of Airpower," *Air Force Magazine*, January 1991.

[3] Giulio Douhet. *The Command of the Air* (1921). Reprinted by Office of Air Force History, 1983.

[4] See, e.g., Adm. Carlisle A.H. Trost, "Maritime Strategy for the 1990s," *US Naval Institute Proceedings*, May 1990.

[5] James W. Canan, "Global Power From American Shores," *Air Force Magazine*, October 1989.

[6] "The US Air Force and National Security: Global Reach—Global Power," USAF white paper, June 1990.

USAF Photo by MSgt. Bill Thompson

Desert Storm ground crews upload A-10 attack aircraft from the 23d TFW, England AFB, La., with 30 mm cannon rounds, Mk. 87 cluster bombs, AGM-65 Maverick missiles, and AIM-9 Sidewinder missiles.

USAF Photo by SSgt. Dean Wagner

Elements of Saddam's warmaking capacity lie damaged in the Euphrates River valley. Either way—whether the Iraqis used their equipment in battle or tried to hold it back in protected positions—coalition firepower took a tremendous toll.

4. Plan of Attack

Targets for the Persian Gulf air campaign are seen in this detail of a map that hung in the "Black Hole," where Glosson's planning and operational action group labored during the war.

At Schwarzkopf's request, the Air Force develops a strategic bombing campaign.

For years, Col. John A. Warden, the US Air Force's honcho for strategic war planning, had promised his wife, Margie, that they would take a Caribbean cruise someday. Someday arrived. And that's where they were—on a cruise ship south of Cuba—when he got the news of the invasion of Kuwait August 2 on the ship's Ocean News television program. The frustrated Warden was unable to get back to Washington until early Sunday morning, August 5.

Monday, in the Pentagon, Warden convened a small task force of planning and operational staff officers to develop a basic conceptual plan for the defense of Saudi Arabia. Most of these officers were assigned to the *Checkmate* division of the Air Staff.

The *Checkmate* staffers were old hands at analyzing operational aspects of a possible war with the Soviet Union. They were experts at computerized wargaming and combat simulation. Months before, when Saddam Hussein had begun his belligerent posturing toward Kuwait, they had begun to talk basic planning concepts for a war that might be fought in defense of Saudi Arabia.

Warden assembled his group in the *Checkmate* office suite, which is an austere, restricted access vault several floors below ground level in the basement of the Pentagon. There, in a large briefing room with walls covered by floor-to-ceiling maps of the Soviet Union and eastern Europe, he stood before a large greaseboard and conducted a brainstorming session. As worthwhile ideas were expressed, he scrawled them on the board. By the end of the day, they had outlined a plan.

The group continued to work all day Tuesday. On Wednesday, August 8, Warden was called to the office of Gen. John M. Loh, the Air Force Vice Chief of Staff. "General Schwarzkopf has requested us to develop a strategic air campaign plan," Loh said. "What do you have to answer the mail?"[1] Schwarzkopf and Horner had developed a bare bones plan of their own for the deployment and reception of aircraft into Saudi Arabia and for defense against an attack by Saddam. Their staffs were almost swamped with detailed planning for the reception and beddown of coalition forces in the Persian Gulf.

Warden's plan was for an attack into Iraq, with the purpose of forcing Saddam to withdraw from Kuwait. He had already named the plan "Instant Thunder" to emphasize it would be the direct opposite of "Rolling Thunder," the gradually escalating air war over North Vietnam. He told Loh they were just finishing something he thought would be appropriate. In the afternoon, he gave Loh a twelve-page brief that described a conceptual strategic air campaign against Iraq.

Loh liked it and suggested a few changes. Gen. Michael Dugan, the Chief of Staff, liked it, too. On Friday, August 10, Warden and a small team of his officers, along with Maj. Gen. R. Minter Alexander, USAF Director of Plans, briefed the plan to General Schwarzkopf at his headquarters at MacDill AFB, Fla.

[1] Col. John A. Warden, interview, April 16, 1991.

Five Strategic Rings

The plan was based on concepts stated by Warden two years before in his book, *The Air Campaign.*[2] In the book, Warden postulated five concentric "rings," or "centers of gravity," for strategic planning. The center ring, and the most important one, is the enemy's leadership. Outside that is key production—oil and electricity, for example. The third ring is infrastructure—roads, railroads, lines of communication. The fourth ring is population. The outside ring is fielded military forces.

The *Checkmate* group roughed in their ideas on the greaseboard, with the five strategic rings marked across the top.

"By attacking leadership," said Lt. Col. Bernard E. Harvey, a key member of Warden's brain trust, "we meant to attack leadership facilities, and we did that throughout the war. The places where Saddam and his other leaders would direct operations are certainly military targets.

"The target, really, was Saddam's regime. What we wanted to do was isolate them and incapacitate them. Isolate them so Saddam could not lie and tell the people we were attacking them directly. Isolate him from his military forces so he couldn't order the army to attack or use weapons of mass destruction, or, if he could order them, not be able to orchestrate their activities.

"We wanted to inflict strategic paralysis on his regime so they weren't even able to perform the normal functions of government."[3]

Also under leadership, Warden listed telecommunications and command, control, and communications, because Saddam used them so extensively. He employed television not only to disinform but also to intimidate and to maintain his iron grip on the people.

The telephone system was another tool for domination. "We discovered that almost the primary function of the telephone system was to allow surveillance of the population," Harvey said. Most phone calls funneled back to a very small number of buildings in Baghdad.

"In fact, we found out that more than half of Iraqi military land communications ran through the commercial telephone system. So the telephone system became a doable target."

Doable meant "without unnecessary civilian casualties or collateral damage," he said. "It would have taken in the vicinity of 10,000 bombs in World War II to inflict the damage we did to the Al-Karakh International Telecommunications Center building in downtown Baghdad with one smart bomb. And, of course, we would have killed thousands of civilians and destroyed other facilities we didn't want to destroy."

Under "Key Production," the group listed, among other things, electricity. "We didn't want to destroy his electrical system for ten years," Harvey said. Rather than targeting generator buildings, the group targeted the switching grid yards that stood next to all electrical generating plants. "Then, once the war is over, if outside assistance were able to be flown in, in a matter of a couple of months, a switching yard could be restored." Sometimes transformers were targeted. They are easier to replace than generating facilities.

Under "Infrastructure," they listed railroads, roads, and bridges. "We intended only to destroy a couple of railroad bridges to cut communications between Baghdad and Basra," Harvey said. "Later on, when it became necessary to build more than just a strategic plan, highway bridges were added as a way of isolating the army in Kuwait."

Under "Population," the group listed "psychological operations."

"We avoided attacking the population at all costs," Harvey emphasized. By dropping leaflets and "other psychological warfare operations I can't go into," he said, "we simply told people to stay home, to stop working for the regime, and to assure them we did not want to hurt them.

"Psychological operations had a significant impact on the army in Kuwait. A lot of enemy prisoners of war had leaflets in their pockets or said that they had read them."

The last ring was "Fielded Forces."

"We needed to take away Saddam's threat to his neighbors and the region," he said. "We had to try to take out his ballistic

[2] John A. Warden III. *The Air Campaign: Planning for Combat*. Published originally by National Defense University Press, 1988. Pergamon-Brassey's, 1989.

[3] Lt. Col. Bernard E. Harvey, interview, May 9, 1991.

missile capability, his long- range aircraft, and, of course, we needed to take apart the Republican Guard. And, first, we had to take out his strategic air defense systems to be able to hit all the other targets."

Not the AirLand Battle

Sitting at the conference table in a large office at CENTCOM, with the bright Florida sunshine streaming through big windows, Warden was conscious that the air campaign he was proposing to General Schwarzkopf did not follow the dictates of the Army's AirLand Battle doctrine. That doctrine postulated a relatively short air campaign followed by a ground force attack with air support.

Warden's Air Force plan was designed virtually to destroy Saddam Hussein's warfighting capability before a coalition ground attack took place.

That appealed to Schwarzkopf. He knew that, while his mission at that time was defensive, the President's stated objectives to restore the Kuwaiti government, protect regional stability, and remove the Iraqi army were inherently offensive operations. It would take months to build up his ground forces enough to fight an offensive campaign. Only airpower could go on the offensive quickly.

While Warden briefed his plan, Schwarzkopf was rather quiet (for him) and asked few questions. When it was over, he expressed confidence that the plan could be carried out, and told Warden to lay it before General Powell.

Returning to Washington, Warden briefed the plan to the Chairman of the Joint Chiefs in his office on the second floor of the Pentagon. Powell listened intently and said he liked the plan—so far. Warden was feeling very confident about it. "I think the Iraqis will withdraw from Kuwait as a result of the strategic campaign," he recalls telling Powell.

"Destroy Them"

"I don't want them to withdraw," Powell replied. "I want to destroy them. You need to have another phase to do that. I want to kill all their tanks."

"So, at that point, then," Warden says, "we started working not only the strategic campaign but also the beginning of what we came to call 'the operational level campaign,' which was the direct attack on the Iraqi army in Kuwait itself."

Powell directed Warden to add Army, Navy, and Marine Corps officers to his *Checkmate* planning team. "You're a joint group now," he said.

"We called the Army and Navy planners," Warden said, "and within a few hours, we had Army and Navy aviators working in the basement with us. We had about 100 people at that point working out of *Checkmate*, of which maybe twenty to thirty percent were Navy and Marine."

"We worked out of the *Checkmate* war planning room, Army, Navy, Marine, and Air Force planners, for over a week," Harvey recalls, "sitting around the conference tables nominating targets and battling to come up with a good consensus."

"Soon," Warden said, "all the Soviet and Warsaw Pact wall maps were covered by big maps of Iraq, Kuwait, and the whole war zone. On one wall, we had a huge satellite picture of Baghdad. Intelligence people and others who had worked in Baghdad, like Ambassador Glaspie, for example, were invited in to help us identify targets. Standing in front of the satellite photo, they would say, for example, 'There was a military command center on the second floor of that building. I drove by it on the way to work.' We'd check the information against other sources, and if it checked out, we'd put it on our list of targets."[4]

The result, Warden remembers, was "a full draft operations order that went down just short of flag level."

They briefed the expanded plan to Schwarzkopf on August 16. "He said some really nice things about airpower," Warden said. "that, in fact, the strength of the United States is in its airpower. He said that he would not be confident of driving the Iraqis out of Kuwait with ground forces alone, even if he had twelve months to do a buildup, because Iraq had one of the best defensive armies in the world and probably *the best* defensive combat engineers in the world.

[4] Warden interview, April 16, 1991.

So, he was very enthusiastic about the application of airpower."

Schwarzkopf directed Warden to take his plan to Horner, who was then in Riyadh. "Brief him," Schwarzkopf said, "and hand it off to him." Warden took along three key staff officers who had helped him develop the plan. They were Harvey and two other lieutenant colonels, Ronnie Stanfill and David A. Deptula.

Horner, who already knew the objectives of the air campaign, listened carefully during the briefings August 21-22, but felt the concept would need significant work to make it a usable operational plan. Warden returned to Washington, but at Horner's request, the three lieutenant colonels remained behind.

The next day, Harvey and Deptula presented the briefing to of the CENTCOM and CENTAF staffs. Horner had already told Glosson to develop the concept into an operational plan.

That evening, Glosson approached the group of young officers and said, "I hope you guys brought more than three days' supply of underwear."[5] The three extended their stay. Deptula remained for the duration of the war as one of the first members of Glosson's "Black Hole" special planning and operational action group.

Setting up initially in a large room next to Horner's office in the Royal Saudi Air Force Building, Glosson went to work. He tasked each wing deployed to Saudi Arabia to assign two aircrews who were expert in employing that wing's weaponry. CENTAF operated the Air Force computer-aided force management system. As more wings arrived, Glosson's staff grew.

General Horner tasked Glosson to prepare an executable air tasking order within a week. The ATO, issued every day, would provide detailed information on each day's flying activities, including assigned targets, type and number of weapons to strike them, which aircraft would carry them, from what bases, air refueling tracks, aircraft and altitudes, as well as quantities of fuel to be transferred to the fighters, takeoff and landing times, restricted areas, intelligence information, and other information vital for each flight. The tracks and altitudes of all supporting aircraft, like AWACS, Joint STARS, and others had to be factored in.

The Target List Grows

Every day, there were new coalition air force assets to be assigned to targets in anticipation of the beginning of the war. New targets were continually added to the list as intelligence became aware of their significance. More weapons and types of weaponry became available. Weapons were matched carefully against targets to achieve specific effects. Strike packages of fighter-bombers, electronic warfare and electronic combat aircraft, air-superiority fighters, and defense suppression aircraft had to be assembled. At the same time, the coalition air forces were flying hundreds of training sorties all over the Persian Gulf area.

Deptula became Glosson's chief planner for the strategic campaign. "There were long, long days," Deptula said, "and basically, what we would do was write out what became known as the master attack plan, one single document that would lay out sequentially the time, where we were going, what we were attacking, with what, and how we were attacking, in a logical format. That's what we did for five months. Prior to the execution of the plan, and as new information became available, we revised it and fine-tuned it."

The Black Hole created an air campaign with five basic objectives: Isolate and incapacitate Saddam's regime, gain and maintain air superiority, destroy his weapons of mass destruction (nuclear, chemical, and biological weapons and production facilities), eliminate Iraq's offensive military capability, and render the army in the Kuwaiti theater of operations ineffective.[6]

Extending from those objectives, Deptula said the people in the Black Hole developed twelve target sets, or groups of targets, to be hit. The leadership and command and control set, for example, included not only control nodes in the communications network but also television towers and transmission facilities. The primacy of air superiority generated a strategic air defense network target set and an airfield target

[5] Lt. Col. David Deptula, interview. May 2, 1991.

[6] Horner, Senate Armed Services Committee, May 21, 1991.

set. There was a chemical target set and sets for Scuds, military production, storage and support, the Republican Guard, electric grids, and oil production, transportation and refining, bridges, and lines of communications.[7]

"Creating each day's attack plan was more complex than dealing with the target sets individually," Deptula said. "Elements of each target set had to be interrelated and treated as parts of a comprehensive plan."

The master attack plan was the engine of the planning process, since it provided a detailed script of what was to happen when, and exactly who was to do it, and with what.

"The best weapon system to achieve the desired effect was selected—regardless of service or country of origin," Deptula said. "General Horner requested weaponry not already in the theater, if we needed it, through the CINC."

Force packages—groups of attacking aircraft—were constructed to exploit specific coalition advantages and enemy weaknesses. For example, night operations were stressed, as were stealth, precision weaponry, cruise missiles, reconnaissance drones, night-capable attack helicopters, and in-flight refueling options.

Weapon system experts from CENTAF staff and field units worked with specialists on intelligence, logistics, and weather. They factored in such specifics as bomb loads and aimpoints. According to their degree of participation in operations, the Royal Air Force, the Royal Saudi Air Force, and other coalition air forces also provided experts.[8]

During the months before Operation Desert Storm began, the Black Hole began tasking groups of aircraft—as many as eighty—to operate together as they would in the war. They did this in southern Saudi Arabia, far beyond the surveillance of Iraqi radar.

The Offensive Begins

Finally, the air offensive began in the early hours of January 17. "We had 160 tankers airborne at one time," Deptula said. "Tankers were stacked with only 500 feet of altitude separation between them. The weather was marginal to bad. Hundreds of fighters rendezvoused with their tankers, sometimes in clouds. The grand air armada, with more than 300 strike aircraft, plus support birds, joined up. Everybody flew exact headings and altitudes, and there weren't any midairs [midair collisions].

"For some time, we had been flying a tanker or two straight for the border, turning back before crossing it. The Iraqis were used to seeing that on their radars. The big difference on the first night of the attack was, when he turned around, a whole mess of F-117s kept on going. F-117s the Iraqis couldn't see. [One of] those F-117s dropped the first bombs on Iraq, taking out an interceptor operations center in the southwest corner."

In Horner's headquarters, there was silence as the clock ticked toward H-hour, 3 a.m. According to Deptula, "General Horner sent Buck [Maj. Mark B.] Rogers upstairs to his office. He said, 'turn on the TV and see what's on CNN.' After a while, Buck called down and said "Baghdad just went off the air!" There's a cheer. I look at my watch and it's exactly 3 a.m." ■

[7] In military usage, "lines of communication" are highways, railroads, navigable waterways, and other access routes.

[8] Deptula interview, Nov. 22, 1991.

5. Onslaught From the Skies

An F-4G Wild Weasel, carrying HARM missiles, glides over Bahrain during Operation Desert Storm. When Weasels were in a combat area, the Iraqi radars did not survive if they operated for more than a few seconds.

USAF Photo by TSgt. Rose Reynolds

Within days, the coalition had wrecked Saddam's command and control and put his air force out of action.

In the air armada that flew on the first night of Desert Storm, virtually every type of attack aircraft possessed by the coalition countries ranged through the flak-lit Iraqi skies.

On the east, Navy and Marine fighters flashed across the coastline to hit airfield runways and coastal defenses. A-6 Intruders hit airfields in Kuwait and naval facilities on the narrow neck of Iraq between Kuwait and Iran. The A-6s were supported by F/A-18 Hornets in their air superiority mode, while EA-6B Prowlers and USAF F-4G Wild Weasels provided jamming and suppression of enemy air defenses.

F-16s equipped with LANTIRN and F-111s flew into Kuwait from the south to attack military installations, troop concentrations, and airfields. They were supported by USAF and Marine defense suppression aircraft, which hooked in across Kuwait's western border.

Coordinated strikes by Air Force, Marine, and British attackers were directed against airfields, strategic installations, and Scud missile sites in southwest Iraq. These included carefully timed attacks by F-111s and F-15Es, followed by British and Saudi Tornados, as well as strikes by B-52s and F-15Es.

B-52 heavy bombers and some of the F-111s dropped area denial weapons with time-delayed fuzes to close several of Saddam's airfields.

Navy A-6s and British Tornados, supported by Navy defense suppression aircraft, coordinated their strikes against airfields to the west of Baghdad.

In the west, Air Force F-15s were joined by Navy F-14 Tomcats, flying from carriers in the Red Sea, to protect the attack flights hitting airfields, Scud sites, and nuclear facilities. Air Force EF-111s provided jamming for strike packages, while F-4G Wild Weasels launched HARMs to take out Iraqi missile direction sites.

Also in the west, Tornados packing British JP233 cratering munitions or Air-Launched Antiradiation Missiles, hit runways, installations, and fighters on airfield ramps.

Precisely-defined targets, including leadership and air defenses in Central Baghdad, were taken out by F-117s, Air-Launched Cruise Missiles, and Navy TLAMs.

The B-52 in Desert Storm

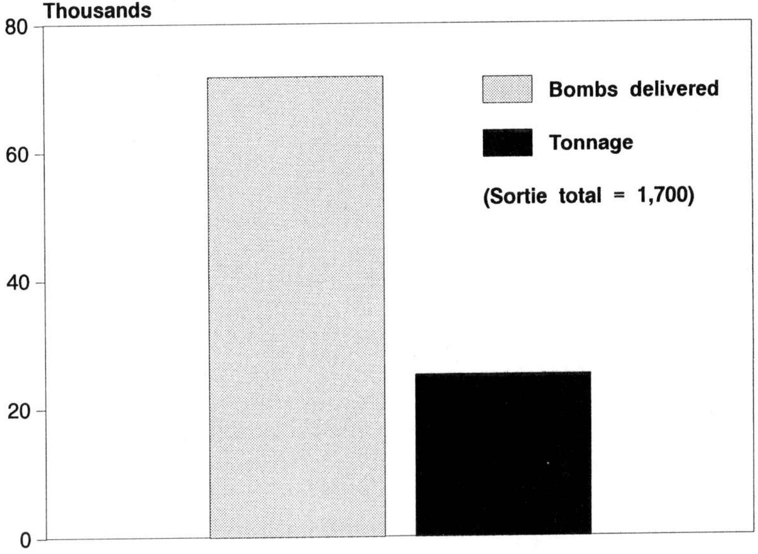

F-117 Stealth fighters ranged far and wide, over hardened command, control, and communications sites, and chemical, biological, and nuclear production and storage points. By dawn, the F-117s had decapitated Saddam's control apparatus. They, along with Navy TLAMs, had virtually shut down his electrical production capability.

Nearly 100 aircraft struck Iraqi air defense positions. Waves of F-16s hit SAM sites and AAA emplacements. F-111Fs and F-15Es, operating at low level in the darkness of the first night, struck airfields and Scud sites.[1] British and Saudi GR1 Tornados cratered airfield runways and hit support structures.

A Thunder of Engines

A dozen B-52Gs unleashed area denial weapons, struck storage areas, and cratered runways, helping to paralyze Saddam's air force.[2] The big bombers, navigating by high-resolution radar and Navstar Global Positioning System satellites in space, roared across the desert at altitudes of less than 400 feet, stunning defenders with the thunder of eight engines as well as with the ordnance they delivered.

F-4G Wild Weasels zeroed in on SAM guidance radars, evading SAMs as they flew toward their targets. The exchange was fierce. One Weasel crew dodged five SA-2 SAMS before destroying the Fan Song radar that controlled the battery. At one point, more than 200 High-Speed Antiradiation Missiles (HARMs) were in flight simultaneously, launched by Weasels and Navy and Marine electronic hunter-killer aircraft.

The Iraqis quickly figured out that turning on their guidance radars invited a Weasel attack, so, after the first night, they shut down whenever Weasels were around, which was nearly always.

Saddam's most critical assets, his command, control, communications, and intelligence (C^3I), integrated air defenses, and power generation capacity, were inoperable. The coalition knocked out his microwave towers, telephone exchanges, relay stations, cables, and transmission lines early.

With air defense sector control sites, integrated operations centers, and the air defense headquarters crippled or destroyed, antiaircraft and SAM installations had to operate independently and ineffectively.

In that first night, more than 650 aircraft, including almost 400 strike aircraft, attacked Iraq. There were 530 from the Air Force, ninety from the Marine Corps and the five Navy carriers, twenty-four from Great Britain, and twelve each from France and Saudi Arabia.

During the first twenty-four hours, fixed-wing aircraft flew 812 strike sorties and the Navy launched 116 Tomahawk missiles against strategic targets, many of them in Baghdad.[3]

By the end of the second week, even Saddam's backup communications were crippled, and he was using messengers to carry dispatches from Baghdad to his troops in Kuwait. The trip took more than two days.[4]

Another measure of the damage to Saddam's infrastructure was that by the sixth day of the war, electronic emissions from the radars controlling his SAMs, AAA, and early warning network had dropped off by ninety-five percent.[5]

Neutralizing Iraqi Airpower

The Iraqi air force never really got off the ground after the first day, when it took

Iraqi Radar Activity

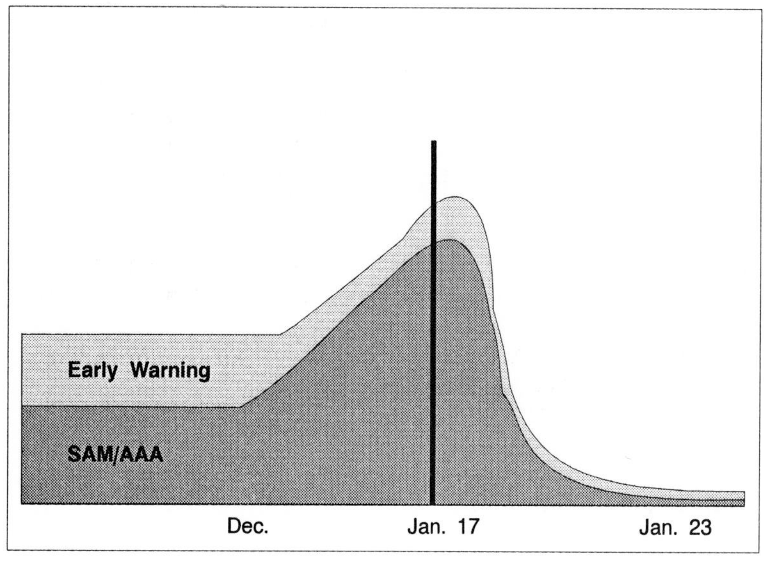

[1] USAF white paper, September 1991.

[2] Capt. Douglas R. Fries, letter, Dec. 3, 1991.

[3] *Conduct of the Persian Gulf Conflict.*

[4] USAF white paper, September 1991.

[5] Gen. Colin Powell, Pentagon news conference, Jan. 23, 1991.

Date	Airman	Unit	Aircraft	Target	Weapon	Location
1/17	Capt. Jon Karl Kelk	58th TFS, 33d TFW	F-15C	MiG-29	AIM-7M	vicinity of Mudaysis
1/17	Capt. Steven Wayne Tate	71st TFS, 1st TFW	F-15C	Mirage F1	AIM-7M	SE of Baghdad
*1/17	Capt. James A. Denton Capt. Brent D. Brandon (EWO)	390th ECS, 366th TFW	EF-111A	Mirage F1	acm	Iraq
1/17	Capt. Robert Evan Graeter	58th TFS, 33d TFW	F-15C	Mirage F1	AIM-7M	vicinity of Mudaysis
1/17	Capt. Robert Evan Graeter	58th TFS, 33d TFW	F-15C	Mirage F1	AIM-7M	vicinity of Mudaysis
1/17	Lt. Cmdr. Mark Irby Fox	VFA-81, CVW-17, *Saratoga*	F/A-18C	MiG-21	AIM-7M AIM-9M	W Iraq, 40 m N of border
1/17	Lt. Nicholas Mongillo	VGA-81, CVW-17, *Saratoga*	F/A-18C	MiG-21	AIM-7M	W Iraq, 40 m N of border
1/17	Capt. Rhory Roger Draeger	58th TFS, 33d TFW	F-15C	MiG-29	AIM-7M	W of Baghdad
1/17	Capt. Charles Joseph Magill (USMC)	58th TFS, 33d TFW	F-15C	MiG-29	AIM-7M	W of Baghdad
1/19	Capt. Lawrence Edward Pitts	58th TFS, 33d TFW	F-15C	MiG-25	AIM-7M	vicinity of Mudaysis
1/19	Capt. Richard Craig Tollini	58th TFS, 33d TFW	F-15C	MiG-25	AIM-7M	vicinity of Mudaysis
1/19	Capt. Craig William Underhill	58th TFS, 33d TFW	F-15C	MiG-29	AIM-7M	vicinity of Mudaysis
1/19	Capt. Cesar Antonio Rodriguez	58th TFS, 33d TFW	F-15C	MiG-29	acm	vicinity of Mudaysis
1/19	Lt. David G. Sveden	525th TFS, 36th TFW	F-15C	Mirage F1	AIM-7M	Iraq
1/19	Capt. David S. Prather	525th TFS, 36th TFW	F-15C	Mirage F1	AIM-7M	Iraq
1/24	Capt. Ayedh Salah al-Shamrani	13th FS, RSAF	F-15C	Mirage F1	AIM-9M	NW Persian Gulf
1/24	Capt. Ayedh Salah al-Shamrani	13th FS, RSAF	F-15C	Mirage F1	AIM-9M	NW Persian Gulf
1/26	Capt. Rhory Roger Draeger	58th TFS, 33d TFW	F-15C	MiG-23	AIM-7M	NW of Mudaysis
1/26	Capt. Anthony Edward Schiavi	58th TFS, 33d TFW	F-15C	MiG-23	AIM-7M	NW of Mudaysis
1/26	Capt. Cesar Antonio Rodriguez	58th TFS, 33d TFW	F-15C	MiG-23	AIM-7M	vicinity of Mudaysis
1/27	Capt. Jay T. Denney	53d TFS, 36th TFW	F-15C	MiG-23	AIM-7M	SE of Baghdad
1/27	Capt. Benjamin Dean Powell	53d TFS, 36th TFW	F-15C	Mirage F1	AIM-7M	SE of Baghdad
1/27	Capt. Benjamin Dean Powell	53d TFS, 36th TFW	F-15C	MiG-23	AIM-7M	SE of Baghdad
1/27	Capt. Jay T. Denney	53d TFS, 36th TFW	F-15C	MiG-23	AIM-7M	SE of Baghdad
1/29	Capt. Donald Scott Watrous	32d TFS, 32d TFG	F-15C	MiG-23	AIM-7M	Erbil, Iraq
1/29	Capt. David Glen Rose	58th TFS, 33d TFW	F-15C	MiG-23	AIM-7M	SE of Kirkuk
2/2	Capt. Gregory P. Masters	525th TFS, 36th TFW	F-15C	Il-76	AIM-7M	Iraq
2/6	Lt. Robert William Hehemann	53d TFS, 36th TFW	F-15C	Su-25	AIM-9M	E of Baghdad
2/6	Lt. Robert William Hehemann	53d TFS, 36th TFW	F-15C	Su-25	AIM-9M	E of Baghdad
2/6	Capt. Thomas N. Dietz	53d TFS, 36th TFW	F-15C	MiG-21	AIM-9M	E of Baghdad
2/6	Capt. Thomas N. Dietz	53d TFS, 36th TFW	F-15C	MiG-21	AIM-9M	E of Baghdad
2/6	Lt. Donald Stuart Brooe Cdr. Ronald Dean McElraft (RIO)	VF-1, CFW-2, *Ranger*	F-14A	Mi-8 Hip	AIM-9M	Southern Iraq
2/6	Capt. Robert Raymond Swain	706th TFS, 926th TFG	A-10A	MBB BO.105	guns	W of Ali al Saleem
2/7	Capt. Anthony Richard Murphy	58th TFS, 33d TFW	F-15C	Su-22/20	AIM-7M	SE of Kirkuk
2/7	Capt. Anthony Richard Murphy	58th TFS, 33d TFW	F-15C	Su-22/20	AIM-7M	SE of Kirkuk
2/7	Col. Rick N. Parsons	33d TFW	F-15C	Su-22/20	AIM-7M	SE of Kirkuk
2/7	Maj. Randy W. May	525th TFS, 36th TFW	F-15C	helicopter	AIM-7M	Iraq
2/11	Capt. Steven B. Dingee	525th TFS, 36th TFW	F-15C	Mi-8 Hip	AIM-7M	W of Mosel (shared)
2/11	Capt. Mark T. McKenzie	525th TFS, 36th TFW	F-15C	Mi-8 Hip	AIM-7M	W of Mosel (shared)
*2/14	Capt. Richard Timothy Bennett Capt. Daniel Bruce Bakke (WSO)	335th TFS, 4th TFW	F-15E	helicopter	GBU-10	NW Iraq, near al Qalm
2/15	Capt. Todd Kevin Sheehy	511th TFS, 10th TFW	A-10A	Mi-8 Hip	guns	over Nukhayb, Iraq
3/20	Capt. John Terry Doneski	53d TFS, 36th TFW	F-15C	Su-22	AIM-9M	Tikrit
3/22	Capt. Thomas N. Dietz	53d TFS, 36th TFW	F-15C	Su-22	AIM-9M	between Kirkuk & Tikrit
3/22	Lt. Robert William Hehemann	53d TFS, 36th TFW	F-15C	PC-9	acm	between Kirkuk & Tikrit

As of this printing, not credited as official victory. acm = air combat maneuvering.

Sources: Frank Olynyk, Bill Strandberg, Jr., and USAF.

heavy losses, and was soon driven underground. Iraq began hiding its fighters in hardened aircraft shelters. Apparently, Saddam thought the coalition could not sustain the pace of the war for more than a few days, after which he could bring his aircraft out of the shelters for a counteroffensive.[6]

Despite its early successes, the coalition feared that Saddam might be able to mount one massive air strike against allied bases, creating the effect of an "Air Tet." (North Vietnam's surprise Tet offensive in 1968 was of limited military value, but the psychological impact was a turning point in the war.)[7]

Consequently, coalition fighters went after every Iraqi airplane they could catch, struck hard at the air bases and runways, and from the seventh day of the war on, pounded the hardened aircraft shelters relentlessly.

The coalition air forces worked well and effectively together in the neutralization of Iraqi airpower. The first day, Horner said, "we had American F-15s escorting Saudi aircraft. The Navy was providing ECM jamming. A Saudi airplane put four craters on the runway, and I'll tell you right now, we couldn't have taken a pickup truck and laid those bombs out there more accurately."[8]

Before the onset of Operation Desert Storm, the Iraqis had been flying at a daily rate of about fifty-five fighter sorties and forty support sorties. They got twenty-five fighters into the air the first night. Within ninety minutes, US Air Force F-15s had shot down four of them and an EF-111 had driven a fifth into the ground with air combat maneuvering.

The Iraqis averaged thirty fighter sorties a day for the first week, and by the end of that week had lost fourteen fighters in aerial combat. No coalition aircraft had been shot down by Iraqi fighters.

The first Iraqi fighter to fall was a MiG-29, shot down by Capt. John K. Kelk, flying an F-15C on combat air patrol for strike flights near Mudaysis. Ultimately, Kelk's unit, the 33d TFW from Eglin AFB, Fla., would claim fourteen aerial victories in the Gulf War and dub itself "the largest distributor of MiG parts in Southwest Asia."

Maj. Robert E. Graeter, also of the 33d TFW, was a flight leader that first night, and was credited with two victories. "We flew into Iraq just after the first F-117s and F-15Es had penetrated for their bombing attacks," Graeter said. "Since they would be coming out as we went in, anything flying over Iraq would be enemy, and we could hit them.[9]

"My route was to check out a field southwest of Baghdad called Mudaysis, where the Iraqis had twelve to eighteen fighters, and then go northwest to two other fields, H2 and H3, where there were large numbers of fighters.

"Evidently, some of them had launched when the strike forces started hitting their targets. We can see some bogeys on our radar scopes, and a whole train of F-15Es, as they roar around on the deck. I pick up a low target coming out of Mudaysis at about twenty-five miles. He's not squawking anything on his IFF.

"Just then, AWACS comes up on the radio and calls bandits southwest of Mudaysis. I break lock on the bandit and now I can see two more bandits, in trail, coming out of the same field, so my radar picture fits with what AWACS says.

"I lock onto the lead bandit and another pilot in the flight locks up the trailing bandit. I shoot an AIM-7 [radar-guided Sparrow] at the bandit at a range of eight and half miles, and turn left to offset from the missile I launched. I'm up at 20,000 feet and he's at 7,000.

"As I come downhill towards him, my missile impacts. He's now at my right, two o'clock, and that's where I see the big, big, long fireball. He just took off and he's full of fuel.

"The missile explodes first, a cone shaped flash, then there's the initial big explosion of the fighter, then the fireball coming out of the explosion. Flaming chunks start falling out of the fireball. It lights up the clouds, the ground, and reflects in my cockpit. He's about three miles away. He was an F1 Mirage.

"At this point, the trailing fighter, the one the other pilot in my flight is locked

[6] USAF white paper, September 1991.

[7] *Conduct of the Persian Gulf Conflict.*

[8] Horner, CENTCOM news briefing, Jan. 18, 1991.

[9] Maj. Robert E. Graeter, interview, July 8, 1991.

onto, turns and runs. But then we see another fighter, apparently the wingman of the Mirage I shot down, suddenly turn hard right. He's only at about a thousand feet when he starts the turn, and he just rolls over and crashes into the ground about two miles in front of me.

"Now there's fire everywhere. We decide to leave. There are two fireballs, and the base they came out of is right over there, with a lot of airplanes on it. We climb up and head for H2 and H3, but none of their planes are up.

"We head back across the border. Later, we are told that the Iraqis had eight planes up in the western sector, which was our responsibility, and we got three of them. So, altogether, we got forty percent of their force. I got credit for the one I shot down and the one that crashed."

On January 23, Air Boss Horner ordered coalition air forces to begin attacking the Iraqi fighters in their shelters, using laser-guided bombs designed for penetration of hard targets.[10]

Two days later, the Iraqi air force, after taking stock of what was happening, "flushed" to Iran. Coalition leaders do not know for sure what Saddam had in mind. Perhaps he believed he could bring the fighters back when the war was over. (Iran expropriated the Iraqi aircraft and added them to its own air force.)

About 120 aircraft tried to escape to Iran.

[10] USAF white paper, September 1991.

Iraqi Flight Activity

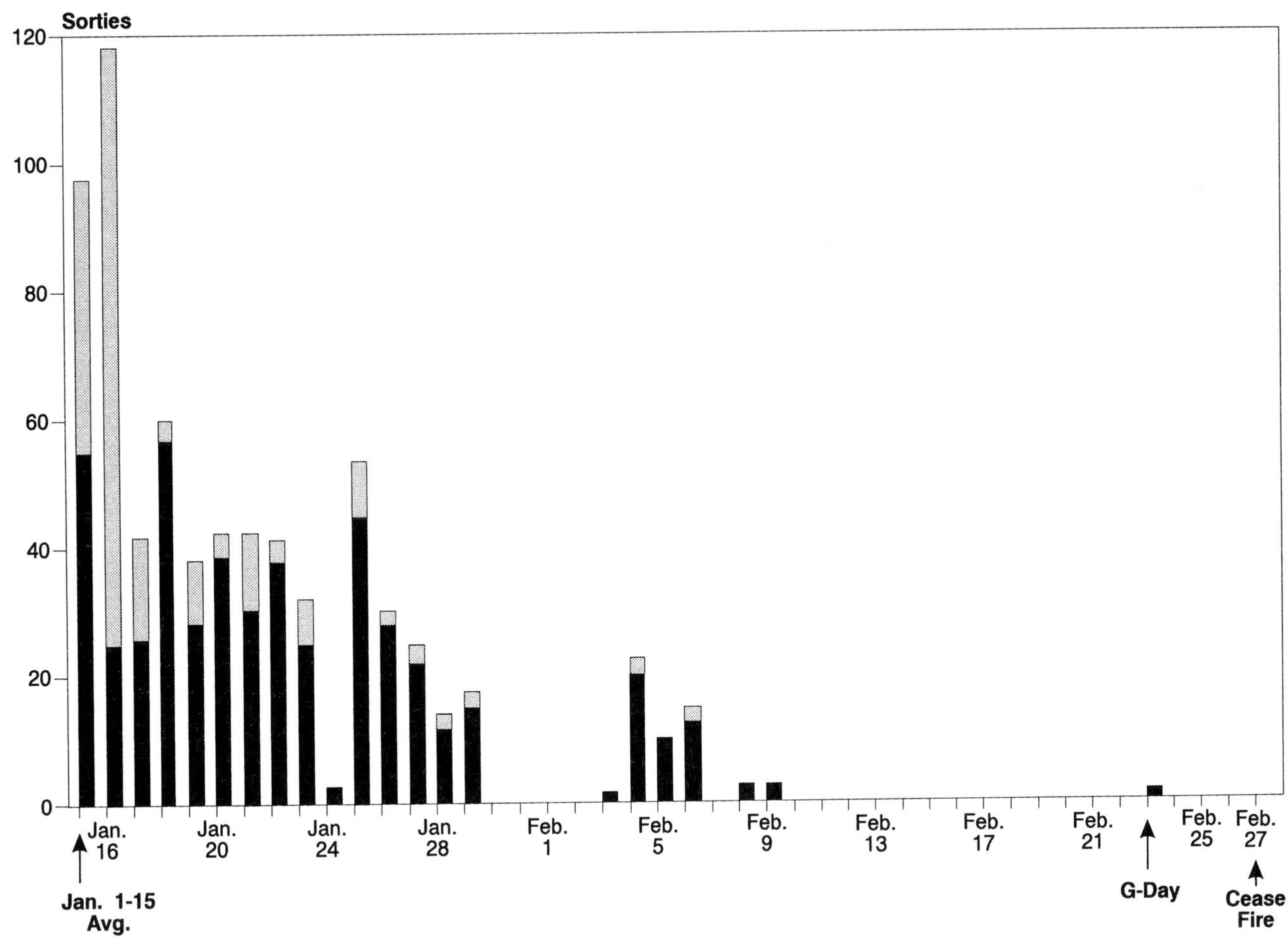

Source: Air Force Briefing.

Some ran out of fuel and crashed. Others were shot down by US Air Force F-15s on "barrier patrol."

The Iraqi air force was never a factor in the fighting, although it continued sporadically to put up sorties and took several losses in March, after the cease fire date.

Perhaps the strangest aerial engagement of the war came on February 14, when Capt. Tim Bennett and his WSO, Capt. Dan Bakke, on Scud patrol near al Qahn, were notified by an E-3 AWACS that Hind helicopters were attacking a special forces team in northwest Iraq.[11]

[11] Capt. Richard Timothy Bennett, interviewed by Frank Oliveri, *Air Force Magazine*, Oct. 11, 1991.

"They asked us if we could go give them a hand," said Bennett, who on February 14 was flying an F-15E configured for Scud attack. "As we get over there, as we turn, we start getting contacts on the helicopters on the radar, but all we're carrying are AIM-9s, you know, heat-seeking missiles, and laser-guided bombs."

They definitely had helicopters on radar, but were not yet certain they were hostiles. "We were worried that they might have sent a Special Ops chopper in there to extract them," Bennett said. He conferred with the AWACS, and all five of the helicopters were declared hostile.

Bennett and another F-15E flying on his wing dropped down through the cloud cover, which was heavy. As they popped out of the weather, they could see the helicopters maneuvering and deploying troops on the ground.

The F-15E cruised in at 1,500 feet with AAA coming up around them. "Dan and I talked real briefly about what we'd do," Bennett said. "We decided we'd drop a bomb first. That way, if a helicopter was sitting on the ground, we'd take it out. If it wasn't on the ground, we'd get rid of the troops that it had just dropped off and give them something to think about while we took care of the rest of them.

"What happened was, the guy was setting down when we decided to designate. We still had a radar contact on him, so we had the AIM-9 looking at him. I was basically working the air-to-air radar and Dan was working the targeting pod with the laser-guided bomb. So we let the bomb go, and the bomb was sailing through the air.

"Right at that time, I'm waiting for the helicopter to come up, and if he comes up, I'm going to hit it with my AIM-9. As he comes up and starts moving—at that time, the radar is seeing him moving at about 150 knots, moving away—I'm thinking there is no way in hell the bomb is going to make it, so I uncage the AIM-9.

"I'm getting ready to shoot it, just waiting to get in range, when the bomb comes right into the field of view, right into the chopper, and blows it all to hell. It just disintegrated. You know, that's a 2,000-pound bomb that hit it. When he picked up, he was kind of coming at us, so the bomb had enough energy to make it to him."

It was the first time in the history of aerial warfare that one airplane had "shot" another one down with a bomb.

In the final accounting, the coalition destroyed thirty-five fixed-wing Iraqi aircraft in the air and more than 200 on the ground. About 375 of Iraq's 594 aircraft shelters were wrecked. Allied intelligence is not

Iraqi Air Force Attrition

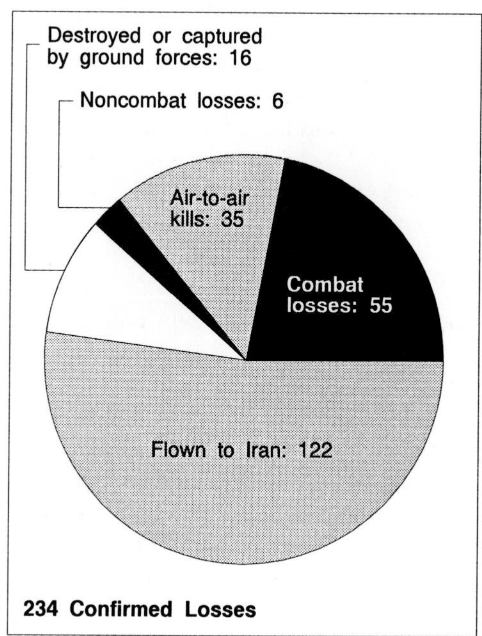

Source: Department of Defense.

certain how many aircraft were destroyed inside the shelters.

The Scud Chase

Saddam had lost many—but not all—of his weapons in the initial attacks. Early in the evening on the first day of the war, he launched two Scud ballistic missiles at Israel. They plunged into the sea, not far offshore.

No damage was done, but the act enraged the Israeli government. The coalition had a new problem on its hands. If Israel struck back, that would almost certainly split the coalition because some coalition states could not ally themselves with the Israelis.

The next night, at 2:15 a.m., six more Scuds landed in and around Tel Aviv. Several people were injured. At 4:45 a.m., Saddam launched his first Scud at Saudi Arabia. It was intercepted and destroyed at 17,000 feet by a US Army Patriot air defense missile. In no previous war had a missile shot down another missile.

Both to defend Israel and keep it out of the war, the United States diverted a shipment of Patriots consigned to Saudi Arabia and delivered them to the Israelis instead.

Intercepting Scuds in the air, just before they hit their targets, was not the preferred way of dealing with them, though. It was much better to catch them on the ground before they launched.

The Iraqi missiles were frequently termed "Soviet-built Scud Bs" in press reports, but they were actually an Iraqi modification called the *Al Hussein*. This variant has expanded fuel tanks and a smaller warhead, 350 pounds rather than 1,000. The *Al Hussein* has a range of 382 miles, more than enough to attack all of Israel and the major cities of Saudi Arabia. It is not very accurate. The batteries expect nothing better than to land their shots somewhere within a mile and a half of the aiming points.

Horner had targeted Scud sites known to the coalition in the initial attack on January 17. The first strike aircraft into Iraq, after the F-117s, were F-15Es assigned to hit the westernmost Scud sites that posed the most immediate threat to Israel. Plants believed to be producing chemical warheads for these missiles were also attacked the first day.[12]

As the Iraqis began firing Scuds from mobile launchers, the air effort shifted to locating and destroying the TEL [transporter erector launcher] vehicles. Ultimately, the equivalent of three squadrons was assigned to this mission.

"The first night we were tasked against Scud sites in western Iraq. We also attacked airfields and communications sites," said Lt. Col. Stephen Pingel, commander of the 335th TFS from Seymour Johnson AFB, N.C. "The second night, we attacked power plants, including one just north of Basra. We went against Iraqi POL production and storage areas.

"But Scud hunting turned out to be a very difficult thing. A fixed site was little more than a small concrete pad in the desert that had been surveyed so the launching crew knew the exact coordinates. They needed the location to tell the Scud's navigation system where it was coming from and where it was going. They sometimes had a spindly crane that, from the air, looked like part of a toy erector set, to lift the Scud into launch position.

"The sites were empty until a Scud was trucked onto it. So, unless you caught them with a Scud in place during the fueling and launching process, which could take an hour or so, the site wasn't much to see and certainly didn't stand out as a target."[13]

Two "Scud boxes," were established, one in the west, over the area from which the missiles were launched at Israel, and one in the south, where they were launched at Saudi Arabia.

Patrolling these boxes were Air Force F-15Es, F-16s, and A-10s, Navy A-6Es, and British Tornados. They looked not only for Scud launches in progress but also for TEL vehicles on roads or beneath overpasses. USAF RF-4Cs and Navy F-14s flew reconnaissance missions to discover launch sites.

At night, the Joint STARS side-looking radar could spot TEL locations and pass the information by datalink to air and ground commanders and to airborne F-15Es. U-2

[12] *Conduct of the Persian Gulf Conflict.*

[13] Lt. Col. Stephen Pingel, interview, May 31, 1991.

and TR-1 strategic reconnaissance aircraft cruised high above the search areas, their long-range sensors probing, recording, and reporting Scud launchpoints and data on missile trajectories. American and British special operations forces, on the ground deep in Iraqi territory, hunted TELs and, when they found them, called in air strikes.

F-15Es equipped with LANTIRN also hunted Scuds at night, when the plume from a missile in flight was visible and the launch site could be pinpointed. The F-15Es promptly attacked the site and the launcher, but the supersonic Scud itself was too fast for intercept by an air-to-air missile. The Scud patrols had to work quickly because the Iraqis could drive the launch vehicle away minutes after they fired a missile.

RAF reconnaissance Tornados formed "look and shoot" teams with strike Tornados and used their sensors to find Scuds. US F-16s and A-10s patrolled assigned areas, on the watch for TELs. B-52s and F-117s took out Scud storage and production facilities.[14]

"B-52s were used to deter Scud launches," said Maj. Gen. John A. Corder, CENTAF Director of Operations. "They flew along roads we knew were used by the Scud launchers to get to their launch points, especially in the western box, where Scuds had been launched at Israel. The Buffs[15] would drop a bomb or two every fifteen or twenty minutes. All night long. Along with the F-15Es, that kept a lot of movement down."[16]

Hardest to find were the mobile launch sites. These were no more than level spaces along the roadside that the Iraqis had surveyed ahead of time so launch crews would know their exact locations for aiming purposes. The crews hid the Scuds and launchers, often in residential areas, by day and moved them to their launch sites at night.

Altogether, CENTAF flew 2,493 sorties in what became known as the "Great Scud Hunt," most of them in the first three weeks of the war. They did not get all of the Scuds, but they definitely reduced and suppressed Saddam's terror weapon. Scud launches averaged five a day for the first ten days of the war, and then dropped to an

[14] USAF white paper, September 1991.

[15] B-52 nickname, derived (approximately) from "big ugly friendly fellers."

[16] Maj. Gen. John A. Corder, interview, July 8, 1991.

Scud Launches

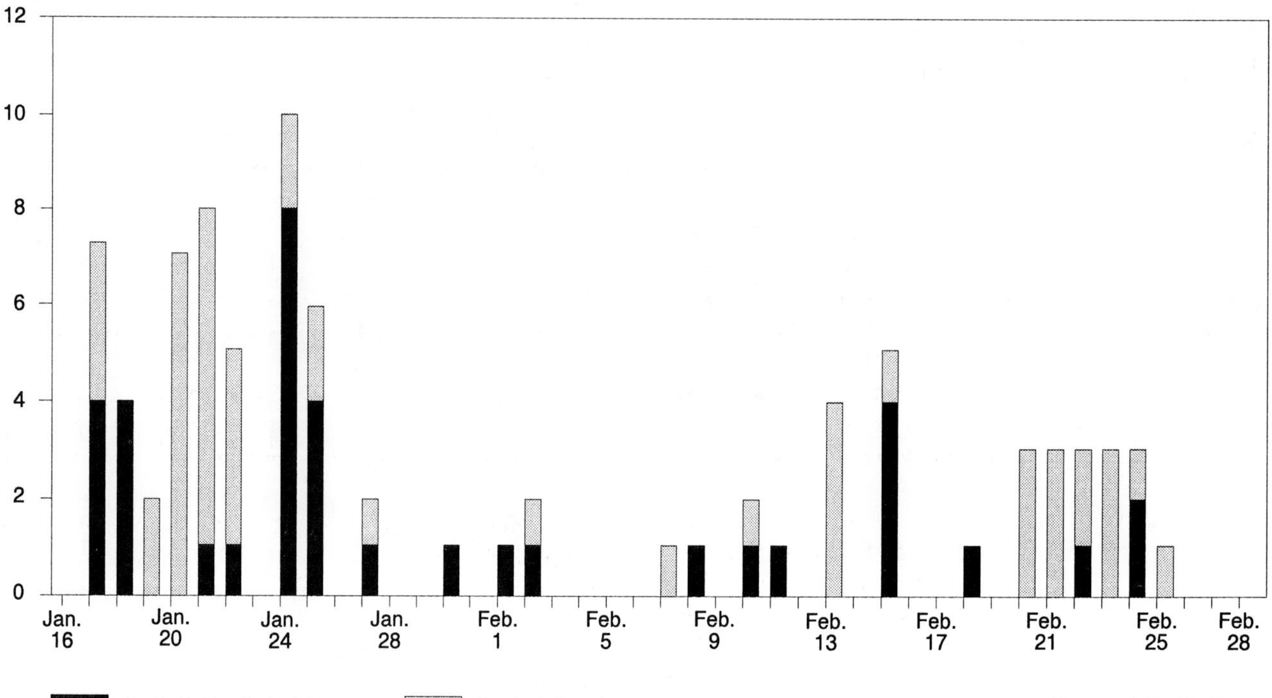

Source: US Air Force.

Sorties Against Scuds

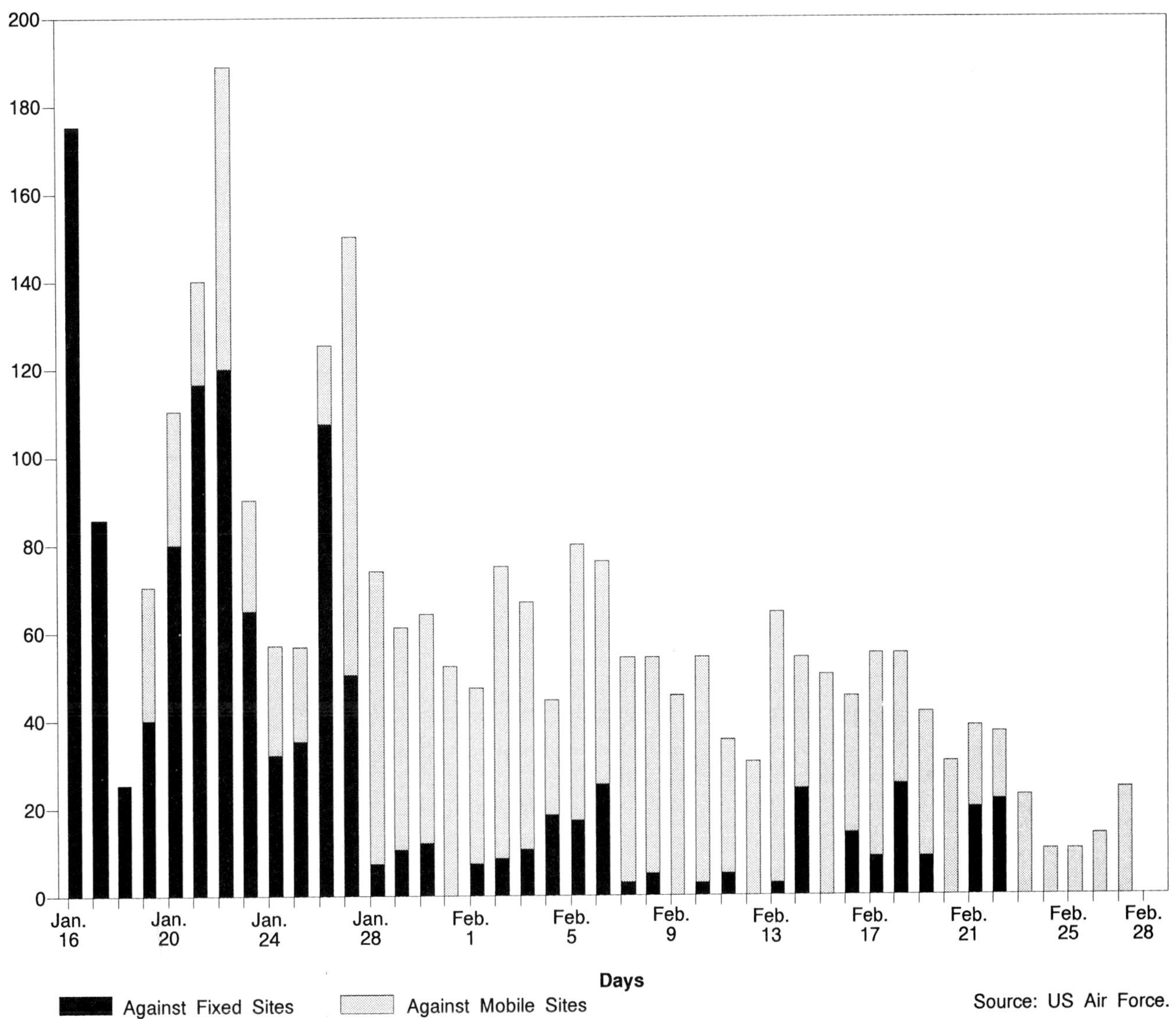

Source: US Air Force.

average of one a day for the next thirty-three days.

The Great Scud Hunt also forced the Iraqis to use unprepared and unsurveyed launch sites, degrading the accuracy of a missile that was not accurate to begin with.

The last launch of a Scud against Israel was February 25. A Patriot shot it down. On February 27, a force of Scuds, probably preparing for a mass launch against Israel, was destroyed in the western launch box.[17]

The "Second Front"

Adding further to Saddam's problems, the coalition opened a "second front" on Iraq's northwest border the third day of the war. "Proven Force," a composite force under the command of Maj. Gen. James L. Jamerson, USAF, operated from Incirlik AB, Turkey. The air arm, the 7440th Provisional Wing, was commanded by Brig. Gen. Lee A. Downer, Inspector General for US Air Forces in Europe.

The Proven Force deployment was conceived by several young officers in the 52d TFW at Spangdahlem AB, Germany. The transformation from concept to combat operation was swift.

[17] USAF white paper, September 1991.

"They had been digesting intelligence reports on the Iraqi electronic combat order of battle," said Gen. Robert C. Oaks, Commander in Chief, US Air Forces Europe.[18]

"They deduced the F-16/F-4G Wild Weasel team concept they were using in training at Spangdahlem would be very effective against Saddam's command and control system, not only in western Iraq but throughout the country."

The officers developed a detailed concept of operations and presented it in a briefing at Wiesbaden, Germany, to Brig. Gen. Glenn A. Proffitt II, Commander, 65th Air Division, who runs USAFE's electronic combat operations.

Oaks visited Wiesbaden, was impressed with the idea, and invited the officers to brief his staff at Ramstein. Together, they expanded the plan to encompass a full-blown task force that became Proven Force.

Oaks briefed Gen. John Galvin, Supreme Allied Commander Europe, at his headquarters in Mons, Belgium, September 4-5. Galvin immediately took the idea of a "second front" at Incirlik AB, Turkey, to Gen. Colin Powell, Chairman of the Joint Chiefs of Staff, and to Schwarzkopf.

"It was immediately obvious to all of us that, operationally, it was a very good and very doable idea," Oaks said. "But it was just as obvious that securing the political approval from the Turks might prove difficult."

On September 18, USAFE began deploying aircraft to Incirlik to participate in a NATO exercise, Display Determination 1990. Other deployments followed. A Joint Task Force staff was established at USAFE headquarters December 27.

On January 16, with some aircraft that would become part of Proven Force already in place, the first elements of the JTF headquarters moved to Incirlik.

The next day, the first day of Desert Storm, the Turkish parliament approved the use of Incirlik Air Base to carry out UN resolutions. A-10s, F-15s, EF-111s, EC-130s, F-111s, F-16s, and F-4Gs moved to Incirlik, and Proven Force aircraft began flying combat sorties over Iraq.

Downer's force was originally assigned seventeen strategic targets "with more to come," according to Glosson.[19]

"We hit targets assigned to us by CENTAF," said Downer. "They were strategic—command and control, electric power, petroleum production and storage, chemical, biological and nuclear production factories, airfields, and storage areas of all kinds. By the end of the war, we had been assigned and hit over 100 strategic targets. Some of the targets were huge, and we hit them over and over."

To keep the command and control lines clearly defined the first few days, Horner established a coordination line. "We were responsible for anything in Iraq above thirty-four degrees, thirty minutes, north," Downer said.

The Proven Force operation was soon integrated into the broader campaign directed by the Black Hole. "We produced an air tasking order for the targets we'd been assigned, transmitted it to Riyadh, and they folded it into the overall ATO," Downer said.

Downer was also prepared to hit non-strategic targets. "Saddam had a corps near the border with several divisions in it, including one Republican Guard division. They were dug in near where the Turkish border meets Iraq. We developed a great plan to take them out if they began to move, either against Turkey or to reinforce towards the southeast."[20]

Essentially, Downer ran a composite task force, about 130 aircraft, which conducted operations over northern Iraq. It included twenty-eight F-15C air-superiority fighters; forty-six F-16C, F-111E, and F-4E strike aircraft; thirty-two EF-111A electronic support aircraft, F-4Gs, and F-16Cs teamed with the Wild Weasels; and about thirty other aircraft, including AWACS and tankers.[21]

"Most of the aircraft at Incirlik came out of US Air Forces in Europe," Downer said, "but the tankers came from Dyess AFB, Tex., part of Strategic Air Command; the AWACS from their main base at Tinker AFB, Okla. Some of the F-4Es came from Clark AB in the Philippines. The people

[18] Gen. Robert C. Oaks, interview, Jan. 15, 1992.

[19] Glosson interview, March 5, 1992.

[20] Brig. Gen. Lee A. Downer, interview, Aug. 5, 1991.

[21] USAF white paper, September 1991.

came from all over the Air Force, including the Air National Guard and the Air Force Reserve.

"A big part of our job was hitting storage areas. Some of them were incredibly large—twenty or twenty-five square miles.

"Near cities like Mosul or Kirkuk, or in one huge valley full of storage areas for ammunition, chemical and biological weapons that we called 'Happy Valley,' the skies looked exactly like those over Baghdad that everyone saw on television. The defenses were most impressive."

Downer speculated on why so few coalition aircraft fell to the air defenses: "First of all, there were the Wild Weasels. Firing the HARM, they were lethal almost every time. Saddam's radar operators soon figured out that they were being targeted by the weasels, so they just didn't turn it on. They began to fire SAMs ballistically. The antiaircraft rounds appeared to be fired barrage style. The gunners did not track our aircraft.

"In a longer war, the AAA gunners might have learned how to do it. Our experience in Vietnam says that the average gunner did not really get good until after he had actually hit one of our airplanes. Then, he began to figure out what it took to hit the target, and then he became lethal because he knew how to lead the target, how to track it, and how to fire only when the target is in range."

Campaign in the North

There were unique aspects to the war in northern Iraq. "One day, early on," Downer said, "we went to attack an airfield near Mosul. There were four big, fat Boeing 757s parked on the ramp. The Iraqis had stolen them from Kuwait Airways and were probably going to use them to transport their troops. We eliminated the airliners from further involvement in the war.

"On another field, farther south, we spotted a Russian-built transport, [an Il-76] Candid, which is about the size of our C-141 transport. The first fighter in to attack that night was a Wild Weasel.

"It was armed with Maverick air-to-ground missiles. We had run out of SAM sites to hit, so the Weasels had started carrying Mavericks instead of HARMs. The Weasel crew rolled in, lined up, and blew the tail off the Candid with one shot."

From time to time, the Incirlik provisional wing heard from Colonel Warden's *Checkmate* division back in the Pentagon basement. "They were analyzing data independently," Downer said, "and, apparently, they had a direct feed from some of the intel sources.

"One of the *Checkmate* people called our command post and said, 'There are twenty Russian-built [Su-22] Fitter jet fighters sitting in the parking lot of the main train station in Kirkuk. We will send you imagery.'

"We began to generate a strike mission for takeoff first thing in the morning. Before long, the photo got there, and sure enough, we could see this large parking lot, and Fitters parked all over it. Most probably, they had been moved there by rail.

"We launched the strike force. When the force got to Kirkuk, they found that, during the night, the Iraqis had moved the jets to a big traffic circle, maybe a hundred meters away from the train station. They had parked them in a daisy ring around the circle. There it was, a perfect circle, a beautiful target for the F-16 guys, with enemy aircraft parked all around it!

"But the circle was in the middle of the urban section of Kirkuk. They had to put all the bombs inside the circle, or there would be civilian casualties and collateral damage. That really wasn't much of a problem, because the F-16 is equipped with a state-of-the-art weapons delivery system—it's really accurate.

"They were armed with 500 pounders, with fuzes set to go off about ten feet above the ground. In Vietnam, we called them 'daisy cutters.' Remember, we were after airplanes, not structures or tanks.

"They attacked and wiped out the Iraqi fighters parked around the circle. There was very little cratering, but shrapnel sprayed over all the airplanes. The next day, we saw that the Iraqis had heaped up several junk piles in that traffic circle, so we concluded we were successful. And there was no damage apparent outside the circle."

Later in the war, Downer said, his forces ranged south of the coordination line. "We had done enough on petroleum and electricity. We kept on hitting the nuclear, chemical, and biological stuff, but we also started hitting targets farther south.

"In fact, our last mission, in the early morning hours of February 28, 1991, the day the war was declared over, we hit Taji, a big military-industrial complex just north of Baghdad. Fourteen F-111s out of Incirlik followed sixteen B-52s. That was a pretty impressive raid."[22]

In some ways, the provisional operation at Incirlik was a preview of how the US Air Force will be organized in the future. Soon after he became Chief of Staff, Gen. Merrill A. McPeak began to restructure the force, creating "composite wings" with a broad range of capabilities to replace the traditional wings, most of which were organized for specialized and limited functions.

Two weeks after the Gulf War began, McPeak pointed to the composite wing already operating at Incirlik as an example of what he had in mind.[23]

[22] Downer interview.

[23] Gen. Merrill A. McPeak, Air Force Association Symposium, Jan. 31–Feb. 1, 1991.

Flying out of Incirlik

Lt. Col. Terry Simpson, an F-111 weapons systems officer (WSO) and commander of the 55th Tactical Fighter Squadron, RAF Upper Heyford, flew out of Incirlik during the Gulf War. For most missions, the Aardvark crews flew to orbit points in Turkey.

"We had hold points so we could zero out our timing and make sure we started each mission at the right instant to hit our TOTs [time on target] exactly," he said. "Timing is critical when you have fifty to seventy airplanes at a time out there with lights off.

"The first night, there was a lot of silence in the cockpit," he said. "My pilot, [Capt.] Mac McEntire, and I had the intercom on 'cold mike' most of the time, talking to ourselves rather than to each other. We were saying things like 'This isn't really happening—but it is.'

"Our target that first night was a power station at the bottom of a dam near Mosul. It was in a valley, of course. We wanted to release our bombs at 200 feet above the ground. The valley below the dam was deep, so we couldn't attack by flying up the river. We'd be too low to avoid colliding with the dam. Besides, attacking from that direction, some of our bombs might actually hit the dam. We were prohibited from striking dams because of the flood threat to the local civilian population. So we planned attacks back and forth across the river."

Simpson that night was also mission commander for the entire F-111 attack, which hit several targets besides the power station. "We were a flight of four. Two birds were to attack from the west and two from the northeast, one at a time. The first guy was to hit it from the east. We were to hit it from the west. The third bird was to come in from the east, and then our wingman would attack from the west. We timed it so the alternating attacks came from opposite directions, hoping to confuse the gunners."

The first aircraft aborted on the way to the target, so Simpson's bird made the first attack. The lights in Mosul were on. They knifed down from cruise altitude to attack altitude.

"They obviously didn't expect us," Simpson said. "Then, as we descended and turned toward the IP [initial point] about thirty miles out, they picked us up and AAA started coming up. It was light, scattered here and there. They seemed to be probing for us. Probably didn't have us on radar, but heard our engines in the night.

"Once we're down low, we can see a lot of stuff going off. Lots of muzzle flashes and tracers from small arms fire. As we make the final turn, the big AAA intensity increases dramatically and the lights of the city start to go out. Whole sections go off at a time. In about a minute, the whole city is blacked out.

"Now we're pressing in closer and the city and river valley are off to the left and there's a high ridge to the right. A lot of AAA is coming down towards us from the ridge. Mac is flying us right through it. Dodging the bursts and tracers, he stands us on one wingtip and then the other. He has to look at this stuff. I look up from my scope now and then, take a deep breath because of what I see, and then go right back in the scope."

Simpson liked what he saw on his radar. "Down low, we couldn't see the dam because it was in the valley. But I could see the hilltop we were using as an offset aimpoint clearly. I knew our exact position in relation to the target."

They were at 200 feet, blasting along through clear air between the flak bursts at more than 550 knots. There was apprehension in the cockpit. "Our training took over," Simpson said. "We were going on instinct. We were going to bomb that target, no matter what." The AAA bursts got thicker and closer. So did the SAMs. "I counted four of those little corkscrews—SA-7 shoulder-mounted infrared missiles—on my side. Mac saw several on his side." Mac actuated countermeasures equipment.

Mac started to deviate to the right of their planned course. "This stuff is really getting heavy over here," he told Simpson. "It's heavy over here, too," replied Simpson.

"It was okay for him to deviate to the right, as long as he didn't move over too far," Simpson continued.. "I still had a good lock on the target location.

"So, we're roaring through there, talking in high-pitched voices. 'Oh, man, this is bad. I don't like this at all.' 'I don't like it, either. Keep pressing in.' Finally, I say, 'Mac, we've got to come left.' He says, 'hey man, they're shooting like crazy over here.' He was right. The sky was brighter than noontime. Muzzle flashes, I guess. You could read a map, it was so bright. 'They're shooting just as hard on this side,' I say. 'Turn left. We've come this far. Let's hit this target.'

"Mac turned left. We were now right on!" Simpson described the final run.

"Halfway between the IP and the target, I switched to bombing mode, and the INS [Inertial Navigation System] readout changed from miles to thousands of feet. Even though we were screaming through there as fast as we could, it seemed to take ten years for the readout to count down to zero and for the green light to come on.

"Then, the most gratifying thing in the whole world was hearing that *thump, thump* of the bombs coming off, and then to look down at my panel and see the stations are all clear. The guys coming in from the other direction saw our bombs hit and watched sparks flying between the transformers.

"Now, I'm saying, 'let's get the hell out of here!' So, Mac whips the thing around and we start screaming out. We probably got up to Mach 1.4, because once you clean off those bombs and get those wings swept back, that thing will run like a scalded-ass ape."

They turned hard to the right off the target and flashed over the lake behind the dam. There were no AAA sites on the water, so they had fifteen or twenty miles of tranquility, and then flew back into the AAA barrage over land.

"We deviated around and through it, and finally crossed back over the border into Turkey," Simpson said. There were three minutes of peaceful flight in the blackness. "Then," Simpson said, "we turned and looked at each other, which is unusual in a side-by-side airplane—usually you're too busy with your crew duties, and you're looking ahead or out the side. And we reached over, and we hugged each other, and then we gave a 'high five' and said, 'Oh, my God, I don't want to do this again!'"

But they did do it again. Simpson flew seventeen more missions with Mac, and both of them flew missions with other crewmembers before the war ended.[24]

[24]Lt. Col. Terry L. Simpson, interview, Aug. 9, 1991.

Adjusting the War Plan

Early successes having exceeded expectations, the coalition began making adjustments to the war plan. The air campaign, as originally conceived, was to unfold in four phases:

- Phase I. Attack strategic "centers of gravity" deep inside Iraq, mainly around Baghdad.

- Phase II. Gain air superiority, neutralize the Iraqi air force, and take out the integrated air defense system.

- Phase III. Isolate the Iraqi army, methodically destroy its armor, artillery, and vehicles while continuing phase I and II attacks.

• Phase IV. Support the coalition ground attack.

As it happened, most enemy "centers of gravity" were knocked out quickly, the integrated air defense system was virtually destroyed within thirty-six hours, and the Iraqi air force was beaten in the first round. Coalition air forces did not wait, as planned, for the fifth day of the war to attack the Iraqi field army. They hit it the first day, and every day thereafter, relentlessly, until the cease fire.

As the war progressed, Glosson's team in the "Black Hole" constructed the master attack plan and directed the ongoing preparation of air tasking orders to fit circumstances as they unfolded.

The daily tasking process began at Horner's 7 a.m. staff meeting, with discussion of the previous day's results and CENTCOM's updated objectives. The planners then worked the new guidance, new intelligence information, bomb-damage assessments, weather forecasts, and other considerations into a revised attack plan, which had to meet with Glosson's approval by 8 p.m.

The new plan went next to the intelligence people, who specified aimpoints (bunker doors, building air shafts, etc.) for each target. Other planners produced worksheets with additional numbers and details.

By 4:30 a.m., the target planning worksheets were in the hands of the team that processed the Air Tasking Order. These people used a computer-aided force management system (CAFMS) to blend in still more factors—tanker tracks, airspace deconfliction (making sure that two groups of aircraft are not sent to exactly the same point at the same time), Identification, Friend or Foe (IFF) "squawks"—and turn out an operations order the force could execute.

The ATO would be delivered, either by computer or messenger, to units between 5

The Air Campaign: Original Plan

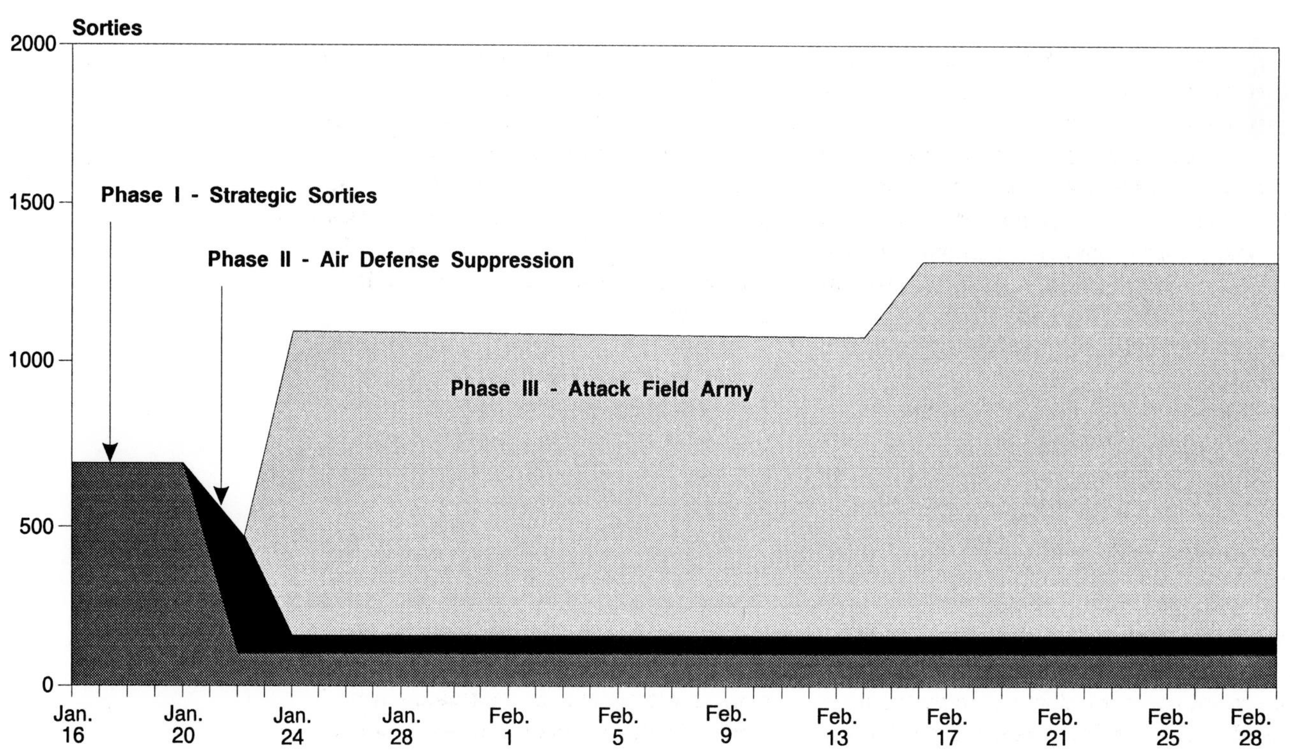

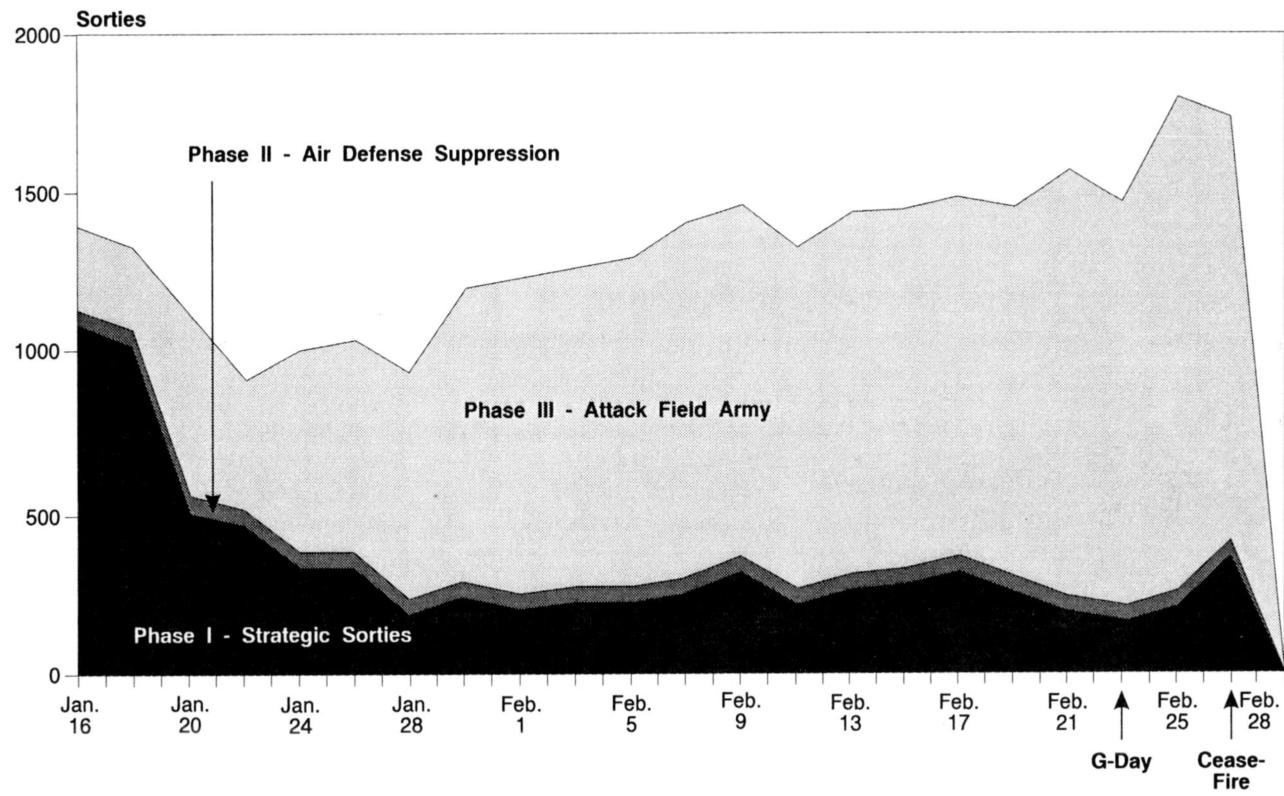

p.m. and 7 p.m. The execution day began the following morning at 5 a.m. and covered the next twenty-four hours.

The Black Hole was handling three "wars" concurrently: changes to the execution war of "today," changes to the ATO working for "tomorrow," and planning for the "day after tomorrow." Aircraft, weapons, and targets were shifted constantly to adjust to changes in weather, BDA reports, Scud attacks, and other variables.

"Here's an example of how the attack plans were developed," said Lt. Col. David A. Deptula, Director of Strategic Planning in the Black Hole. "Early in the war, one of the key military production targets was Latifya liquid propellant production facility [near Baghdad], which manufactured Scud fuel.

"The large number of aimpoints to put the plant out of production drove the large number of bomb droppers in the attack package. The array of defenses surrounding it and the proximity to Baghdad required a large SEAD [suppression of enemy air defense] and EC [electronic combat] complement. Additionally, the size of the attack package and potential interceptor threat dictated a large force protection element. The entire strike package was on the order of 600 aircraft.

"Putting together an attack plan involves many more considerations than just matching strikers with targets. To ensure the highest probability of success of this particular attack, the hostile potential of two large airfields had to be neutralized. In and of themselves, they were also priority targets because of their strike, chemical, and interceptor capabilities.

"I sequenced the strike packages from west to east, hitting Al Asad from 6:30 a.m. to 6:50 a.m., Al Taqaddum from 7 a.m. to 7:10, and finally the Scud fuel factory between 7:10 and 7:30 a.m.

"In this manner, the principal strike package against Latifya was assured of protection from any flank attack out of the west, and the sequencing also enabled deconfliction of three large strikes made up of over 150 total aircraft in about an hour. Concentration of force was another element in this particular attack, which made it quite successful.

"This was just one hour of a twenty-four hour day that was filled with attacks like these and reflects the timing and coherency that went into the planning of each day's master attack plan.

"The daily ATO, which was written from the master attack plan, told the units carrying out the attacks the details required for execution, such as TOT [time on target] spreads, tanker track assignments, entry/exit points for safe passage procedures, and so on.

"Even with all these details, however, there were always changes that had to be dealt with, and the flexibility and initiative on the part of the aircrews flying the missions is what really made the air campaign a success."[25]

[25] Deptula interview, Jan. 8, 1992.

[26] Capt. Larry C. Hills, interview, Aug. 8, 1991.

[27] 1st Lt. Jeffrey W. Kelly, interview, Aug. 8, 1991.

USAF Daily Fighter Sorties

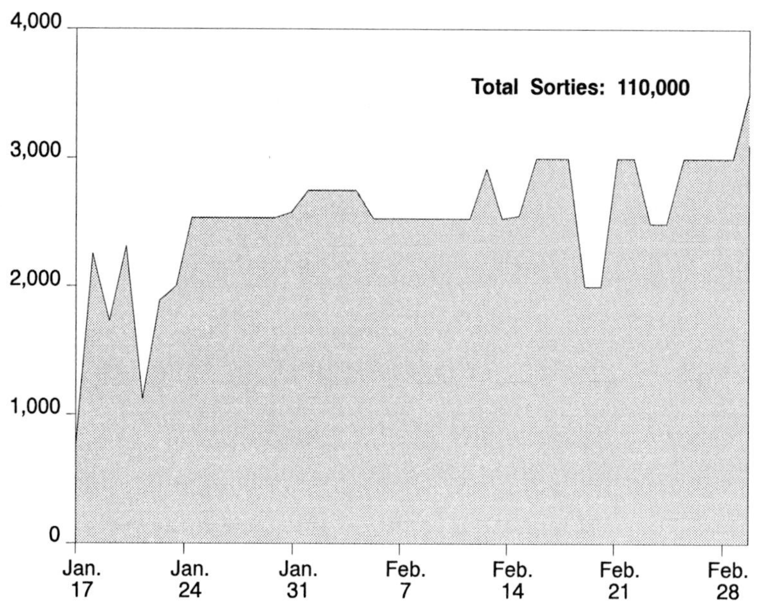

Sources: CENTCOM, US Air Force.

Planning in the Wings

When a flying unit received the daily ATO, it began planning the fine points of the mission. "There'd be a detailed briefing," said Capt. Larry C. Hills, an F-111 pilot in the 48th TFW, deployed out of Lakenheath in Britain. "Everybody was told what the target was and how many birds were going to attack it. We had to make an attack plan.

"To complicate the job for the Iraqi air defenses, we'd be attacking the target from different directions, tossing bombs from different tracks. We had to take into account the predicted wind because it might blow the smoke from the explosion of a bomb just released by an aircraft up ahead between you and your target, and obscure it. There were a lot of other details to work out. We'd discuss these things and formulate the attack plan.

"So, we would concentrate on how we were going to deconflict ourselves, both in flight paths and in time. Deconfliction assures we won't have two fighters trying to occupy the same space at the same time, or someone passing over an aimpoint at low level, just as somebody else's weapon goes off below him. We also took into account the locations of AAA and SAMs predicted by the intelligence people. They were pretty good at that."[26]

"On one mission," said 1st Lt. Jeffrey W. Kelly, Hills's weapon systems officer, "we had planned three holding points near the target, where birds would orbit before starting their timed runs. We each had two laser-guided glide bombs, so we planned two TOTs for each of us. You just had to be exactly on time, airspeed, and altitude.[27]

"For the first weapon, I just couldn't get a 'Ready' light. That meant we couldn't drop. We went back to our orbit point and got ready to go in and hit our second TOT while I tried to fix the system. We suddenly realized we were orbiting near three SA-8 missile sites. Why they didn't hit us, I'll never know.

"We did a couple of 360 degree turns and it was time to hit our second TOT. Just then, we got a 'Ready' light, so we blasted on in and released the weapon. Then the release system went out again. That was okay, because we had missed our TOT for the first bomb anyway. We brought it home. But the system was up long enough to take out one of our targets, which was an aircraft bunker."

Being professional in the combat zone takes courage and determination. "We often had to deviate from our planned routes somewhat to get around ground fire," said Kelly.

"I thought they'd run out of bullets, they were putting so much out at us. As soon as they heard an aircraft sound, they'd throw it up in all directions. You'd see it around you, in front of you and behind you. That's when I'd go back to my radar work, and let Larry figure out a way through it."

"Sometimes you just had to go straight through it, just push the throttles up and go straight through," added Hills. "Sometimes you could see it coming up like spray from a big garden hose or a water sprinkler—red, orange, white. It arced over, ran out of energy, and the tracers would burn out. You might have to move over in one direction, or deviate from the course in the other direction. So, as you're roaring along, the adrenaline is flowing and the apprehension level is pretty high."

"We have an infrared picture in the cockpit," Kelly said. "I shoot a laser beam out to designate the target for the GBU-24, the 2,000-pound glide bomb.

"When you release the bomb, it sounds like you're dropping a house off the side of a cliff. We're going pretty fast, almost Mach 1, so the bomb has a lot of energy imparted to it by the aircraft momentum.

"Its movable fins put it in a glide, and the bomb will climb up and fly. At a certain point, its seeker head comes alive and it homes in on my laser beam reflecting off the target."

"While this is going on, we are turning away to avoid the defenses around the target," Hills continued. "But there is still plenty of AAA trying to reach us. I wanted to turn away more, to avoid the AAA, but you can't turn too far or the pod on the bottom of the aircraft can't keep the laser spot on the target. If that happens, the bomb goes stupid.

"So, I'm listening to Jeff, over there in the right seat, saying, 'Waiting for the bomb to come into view.' It's a long time from when the bomb comes off until it impacts.

"Then, Jeff sees it on the tube as it hits the bunker. He calls, 'Impact.' It penetrates and there's an explosion, like an atom bomb going off, and two or three terrific secondaries. So, we break hard and start the egress.

"I let go of everything and reengage the computers and the terrain-following systems and let them take the airplane down to 200 feet. We're doing almost 600 knots, and at that speed, at night, the computers can do a better job of flying the F-111 than I can.

"Our best friend is the night. But at night, there's no horizon, except what you get from AAA flashes, and that's not enough to fly that fast on the deck.

"The egress was worse than the trip in. Going in, the defenses wake up as you approach them. On the way out, once the bombs have gone off, it's like you've stirred up some hornets! They're everywhere.

"They know we're coming out, they hear us, they're mad, and they're just throwing everything at us. SAMs are in the air. So are interceptors. I was scared. I was pumped up because it was happening so fast. And then we were out of there, and we were coming back home. What a feeling!" ■

6. The Awesome Weapons of Aerial Warfare

An F-15E crew signals "thumbs up" as it sets forth on Scud Patrol. This dual-role variant of the F-15 air superiority fighter, fairly new in the Air Force lineup, performed exceedingly well in the Gulf War.

USAF Photo by TSgt. Hans Deffner

Never before in history had air forces been so superbly equipped for their task.

The heart of Saddam's ability to wage war was demolished in the first hour of bombing, but the Gulf War would go on for forty-three days. During the course of it, the combined air forces of the allied coalition would demonstrate the awesome capabilities of modern aerospace systems and weapons.

The opening attack actually came at 2:20 a.m., forty minutes ahead of H-hour, when a task force of ground-hugging American helicopters crossed the border into far western Iraq.

Task Force Normandy consisted of two teams of helicopters. Each team was led by two US Air Force Special Operations Forces MH-53J Pave Low helicopters, followed by four US Army AH-64 Apaches carrying laser-guided Hellfire missiles.

Their mission was to destroy two radar sites north of the Saudi Arabian border. The sites controlled four Iraqi fighter bases and were linked into the communications network for the Intercept Operations Center in Baghdad.

In the lead Pave Low was Maj. Bob Leonik. The Air Force helicopters were equipped with state-of-the-art, terrain-following radar and a navigation system linked electronically to signals from the satellites of the Global Positioning System (GPS).

They provided precise navigation data to guide the forces sweeping at an airspeed of 120 knots through the darkness over the rough bluffs, mesas, and dry river courses of the desert of western Iraq. There were no accurate maps of the area, and the Pave Lows' navigation systems were ten times more accurate than the Apaches'.[1]

The eight Apaches, each with eight Hellfires, thirty-eight rockets, and a 30-mm chain gun, provided the required firepower. The mission was commanded by Army Col. Dick Cody.

"Neither the Pave Lows nor we had ever flown in that area," he told a reporter. The terrain was entirely different from where they had trained. "You had mesas and a little bit more terrain, which made it more dangerous. The Pave Lows had terrain-following radar ... our FLIR [forward-looking infrared radar], coupled with our night vision goggles, was just working great. So you had two different systems backing each other up."[2]

Just south of the targets, the Pave Lows peeled off and flew back to a rendezvous point. The Apaches continued toward the targets and began to slow down. "OK, I've got the target area," CWO2 Thomas "Tip" O'Neill told his pilot.

Adjusting his IR equipment, O'Neill's pilot, CWO3 Dave Jones, moved in on the first building to be hit. "There's the generator right there."

"Party in ten," said 1st Lt. Tom Drew in the lead AH-64. They would fire their missiles in ten seconds.

One for Saddam

"This one's for you, Saddam," whispered Warrant Officer Jones.

At 2:38 a.m.,[3] "LAUNCH" flashed on their FLIR screens. As the missiles roared away toward the targets, the attackers, looking at their screens, could see figures start

[1] Richard Mackenzie, "Apache Attack," *Air Force Magazine*, October 1991.

[2] Mackenzie, "Apache Attack."

[3] Slight variations reported for exact minute this attack began. Some official sources record it as 2:39 a.m.

to run out of the buildings. They didn't get very far before they were surrounded by flame and shrapnel.

"Just incessant fire," Colonel Cody recalls. "Missile after missile, rocket after rocket, 30-mm after 30-mm coming from four aircraft they [couldn't] even see. When we closed in to 4,000 meters, we engaged their ZSUs [Soviet antiaircraft guns] and antiaircraft artillery and put them out."

The scene was the same at the other radar site. They destroyed all the buildings and equipment at both sites in nearly-simultaneous attacks. It was all over in four and half minutes.

They had knocked out the radar in a corridor of the Iraqi air defense system, opening the way through which coalition nonstealthy attack fighters, principally nineteen scud-hunting F-15Es, could flow on their way to targets in the west of Iraq.

The lead F-117s were already deep into Iraq, pointing toward their targets. Minutes later, at H minus nine minutes, an F-117 blinded another Iraqi air defense sector by dropping the first bomb on Iraq, knocking out a sector air defense headquarters in the southwestern corner of the country. All the sites were caught by surprise.

"As a result," said General Glosson, CENTAF's Director of Air Campaign Plans, "we were able to retain total tactical surprise until the bombs started falling on Baghdad."[4]

Helicopters and TLAMs

The Air Force MH-53J Pave Low helicopters were ideally equipped to act as pathfinder for the Army Apaches. In addition to GPS and FLIR systems, the Pave Low can couple its terrain-following radar to the autopilot. It has secure communications and advanced electronic countermeasures (ECM) as well as chaff and flares to confuse enemy air defenses.

Even so, it was a demanding night.The helicopters came in by a circuitous route, flying a nap-of-the-earth profile, descending into wadis, and hugging the desert floor.[5]

For defense, the MH-53J carries 7.62-mm miniguns, six-barreled Gatling guns that can shoot up to 6,000 rounds per minute. It is extremely effective in firefights, but (although Task Force Normandy had to dodge two SAMs on its way out of Iraq), that was not the MH-53J's job on this mission.

The fireworks were the assignment of the Army AH-64 Apaches that followed the MH-53Js to the Iraqi radar sites. The Apache attack helicopter fairly bristles with ordnance. It has a 30-mm chain gun, for which it carries 1,200 rounds of depleted uranium ammunition, but its big punch is AGM-114 Hellfire missiles. The Apache can pack up to eight of these.

Its primary sensor is the target acquisition and designation system (TADS) that magnifies as well as illuminates.

Eyewitnesses said that when the Hellfires hit, the Iraqi radars evaporated in clouds of smoke and flame.[6] At the moment the Apaches destroyed the radars, the first Tomahawk Land Attack Missile (TLAM) was cruising low across the desert toward Baghdad. Since winds along the way could affect its programmed speed, the TLAM was assigned a five-minute window for impact rather than an exact time on target.

It was to strike Baghdad between 3:06 a.m. and 3:11 a.m.

The first Tomahawk had been launched at 1:30 a.m. by the guided-missile cruiser USS *San Jacinto*, steaming in the Red Sea. In short order, the USS *Bunker Hill* in the Persian Gulf and then the battleships USS *Wisconsin* and USS *Missouri* opened fire. The initial attack was by fifty-two Tomahawks. Some 100 were fired on the first day of Desert Storm.[7]

The TLAM is propelled from the launch tube by a rocket booster that burns for about twelve seconds. At the end of the booster burn, a small turbojet engine kicks in and the missile extends its wings and tail for the cruise portion of the flight.

It flies to the target at a speed of about 450 knots, approximately 520 miles per hour. An inertial navigational system provides guidance until landfall. After it crosses the coastline, the missile uses its TERCOM[8] radar altimeter to compare the topography along the route with detailed contour maps

[4] Maj. Gen. Buster C. Glosson, interview, May 28, 1991.

[5] USAF white paper, September 1991.

[6] Mackenzie, "Apache Attack."

[7] *United States Navy in Desert Shield/Desert Storm*, Department of the Navy, May 15, 1991.

[8] Terrain contour matching system.

stored in its computer memory and adjusts its flight path accordingly.

As the Tomahawk approaches the target, a small digital camera compares the view with a stored image for final adjustments to the target. The Tomahawks used in the Gulf War weighed 3,275 pounds and had a 264-pound warhead and a range of 800 miles.

Stealth in the Night

No coalition aircraft or weapon, however, jolted Saddam more severely that first night than the F-117 Stealth fighter. *[See chapters 1 and 9.]* It swept in on its targets undetected, and delivered a punishing blow.

The F-117s employed two 2,000-pound GBU-27 laser-guided bombs (LGB). A regular 2,000-pound gravity bomb is converted into the GBU-27 with a Texas Instruments guidance kit inside the seeker head on the nose of the bomb, and controlled, movable winglets aft that receive input from a guidance unit. The bomb carried by the F-117 has a reduced wing assembly so it can be tucked inside the weapons bay. The GBU-27 uses a BLU-109 (I-2000) steel-encased warhead to penetrate hardened structures such as aircraft shelters and command-and-control bunkers.

The air defense headquarters in Baghdad was destroyed by an F-117A that dropped an LGB down the air shaft of the hardened concrete structure. Another air defense sector operations center in western Iraq was destroyed when a second F-117A put an LGB through a hole made by the GBU-27 of an earlier F-117A attack. The headquarters of the Iraq Air Force was also destroyed the first night by an F-117A.

Horner, in a press conference, riveted his audience to the television screen when he said, "This is my counterpart's headquarters in Baghdad. This is the headquarters of the air force." Millions of people saw the building's lower floors billow out when the weapon exploded deep down the air shaft.[9]

Maj. Jon Boyd of the 37th TFW, piloting an F-117A, flew and fought on the first night. "We were going after some of the more critical targets—command, control, and communications—those types of things, not so much hardware as C^3," Boyd said. Their job was to make sure the targets were knocked out.

"So CENTAF was going after some fairly critical, time-sensitive nodes .... We were backing each other up, in case the target was missed. We were supposed to take a look-see to make certain the target was hit, hit it if it wasn't, or go on to another target, and continue to dismantle the C^3 structure—that was our primary job."[10]

F-117s flew thirty sorties the first night. They were particularly devastating throughout the war, destroying hardened targets by dropping smart bombs on laboratory, research and production facilities, flying unscathed over the most heavily defended parts of Iraq. F-117s constituted less than two and a half percent of all coalition fighter and attack aircraft in the Gulf War, yet they attacked thirty-one percent of strategic Iraqi targets the first day. Overall, the F-117 flew only two percent of the combat sorties throughout the war but attacked more than forty percent of the strategic targets.[11]

Months after the war, analysts in the Office of the Secretary of Defense questioned whether the F-117 had actually penetrated the Baghdad defenses without escorts or jamming support.[12]

The Air Force refuted this allegation, declaring that while other aircraft operated in the same vicinity at times, in only one instance were they there to support the F-117s. "They did benefit from the fact that there was a lot of confusion in there," said USAF Chief of Staff McPeak. "We created pandemonium [in the area around Baghdad] but some of the stories I've read would make you think we had Wild Weasels on one wing and the EF-111 on the other and a Compass Call at six o'clock [astern] to get those guys across Baghdad. That is absolutely untrue."

The F-117s, McPeak said, "were the only aircraft that we fragged[13] into downtown, inside the city limits—the only one we could do that with because the threat down there was genuine."[14]

[9] Lt. Gen. Charles Horner, CENTCOM news briefing, Jan. 18, 1991.

[10] Maj. Jon Boyd, interview, May 10, 1991.

[11] USAF white paper, September 1991.

[12] "OSD 'Lessons Learned' Questions USAF Claims of F-117, PGMs, F-16 CAS Success," *Inside the Air Force*, Nov. 8, 1991.

[13] The "frag," or fragmentary order, is a part of the Air Tasking Order. Units or aircraft are "fragged" to execute it.

[14] Gen. Merrill A. McPeak, Air Force Association Symposium, Jan. 30, 1992.

The Winning Combination

The initial air tasking order called for coordinated attacks by the air armada throughout Iraq and Kuwait. Sweeping the area for enemy fighters across Iraq were twenty F-15Cs.

Steve Tate from the 1st Tactical Fighter Wing, Langley AFB, Va., led a four-ship flight of F-15s on January 17. They had launched at 1:30 a.m. and refueled in the air. Tate decided to split off his second element of two Eagles into a separate orbit some miles away to provide better radar coverage.

Tate's radar soon detected an Iraqi Mirage F1 closing on the leader of his second element. He called out the "bandit" to the flight, locked onto the Mirage with his radar, and squeezed off an AIM-7M Sparrow missile.

The F1 was twelve miles away, but the missile struck it head-on. The aircraft exploded and dissolved into a bright ball of orange fire.[15]

[15] Julie Bird, "1st TFW Eagle Might Claim 1st Air Kill in War," *Air Force Times*, Jan. 28, 1991.

Coalition fighters shot down a total of thirty-five Iraqi fixed-wing aircraft during the war. Of these, thirty were downed by USAF pilots flying F-15 Eagles. A US Marine pilot on exchange duty with the Air Force bagged one. A Saudi pilot, also flying an F-15, shot down two Iraqi aircraft, and the other two were taken by US Navy pilots in F/A-18s.

Several factors account for the preeminence of the F-15 in the air-to-air war. Throughout the conflict, it was employed primarily in the air superiority role, and in that, the F-15 is better than any other aircraft flying today.

The Navy's F/A-18 is an excellent airplane, but it is a "swing role" fighter, employed for air-to-ground as well as air-to air missions. It did not fly as many air superiority missions as did the F-15.

The F-15s repeatedly flew deeper into Iraq than some other coalition aircraft. The Navy's primary air superiority fighter, the F-14, for example, flew extensive fleet air defense, closer to the Persian Gulf or the Red Sea and Kuwait, where no Iraqi aircraft were operating.

The Eagle also had the range and endurance to orbit in the corridor between Baghdad and the Iran—Iraq border, a high-traffic area for Saddam's fighters. All in all, F-15 pilots were flying the right fighter in the right place at the right time, and they performed as they had been trained.

The dominant air-to-air weapon of the war was the AIM-7M Sparrow. It was used by US pilots in twenty-nine aerial victories and by the Saudis in two.

The radar-guided AIM-7, therefore, was credited with three times the number of victories as the heat-seeking AIM-9M Sidewinder (ten, all US).

(The statistics are muddled a bit because a Navy F/A-18 pilot fired both an AIM-7 and an AIM-9 to down one Iraqi MiG-21.)

That pattern was the reverse of the US experience in the Vietnam War, where nearly all of the missile victories were with Sidewinders. Back then, the Sparrow was new in service. The pilots were more familiar with the AIM-9, which was also easier to employ.

The Vietnam-era Sparrow had several limitations. It depended for guidance on the radar of the launching fighter. If the launching aircraft had to turn and maneuver too much, the missile could not hold a lock on the target. The rules of engagement restricted the pilot from launching missiles without visual identification of the targets. That meant they had to be close, and the radar-guided AIM-7 of that era worked best at greater range.

By the time of the Gulf War, the Sparrow had been improved considerably. Today, for example, it can be launched much closer to the target. Maneuvering parameters are much expanded.

The big difference, however, is AWACS. Controllers can provide positive identification of targets well beyond the visual range of the attacking fighters. This increases the utility of the Sparrow, which has a longer range than the Sidewinder. Also, air superiority fighters like the F-15 now have their own identification equipment to complement the AWACS capability.

The AIM-7 Sparrow has become the weapon of choice for medium-range attacks, with the Sidewinder preferred at shorter ranges. Given AWACS and other features of modern aerial warfare, relatively fewer engagements are at close range.

Electronic Battle

Among the most dangerous missions of the war was the suppression of Iraqi SAMs and radar sites by USAF F-4G Wild Weasel aircraft. SAM suppression was also flown by Navy and Marine Corps EA-6Bs and F/A-18s.

A Wild Weasel two-man crew first detects the emissions of an enemy radar site, locks onto the emitter, and launches a High-Speed Antiradiation Missile that homes in on the site and destroys it. During Desert Storm, more than 1,000 AGM-88 HARMs were fired, virtually shutting down Iraqi radar.[16]

The opening F-4G assault was led by Lt. Col. George Walton of the 35th Tactical Fighter Wing, George AFB, Calif. Together with Wild Weasels from Spangdahlem AB, Germany, forty-eight of these hunters stalked and attacked Iraqi targets night and day. Walton's squadron, the 561st, flew out of Shaikh Isa in Bahrain.

"On the first night," he said, "the most emotional thing I can remember was taxiing out of the ramp area toward the runway and seeing, on a pole on top of the last revetment, an American flag. It was spotlighted, waving in the early morning breeze. We hadn't had an American flag up on the base until then, in deference to the Bahrainis.

"There's this huge red, white, and blue banner. What a feeling of pride. As we taxied past the quick-check area, just before the runway, all the maintenance guys and the media people are lined up, and there is hardly a dry eye among them. I mean, they're all crying. Well, there were some wet eyes in the cockpits as well."[17]

Walton led twelve F-4Gs against radars around Baghdad. "It was a target-rich environment," he said. "The emitters came on and stayed on for the entire flight of the missiles. Later in the war, they would stop emitting as soon as they saw our acquisition radar signature. They soon figured out that our missiles homed in on their signals. But that first night was really good, and we did good work."

Walton described the first suppression attack on Baghdad. "We were operating on the southern perimeter. This was a joint attack on the enemy air defenses of Baghdad by the Air Force coming in on the south and southeast, and the Navy, the Red Sea battle group, coming in on the west. We were supported by Air Force EF-111 jammers.

"We came up through the perimeter of the city and got as deep as we could to get as many of those deep threats as possible, without going over the center of the city. Over the center of Baghdad was the last place anybody wanted to be. The operation was well-timed and extremely well-executed. I believe it was one of the largest SEAD [suppression of enemy air defenses] packages ever thrown together on that first night."

He is probably right. At one point, more than 200 HARMs were in the air simultaneously, each zeroing in on an emitting Iraqi radar.[18]

The disruption of radar and communications was coordinated by area-jamming and suppression aircraft, including Air Force EF-111 Ravens, Navy and Marine Corps EA-6B Prowlers, and Air Force EC-130 Compass Call aircraft. These standoff jammers were very effective throughout the war and were an important reason allied aircraft losses were so low. Only thirty-nine American and allied aircraft were lost in combat during the war.

"They threw everything at us that night," Walton said. "I saw one of the most fantastic fireworks demonstrations I've seen since years ago. Baghdad was lit up like a Christmas tree.

"There were other fireworks, too, as we were coming out. That Mirage that Steve Tate splashed couldn't have been more than four or five miles off our left side as we're heading south, and I think that guy was probably beaming us or looking in our general direction trying to convert [move to a position behind Walton's tail] when Steve Tate shot it down."[19]

[16] Bruce D. Nordwall, "Electronic Warfare Played Greater Role in Desert Storm Than Any Conflict," *Aviation Week & Space Technology*, April 22, 1991.

[17] Lt. Col. George W. Walton, interview, July 18, 1991.

[18] USAF white paper, September 1991.

[19] Powell, "Voices From the War."

Aardvarks Against Airfields

Streaking in from Taif in southwestern Saudi Arabia were F-111Fs of the US 48th Tactical Fighter Wing from RAF Lakenheath and, from Incirlik, Turkey, F-111Es of the 20th TFW, RAF Upper Heyford, England. The F-111Es carried GBU-15s and CBU-89s.

Although the targets varied, airfield attack was on the top of the list. The CBU-89 is an area denial cluster bomb designed to deliver scores of land mines. The F-111F proved ideal for the tasks at hand, blowing in at low level and striking targets deep inside Iraq with precision.

Capt. Stephen M. Ling, a WSO in the 492d TFS, RAF Lakenheath, remembers his first mission. "It was go up, hit the tanker, let down at the tanker track, go low level all the way up to H3, an airfield in the west end of Iraq, and drop some Gator mines on it. It had more AAA defending it than they had in Hanoi during the southeast Asia war.

"As we were letting down on the way in, we had the first 'mission jitters,' I guess you'd call it. The hollow feeling in the pit of your stomach. All you can think about is 'are we going to make it back? Are we going to be able to get there, drop the bombs, and do our stuff?' But by the time you cross the border, you are so busy doing your job you forget about all that.

"All the jitters are gone, and now I'm busy concentrating on looking out for the bad guys, updating my computers and bombs and everything.

"Anyway, our whole mission from border to border crossing is twenty minutes. Two minutes after we cross the border, we had two Mirages try to shoot us down. We were at 1,000 feet, actually had dropped down to 400 feet by then, and they were coming in at 1,000 feet off our right side. I picked them up because we were getting some RHAW [radar homing and warning] hits from them.

"They had their wingtip lights on! As they were coming in this way, we stuck it down to 200 feet. My old F-4 days are coming back, and I'm saying to my pilot, 'Come on, we can turn, we can turn, we can do it, and we've got two kills the first night of the war! But then reason prevails—we've got a mission, and it's not shooting down Mirages.

"We just got down to 200 feet and pushed it up to about .95 Mach, made a couple of hard turns and lost them. They were hand flying their birds at that low altitude and we were in automatic TF (terrain-following) mode. They couldn't hack it and we lost them back at four o'clock.

"About a minute after that, we get a big floodlight from the ground—one of the guard towers inside the border there. As soon as they light us up, the AAA starts coming up. We kind of edged underneath it and the red tracers went arcing over us because they couldn't depress their guns enough.

"After we blew through there, we turned back toward H-3. Someone else's bombs went off and the entire sky lit up. It must have been a twenty-five-mile diameter circle with nothing but red tracers and flak going up. We maneuvered our way through it and dropped the mines.

"We get an indication in the cockpit that the canisters, four of them, are going off, but we can also see a flash of light behind it, as each one departs. We counted four flashes. Then we got out of there. We logged seven and a half hours that night. That's how far we had to go."[20]

The F-111F is designed for long-range, interdiction missions. The Pave Tack targeting pod carried in its weapons bay can acquire, track, and designate targets for laser, infrared, and electro-optical guided weapons. The swing-winged F-111F is powered by two Pratt & Whitney TF30-P-111 engines with 25,100 pounds of thrust in afterburner. The F-111F dashes at up to Mach 1.2 at sea level and has exceptional navigation and radar bombing capabilities.[21]

Originally introduced in 1965 as the TFX—"the airplane that can do everything"—the F-111 soon found itself derided as the airplane that couldn't do anything. It was plagued by problems with engines, avionics, and wing spars, and seemed to be grounded as often as it was flying.

From that dismal start, however, the

[20] Capt. Christopher M. Ling, interview, Aug. 8, 1991.

[21] General reference for USAF aircraft and systems in this chapter is Susan H.H. Young, "Gallery of USAF Weapons," *Air Force Magazine*, May 1991.

F-111 eventually recovered and went on to have a distinguished and sometimes spectacular career.

The newest Aardvark, the F-111F, ended production in 1974, but has had a complete avionics upgrade since then and is now equipped with all digital systems, a new attack radar, and a modernized terrain-following radar. The most significant improvement may have been the addition of the highly-accurate Pave Tack weapons delivery system, which F-111F crews used with telling effect in the April 1986 El Dorado Canyon raid on Libyan military installations.

When the Pave Tack pod is not in use, it tucks up into the aircraft's weapons bay. That means a reduction in aerodynamic drag, which improves both airspeed and fuel economy on the way to targets and back.

Operating at low level at night, the Aardvark can be awesome. "Often the F-111 crews would see through their rear view mirrors a gun open up, shooting at the sound," a 20th TFW unit history of the Gulf War said. "One of the other names for the F-111 is 'Whispering Death,' the reason being that when the jet is at full gallop, little noise is projected forward so the gunners didn't hear them coming and routinely fired at where they had just been."[22]

Funky Chicken Maneuvers

Airfields were, indeed, tough targets. "For us air-to-ground guys, the first week was the worst," said Capt. James J. McGovern, an F-111 pilot in the 48th TFW. "After that, we had really beaten the bejesus out of everybody, and you could tell there was less AAA, fewer SAMs, and less air-to-air activity.

"We were hitting an airfield near Baghdad named Al Habbiniyah. We flew right underneath a MiG cap[23] that Intel said consisted of three or four MiG-29s. They jumped us, but we defeated the attack and continued. They actually got a missile launch on the guy behind us, but he broke hard and evaded it.

"We climbed to medium altitude just before reaching the airfield and got lit up by a SAM site. We were carrying 2,000-pound bombs to deliver on the runways. They launched a big red flare which lit up the whole area, including us. We dropped our bombs and tried to get out of there.

"There were two Mirage F1s circling around there, and now that we're lit up, they came in. They had these floodlights on the wingtips that they use for dogfighting. They are almost the size of landing lights.

"So, I got this huge beam high and from the left side, and it lit up the cockpit just like daytime. A second later, another one comes low on the other side. It's like wolves coming in at you out of the forest. So we just start doing the 'Funky Chicken'—tight maneuvering—because they are close enough to use either heat-seeking missiles or guns. There's pandemonium in the cockpit. My WSO is trying to call positions on the one on his side, but I'm trying to get away from the one on my side.

"I did a couple of turns, and when their noses were pointed away, I rolled inverted and lit the afterburners, which we're never supposed to do at night because it gives the other guy such a good infrared target. But, I'm out of airspeed and ideas, so I go into min burner [minimum afterburner]. Fortunately, once you point the F-111's nose toward earth, she accelerates like a sled going down a ski jump. We went supersonic, inverted, forty-five degrees nose low, and six or seven seconds later, we're going through Mach 1.1, so I level off at 1,000 and then drop down to 200 feet. In the space of maybe thirty seconds, we were down to 200 feet, supersonic, out of Iraq, and not looking back."[24]

The GBU-15 is a modular bomb consisting of a 2,000-pound body, a Maverick TV or imaging infrared (IIR) seeker head, a control/datalink unit, and a cruciform wing. When the glide bomb is launched toward the target, the weapon system officer (WSO) in the F-111F continues to refine the aimpoint, since the GBU-15 transmits the TV or infrared picture its seeker head sees to the launching aircraft. The thirteen-foot glide bomb has a total weight of 2,500 pounds and a range of up to fifty miles, depending on the launch speed and altitude.[25]

[22] 20th TFW history, undated.

[23] A cap is combat air patrol, or protective air cover. Aircraft flying it are said to be "capping."

[24] Capt. James J. McGovern, interview, Aug. 8, 1991.

[25] *Jane's Air-Launched Weapons*, 1990.

"About the third night of the war," McGovern said, "we were ordered to go up north and find what they thought was a chemical storage center. We found it—a twenty-five-square-mile area of nothing but hardened bunkers. They were camouflaged with an earthen shell.

"I took out one of the bunkers. There was a huge secondary explosion. I employed two 2,000-pound LGBs on it. It was just like you saw on television. In the cockpit, on the display, you can see the road coming up, then you see a big, square door, and then you see the big mound of earth behind it. The first weapon went into the door and took it out. The second one, about four seconds later, shot right through the opening and then the huge secondary explosion just blew the roof off."[26]

Tornado in the Storm

Of the sixty combat aircraft the Royal Air Force deployed for Operation Desert Storm, forty were GR1 Tornados. The RAF used the Tornado to deliver the JP233 airfield denial weapon in the face of very heavy air defense weapons. This twin-engine, swingwing fighter bomber has much the same capability as the F-111.

It is capable of supersonic speeds at low altitude, is air refuelable, has excellent ground mapping radar and FLIR. The Tornado was designed for high-speed, low-altitude, precision attack and is all-weather-capable, day or night.

To deliver the JP233 effectively, the Tornado must fly low, 100 to 150 feet, and obliquely over a runway at 450 knots. The system consists of two complementary submunitions: a runway cratering bomblet (SG 357) and an area-denial weapon (HB 276). The Tornado carries two dispensers mounted in tandem under the fuselage. Each dispenser holds thirty cratering munitions and 215 area denial munitions.[27]

Between January 17 and January 23, the RAF lost six Tornados on low level missions, although only one was shot down while actually employing JP233s.[28] After January 23, Horner directed all coalition aircraft to operate at medium altitudes.

On the tenth day of the air war, coalition aircraft began the systematic bombing of Iraqi hardened shelters protecting aircraft and ballistic missiles.[29] Before the war, Iraq had hired British, Belgian, and Yugoslav firms to design and build more than 600 hardened shelters.[30] Protected by sand berms, the typical shelter had a steel and concrete roof four feet thick. The strong blast doors weighed forty tons, and were protected by concrete blast walls two feet thick. The shelters designed and built by the Yugoslavs were specially toughened, with roofs twelve feet thick.

Against these shelters, allied aircraft most often employed the BLU-109B (I-2000) 2,000-pound bomb in both the "dumb" (or gravity) configuration and smartened up as an LGB. The LGBs were dropped with extreme accuracy, usually down a shelter air shaft, but, in many cases, right through the roof.

Long-Range Eagle

The F-15E, sometimes called the "Strike Eagle," is a dual-role variant of the F-15 air superiority fighter and an extremely valuable weapon for long-range interdiction. It has been especially equipped to operate at night and in bad weather and has a crew of two. The weapon systems officer in the rear cockpit utilizes four multipurpose cathode ray tube (CRT) displays for radar, weapons selection, and monitoring enemy radar.

The front cockpit has a wide-field-of-view head-up display and three CRTs. The F-15E synthetic aperture radar provides high-resolution, TV-quality images. The aircraft has an automatic terrain-following system that can be coupled with the flight controls, and a highly accurate ring-laser gyro INS.

The Eagle can carry 24,500 pounds of ordnance. Conformal fuel tanks reduce drag and increase the range. The first operational wing equipped with the F-15E was the 4th Tactical Fighter Wing stationed at Seymour Johnson AFB, N.C. Although still converting to the F-15E at the start of the air war, the wing deployed forty-eight of them to Saudi Arabia.

[26] McGovern interview.

[27] *Jane's Air-Launched Weapons*, 1990.

[28] British Ministry of Defence Briefing, April 19, 1991.

[29] Col. John A. Warden, interview, May 17, 1991.

[30] Gen. Merrill A. McPeak, Pentagon news briefing, March 15, 1991.

Key to the F-15E's capability to find the Scuds at night was the Martin Marietta LANTIRN (Low-Altitude Navigation and Targeting Infrared for Night) system. It consists of two pods, one for navigation and the other for targeting, mounted under the fuselage. Although there were enough navigation pods to equip all F-15Es and some F-16s deployed in the Gulf War, only twenty-two targeting pods were available.[31]

The navigation pod contains terrain-following radar, the returns from which can be displayed in the cockpits, and a wide-angle FLIR for night navigation. The targeting pod has a wide and narrow field-of-view FLIR and a laser designator, both of which can track targets by either manual or automatic mode of operation.

Working against the Scuds, the F-15E utilized its radar to detect the launchers and then employed the LANTIRN to pinpoint the target. A typical Scud patrol mission lasted up to six hours and was flown as a two-ship formation. The leader usually carried four 2,000-pound GBU-10 LGBs. The wingman carried either six CBU-87 combined effect munitions (CEM) cluster bombs or a dozen Mk 82 500-pound bombs. The F-15E proved extremely effective against Scuds and against a wide-range of targets, including enemy armor.[32]

The F-15E pilots preferred to operate at low level, for which their aircraft was designed. "If it wasn't for our low-level capability, I wouldn't be here," said Capt. Mark F. Wetzel. "On the first night, we were part of a six-ship attack on H-2, one of Saddam's airfields out west. AWACS called two bogies [aircraft, probably hostile] airborne, but they didn't see us.

"We completely surprised them. The runway and taxiway lights were still on, and the rotating beacon [which all airfields have] was still going around. We didn't need the infrared. We could see everything. Everybody roared in at 300 feet and we each hit our target on the airfield, almost simultaneously. We were almost gone when the stuff started coming up.

"Now is the part where flying low level saved me. On our egress route, we were still at 300 feet. AWACS came up again and changed the bogies to bandits, meaning they were positively identified as Iraqi aircraft.

"Just then, a MiG went over us at about 7,000 feet. If we had been higher, he could have targeted us, and we'd have been toast.

"The F-15E crew behind us picked him up on radar and was about to take a missile shot when another air-to-air missile flashed by them and blew up the MiG they were about to shoot.

"Another MiG had shot it down! We understand the Iraqis were trained to fly into combat with their missiles armed and the trigger depressed, so the first thing the missile locks onto gets hit. The pilot probably thought he was locked on one of us.

"The guys in the other F-15E saw the second MiG turn and fly into the ground. I guess the Iraqis got credit for two kills."[33]

Joint STARS

Joint STARS was still in development when the war started. At General Schwarzkopf's request, the two existing E-8As were deployed to Saudi Arabia in mid-January, hours before the start of the war, although the Air Force was still testing and evaluating them. In fact, at war's end, the aircraft still faced six more years of development before official deployment.

The E-8A is a specially modified Boeing 707-320 with a Norden multimode, side-looking twenty-five-foot radar antenna housed in a "canoe" under the forward fuselage. The radar has a range of more than 155 miles. It operates in the synthetic aperture radar (SAR) mode to detect and locate stationary objects such as parked armored vehicles. The equipment alternates between SAR and a Doppler mode to detect slow-moving ground targets. Together, the two E-8As logged more than 600 hours and flew fifty-four missions with a system availability rate higher than eighty percent.

Joint STARS was able to track anything that moved on the ground. Each night, one of the giant planes orbited for ten hours or more. It provided important information on likely Scud sites and gave Army ground commanders current intelligence about Iraqi troop movements. It provided ground and

[31] Lt. Col. Jack Moffitt, interview, April 17, 1991.

[32] Jeffrey M. Lenorovitz, "Air Crew Training, Avionics Credited for F-15E's High Target Hit Rates," *Aviation Week & Space Technology*, April 22, 1991.

[33] Capt. Mark Wetzel, interview, May 31, 1991.

air commanders what Lt. Gen. Gordon Fornell, commander of Air Force Systems Command's Electronics Systems Division, describes as "this real-time, god's-eye view of the battle."[34]

Joint STARS could even see concertina wire barriers in the desert. It helped Army artillery units spot enemy positions. The aircraft provided real-time radar information that was used by a US VII Corps Multiple Launch Rocket System unit to destroy an Iraqi SA-8 SAM site. "Every place they went, Joint STARS saw them," commented Col. Mendel Solomon, Army Joint STARS program manager and deputy director of the USAF-Army Joint STARS project.[35]

The E-8A was able to locate, identify, and target assembly areas, POL[36] storage sites, convoys, trucks, tanks, SAM sites, and artillery. On the night of February 13, an E-8A detected an Iraqi army division on the move south with more than 225 vehicles. Coalition aircraft, principally F-15Es, attacked and virtually annihilated the force. Coupled with F-16s, Joint STARS was the key to the "kill box" approach to battlefield air interdiction that proved so effective.[37]

The Eminently Versatile F-16

Two hundred and forty-nine F-16s were deployed to the Gulf. Capt. Gregory S. Whiting, a pilot with the 612th TFS out of Torrejon AB, Spain, was deployed to Incirlik, Turkey. He remembers every mission, but one was especially interesting.

"We were tasked to hit the Bayji oil refinery about half way through the war," he said. "Somebody else had hit part of it the night before. They had done a great job, and the smoke was visible for 200 miles.

"My particular target was a group of petroleum storage tanks. The area was heavily defended by Triple A, but we had Wild Weasel support to cut down on the SAM threat. I dropped my bombs on two of the tanks, which blew up, and the fireball exploded two more that were right next to them. There were lots of secondary explosions.

"We all felt good about that mission. Felt good because we were able to hit something and instantly see the results. It was instant feedback." Whiting flew twenty-eight missions during Desert Storm.[38]

The F-16 has a multimode look-down radar, an advanced radar warning receiver, and the pilot enjoys a wide-field of view on his head-up display. The aircraft has internal chaff and flare dispensers to help it evade missiles as well as electronic countermeasures equipment. The Fighting Falcon also has advanced electronic counter-countermeasures equipment, is fitted with an internal gun and carries 500 rounds of 20-mm ammunition.

It was a versatile fighter in the Gulf War, attacking targets by day or night and in bad weather. Equipped with LANTIRN, the F-16 proved to have superb night fighting capabilities, although a shortage of targeting pods kept the F-16 from utilizing all of its capabilities.

F-16s played a key role in the destruction of Iraqi forces in Kuwait and Iraq. In the target-rich environment, Iraqi-controlled Kuwait was divided into fifteen-mile-square grids that pilots called "kill boxes."

Seasoned pilots were assigned to patrol specific kill boxes as "killer scouts," controlling other fighter-bombers as the "fast FACs" had done in southeast Asia. Teaming with the "killer scouts" who marked the targets were the "killer bees," F-16s hauling 2,000-pound or 500-pound gravity bombs, cluster bombs, and Mk 20 Rockeye canisters. By February 17, intelligence estimated that 100 to 150 Iraqi tanks per day were being destroyed through this methodical approach.[39]

Early in the air campaign, twenty F-16s of the Air National Guard's 138th TFS from Syracuse, N.Y., and the 157th TFS, McEntire ANGB, S.C., attacked an Iraqi-occupied air base in Kuwait. More than thirty SAMs plus heavy AAA fire met the F-16s. The sky was filled with flak. On this mission, one F-16 pilot received his baptism of fire. After returning from the mission, the newly-initiated pilot asked another F-16 pilot, a Vietnam veteran, "Are all combat missions like this one?"[40]

[34] Peter Grier, "Joint STARS Does Its Stuff," *Air Force Magazine*, June 1991.

[35] Grier, "Joint STARS Does Its Stuff."

[36] Petroleum, oil, and lubricants.

[37] USAF white paper, April 1991.

[38] Capt. Gregory S. Whiting, interview, Aug. 7, 1991.

[39] Tom Matthews, "The Secret History of the War," *Newsweek*, March 18, 1991.

[40] Maj. Gen. Philip Killey, interview, June 17, 1991.

Coalition Forces Munitions in the Persian Gulf War

Designation	Classification	Specifications
Mk 82	General-Purpose Bomb	500-lb bomb
Mk 83	General-Purpose Bomb	1,000-lb bomb
Mk 84	General-Purpose Bomb	2,000-lb bomb
M117	General-Purpose Bomb	750-lb bomb
BLU-82	Daisy Cutter	15,000-lb bomb
BLU-109 (I-2000)	Improved General-Purpose Bomb	2,000-lb hardened
GBU-10	Laser-Guided Bomb	BLU-109 or Mk 84 + Paveway I or II Kit
GBU-12	Laser-Guided Bomb	Mk 82 + Paveway I or II Kit
GBU-24	Laser-Guided Bomb	MK 84 or BLU-109 + Paveway II or III Kit
GBU-27 (F-117A Wpn)	Laser-Guided Bomb	I-2000 + Paveway III Kit*
GBU-28	Laser-Guided Bomb	4,700-lb + Paveway III Kit**
CBU-52	Cluster Bomb	600-lb antipersonnel
CBU-55	Cluster Bomb (fuel-air)	500-lb with BLU-73/Bs
CBU-58	Cluster Bomb	800-lb with BLU-63/Bs
CBU-87/B	Cluster Bomb (CEM)	1,000-lb with 202 CEMs
CBU-89	Cluster Bomb	1,000-lb with mines***
Mk 20 Rockeye II	Cluster Bomb	500-lb antiarmor
JP233	Dispenser	British airfield denial****
GPU-5 (Gun pod)	30-mm Gatling Gun	Carried by F/A-16
GBU-15	Glide Bomb	Mk 84 + kit. TV or IIR-guided 8 nm.
AGM-84E	SLAM (Navy)	60 nm missile with 500 lb warhead. E/O guidance
AGM-88 HARM	High-Speed Antiradiation Missile (US)	15 nm
ALARM	Air-Launched Antiradiation Missile (British)	30 nm
AGM-86C	Air-Launched Cruise Missile	Range 1,500 + miles launched from B-52G
BGM-71A/C TOW	Antitank Missile	42-lb wire-guided 2 nm
BGM-109/C Tomahawk	Navy TLAM	Sub or ship to land*****
AGM-114 Hellfire	Antitank Missile	95-lb laser-guided 10 nm
AGM-65 Maverick	Air-to-Surface Missile	TV, IIR or Laser-guided 10 nm
AS-30L (French)	Air-to-Surface Missile	Laser-guided 10 nm
AIM-7F Sparrow	Air-to-Air Missile	Semiactive radar 20 nm
AIM-9L/M Sidewinder	Air-to-Air Missile	Heat-seeking more than 5 nm
AIM-120A AMRAAM	Air-to-Air Missile	Fire-and-Forget 25 nm

* GBU-27 is equipped with a special Paveway III Kit with shortened fins.

** Bomb was a "quick reaction" munition especially built to attack Iraq's deep, superhardened bunkers.

*** Submunition is Gator airfield-denial mine.

**** Two dispensers each carries thirty SG-357 cratering submunitions and 215 HB-276 area-denial submunitions.

***** Cruise missile with 800 nm range at 520 mph. Has INS/TERCOM guidance. Warhead 264 lb.

Sources: US Air Force, *Air Force Magazine, Aviation Week & Space Technology,* Jane's Publishing Co.

F-16s flew almost 13,500 sorties during the war, more than any other aircraft. They attacked Iraqi ground forces in Kuwait, joined in the Great Scud Hunt, and destroyed military production and support areas as well as chemical production facilities and airfields.[41]

[41] USAF white paper, April 1991.

[42] Maj. Gen. John J. Closner, interview, May 31, 1991.

[43] Richard Mackenzie, "A Conversation With Chuck Horner," *Air Force Magazine*, June 1991.

[44] Lt. Col. Keith A. Bennett, interview, Aug. 8, 1991.

[45] "Operation Desert Storm." A-10 Briefing. King Fahd International Airport, Saudi Arabia, Spring 1991.

The Warthog is Tough

The aging A-10 Thunderbolt II, affectionately called the "Warthog," performed well in the Gulf War. Designed specifically for close air support, it is armored, can carry a large load, has a 150-mile combat radius, and can remain on station for an hour.

The A-10 lugs a payload of up to 16,000 pounds of mixed ordnance and is equipped with an internal 30-mm GAU-8/A cannon that can fire 4,200 rounds per minute. The armor-piercing depleted-uranium round weighs 2.05 pounds and was designed to kill tanks. The primary weapons are both the cannon and the AGM-65 Maverick. The aircraft has two General Electric TG34-GE-100 turbofans with 9,065 pounds of thrust each.

Col. Bobby Efferson, commander of the A-10-equipped 926th TFG, NAS New Orleans, La., can attest to the toughness of the A-10. En route to a target on a BAI mission, Colonel Efferson's flight was taking heavy AAA when, suddenly, his aircraft was hit by an Iraqi 57-mm round. Wrestling the aircraft to maintain control, Efferson turned toward Saudi Arabia as the A-10 suffered total hydraulic failure. Fighting the aircraft manually, Efferson was able to keep control through approach and landing. With no brakes, he finally ran off the runway at the end of the landing roll. His tires were shredded by shrapnel. Maintenance people counted 327 holes in the aircraft. It was repaired and flying again within the week.[42]

The A-10 performed a wide range of missions with its mixed load of ordnance. Although it was designed to operate at very low altitudes in support of ground forces, heavy enemy defenses forced pilots to fly at medium altitudes—above 8,000 feet—along with the rest of the coalition aircraft.

Horner had ordered all aircraft in the Gulf War to operate at medium altitude. "I think I had fourteen airplanes sitting on the ramp having battle damage repaired, and I lost two A-10s in one day [February 15] and I said, 'I've had enough of this,'" Horner told a reporter.[43] He pulled the A-10s out of Republican Guard areas and assigned them to less heavily-defended targets.

The "Warthog" employed the Maverick as an improvised FLIR and operated at night. It joined in the Scud hunt, flew cap above downed airmen, and attacked armor and troop concentrations.

Lt. Col. Keith A. Bennett, Commander of the 511th TFS, RAF Alconbury, England, remembers one particularly satisfying A-10 mission. "We were up in the triborder area on a beautiful day. The airborne FAC called us in on an artillery site. I rolled in, released, and my ordnance—CBUs—covered the site completely. Suddenly, the whole area started cooking off. They must have been storing ammo right by the guns. It was spectacular. The whole flight got six out of eight guns.

"Then, on the way home, almost down to Bingo [minimum fuel], I looked down and saw an armored personnel carrier, sitting out in the open. And then, coming at right angles, is another APC. He pulls up right next to the other one, like two guys waiting at a stop light. "I said, 'Two, we've got gas for one pass. I'll take the one on the left.' So, I rolled in and shot the one on the left. Then Two rolled in and killed the one on the right."[44]

Extracted from an intelligence debrief of an Iraqi brigadier general who had been taken prisoner is this statement: "Concerning the air attacks, source stated bluntly that they had 'won the war' for coalition forces. Source expressed admiration for the effectiveness of the American A-10 tank-killer aircraft, which heavily attrited his unit. Source also stated that his troops had nicknamed the A-10, 'The Silent Gun.'"[45]

Maverick Delivers a Charge

The Maverick antiarmor missile employed by F-16s, F-4Gs, and A-10s was one of the great weapons of the Gulf War.

The AGM-65 Maverick has been around since the mid-1960s, but has been upgraded and improved several times.

The variant employed in Desert Storm was the AGM-65D with an IIR seeker. The eight-foot missile weighs 485 pounds at launch and has a 126-pound shaped charge high explosive warhead. Maximum range is twelve miles.

To launch the missile, the pilot acquires the target on his Maverick display, sets cross hairs over the target image, then launches the missile. If there is heavy ground fire, he can break away from the target and the Maverick will continue to home in.[46]

Using Maverick at night, A-10 pilots flying at medium altitudes pointed the noses of their aircraft down toward areas of known Iraqi Army concentrations and looked for the unmistakable infrared signature of Iraqi vehicles.

The technique worked well. After the missile was launched, the fighter-bombers could then employ gravity bombs, working off the burning target hit by the Maverick.

One of the most effective methods Horner's aircrews used against enemy armor was "tank plinking." It worked best just after nightfall when F-111s with Pave Tack pods and F-15Es with LANTIRN pods found tanks by detecting their infrared signatures. Even if a tank had not been operated during the day, its metal body retained considerable daytime heat while the desert surroundings cooled down quickly.

That heat made them show up starkly for the IR detectors of the F-111Fs and F-15Es, which then homed unerringly in on the tanks in their desert revetments.

Some soldiers (including Schwarzkopf) disliked the "tank plinking" term, but most airmen (including Horner) liked it, so it took firm root in the lexicon of the Gulf War.

F-16C pilots with LANTIRN pods on their aircraft frequently used their Maverick missile seekers to identify potential targets.

The B-52's Historic Reach

The Department of Defense waited for exactly one year to reveal one of the most extraordinary missions of the war. At 6 a.m., Jan. 16, 1991, seven B-52G heavy bombers took off from Barksdale AFB, La., to strike Baghdad on the longest air combat mission in history.[47]

Each bomber flew a total distance of more than 14,000 miles, refueled four times, and remained in the air for more than thirty-five hours before landing again at Barksdale.

The B-52s carried AGM-86C conventional cruise missile variants that the United States had not acknowledged that it possessed at the time of the flight. The seven aircraft launched a total of thirty-one missiles at eight targets.

"Fired from outside Iraq's air defense network, the missiles attacked high-priority targets, including power generation and transmission facilities and military communication sites," according to Pete Williams, Assistant Secretary of Defense for Public Affairs. The missiles struck about ninety minutes after H-hour.

The Pentagon delayed revelation of the mission, Williams said, because it was not eager to advertise the existence of the new air-launched cruise missile variant and the capability it embodied.

The mission turned out to be one of a kind in the Gulf War. It was mounted at the beginning when Iraq's air defenses were still intact and weapons that could attack from standoff range were at a premium, Williams said.

Although B-52s did not strike again from such distances, the big bombers saw extensive action in the Gulf. B-52Gs operating out of Saudi Arabia, Spain, England, and Diego Garcia flew 1,624 missions and dropped 72,000 bombs. They delivered twenty-nine percent of all US bombs (and thirty-eight percent of the Air Force bombs) during the Gulf War.

The basic B-52 Stratofortress is more than thirty years old, but it held a mission-capable rate of better than eighty percent throughout the war. According to estimates, between twenty and forty percent of Iraqi deserters were influenced in their decision to run by the devastating effect of the B-52.[48]

The Boeing B-52G has undergone numerous modifications, including an electro-

[46] *Jane's Air-Launched Weapons*, 1990.

[47] Pete Williams, Pentagon news briefing, Jan. 16, 1992.

[48] USAF white paper, April 1991.

optical viewing system using FLIR and low-level-light TV sensors to improve low-level night penetration. The aircraft has a crew of six and carried 40,000 pounds of conventional weapons on a typical Desert Storm mission.

Horner controlled seventy-three B-52s. Twenty of them were on Diego Garcia, and another twenty were at Jiddah, Saudi Arabia. The rest of the B-52s flew from bases in Spain and England. Stratofortresses based at Jiddah flew three- or four-hour missions, sometimes two per day. They employed 500-pound and 750-pound bombs (up to fifty-one at a time), Gator mines, and other CBUs.

"Initially, we used B-52s for night strikes," said Brig. Gen. Patrick P. Caruana, USAF, CENTAF Director of Strategic Forces. "But gradually, as we gained air supremacy and found areas where we could operate without concern for air-to-air threats, we went to a twenty-four-hour-a-day operation."[49]

Targets for the B-52s were Iraqi oil refineries, Scud missile sites, airfields, Iraqi Republican Guard divisions, troop concentrations, and logistic complexes. They were also used to breach the huge berms the Iraqis had built up to fend off the expected amphibious attack.

"At the height of the air activity," Caruana said, "we made B-52s available to CENTCOM to put over the Republican Guard, or any targets for that matter, in Kuwait and Iraq, every three hours."

On the night of February 13, an Iraqi armored division began to move and was detected by Joint STARS. A cell of Stratofortresses was directed to attack the lucrative target. In another case, B-52s attacked a rail marshaling yard when Scud missiles were discovered on flat cars.

C-130 Daisy Cutters

On February 7, two MC-130Es, variants of the famed C-130 Hercules transport, of the 8th Special Operations Squadron had a special cargo destined for the Iraqi front lines in Kuwait. Each aircraft held a 15,000-pound BLU-82 bomb, the so-called "Daisy Cutter,"[50] which is the size of a Volkswagen Beetle. The big bombs rolled out the back of the C-130s on cargo pallets.

The two-ship formation was led by Maj. Skip Davenport of Hurlburt Field, Fla. When the bombs detonated, the explosions created a sensation among coalition and Iraqi troops alike.

An Iraqi battalion commander and his staff promptly surrendered and provided US Marines with maps of minefields along the Kuwait border. The Daisy Cutters provided an intelligence bonanza, besides destroying Iraqi minefields and fortifications.

Days before the beginning of the ground war, the C-130s struck a minefield with such spectacular effect that the Iraqis thought the allied invasion was under way. They turned on their air defense radars all along the border, revealing the locations of some that the coalition had not known about.[51]

The AC-130H Spectre gunship is a modified Lockheed C-130H powered by four Allison T56-A-15 turboprops. It is equipped with two electronic counter-measures pods as well as chaff and flares for defense against missiles. It has FLIR and low-light-level television and is equipped with a computer-aimed fire-control system. It is armed with two 20-mm Vulcan cannons and one 40-mm cannon that fire from the left side of the aircraft. In addition, the aircraft is equipped with a powerful and accurate 105-mm howitzer.

AC-130Hs, with F-15Es, were the backbone of aerial attacks on the Republican Guard during the "mother of all retreats" that started in the early morning darkness of February 26.

Phase IV of Desert Storm, air operations in conjunction with surface forces, began well before the "100-hour war" of February 24–28, and the AC-130H was a significant part of it.

A Spectre was lost at dawn on January 31 when it was shot down by an Iraqi SAM while supporting Saudi and US Marine units under Iraqi attack in Khafji, Saudi Arabia. Normally, the Spectres only operated during hours of darkness in areas of moderate threat. The aircraft crashed just off shore

[49] Brig. Gen. Patrick P. Caruana, interview, Oct. 30, 1991.

[50] A "daisy cutter" is a bomb fuzed to detonate in the air, just before it reaches the surface of the earth. There is little or no cratering. The BLU-82, which has a thin casing, gets its tremendous force from blast alone. Another daisy cutter, the 500-pounder mentioned *on page 59*, has a relative thick casing of hard steel and achieves its effect by fragmentation.

[51] Joshua Hammer and Douglas Waller, "Special Ops: the Top-Secret War," *Newsweek*, March 18, 1991.

in the Persian Gulf, killing all fourteen crewmen.[52]

Intelligence Problems

Some Iraqi targets proved tough to hit. A huge nuclear research facility just south of Baghdad was heavily defended by SAMs, AAA, and an earthen berm. The complex, a quarter mile square, was obscured by well-placed smoke pots when two F-16 squadrons attempted an attack. Because of the heavy defenses and the poor visibility, the F-16s lofted the bombs from a safe distance but with poor results.

Two nights later, four F-117s attacked the facility. They destroyed two reactors, some buildings, and damaged two other reactors. After more night attacks, the F-117s destroyed the site. Using videotape from the F-117s' recording systems, damage after each sortie could be assessed and used to plan the next attack.[53]

Schwarzkopf was particularly critical of the Central Intelligence Agency and Defense Intelligence Agency for delayed and conservative reports on targets, enemy capabilities, and bomb-damage assessment.[54]

Arrangements were made to speed up the distribution of intelligence products. For example, key members of the Air Staff in the Pentagon were locating and faxing, through secure communications, overhead intelligence photographs, trying to provide the data in near real-time.[55]

Bomb-damage assessment proved to be a sticky problem during the Gulf War. The reasons are many. For example, Air Force, Navy, and Marine fighter-bombers have few strike assessment cameras (which were once common during the Vietnam War). Theater commanders received good intelligence from Air Force TR-1s, Joint STARS, active-duty and Air National Guard RF-4Cs, Navy F-14 Tomcats, French Air Force Mirage F1s, and Royal Air Force GR1 Tornados.

The Coalition Contribution

The contribution and effectiveness of the allied air forces was notable. The RAF picked up most of the "bridge busting" mission for the coalition forces. Using the thirty-year-old Buccaneer strike aircraft to lase targets, Tornados employed Paveway laser-guided bombs to destroy thirty-three of thirty-six strategic bridges across the Tigris and Euphrates rivers in Iraq, further isolating the Iraqi Army to the south of Baghdad. Performing this dangerous mission, the RAF lost one Tornado to missiles on February 14.

Coalition air forces large and small operated with telling effect. Bahrain, for example, flew more than 130 ground attack sorties with its squadron of twelve F-5s against Iraqi targets in Kuwait and Iraq.[56]

The French Air Force contributed Jaguar A/E fighter-bombers, Mirage F1 air-to-air fighters and Mirage F1RC combat aircraft. In addition, the FAF provided support aircraft, including C-135FRs and Puma air-rescue helicopters that were responsible for the rescue of at least one American pilot inside Iraq. The French were stationed at Al Ahsa AB southwest of Dhahran, Saudi Arabia.[57]

One unusual feature of the French participation was that the Iraqi Air Force was equipped with some of the same equipment as the French Air Force was using against Iraq. For example, both countries employed the French-built Mirage F1, which caused the French to ground the F1 until several days into the Gulf War for fear of allied aircraft shooting them down by mistake.

The French employed the Jaguar armed with the AS-30L laser-guided, air-to-surface missile against Iraqi airfields in Iraq and Kuwait. The missile weighs 1,150 pounds at launch, is equipped with a 550-pound warhead, and has a range of six miles. The missile is launched a safe distance from the target, uses a mid-course inertial guidance system, and is terminally guided to the target by a self-tracking laser illuminating pod carried by the fighter-bomber, allowing the pilot to "fire and forget," breaking away a safe distance from the target.

The SEPECAT Jaguar is an aging fighter-bomber with very limited night and all-weather capabilities. The single-seat fighter is powered by two Adour 7,305-pound thrust engines, has an unrefueled combat range of 500 miles, weighs 34,615 pounds maxi-

[52] Joby Warrick, "Downed AC-130 Found," *Air Force Times*, March 18, 1991.

[53] Douglas Waller, "Armed for Action: High Tech Gizmos," *Newsweek*, June 17, 1991.

[54] William B. Scott, "Triangular Recon Aircraft May Be Supporting F-117A," *Aviation Week & Space Technology*, June 10, 1991.

[55] Molly Moore, "Schwarzkopf: War Intelligence Flawed," Washington *Post*, June 13, 1991.

[56] Alex Renton, "How RAF Tornados Were Lost in the Gulf," *The Independent*, London, England, May 24, 1991.

[57] World Defense Almanac, Vol. 15, Issue 1, 1991.

mum on takeoff, has a top speed of 1,056 knots, and can carry 10,500 pounds of ordnance. The Jaguar can air refuel and proved very successful in the airfield attack role employing the AS-30L.[58]

[58] World Defense Almanac.

A Tough Fight

Iraq had an impressive array of weapons, including the French-made AM-39 Exocet air-to-surface missile with a range of more than thirty miles. The Iraqi Air Force attacked the USS *Stark* with two AM-39s in April 1987, seriously damaging the ship. One Iraqi Mirage F1 was shot down attempting an Exocet attack on coalition warships. Two F1s were shot down over the Saudi oil fields.

The Iraqi Air Force was neutralized within a few days of the air war and could not fend off coalition air forces. Nevertheless, Iraq brought a vast array of ground-based air defenses to bear against coalition air forces. There were few "milk runs" when attacking targets in Iraq or Kuwait.

Iraqi air defense forces provided coverage from the surface to 50,000 feet.[59]

Iraq had hundreds of SA-7 Grails, SA-14 Gremlins, and HN-5A SAMs in its formidable air defense. The destruction of the IADS still left ample firepower for employment against coalition forces. For example, the SA-14 Gremlin is the new Soviet shoulder-launched, heat-seeking missile, an improved version of the SA-7. The missile has good countermeasures against flares and can attack a target aircraft from any direction. The minimum effective altitude is thirty feet and the maximum effective altitude is 17,000 feet.[60]

The Roland missile, built by Messerschmitt-Bölkow-Blohm and Aerospatiale, is difficult to counter because a tracking unit tracks both the target and the missile and generates steering signals to the missile. The Roland has a weight of 149 pounds, a maximum range of 4.3 miles, and a minimum range of 1,500 feet. The missile has a maximum altitude of 18,000 feet.[61]

The Soviet built SA-3 Goa is roughly comparable to the American-built Hawk missile. It has a range of nineteen miles and a maximum altitude of 50,000 feet.

[59] Michael Taylor. *Encyclopedia of Modern Military Aircraft*, 1989.

[60] Tony Cullen and Christopher Foss. *Land-Based Air Defence*, 1990–91.

[61] Cullen and Foss.

Why Weren't They Better?

Iraqi air defenses were thick and provided layered coverage at all altitudes. Why did they not take a greater toll on coalition aircraft? Most important, the Iraqi air de-

Iraqi Antiaircraft Weapons

Weapon	Description	Effective Range
14.5-mm ZPU-1, ZPU-2, and ZPU-4LAAG	Light AAA	5,000 feet
23-mm twin and ZSU-23-4	Light AAA	15,000 feet
37-mm	Medium AAA	10,000 feet
57-mm S-60 and ZSU-57-2	Medium AAA	20,000 feet
85-mm KS-12	Heavy AAA	25,000 feet
100-mm KS-19M2	Heavy AAA	36,000 feet
130-mm KS-30	Heavy AAA	50,000 feet
SA-7 Grail	Manportable SAM (IR)	3.5 nm
HN-5A (Chinese manufacture)	Manportable SAM (IR)	3.0 nm
SA-9 Gaskin (4 mounted on vehicle)	Mobile SAM (IR)	4.3 nm
SA-13 Gopher (4 mounted on vehicle)	Mobile SAM (IR)	6.0 nm
SA-14 Gremlin	Manportable SAM (IR)	4.0 nm
SA-2 Guideline	Command Guidance SAM	25.0 nm
SA-3 Goa	Command Guidance SAM	18.0 nm
SA-4 Ganef	Command Guidance SAM	50.0 nm
SA-6 Gainful	Semiactive Guidance SAM	19.0 nm
SA-8 Gecko	Command Guidance SAM	7.5 nm
Roland (French/German manufacture)	Command Guidance SAM	4.3 nm

Sources: Jane's Publishing Co. *Air Force Magazine.* Bofors Aerotronics.

fenses, built along the Soviet model, depended heavily—almost 100 percent—on centralized control.

Saddam's central command and control facilities and networks were severely damaged in the opening hours of the air war, and he was never able to rebuild them. Most SAM or AAA batteries were forced to operate autonomously, with little coordination or central direction. There was no early warning of incoming coalition attackers. The result was the dense barrage fire Americans saw on television. Most attackers were able to avoid it.

Equally important was the coalition's combination of training, equipment, tactics, weapons, planning, and capability to suppress enemy defenses.

The coalition had an overall air commander. Combat decisions were made by those who understood the risks and the tactics. The commanders in the field were in charge, and the combat aircrews made most of the decisions on tactics and risks. Having the appropriate weapons on hand was also very important. Precision- guided weapons of the right type paid dividends.

Col. Tom Lennon, commander of the F-111F-equipped 48th TFW (Provisional), said, "They [our aircrews] were much better prepared to go into this war than we were when we went to southeast Asia, I can guarantee you that. Our training programs right now are so much better, things like Red Flag, all the NATO exercises we do over here [Europe] continuously, and the weapons deployment training locations we go to, composite force training. Quarterly, we get together with the EF-111s and the Wild Weasels and do composite-type training.

"All those things better prepared us for combat. And additionally, we had five months down there [Saudi Arabia] to do the planning for this campaign for our targets and to train for exactly the type of missions we were going on. You know, we dropped precision-guided munitions in this war that hadn't even been thought of during the Vietnam War."[62]

One of the astounding stories of Desert Storm was the efforts of a "quick reaction team" of the Munitions Systems Division at Eglin AFB, Fla., to build and field a 4,700-pound laser-guided bomb called the GBU-28 in just seventeen days. The bomb was designed to destroy extremely deep and hardened Iraqi command-and-control centers. The weapon had to be able to penetrate 100 feet or more of earth and at least twenty feet of concrete.

The team fabricated the bombs from surplus Army eight-inch artillery gun barrels. The bombs were filled by hand with molten explosives at Eglin AFB and were flown to Saudi Arabia and Nellis AFB, Nev., while the explosive was still warm. Tests were conducted at Nellis verifying the bomb could be dropped from F-111Fs and would produce the proper destructive effects.

Two of the bombs were dropped by two F-111Fs of the 48th Tactical Fighter Wing on two targets north of Baghdad.[63] At least one deep bunker was destroyed. The ground war was in its last day and Iraq's military power was almost destroyed.

Fighting the Oil Spill

In the middle of the war, Iraq began dumping thousands of barrels of Kuwaiti oil into the Persian Gulf. Petroleum engineers and oil field experts advised two courses of action: try to set the oil spill afire, burning off pollutants that would otherwise flow into the sea. Second, they suggested destroying the manifolds, the system of pipes controlling the pressure, at the terminal.

As Schwarzkopf explained it, coalition forces achieved the first of these goals by accident. On January 25, the US Navy in the Gulf encountered a small boat of the kind the Iraqis used for minelaying. A fight ensued, and the Sea Island terminal was set afire by circumstance in the exchange.[64]

The job of destroying the manifolds went to F-111F aircraft with GBU-15 electro-optical guided bombs. They began the operation after dark on January 26.

"We originally had five airplanes fragged for this target," said Colonel Lennon, who flew one of the F-111Fs. "We dropped the first bomb and the Number One aircraft in the flight started to guide it in, using the downlink pod.

[62] Col. Thomas Lennon, interview, April 22, 1991.

[63] Lennon interview.

[64] Schwarzkopf, CENTCOM news briefing, Jan. 27, 1991.

"The downlink pod died, and Number Two had to pick the missile up electronically and guide it in the rest of the way to the manifold. The guidance aircraft were about forty or fifty miles away from the target, basically heading south with the target, off to the right, three o'clock position, in what we call a datalink orbit."

They watched the picture transmitted to their CRTs by the bomb's seeker head and used the datalink to steer the bomb into the target.

"Major Sampson and I went in, and we planned to be at 20,000 feet, Mach 1, and about twenty miles from the target for the release point," Lennon said. "We pickled off the bomb. Then, we just turned as hard as we could to egress the target area to stay away from the AAA that was fragged to be on the coastline there in Kuwait. There were a few SAMs, but with the launch range that we had, we could pretty much stay away from most of them, except for the SA-2.

"So that was a memorable mission. Not necessarily one of the highest threat missions that I'd flown, but it was a good mission ... because all of us in the flight felt it was real important stopping the oil that was flowing into the Gulf."[65] ■

[65] Lennon interview.

USAF Photo by TSgt. Rose S. Reynolds

An F-111 fighter-bomber from the 48th TFW, RAF Lakenheath, taxis on a runway in the crisis area during Desert Shield. The EF-111A in the background, an electronic countermeasures aircraft, comes from Mountain Home AFB, Idaho, home of the 366th TFW.

USAF Photo by SrA. Chris Putnam

Munitions crew members from the 33d TFW load a Sidewinder missile, just one of the many types of munitions available, onto an F-15. "It's like a 7-Eleven," one of the crew said. "The pilots can get any bomb they like."

7. The Attrition of Iraq

Saddam hesitated to put his air force into the air, but lost much of it on the ground anyway. The advancing Army Airborne found the remains of this Iraqi Su-25 Frogfoot, apparently destroyed before it ever got airborne.

XVIII Airborne Corps Photo

Saddam's central control was gone, but his occupation force was still there, dug in and dangerous.

The opening attacks had broken Saddam's central control and his ability to mount a real counteroffensive. Iraqi forces still occupied Kuwait, however, and both the army and the air force still had the means to fight fiercely. Before coalition ground forces could move in, airpower had to reduce the dug-in forces and the infrastructure supporting them in both Kuwait and Iraq.

Around the clock, coalition air forces struck Iraqi armor, artillery, infantry vehicles, the Republican Guard, logistics installations, command posts, and command and control facilities.

Every three hours, US B-52 bombers hammered Saddam's field army. Attack aircraft hit supply depots, headquarters, supply lines, bridges, and individual vehicles. Airfields and strategic targets around Baghdad were still high-priority targets.

At the start of the war, there were fifty-four railroad and highway bridges in Iraq, most of them on roads running southeast from Baghdad to Basra and Kuwait. By the end of the war, coalition aircraft destroyed forty-three of these spans (some had little military significance and had not been targeted) as well as thirty-two pontoon bridges built as replacements. By the third week, supplies reaching Basra, the major transhipment point for the Iraqi army in Kuwait, were insufficient to maintain any sort of combat effectiveness.[1]

F-111Fs and F-15Es, using smart bombs, made smoking ruins of Iraqi armor. "The F-111 and the F-15E took out 100 to 200 tanks a night," General Horner said.[2] The F-111s, sweep-searching with their FLIR pods as they cruised the battlefield, were especially effective at night and twilight, when temperature differences between the cooling metal of the tanks and the ambient heat pulses from the desert stood out for the infrared sensors. Overall, the F-111s destroyed more than 1,000 tanks and armored vehicles, peaking in the period just before the coalition ground offensive, when they were achieving an extraordinary number of armor kills per night.

The Maverick missile, employed by the A-10s and F-16s—and even by the F-4G Wild Weasels when they weren't attacking enemy radars and electronic defenses—was devastating against armor. Coalition forces used 5,500 Mavericks (ninety-nine percent of them fired by the US Air Force) in Operation Desert Storm.[3]

"Flying across the Arabian peninsula, one could see hundreds of blinking anticollision beacons with offensive aircraft coming from bases all over Saudi Arabia as well as Oman, Yemen, Bahrain, and the United Arab Emirates," a unit history compiled by the 36th TFW said.

"B-52s came from the Indian Ocean, Europe, and as far away as Louisiana.... Brigadier General Glosson had mentioned in his pep talk that we were going to use more tankers than were planned to support a war with Russia. Indeed, maps showed there was very little airspace in the northern half of Saudi Arabia that did not have a tanker track in it. For the next two months, the tanker tracks would remain full of fighters, getting gas before long missions into

[1] USAF white paper, September 1991.

[2] Richard Mackenzie, "A Conversation With Chuck Horner," *Air Force Magazine*, June 1991.

[3] USAF white paper, September 1991.

Iraq as well as topping off before working their way back home."[4]

Capt. Ivan Thomas, a pilot with the 10th TFS, remarked on the amount of mission materials created for aircrews to take along on flights in the AOR.

"On a typical sortie at al Dhafra, a pilot would have no less than three maps, a target photo, lineup card, clue card, attack card, and other extraneous pieces of paper.

"All of this information was affectionately called 'Queep.' Sometimes it appeared that if a cockpit wasn't full of Queep, you didn't have enough."[5]

[4] *The Gulf War: The 36th TFW Story*, 1991.

[5] "History of Desert Shield/ Storm," 50th TFW unit history, 1991.

[6] Maj. Gen. John A. Corder, interview, July 8, 1991.

Assigning the Targets

The beginning and middle parts of the war were mostly airpower, and the US Air Force was supplying most of it. Maj. Gen. John A. Corder, CENTAF Director of Operations, explained how the targets were apportioned later in the war.

"Everybody recognized that an airplane didn't fly unless it was in the air tasking order," Corder said.

Horner and Glosson met daily with Schwarzkopf and adjusted the air campaign to meet his requirements as they evolved.

The strategic targets were assigned first, the toughest ones going to the F-117s and the next toughest to the F-111s. Then the Scuds were targeted. F-15Es and the F-16s equipped with LANTIRN were designated for the night attacks on Scud sites, while A-10s, A-6s, and F/A-18s went after them by day.

For tactical targets in the KTO, Corder said, "Glosson or one of his deputies would say, 'Here are the targets and here are the TOTs [times on target]. What do you want to hit, Navy?' And the Navy would say, 'we want to hit these coastal sites, Silkworm [antiship missile] sites, and, because of our aircraft carrier deck cycle time, we'd like these particular TOTs.' Glosson would say, 'okay, you can have that.'

"Then, 'all right, Marines, what do you want to hit?' The Marines would say, 'We want to support our own troops.' Glosson would say, 'okay, here are some targets in the south.'

"The Brits wanted to hit airfields. They got them. Later, they asked for bridges. They got them. It was the same routine with the Italians, the French, and everybody else. Whatever they asked to hit, they got.

"And what they provided came to about twenty-five percent of the effort. Then, when the meeting was over, the US Air Force filled in the blanks and covered the other seventy-five percent."[6]

Dividing the Air Effort
D-Day to Cease Fire

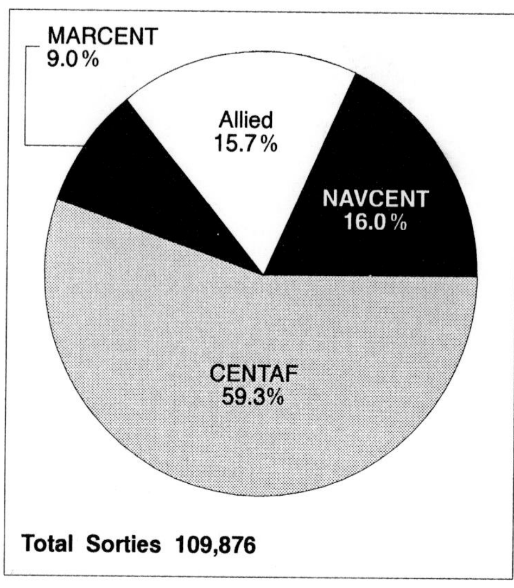

More than half the sorties in the war were flown by CENTCOM's Air Force component, CENTAF. The naval and Marine components, NAVCENT and MARCENT, flew a fourth of the sorties. Special operations forces, not broken out on this chart, accounted for less than 0.5 percent of the total.

Heavy Metal

"You didn't hear much in the media about the F-16 or the B-52, although they did a great job, because those airplanes don't carry equipment that enables them to record what they're hitting in real time," Corder said. "The F-111s, the F-15E's, on the other hand, which also did a great job, did have that equipment, so you heard about them.

"The B-52 was a great psychological thing for our people, especially a few days before the land battle began, when the troops on our side could see the flames in the

Shares of US Air Sorties
D-Day to Cease Fire

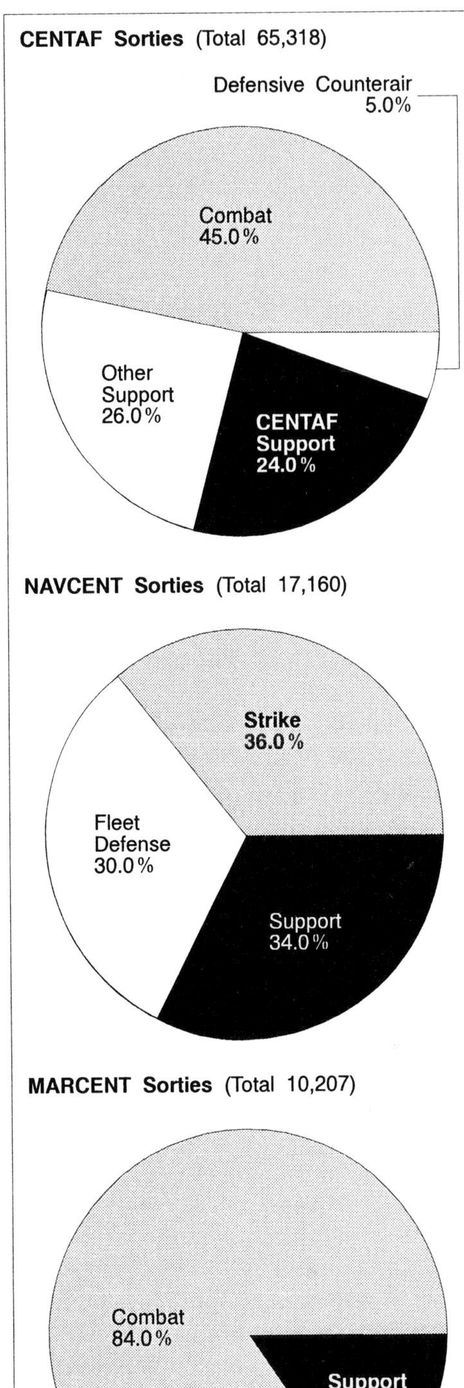

night and feel the ground shake, like an earthquake, when a B-52 strike went in many miles away."[7]

Prisoner interrogations revealed the B-52 as a weapon Iraqi ground forces feared. One Iraqi troop commander, claiming he surrendered because of B-52 strikes, was told that his position had not been hit by B-52s. "That is true," he said, "but I saw one that had been attacked."[8]

When the Iraqis started surrendering, many of the EPWs had punctured eardrums and infected sinuses, the result of the concussions from the huge B-52 bomb loads.[9]

Nothing could match the Stratofortress in putting down massive firepower. "As the deadline [for the ground invasion] approached, the Marines became very concerned," Corder said. "They seemed to worry a lot that they would get bunched up in the Iraqi wire. We put thirty to forty B-52 sorties in front of them every night for several nights before the ground war started."

B-52s were used along enemy front lines in conjunction with aircraft delivering psychological warfare leaflets to warn Iraqi forces of what to expect if they did not leave Kuwait. The leaflets announced that the B-52s were coming, and after the attack, more leaflets reminded the Iraqis where the bombs had come from and said that the B-52s would be back.[10]

"The B-52s were great," Corder said. "They hit some precision targets like airfield runways, and they did good work against area targets. There were plenty of area targets.

"For example, Saddam had a storage area at a place called Taji, which was north of Baghdad. If you can imagine the USAF Air Logistics storage areas at Oklahoma City, Okla., Sacramento, Calif., and Ogden, Utah, put all of them together, and then double that, you'd have some idea of the incredible size of Taji. They hit it again and again."[11]

Concentrating on Kuwait

"Initially, much of the air assets were devoted to strategic targets to make sure we got those down, while we were also

[7] Corder interview.

[8] USAF white paper, September 1991.

[9] Corder interview.

[10] *Conduct of the Persian Gulf Conflict*.

[11] Corder interview.

killing the front-line forces," Horner said. "As we killed off the research and development stuff—storage, those kinds of targets—we brought more and more assets into the KTO. We really started heating the battle up in Kuwait."[12]

By the start of the ground war, the coalition air forces had flown some 67,200 combat sorties. Saddam was not the only one who lost command and control. Many of his corps, division, and brigade commanders were out of touch with their forces.

Vast stores of his equipment were rendered useless. Huge stockpiles of supplies Iraq positioned to support the KTO were depleted or destroyed. The road networks the Iraqis planned to use for replenishment were badly damaged.

These intensive interdiction operations sapped morale in the Iraqi field forces, and according to captured Iraqi officers, fueled the high rate of desertions. The air campaign greatly reduced Saddam's ability to bring his remaining strength to bear against coalition ground forces.

After more than a month of bombardment, however, Iraqi forces were still in Kuwait. They were poorly fed, ill-housed, in poor physical condition, and suffered from low morale. Later, Schwarzkopf would rate the overall effectiveness of the Iraqi forces at the time of the coalition ground attack at about fifty percent. The allied offensive up to that point, largely airpower, had destroyed at least half of Saddam's combat punch.[13]

The coalition air forces achieved this despite bad weather, which was a factor throughout the campaign. Some forty percent of the attack sorties scheduled for the first ten days were canceled because of poor visibility or low overcast in the KTO.

Coalition planners had computed sorties on the basis of thirteen percent cloud cover, average for the region at that time of year. As it worked out, the cloud cover was thirty-nine percent, the worst in the fourteen years that flight weather records have been kept on the Saudi peninsula.

Strikers and Traffic Cops

Saddam had built an enormous military establishment, and it took a lot of destroying. Some targets were suggested from Washington, based on intelligence data from strategic reconnaissance platforms, including satellites and U-2 and TR-1 aircraft. Most targets were identified within the theater.

"Joint STARS was developing targets all night long," Corder said. "We could strike any target within 200 miles of the border in twenty minutes. From the time we were told where it was, we could have an airplane on it in twenty minutes."[14]

Capt. Charles M. Robinson and Capt. Mark L. Wetzel, F-15E crewmembers with the 4th Wing from Seymour Johnson AFB, N.C., described how the strike flights worked with Joint STARS and the command and control aircraft.[15]

"We'd take off from Al Kharj with twelve CBU-87 cluster bombs, filled with a mixture of antipersonnel and antitank munitions," said Robinson. "They're called combined effects munitions—CEM—which were deadly against vehicles. We'd point towards the Kuwaiti border."

"Using our secure radio, we would check in with AWACS, which would clear us into the combat zone and turn us over to Joint STARS," Wetzel said.

"On one mission," said Robinson, "we were sent after a convoy supporting the Republican Guards. Joint STARS gave us the coordinates. We were flying in flights of two."

The weapon system officers conferred by secure radio, comparing pictures from their TSDs (tactical situation or "moving map" displays) with data they were getting from Joint STARS.

"Kuwait is so small, you can fly along the border and see most of the country in the TSD, so it's easy to map out targets," Wetzel said. "We could use the ground mapping radar to update the inertial navigation system, if necessary. It was never more than slightly off.

"After we had identified exactly where we were going, we'd change frequencies to talk to the ABCCC. On other missions, depending where the target was, we'd stay with AWACS. Those two birds were like traffic cops in the sky."

[12] Mackenzie, "A Conversation With Chuck Horner."

[13] *Conduct of the Persian Gulf Conflict.*

[14] Corder interview.

[15] Capt. Charles M. Robinson and Capt. Mark Wetzel, interview, May 31, 1991.

They were cleared into a little area about fifteen miles square. "The whole country was divided into squares, with names like Alpha Six, Brown Six, or Charlie Six," said Robinson. "The hardest part of the mission was avoiding running into somebody else, we had so many airplanes up there, so AWACS or ABCCC would clear you in, clear you out, and warn you of other traffic.

"Then, once we'd located the convoy, we took spacing on the other Strike Eagle so that we'd hit the target almost simultaneously. We wanted one guy's ordnance going off just as the second guy was releasing his over the target. Timing was very important. Don't forget, it's nighttime, and we're flying blacked out. We can't see each other except on radar.

"We angled thirty degrees off the target and rolled in from 25,000 feet. It was a clear night and I could see the convoy through the HUD. It was also picked up by the FLIR system and displayed on one of my MFDs.

"As usual, there wasn't any AAA at first because the people down below didn't know they were going to be hit. I rolled inverted, put the diamond in the HUD near the back of the convoy—the other guys were hitting the head of the convoy—rolled back upright in a thirty-degree dive, and pressed the pickle button. I started the pullout, and we felt the CBUs coming off the racks.

"Just as we pulled out, the other guy's munitions detonated along the front part of the convoy. It was spectacular. Instant shredded trucks. Our stuff hit fifteen seconds later. The convoy was totally disabled. Then, their stuff started coming up and we got out of there."

How the Accuracy Was Achieved

One of the features of the air campaign in the Gulf was that despite the intensity and scope of the bombing, there was very little collateral damage. In previous conflicts, it was deemed a regrettable but inevitable fact of war that some bombs would fall on civilian structures and even residential areas adjacent to military targets. Except in rare circumstances, that did not happen in Desert Storm.

Aerial weapons and delivery systems have come a long way since World War II and the Vietnam War.[16] In those days—indeed, until the last decade or so—weapons delivery was essentially a manual process.

The pilot did most of the precise work required to locate a target. Then he placed his aircraft at exactly the right point in space, at the right altitude, airspeed, dive angle, and heading to make the ordnance hit the target.

He had to hold the aircraft on a set path for a relatively long time, even though he was being bracketed by antiaircraft fire and knew that enemy interceptors might be waiting for him as he came off the target.

It might seem a simple task for a fighter to attack a target on the ground. A streamlined projectile dropped from an aircraft follows a precisely-predictable trajectory from the release point to the target. There are many complications, however, in getting into position to make that drop. One of them is what pilots call the "pucker factor," stress induced by the knowledge that they are targets themselves all through the attack.

To determine the proper release point, the dive bombing aircrew starts with a "minimum safe drop" altitude. At first, over Iraq, Horner decreed that altitude to be 15,000 feet. Only F-15Es and F-111s, equipped to fly and deliver ordnance on the deck at night, could go lower.

After the coalition took out the toughest of the air defenses and as the inaccuracy of the remaining ones became apparent, the minimum safe altitude was lowered to 8,000 feet. To release bombs and pull out above that altitude, pilots had to roll in at 13,000 to 15,000 feet. Eventually, when bad weather cloaked Iraq during the ground war, coalition aircraft were permitted to go as low as required to support Schwarzkopf's advancing tanks and troops.

In the old, manual bombing days, a pilot had to hold a prescribed dive angle and airspeed to get accurate deliveries. Typically, he would consult bombing tables and select, for example, a forty-five degree angle and an airspeed of 450 knots. From another

[16] James P. Coyne, "Bombology," *Air Force Magazine*, June 1990.

table, he would obtain his bombsight setting, which was expressed in mils (an angle of measurement).

His pipper might be squarely on the mark, but if his dive was too steep or he was traveling too fast, his bombs fell long, hitting the ground beyond the target. If he was too shallow or too slow, they hit short. A dive angle five degrees shallow, for example, caused the first bomb to land 130 feet short.

The problem was usually complicated further by crosswinds, headwinds, or tailwinds. Above 3,000 feet, forty-knot winds are common. A strong wind from the left displaces the flight path of a diving aircraft to the right. Wind has negligible effect on the bombs as they fall, but they follow the sideways flight path of the aircraft at release point, so the pilot aims to the left of his target to compensate.

It would seem that the aiming point could simply be offset by a certain number of feet per knot of left crosswind. Winds, however, seldom blow directly on the nose or tail or from ninety degrees to the aircraft centerline. There usually are quartering winds, and it is difficult to apply a rule of thumb correction accurately. In the old days, pilots compensated as best they could with a system they called TLAR, or "That Looks About Right."

Diamond on the Target

By the time of the Vietnam War, modern computers and avionics had begun to transform weapons delivery. The LTV A-7D, an Air Force version of a Navy fighter bomber, represented a quantum leap in the ground attack aircraft. It featured an extremely accurate inertial navigation system, a HUD, and a weapons employment system unparalleled at the time.

It also had a terrain-avoidance system and a reliable radar all-weather bombing system. Equipped with the first truly accurate toss-bombing capability, the A-7D was the forerunner of today's F-16s and F-15Es. (The Navy employed a version of the A-7 in Operation Desert Storm.)

In the Gulf War, F-15Es and F-16s roamed the battle zone at all altitudes. The F-15Es skimmed the earth the opening night to blast Scud sites. Later in the war, F-15Es and F-111Fs swept in for what Horner called "tank plinking."

There were not enough LANTIRN targeting pods available to equip all of the F-15Es during the Gulf War. Nevertheless, the aircrews racked up very high scores with gravity (or "dumb") bombs, thanks to the aircraft's central computer and weapons delivery system, combined with infrared scanning and high-resolution radar mapping.

An F-15E might be directed onto a tank by Joint STARS or locate one with the infrared system or high-resolution radar mapping. The crew designates the tank's position on the radar map, superimposing a diamond-shaped symbol over the target.

As the pilot approaches the target area, he pulls the aircraft up into a steep climb, "popping up" for the bombing attack. When he reaches a precomputed altitude, he rolls the aircraft inverted and pulls the nose down and around toward the target. His infrared system makes the target visible to the eye, even in a night attack. He rolls upright.

His sensors now sweeping the landscape ahead, the pilot tracks the target with his head-up display rather than on the radar map. Through the HUD, he sees the tank and another diamond like the one on the radar display. If the computer is working perfectly, the diamond will be superimposed on the tank. If it is slightly off, the pilot can use a button on his throttle to slew it onto the tank, thus designating the exact position for the weapons system.

In the HUD, the pilot also sees steering symbology, which includes a vertical azimuth steering line. He flies the aircraft so that another symbol, the flight path marker—which represents his aircraft—is superimposed on the steering line.

He is now descending toward the target at a steep angle and at a speed of more than 450 knots. Banking smoothly left or right, he keeps the flight path marker on the azimuth steering line and "kills" any wind drift left or right.

A range caret starts to march down the side of the HUD. When it reaches an "in range" position on the HUD, the pilot depresses the bomb release button on top of the stick. He starts a firm, high-g pullout. At the proper point in his pullout—and that will vary, depending on altitude, airspeed, dive angle, and the number of g's being applied—the bomb will be released to arc precisely into the target. No TLAR about it.

Systems of this caliber enabled aircrews in the Gulf to hit their targets precisely and avoid collateral damage. It also took skill and courage on the part of the aircrews, who often took additional risks to make sure their shots would not fall in the wrong place. The planners were so confident in the aircrews and their equipment that the targeting assignments were precise beyond all precedent. It was not enough to hit a structure. Aircrews were required to land their ordnance at particular points, such as doorways, on the structure.

By the time of the Gulf War, bombing accuracy, as measured by the "circular error probable," had been reduced from thousands of feet to less than ten feet for the F-117.[17]

Bearing the Brunt

The workhorse of the air war in Kuwait was the F-16. The F-16 force (249 of them) flew more sorties (nearly 13,500 of them) than any other strike aircraft in the Gulf. The assortment of missions included duty as Killer Scouts, marking targets for other aircraft to hit.

Each Killer Scout was responsible for a "kill box," fifteen miles square. The crew located targets within that box, and reminiscent of the "Fast FACs" of the Vietnam War, directed air attacks onto the targets.[18]

Every day, all day, coalition aircraft attacked Iraqi forces throughout the KTO relentlessly. "We worked out of a forward operating base, King Khalid City, only forty or fifty miles south of the border," said Capt. Ronald B. Garan, an F-16 pilot from the 363d TFW, Shaw AFB, S.C.[19]

"We would take off and contact the ABCCC [Airborne Battlefield Command and Control Center], which would hand us off to an Air Support Operations Center, or maybe to a forward air controller, flying in an OA-10."

"The FAC would direct us to a map grid and then control our strike," said Maj. Donald K. Kamps, also of the 363d.[20] "On the second to the last day of the war, we were fragged against a column of tanks only about eleven klicks [kilometers] east of friendly troops. The OA-10 marked the location for us with the standard white phosphorus marking rockets. We were carrying the CBU-87, which is a 1,000-pound cluster bomb filled with combined effects munitions. They stopped the tank column.

"On another occasion, we dropped Mk 84 2,000 pounders on dug-in tanks. They were in revetments. We were using an airburst fuze that detonated about fifteen feet above the ground. The orange blast from each bomb would take out two revetments and knock out one tank at the same time."

Saddam took steady losses in main battle tanks, armored personnel carriers, mechanized vehicles, and artillery pieces. His communications were so battered that he may not have realized the extent to which his forces had been reduced.

Daytime Flak

The F-16s flew mostly during the daytime. "We carried six Mk 82 500-pound bombs, or two Mk 84s, which are 2,000 pounders," said Lt.Col. Steve Wood, Operations Officer of the 10th TFS, deployed from Hahn AB, Germany, to Al Dhafra in the United Arab Emirates.[21] "We went after a big petroleum complex north of Basra. There were no SAMs, but there was plenty of AAA."

"You don't see it coming up in the daytime the way you see it at night," said 1st Lt. Aaron Booher, a pilot in the squadron. "You see little puffs, and it becomes a blanket of puffs, and you pull up to get away from it. The only time I saw red tracers was in the late evening.[22]

"When it gets close but not too close, you can see it burst, and you watch the flak fly out in all directions, and then it quickly slows down and falls toward the ground," added Capt. Erik Burgeson. "It gets your attention."[23]

[17] USAF white paper, September 1991.

[18] USAF white paper, September 1991.

[19] Capt. Ronald B. Garan, interview, May 30, 1991.

[20] Maj. Donald K. Kamps, interview, May 30, 1991.

[21] Lt. Col. Steve Wood, interview, Aug. 5, 1991.

[22] 1st Lt. Aaron Booher, interview, Aug. 5, 1991.

[23] Capt. Erik Burgeson, interview, Aug. 5, 1991.

Aircrews from their squadron hit several POL complexes, switched to pontoon bridges, and then were tasked to strike the Republican Guard. Since their base in the UAE was so far south, some of their early missions lasted seven and a half hours.

"Then we started working out of a forward operating base closer to the border," said Burgeson. "We would take off from Al Dhafra with four 2,000 pounders, refuel in the air, bomb the Republican Guard, and then land at our forward location.

"There, we would refuel, load up four more 2,000 pounders, go hit the Republican Guard again, and return to the forward base. We'd refuel, upload some more bombs, hit the Republican Guard, refuel at the forward location, and head back to Al Dhafra. Dropping 24,000 pounds a day made you feel you were accomplishing something. That made a pretty full day."

Weasels Over the KTO

The skies over Kuwait were hostile, with defenses nearly as tough as those in Iraq. "The first few days of the war, we were really busy," said Capt. Steven B. Sokoly, an F-4G electronic warfare officer from the 52d TFW, Spangdahlem AB, Germany.[24] On the second night of the war, he said, "we all split up and went to different patrol areas and altitudes."

"Kuwait City was to our southeast," said Capt. John C. Ustick, a 52d TFW flight commander.[25] "We had taken responsibility that night for the whole northwest corner of Kuwait. We were ready to slam whatever came up. Three and Four [the two ships in the second element of the flight] were working south of the area, and my element was working north.

"We all came under SAM attack. Five SA-2s were launched at Number Three. He was jinking through the clouds. We all were, and we were watching these fiery red dots going over each other's canopies in the night. On top of that, the AAA was incredible, as it was almost every time we were over Iraq or around Kuwait City."

"Practically every kind of radar they had was up," Sokoly said. "We were carrying four HARMs each. You'd get a contact, pop out of the cloud, and just then see your wingman or somebody else pop out of another cloud, in his altitude block. You'd look at him for a split second, and *boom*, see this great big HARM come shooting off his aircraft, and watch it arch up and then down, towards a SAM site."

"The missiles and our airplanes were trailing contrails in the moist night air," Ustick said. "Pretty soon, there were cons everywhere between the clouds as we flew back and forth and the HARMs arched up and down.

"You'd pop out headed north and you'd see some other guy at, say, your one o'clock, pop out headed southwest. *Boom,* a HARM locked on a target would come off him and arch over your head."

"We knocked out SA-2s, SA-3s, Rolands, whatever they had," Sokoly said. "We could tell when we got a kill, because the radar the missile was locked onto would suddenly go off the air."

Later in the war, SAM launches dropped off. "We started doing what we called 'Weasel Police,'" Ustick said. "We'd go up, hit a tanker, and then take up combat air patrol positions over Kuwait or southern Iraq."

"One night," Sokoly said, "we spent four half-hour blocks up there, hunting, going back to the tanker, then back to the patrol area. We hit five tankers. Below us, ten strikes went into Kuwait. Not one SAM came up, and we didn't shoot a single missile."

There was good reason for that. "When the President doubled the size of the forces in Saudi, we got another 120 aircraft," Corder said. "Guard and Reserve F-16s went into Al Kharj and we got some F/A-18s from the Marines for the first two days.

"So, the first morning of the war, we were able to mount a very large bombing campaign against the SAM sites. We knew where they were, and we hit them.

"After that, every time somebody fired at us, we sent Wild Weasels and fighter-bombers in, and took them out. Soon, we had air *supremacy* above 15,000 feet, because that was the limit of their hand-held infrared missiles. We had air *superiority* above 5,000 feet. There were still a lot of ground defenses around targets, though. But,

[24] Capt. Steven B. Sokoly, interview, Aug. 6, 1991.

[25] Capt. John C. Ustick, interview, Aug. 6, 1991.

with the accurate employment systems we had, we never had to go below those altitudes.

"Eventually, we knocked out so many of their air defenses, we felt safe moving the orbits of both AWACS and the tankers a hundred miles north of where they had been. There was some airspace we had paid the price of admission for, and we owned it."

When the Iraqis began sending aircraft to Iran, coalition air planners were unsure what to make of it. "We were ready for anything. We didn't know what they planned to do with them, flying out of Iran.

"For a while, the Navy reserved a lot of their sorties for fleet defense. I can't say I blame them for that, because we just didn't know what to think, initially.

"But, then, Iran announced they were expropriating the planes and we began to realize they would stay neutral. It took us two or three days to understand that."[26]

[26] Corder interview.

US Aerial Munitions Expended

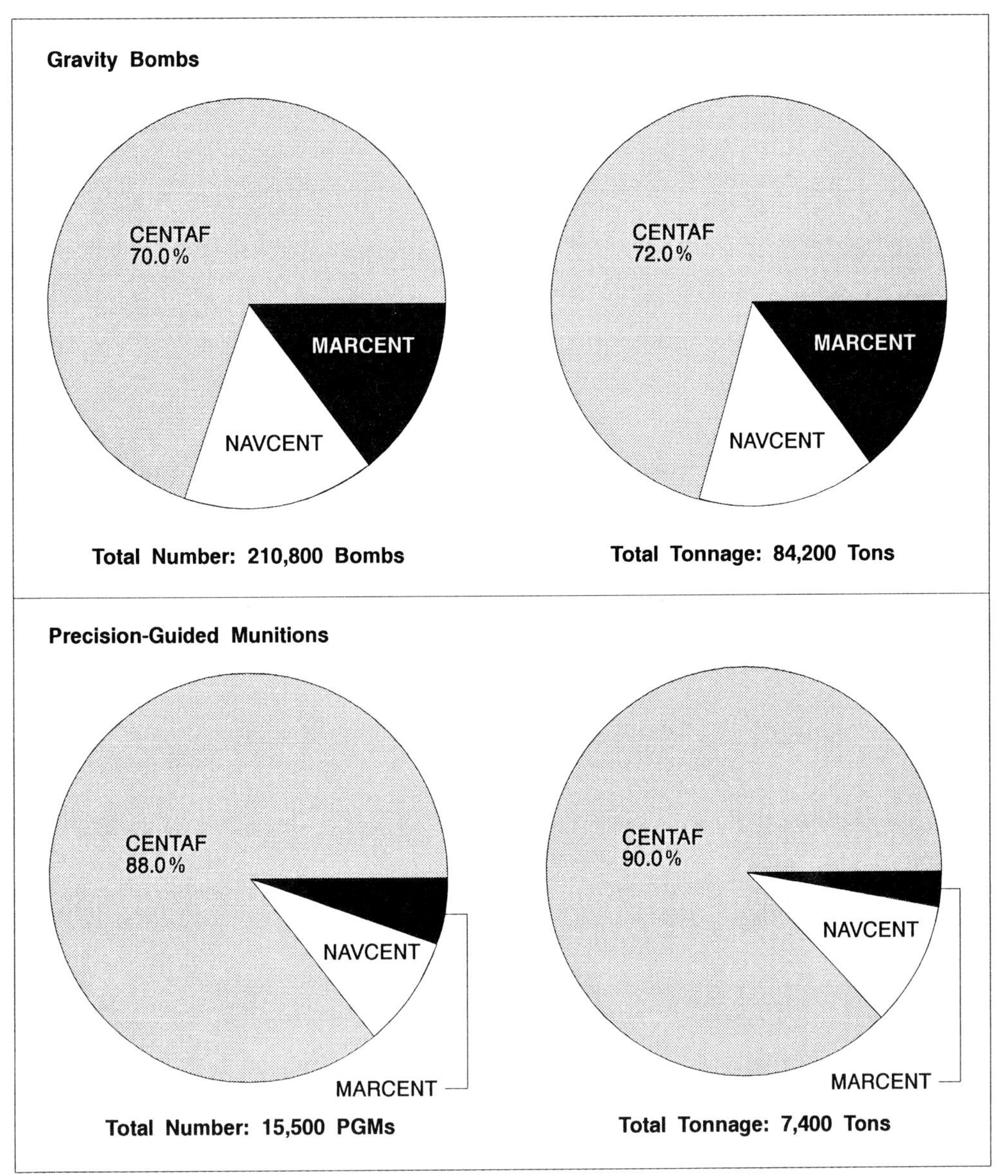

The Attrition Continues

Meanwhile, the attrition of Iraq continued, with emphasis on the Republican Guard. "We always hit the Republican Guard with the B-52s and other aircraft," said Corder. "We hit them all over, putting a lot of effort in the north, then moving slowly south, to squeeze and squeeze and squeeze them. And we always had aircraft attacking the miles of concertina wire they had strung along the south edge of their defenses. We constantly hit artillery emplacements and artillery pieces whenever we found them, which was often, and we dropped plenty of antipersonnel weapons."[27]

The A-10 demonstrated its value in a variety of missions, although its vulnerability to guns and missiles eventually caused Horner to limit its use in high-threat areas. It was devastatingly effective against Scuds and on armed road reconnaissance missions, in part because its pilots used binoculars as an aid in targeting, something no other fixed-wing aircrews did.

The principal Gulf War weapon for the A-10 turned out to be the Maverick missile rather than the much-touted 30-mm GAU-8 rotary cannon. Overall, Warthog pilots destroyed 1,000 tanks, 2,000 other vehicles, 1,200 artillery pieces, and two helicopters (which they shot down by cannon).[28]

The coalition struck early at Iraq's fuel refining and production capability (but not its crude oil production system, which was not targeted), sharply limiting the supply of fuel for tanks, aircraft, vehicles, and other military equipment.[29]

Capt. Brian S. Brandner, an F-111 pilot, and weapon system officer Capt. David B. Schapiro were deployed from Upper Heyford, UK, to Incirlik AB, Turkey, as part of Proven Force. They flew their first mission at night against an oil pumping station in a petroleum complex in western Iraq.

"It was the second day after Proven Force arrived," said Schapiro. "We went into mission planning kind of nervous about what was going to happen. Before the mission, I just wanted to be by myself for about ten or fifteen minutes to reflect on what might happen to us. But once we started engines and took off, I focused on the job and all the nerves started to go away."[30]

"The thing that was going through my mind," Brandner said, "was that it's not a game, this is the real thing. Having talked about the AAA and SAMs with the guys who had flown the night before, I had this notion that, if I had to die, this was the night to do it.

"Walking out to the jet was the longest walk in my life. I don't think anybody was more scared than I was. I really didn't become at ease until the first AAA came at us. That was it. Something just snapped. The fear was there, but I was in control of it and ready to press on with the mission.

"After we defeated the first two or three threats, I realized, 'hey, this is survivable,' and we went on from there. We ingressed on the deck. Two hundred to three hundred feet. About 500 knots. It was pitch black. A couple of times, the automatic system went out and we were hand flying, using the radar system to be sure we'd stay clear of the terrain."[31]

"We were the fourth aircraft in sequence to hit the target," Schapiro said. "There were two initial points, two aircraft on each IP, and then we had separate DMPIs, designated mean points of impact, in the complex."

"Timing was important," Brandner said. "In fact, it was the paramount consideration. We'd be dropping bombs on each other if our timing was off. We put half of our weapons into the complex. Unfortunately, we apparently hit a bird on the way into the target and it hit the key electrical connection on our right wing, and that prevented half our bombs from dropping, so we brought them home. It was kind of interesting, landing with six bombs under one wing."

That wasn't their only problem, however.

"We had AAA and ground fire, red, orange, white, multiple colors," said Schapiro. "And then, when we climbed to get over the densest AAA, they launched SAMs. Apparently, the SAMs were being fired ballistically. Our radar warning gear never showed indications they were trying to track us.

[27] Corder interview.

[28] USAF white paper, September 1991.

[29] *Conduct of the Persian Gulf Conflict.*

[30] Capt. David B. Schapiro, interview, Aug. 9, 1991.

[31] Capt. Brian S. Brandner, interview, Aug. 9, 1991.

"We made it back okay. It was a very interesting first mission. After we had flown a number of missions, it became, definitely not routine, but not so much scary, more like, very exhilarating," Schapiro said. To say the least.

International Teamwork

"We hit a few bridges here and there during the first couple of days," said Corder. "After about the fourth day of the war, we started going hard against bridges, to seal everything off.

"They started putting up pontoon bridges to replace the permanent structures we'd knocked down. For three or four nights, they were putting up pontoon bridges as fast as we could knock them down. Then they began to run out of bridges.

"So, they'd put one up for a few hours at night, and then take it down. To counter that, we put patrols every thirty minutes over the Tigris and the Euphrates and we'd catch them, and we'd knock the bridges down.

"The F-111s were in after bridges at night, and the British and the French were in there in the daytime, dropping precision-guided bombs. The Tornados dropped laser-guided bombs from 15,000 feet, although they were not equipped with laser designators. British Buccaneers equipped with laser pods designated the aimpoints for the bombs.

"The attackers bombed the bridge abutments, the ends of the bridges, with pinpoint accuracy. Only occasionally would you see a miss. And that took care of the Iraqi bridge system."

The coalition air forces worked very well together. "We never had any real command and control problems with anybody," Corder said. "The British, French, Italians, Saudis, Kuwaitis, Bahrainis, the Navy, the Marines—they all flew under one control.

"Everybody took tough missions. No country, proportionately, took less than any other. Some countries had restrictions, however. The Canadians could not fly air-to-ground and were not permitted by their government to overfly the battle area."

"Initially, the French said they could only fly in Kuwait. Then they said they would fly in Iraq, but only in support of their own forces. But, once the war started, they loosened up a bit and carried their share of the load.

"The British more than carried their share. They went after every tenth target we had. The Saudis were great air-to-air guys, and they flew in some of the dirtiest weather of the war, in the blackest night.

"Regarding the contribution of the Navy and the Marines, we were very happy with every sortie they would give us. They did good work, given the weapons they had. They only had about 500 laser-guided bombs on all six carriers.

"Originally, the Marines planned to hold much of their effort back, not available to the Joint Forces Air Component Commander, in case their troops needed it. But, as January 17 approached, they were much more forthcoming."

Corder expressed surprise when told that some sources said the Navy and Marines had not been assigned as many combat sorties as they wanted.

"General Horner was always asking, 'what do you want, how can we help you, what do you need?' We gave them thousands of 500-pounders, gave them HARMs, whatever they needed to keep going. We even flew copies of the ATO out to helicopter pickup points for them because their communications and computer systems weren't set up to handle it electronically."[32]

[32] Corder interview.

Tankers and Jammers

Aircraft striking deep into Iraq needed aerial refueling to reach their targets and return. Refueling was also required by those flying extended Scud searches.

"The US Air Force provided tanker support on a proportional basis," Corder said. "The Italians, for example, had their own tankers, but they didn't have enough. We trained them to use our probe and drogue systems on the KC-135 and the KC-10s, and we provided tankers based on how many sorties they made available for the ATO.

"At one point, the Navy wanted to fly F-14s from their carriers in the Red Sea to the area around Basra. That's like flying from Florida to Pennsylvania to get into the fight. So, General Horner gave the Navy tankers in proportion to the number of Navy sorties in the ATO.

"Of course, a huge number of them were used flying those F-14s all the way from the Red Sea, and that bothered the Navy commander in the [Persian] Gulf because he wanted more tankers than he was getting for his airplanes. The Navy finally moved one of their carriers from the Red Sea to the Arabian Gulf, giving them four in the Gulf, which was closer to the action."

Electronic countermeasures, jamming, and defense suppression were also in high demand. Among those supplying these commodities were Air Force EF-111 Ravens and F-4G Wild Weasels, Marine and Navy EA-6B Prowlers and F/A-18 Hornets, and Air Force EC-130 Compass Call aircraft.

"There are several electronic warfare success stories," said Corder. "The F-4G and HARM combination is one. After the first four or five days, the Iraqi radar stopped coming up when the Weasels were in their areas. Their passive systems could pick up the signature of the F4G nose radar. They would immediately shut down. Now, that's intimidation.

"Another [success story] is the EF-111. Saddam's 1970–1980 vintage air defenses were duck soup for the EF-111, which could jam the Spoon Rest, the Flat Face radars, and the SA-2 and SA-3 missiles. The EF-111 jammed his other systems, too. Compass Call EC-130s jammed the Iraqi military communications very well.

"Aircraft self-protection systems worked perfectly against radar-guided missiles. The people who were shot down were hit by guns or infrared missiles. We do need an IR warning system, something that doesn't exist right now.

"So, our electronic combat equipment worked against older systems. I think it's safe to say that our stuff will work against the modern systems, too. We have a reasonable capability against them, I believe, but it's one of those things you never know until you get into combat.

"Electronic combat proved itself in this war. I wouldn't say we're bulletproof, but electronic combat should be given a lot more credit than it has gotten in the past.

"Talk to the combat aircrews," he said. "Ask if they'd rather go against the SAMs *without* the Wild Weasels. They want electronic pods on their airplanes now. In the past, many fighter pilots thought the centerline[33] was a place for a fuel tank, not a pod. I don't think you'd find many that don't want electronic combat gear now."

Deconfliction and the ACE

One of the biggest dangers aircrews faced over the Saudi peninsula was mid-air collision with another coalition aircraft. The sky was crowded all over, but the risk was especially sharp at lower level. There was an additional hazard to crews overflying target areas just as ordnance delivered by a previous crew exploded.

In the beginning of the air war, as Task Force Normandy was mounting its corridor-opening operation, Special Operations forces emplaced radar beacons along the northern Saudi border. These beacons established positive location points for coalition pilots entering and leaving Iraqi airspace.[34] Specific entry and exit corridors were established, too.

"The primary mission of AWACS was air defense," Corder said. "In the beginning, they would find the enemy planes and put our people in the best position to start the fight. The first night, the Iraqi airplanes started turning into fireballs and they didn't even know what was happening. The Iraqi air force just became chaotic and our guys went in there and cleaned them up.

"After the Iraqis stopped flying, the AWACS became a traffic advisory agency. They assisted in rendezvous between tankers and fighters, for example. AWACS cleared all the coalition aircraft into and out of the kill boxes over Iraq.

"We put an Airborne Command Element, or ACE, headed by a colonel, on the AWACS. With him, he would have an air-to-ground expert, an air-to-air expert, and a tanker expert. The ACE would make quick reaction decisions on diverting groups of fighters from one target area to

[33] Station for carrying stores underneath the fuselage.

[34] *Conduct of the Persian Gulf Conflict.*

another, depending on orders from General Horner.

"There might be a situation, on the other hand, where eight thirsty fighters come out of the battle area at the same time, and they all head for the same tanker. The ACE would decide who refuels first and who goes to another tanker. Suppose the weather has turned sour at one fighter base in Saudi Arabia—the ACE decides where the fighters from that base land."

Battle for Khafji

It is still unclear why Saddam Hussein ordered an attack on Khafji, just inside Saudi Arabia, on January 29. His intention may have been to probe the coalition forces generally. Perhaps he even meant to provoke the ground battle he had repeatedly said he wanted.

As for his tactics, he may have hoped to attack, then withdraw while keeping contact with the coalition forces, pulling them back into his defensive positions, and setting the stage for a protracted and bloody ground engagement.

Saddam probably started his preparations for the Khafji assault on January 22. Unfortunately for him, an E-8A Joint STARS aircraft was on the job, using its moving target indicator and side-looking radar to look deep into the battle area.

Joint STARS operators detected an armored division assembly area and a convoy of more than sixty vehicles moving through the night toward Saudi Arabia. They called in two A-10s and an AC-130 gunship and vectored them onto the convoy and the staging area with the result that seventy-one vehicles were destroyed. Saddam therefore started his attack on Khafji short-handed.

When the battle began, Saddam threw three mechanized brigades and an offshore landing force into his attack. US Marines and Saudi National Guardsmen defended the city. They destroyed armored vehicles with TOW missiles, and Qatari tank forces took a heavy toll of Iraqis.

Land and sea-based coalition forces destroyed the offshore landing force. Coalition air forces attacked the Iraqis in and around Khafji. After two days of fighting, most of Saddam's remaining forces withdrew and the rest surrendered. They lost more than 200 vehicles.

The coalition had won its first victory, but at a price. An AC-130 gunship was shot down by an Iraqi SAM, with the loss of all fourteen crew members. In a "friendly fire" incident, seven Marines were killed when a Maverick missile fired by an A-10 struck a light armored vehicle.

If Saddam had in mind pulling the coalition ground forces back onto his entrenched defenses, the ploy did not work. Schwarzkopf did not pursue the retreating Iraqis on the ground, but instead let airpower take care of the remnants.

After Khafji, the start of the ground war was less than four weeks away. Schwarzkopf had already begun preparation for his "Hail Mary" move to the west. Coalition air forces continued their campaign of attrition.

On the eve of the ground war, the coalition had destroyed sixty percent of the Iraqi tanks, sixty percent of the artillery, and forty percent of the armored vehicles.[35]

To put those percentages in perspective, it was once customary to regard a military force as utterly defeated when it had been "decimated," or reduced by ten percent. The Iraqi forces had been decimated several times over in the air campaign.

That attrition was considerably greater than the level Schwarzkopf had decided was necessary before he could launch a ground attack. ■

[35] USAF white paper, September 1991.

BILL ANDREWS

8. Collateral Damage, Casualties, and POWs

Capt. William F. Andrews, an F-16 pilot, was shot down and captured on his thirty-fifth mission. He witnessed coalition firepower from the ground and saw its effect on his captors.

Casualties and losses are inevitable in war, but in Desert Storm, the rates were amazingly low.

It was obvious to everyone, including the Iraqis, that the coalition was at pains to avoid collateral damage and civilian casualties.

Iraqi soldiers took shelter in civilian areas when they could, and Saddam regularly moved military assets into residential neighborhoods, where he had high confidence they would not be bombed.

As an indication of how well the Iraqis understood coalition policy in this regard, reconnaissance found two MiG fighters parked next to the Saqqara pyramid in Ur, an archaeological and religious site.[1]

Some civilians were killed or injured by the air attacks, and there was some collateral damage. Saddam, amplified by western journalists reporting from Baghdad, played on such happenings as much as he could in the court of world opinion.

Two strikes—one in January against what Iraq said was a "baby milk plant" and the other on February 14, when 100 or more civilians were killed in a hardened bunker—made major headlines and were prime topics for the evening news.

On January 23, after an escorted tour of the wreckage by Iraqi officials, CNN reporter Peter Arnett broadcast Saddam's claim that coalition bombs had destroyed the only factory in his country that made infant formula. Reporters also tracked down New Zealand technicians who said the structure had produced dairy products when they had been there the previous year.[2]

US officials in Washington and Riyadh said it was a biological warfare facility. "It's surrounded by a high military fence, it has guard posts in all four corners, and it was painted with camouflage paint and defended," Schwarzkopf said. "That's not something you normally do with an infant formula plant."[3]

CNN's own book on the Gulf War noted that the lettering, "Baby Milk Plant Iraq," that workers wore around the bombing site was in English, and that the "Baby Milk Plant" sign (untouched by the strike) propped against a fence led off in English.

Arnett stuck to his story. "Whatever else it did, it did produce infant formula," he said.[4]

The conflicting statements left the situation ambiguous enough for people to believe what they wanted to believe. It would be several months yet before the extent of Saddam's biological, chemical, and nuclear weapons manufacturing ventures came to light. Had it been known at the time, it might have had some impact how the public interpreted the "baby milk" plant incident.

Tragedy in the Bunker

The bombing of the bunker was more serious and more tragic. Iraqi Foreign Minister Tariq Aziz first claimed that at least 400 persons, some of them women and children, had been killed and many more had been injured when two laser-guided bombs destroyed a hardened bunker in Baghdad at 4:30 a.m. February 14.[5]

US officials said the structure had been identified by intelligence agencies as a military command and control facility. It was originally built as a bomb shelter, they said, but later converted for other use.[6]

[1] CENTCOM Chronology of Significant Events, 1991.

[2] Al Kamen, "Accounts Differ on Role of Bombed Iraqi Factory," Washington *Post*, Feb. 8, 1991.

[3] Schwarzkopf, CENTCOM press briefing, Jan. 27, 1991.

[4] Allen, Berry, and Polmar. *War in the Gulf*. CNN, 1991.

[5] Rick Atkinson and Dan Balz, "Bomb Strike Kills Scores of Civilians in Building Called Military Bunker by US, Shelter by Iraq," Washington *Post*, Feb. 14, 1991.

[6] Lt. Col. Bernard E. Harvey, interview, Jan. 16, 1992.

Photo by Eric Hehs/General Dynamics Code One

The building was hardened and surrounded by barbed wire. Numerous radio antennas were visible on the roof. Intelligence sources had observed many Iraqi military and civilian officials going in and out of the building, and military vehicles parked around it.

After the war, when neutral international agencies were permitted into Baghdad to assess the bomb damage, it was determined that the bunker housed one of ten regional military centers. It was apparently also used as an air raid shelter for families of the Iraqi elite.

The casualty count from the bunker varies. Greenpeace, for example, sets the figure precisely at 311 killed.[7] A US Air Force report puts it at "100 or more."[8]

One unresolved question is why the civilians grouped into a facility with military trappings at all. Iraqis had already seen enough of the bombing to realize that they would have been much safer in a residential area, where no bombs fell. Iraqi officials had already advised the families of the elite to take shelter elsewhere.

"The bunker was a military target," said Horner. "It was being used for military purposes. It was one of several that were targeted and struck. The only thing I could think of while I was trying to figure out what happened was [that Iraqi military] guys on the third floor down [in the underground bunker] had probably brought their families in. It's a horrible tragedy."[9]

Exercise of Restraint

Coalition air forces conducted the campaign with such accuracy and carefulness that when a bomb did fall wrong, it was an occasion for comment.

Even a few of the precision-guided weapons went astray. That was the case, for example, when a smart bomb, intended for a bridge at Fallujuh, missed the targets and killed 130 Iraqi civilians in a nearby residential area.

That, however, was a rare exception. Bombardment in Operation Desert Storm was conducted with a precision never before seen in warfare. That, along with the coalition's restraint and its extraordinary effort to avoid collateral damage, preserved far more of Iraq's civilian infrastructure than would have been the case otherwise.

No part of Iraq was targeted more heavily than Baghdad, and reporters who were there during the war or who visited afterwards were struck by the extent to which nonmilitary areas of the city were spared.

In April, *New Yorker* magazine reporter Milton Viorst traveled through postwar Iraq. He wrote of the contrast between what he saw in Baghdad and the destruction of the Axis capitals, Berlin and Tokyo, in World War II:

"Oddly, it seemed, there was no Second World War-style urban destruction, despite the tons of explosives that had fallen. Instead, with meticulous care—one might almost call it artistry—American aircraft had taken out telecommunications facilities, transportation links, key government offices, and, most painful of all, electrical generating plants .... the central post office, in downtown Baghdad, was struck with such exquisite accuracy that three of its four brick walls remained standing, but the interior was transformed into a maze of twisted girders and piles of debris."[10]

Coalition Losses

The coalition forces took some casualties, although the rate was only a fraction of the tens of thousands killed and wounded

Coalition Casualties

	Battle Deaths	Non-Battle Deaths	Wounded
Air Force	20	6	9
Army	98	105	354
Navy	6	8	12
Marines	24	26	92
Total US	148	145	467
Coalition Allies	99	Unknown	434
Total Coalition	247	Unknown	901

Sources: CENTCOM, Department of Defense.

[7] Arkin, William, *Greenpeace*, interview, Jan. 15, 1992.

[8] USAF white paper, September 1991.

[9] Mackenzie, "A Conversation With Chuck Horner."

[10] Milton Viorst, "Report From Baghdad," *The New Yorker*, June 24, 1991.

that some had estimated before the war. Sen. Tom Harkin (D-Iowa), for example, had warned that 20,000 American lives might be lost.[11]

Of the twenty US Air Force aircrew members killed in action, fourteen were lost on the same mission, when an AC-130H gunship of the 16th Special Operations Squadron, Hurlburt Field, Fla., was shot down while supporting US Marines and Saudi National Guardsmen during the Battle of Khafji.

Overall, enemy fire killed 148 US military members and wounded another 467. The Iraqis rarely hit what they were shooting at with their artillery and tank guns, but they lost tens of thousands of their own troops.

Toward the end of the war, a reporter asked Pentagon briefer Lt. Gen. Thomas Kelly about the "furious twelve-hour tank battle" as the remnants of two Republican Guard divisions tried to escape to Basra.

"Just how furious it was remains to be seen, since I just got through telling you that only two US tanks were damaged," Kelly said. "There was a lot of shooting going on. We've heard that the Iraqi tankers said 'we couldn't even see you with our sights and you were hitting us,' which is a pretty good way to do it."[12]

After the war, it became a major theme for commentators that "friendly fire"—bombs and bullets from coalition forces—accounted for an unprecedented percentage of the total coalition casualties. That was true, but the consideration given short shrift in such commentaries is that it was true only because the enemy inflicted so few casualties on the coalition that the total was astoundingly low.

Friendly fire killed thirty-five Americans and wounded seventy-three. Of these, twenty-four were killed in ground-to-ground attacks, while eleven were killed in air-to-ground attacks. Fifty-eight were wounded in ground-to-ground attacks, and fifteen were wounded in air-to-ground attacks.[13] There were no air-to-air casualties.

In many instances, coalition forces had moved forward so fast that they were behind Iraqi positions on the battlefield. Their vehicles were sometimes mistaken for Iraqi vehicles by artillerymen, tankers, and airmen who were employing their weapons over distances of up to three miles.

Coalition vehicles were marked with a large, inverted "V" on the sides and a fluorescent panel on top. The "V" symbols were made with fluorescent panels, white luminous paint, black paint and thermal tape.[14]

That worked well enough for close-in encounters, where the vehicles could be seen with the naked eye when visibility was good. It did not work well in haze or smoke or during night operations.

At times, howling desert winds called *shamals* blasted troops and equipment with grit and reduced the visibility.[15] Dust and mud coated vehicles, which made the "V" markings hard to see.

Even with the magnification of high-technology optics, the markings were not large and visible enough to show up on the scopes of weapons operators firing from miles away.

This is not to say that coalition fire was careless. Artillery, tanks, and helicopters were under the radio control of parent units at all times. Fixed-wing aircraft were under the control of a forward air controller. To reduce the risk of US forces firing on other coalition forces, FACs, Special Operations teams, or Marines from an air naval gunfire liaison company were assigned to all non-American units.

Often, when asking permission to open fire, operators stated the location of their targets with the precise coordinates provided by the Navstar Global Positioning System. Before weapons were fired, each target had to first be declared hostile by the supervising authority.

Still, there were mistakes. In one case, an operator reported the wrong coordinates for a targeted vehicle and was given permission to launch. Two Americans died and six were wounded.

In another case, a FAC cleared the release of a Maverick against a vehicle, but the weapon locked onto and hit a different vehicle. Seven Americans died.

"Simply stated," the Pentagon acknowledged in its interim report on the war, "the

[11] Sen. Tom Harkin, "The Obligation to Debate," Jan. 14, 1991.

[12] Kelly, Pentagon news briefing, Feb. 28, 1991.

[13] USAF white paper, September 1991.

[14] *Conduct of the Persian Gulf Conflict.*

[15] USAF white paper, September 1991.

basic problem is that we can shoot farther than we can identify targets."[16]

Shortly before the ground war started, the Director of the Joint Staff, Air Force Lt. Gen. Michael P.C. Carns, asked the Defense Advanced Research Projects Agency (DARPA) for any solutions it could provide to prevent friendly fire hits on Army and Marine vehicles.

In the astoundingly short time of twenty days, the "DARPA Light" was delivered to the theater of operations on February 26. This flashing infrared beacon is powered by alkaline flashlight batteries.

Its beam, directed toward the sky, is visible through standard night vision goggles up to five miles away on a clear night. Unfortunately, only 190 of them could be delivered to the combat zone before the war ended.

About 15,000 "bud" lights, similar to but simpler than the DARPA Light, were also shipped to the theater of operations and were used to mark tanks and tank fire zones.[17]

Desert Storm Coalition Aircraft Losses

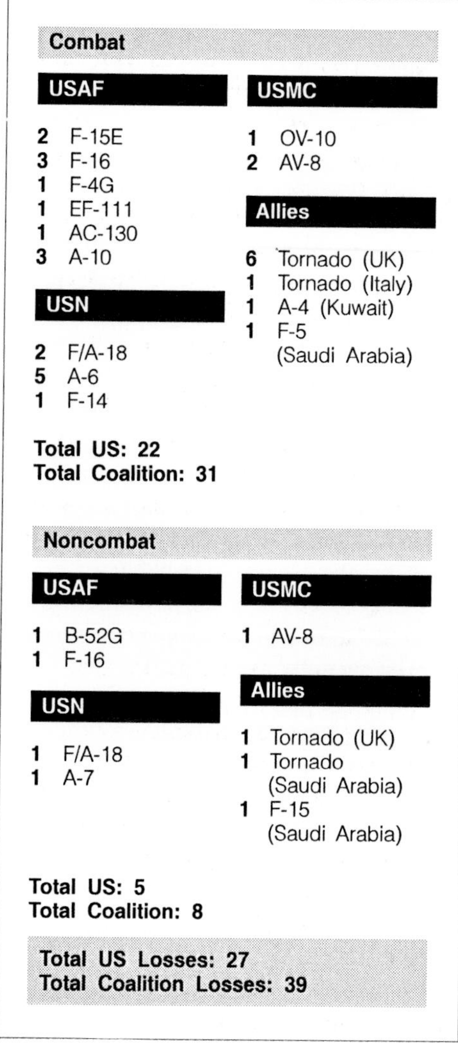

Combat

USAF		USMC	
2	F-15E	1	OV-10
3	F-16	2	AV-8
1	F-4G		
1	EF-111		
1	AC-130		
3	A-10		

USN		Allies	
2	F/A-18	6	Tornado (UK)
5	A-6	1	Tornado (Italy)
1	F-14	1	A-4 (Kuwait)
		1	F-5 (Saudi Arabia)

Total US: 22
Total Coalition: 31

Noncombat

USAF		USMC	
1	B-52G	1	AV-8
1	F-16		

USN		Allies	
1	F/A-18	1	Tornado (UK)
1	A-7	1	Tornado (Saudi Arabia)
		1	F-15 (Saudi Arabia)

Total US: 5
Total Coalition: 8

Total US Losses: 27
Total Coalition Losses: 39

Losses and Rescues

Fourteen USAF aircraft were shot down by SAMs, AAA, or ground fire. The loss rate was one twentieth of one percent, compared with predictions that ranged from a low of one half of one percent to a high of ten percent. Glosson was more optimistic than most. When he briefed President Bush in October 1990, he estimated the coalition would lose no more than eighty and probably less than fifty aircraft.[18]

If an airman went down in hostile territory, he knew that search-and-rescue helicopters would get him out if there was any way to do so. On January 21, Air Force A-10 pilots and the crew of an MH-53J special operations helicopter teamed up to rescue Navy pilot Lt. Devon Jones, whose F-14 had been shot down the night before.

The rescue teams knew that Jones was on the ground, but they did not know exactly where he was. Coalition aircraft, including an MH-53J Pave Low helicopter, flew search patterns for two hours some 165 miles deep in Iraq, but were unable to find Jones at first.

The chopper was returning to base when other searchers picked up a radio contact from Jones and AWACS directed the rescue team back in.

"We refueled and took off again, this time flying with another special ops chopper 186 miles into Iraqi territory," said Sgt. Ben Pennington, an Air Force "PJ," or pararescueman, aboard the MH-53J. "We were about thirty miles from Baghdad and could see thick smoke rising from the city. As we made our final approach, a truck appeared from nowhere."[19]

That was the Iraqi army, which had also figured out where Jones was. It was also the cue for Capt. Paul T. Johnson and his

[16] *Conduct of the Persian Gulf Conflict.*

[17] *Conduct of the Persian Gulf Conflict.*

[18] USAF white paper, September 1991.

[19] CMSgt. Vickie M. Graham, "Desert Rescue: a Tale of Two PJs," *Airman*, August 1991.

wingman, Capt. Randy Goff, from the 354th TFW, Myrtle Beach AFB, S.C., to swing into action. They had been flying low, 500 feet above the scene and dodging heavy ground fire, covering Jones until the rescue helicopter arrived.[20]

Johnson and Goff rolled in on the Iraqi trucks and demolished them. As soon as the helicopter touched down, Pennington jumped out and sprinted fifty yards to Jones, who was somewhat dazed.

"I knew I had to get him out as fast as I could," Pennington said. "He was defenseless, and I didn't know if there was anyone left alive in the truck.

"I could see him pretty well because I was wearing goggles, but with all the sand kicked up by the rotors, it was like running through a car wash with blowing sand instead of water.

"He knew who we were once we were on the ground. I think the A-10 guys told him we were his taxi ride home." Pennington helped Jones aboard the MH-53J, and the crew wasted no time in getting airborne again.

"He'd been on the ground about ten hours and kept asking about his backseater, but we didn't know anything," Pennington said. "When we crossed the border, it was like a 100-pound weight had been lifted from my shoulders."[21]

It had been a grueling mission, lasting six hours, for Johnson and Goff, too. They had taken off with the intention of attacking a Scud missile site, but were diverted to the rescue effort.

They refueled in the air six times and flew deeper into Iraq than any other A-10 had gone before. For their actions on January 21, Johnson was awarded the Air Force Cross and Goff the Distinguished Flying Cross.[22]

Captured by the Iraqis

Unfortunately, the rescue teams could not reach all of the downed airmen in time. Eight from the US Air Force and three from the US Navy were taken and held by the Iraqis as prisoners of war.

One of these was Capt. William F. Andrews, an F-16 pilot from the 10th TFS, Hahn AB, Germany, who was shot down and captured on his thirty-fifth mission.[23]

On February 27, he was leading a flight of four F-16s searching for Iraqi armored units on the move. As he dropped below the clouds for a closer look, he was hit by a SAM.

"It hit my plane violently, throwing it out of control immediately," Andrews said. He ejected almost instinctively. "If I had hesitated at all, I wouldn't have survived."

As soon as his parachute opened, Captain Andrews unsheathed his survival radio and told the other airmen in his flight where he was going to land.

On the ground, however, Iraqi troops surrounded him. He had broken his leg, either in the ejection or during the landing. He decided to surrender, but kept radio contact with the flight as the Iraqis approached.

"As they got within twenty feet, I saw some other forces launch SAMs at my flight, so I radioed them to make a SAM break[24] and to employ countermeasures [flares] against the missiles," Andrews said. It worked, and none of them were hit.

The Iraqis didn't like that at all. They began shooting at Andrews. He dropped the radio, and the Iraqis blew it to pieces with their automatic rifles.

The Iraqi soldiers helped Andrews make crude splints for his leg, then threw him into a truck and started across country. After a while, the truck broke down. About then, a coalition aircraft swooped down and dropped cluster bombs, which detonated less than 1,000 feet up the track the truck had been following.

"I was lucky the vehicle broke down when it did," he said. "Just to see the coalition firepower was awesome. I had always wondered what it was like, but I didn't need a demonstration that close."

Andrews's captors were shaken by the attack. They broke camp in a hurry that night, and in the darkness and confusion, Andrews was able to slip away and hide.

He hoped to stay hidden until rescued, but some Iraqi soldiers looking for deserters found him the next day. They turned him over to other troops, who delivered him to Baghdad three days later.

20 "Air Force Cross Recipients," TAC news release, Jan. 27, 1992.

21 Graham, "Desert Rescue."

22 TAC, Jan. 27, 1992.

23 Sgt. Michael C. Leonard, "Former POW Talks About Confinement," *Capitol Flyer*, Andrews AFB, Md., March 22, 1991.

24 Hard turn and dive to elude or outmaneuver a climbing SAM.

The Iraqis Andrews had encountered thus far had not been cordial, but they didn't torture him. That changed when he reached Baghdad.

"They slapped my injured leg around, or slapped me about the head and shoulders with something that felt like a hammer to try to get answers out of me," he said.

Between interrogations, he was kept in solitary confinement. His cell was about ten feet square and had concrete walls. There was a light fixture, but it wasn't illuminated because there was no electricity in Baghdad. The only light came through a small ventilation slit in a wall about eight feet off the floor.

"I would prop myself up and let the sun hit my face to cheer me up," he said. "It usually lasted about thirty minutes."

The cell had a barred door, but a blanket had been hung across the doorway to prevent him from seeing other prisoners of war. He slept on a foam rubber mat on the floor, and had two blankets. He was able to converse in quiet tones with other POWs, although they could not see each other.

"The prison guards told us we wouldn't be there very long," Andrews said. On March 4, the Red Cross arrived to take charge of the prisoners.

Andrews was flown to the hospital ship USS *Mercy*, then on to Andrews AFB, Md., where he underwent extensive orthopedic care.

"I'll be toting around an extra two pounds of metal in my leg," he said, "but hopefully, I'll be flying again pretty soon."

Andrews returned to the 10th TFS at Hahn in May 1991. He was awarded the Air Force Cross.

A Minute Too Late

Airmen take it hard when another airman, down in hostile territory, cannot be rescued. Hardest of all, perhaps, is when the rescue comes close but still does not succeed.

Capt. Dar Kemp described the mission on which he responded to an emergency locator beacon and was soon talking by radio with the airman on the ground, a fellow A-10 pilot whose aircraft had been shot down by an Iraqi missile.

"He was alive and uninjured," Capt. Kemp said. "He said he was very close to a road and he could see vehicles beginning to stop. As he was talking to me, I was rushing to his approximate location as fast as my Hog would take me, reassuring him all the while that he would be okay.

"Then I noticed a very distinct change in his cool, collected manner. He said there were Iraqis running toward him with guns. I was now only five miles away and closing fast when the downed pilot made his last transmission. He said, 'Guys, it's all over. They have guns pointing at me and they want me to raise my hands. Thanks for your help.'

"A second later, I heard some Iraqi voices and then the sound of the radio being ripped from his hands. Needless to say, my heart went out to him. Looking down at his crashed airplane and all the vehicles around, I couldn't help but wonder why fate had dictated that I arrive just one minute too late to help him."[25]

Major Tice's Story

Everyone who flies in combat knows he may be shot down. Each man deals with it in his own way.

One pilot who was shot down and captured early in the war was Maj. Jeffrey S. Tice, an F-16 pilot from the 401st TFW, Torrejon AB, Spain. He was deployed to Doha, in Qatar. He survived to tell his story.

"It was January 19, the third day of the war," Tice said, "and it was my second mission. It was the first daylight raid in the Baghdad suburbs. We had a pretty big strike package, with sixteen F-16s from our squadron, forty-eight F-16s from other squadrons, along with F-15s for air superiority, EF-111s for jamming, and F-4G Wild Weasels to take out the SAM sites.[26]

"We had medical call signs that day," he recalled, "and I was Stroke [flight call sign] lead. My flight was tail-end Charlie for the whole armada. We had three separate targets, and mine was an oil production facility. Each of us carried two 2,000-pound dumb bombs.

"We started picking up heavy caliber flak about fifty miles into Iraq. It was ex-

[25] Capt. Dar Kemp, "A Minute Too Late—No SAR Required," 511th TFS, 1991.

[26] Maj. Jeffrey S. Tice, interview, Aug. 7, 1991.

ploding in and around our formation, at our altitude. We had to do a lot of jinking[27] to avoid it.

"So we got pretty well strung out. Our group of twelve birds was still several minutes south when the EF-111s started jamming and the F-4Gs started lobbing in their HARMs. Up ahead, the first group of F-16s aborted because of weather over their target.

"The weather started to thin out beneath us as we approached Baghdad, and more AAA was coming up. It was well beneath our altitude and, therefore, nothing to worry about, but it was thick enough to walk on.

"The second group of F-16s finished their attack and egressed the area. The suppression birds went with them, I think. We started to pick up some SAM launches. As we approached the target area, the weather was clear and a million, and we could see the target from the IP [initial point], twenty miles away. Of course, that meant we stuck out like a sore thumb, too.

"I rolled in with my Number Three man just as we really started to pick up a lot of SAM activity. They were launching them ballistically, to scare us, and they were doing a good job of that.

"We rolled in, pickled off our bombs, and got some beautiful secondary explosions as we came off the target. I was really proud of my score."

Tice paused as he thought of what happened next.

"As I turned south to egress, another bunch of SAMs came up and I called for a SAM break. I saw Mike Roberts take a missile right through his airplane, and he went down right then and there. He really got speared. There was no chute."

Tice paused again.

"At this point, my wingman and I were struggling hard to 'get out of Dodge' without taking too much more heat. We were the last ones out. We each had eight or ten SAMs fired at us, and we jinked hard as often as we could. They were fired ballistically, but they shook you up as they went by."

By now, Tice said, they were fifteen miles south of the target and starting to fly back over the weather they had flown above on the inbound trip.

"I saw another launch over by the river, from one of their sites that had really been paying us a lot of attention. This one was different because I was getting signals on my radar warning receiver that said, 'Yes, this one's looking at you.'

"I got a strong signal it was locked on. 'This one's got my name on it,' I thought as it made a big, arcing turn toward me. I was really sweating, now. I nosed over to get some more energy, some more airspeed, and the missile changed its course and then I was absolutely positive it was after me.

"It got close enough that I could see the plume coming off the rocket motor, and I started doing a last ditch maneuver, a big old barrel roll to try to outturn it and make it overshoot. I was inverted as the missile went by, and I thought 'Ah, great, it missed me.'"

No Miss

But it hadn't missed him. Next, Tice said, "It detonated behind me, and shrapnel from the exploding warhead just tore the aft end of my airplane all to shreds. I got all the fire and warning lights in the cockpit, and I realized it hadn't missed.

"The jet was still flying, though, so I got it back under control and radioed the mission commander that I'd been hit and had lost most of my systems."

The mission commander told Tice to punch out. "'No,' I said,'" Tice remembers. "'I've got plenty of altitude,' I said, 'and the aircraft is controllable.' Actually, my instruments had been pretty much shot out, I was on fire, and all the hydraulic fluid and fuel and oil were streaming out behind me."

The engine was producing enough power to climb, so Tice climbed above 30,000 feet as he headed south. Finally, the oil supply drained out, and the engine seized. Tice lowered the nose and let his F-16 glide. He flew the aircraft down to about 20,000 feet when it went out of control.

[27] Changing altitude and heading at frequent intervals.

He was 160 miles from the border. On the ground, he might be able to hide out in the desert until rescuers arrived. He punched out, uninjured. His parachute opened. He descended through the clouds and realized he was over a marshy area. In desert country, water means people, and sure enough, he saw several black tents off to his right.

"I saw muzzle flashes and heard bullets whizzing by me as I descended," Tice said. "When I hit the ground, I got out of my chute and started running. Someone stitched a line of automatic rifle fire in front of me. I stopped."

He was surrounded by a dozen or more Bedouins, who took away his survival radio when he tried to report himself surrounded. They roughed him up, bound him, and shot wildly into the air in celebration of their capture.

"These guys weren't wearing any shoes and their teeth were rotten," Tice noted, "but, boy, they had brand new AK-47s. I tried to converse with them, but the only English word they seemed to know was 'Bush.'"

That night, they roughed him up again. The next morning, they threw him into the back of a truck, drove to a nearby town and handed him over to the local police, who, in turn, turned him over to the Iraqi army.

Interrogation and Beatings

"On the early morning of January 21, I was driven to Baghdad, thrown into an underground bunker, and interrogated for the next couple of days," he said.

Tice's interrogators spoke English with a heavy accent. They kept him blindfolded and asked him numerous basic military questions, but they did not probe for truly significant or classified information.

"They obviously weren't well trained for military interrogations," he said. "They were interested in propaganda. What they really wanted was for me to make a video tape. I refused."

They beat him severely. The interrogation went on for about forty-eight hours, Tice estimated. When he still refused to make their video, "they really turned up the volume. They wired me up for shock therapy."

His captors hooked electrodes to his ears and his chin. Tice did not know the electrical source, because he was blindfolded. "Maybe it's a car battery," he thought.

"The shocks only hurt a lot the first couple of times. Then I pretty much got numb. But it was very tiring, you know, just physically tiring. Besides, I was hungry, needed sleep, and still blindfolded. I needed to go to the bathroom. They knew how to torture people. I could tell they were the kind that really enjoyed torturing people."

On the third day, after about eight hours of electrical shocks, Tice agreed to make the video. "They told me what to say. I said it, imitating their accent as well as I could. Finally, after the video, they gave me the first food and water I'd had in three days."

Afterwards, Tice said, there were regular "maintenance" beatings. He was kept isolated in a five foot by six foot cell with one window. He was moved to five different prisons. Every two days, he was awakened at night, taken to a bunker, beaten, and interrogated.

"But, as long as I could hear bombs falling around Baghdad, I knew that, eventually, everything was going to be all right. In one prison, there was a small louvered window, and every night I would look up through the louvers and wait for what I called the midnight show. It lifted my spirits to hear the bombs going down and the Triple A going off."

Roberts Made It, Too

At the fifth and last prison, Tice encountered thirty-one prisoners, mostly Americans, but including British, Italians, and a Kuwaiti. He was overjoyed to discover that one of the prisoners was Mike Roberts, who had passed through the clouds and out of Tice's vision before his parachute opened. He was not badly injured.

After forty-three days, Tice was permitted a sponge bath and a shave with cold water. On March 4, the prisoners were turned over to the International Red Cross, who bused them to a hotel, where they were given clean clothes, beds, hot baths, and decent food.

On March 6, Tice flew out of Baghdad by Swissair.

"At the border," he said, "a pair of F-15 Eagles joined up on us. Everybody started to cheer. Then three Tornados joined up on the other wing, and the British contingent led us all the way back to Riyadh. It was great."

"But I regret one thing," Tice concluded. "I only got one and a half combat sorties." ■

The Military-Media War

The reporters reporting on the Gulf War became a story themselves. Never before had an armed conflict been so televised, and the world watched not only the war but also the conduct of the news media.

Many viewers were appalled by what they saw, and even some members of the press were struck by the spectacle of it.

"The Persian Gulf press briefings are making reporters look like fools, nit-pickers, and egomaniacs," wrote Henry Allen of the Washington *Post*.

The slant some of them put on their reports did them no more credit than did their behavior in the press conferences.

"They talk about war as if it were a matter to be hashed out with a psychotherapist, or a matter to be discussed in a philosophy seminar," Allen observed. "A lot of them seem to care more about Iraqi deaths than American deaths, and after the big oil spill in the Gulf, they seemed to care more about animals than people."[1]

Military-media relations, never cordial, went further downhill during the Gulf War. Reporters complained on radio and television, in print, and to Congress that the military did not allow them to go wherever they wished, find out whatever they wanted to know, and use the information as they saw fit.

"The US military in Saudi Arabia is trampling on the American people's right to know," said Walter Cronkite. That the public seemed to take the military's side in the confrontation, he said, "can only be because the press has failed to make clear the public's stake in the matter."[2]

Columnists Jack Anderson and Dale Van Atta took that one step further. "The public's right to know is not surrendered in a war," they said. "And even if the majority of the public is willing to surrender it, the press will not."[3]

What the public may have realized was that it was being well informed—if not inundated—by all the facts and figures flowing back from the Gulf. The clash of the military and the media obscured the reality that the war was actually well covered, with credit due to both the government and the press.

The armed forces made public an extraordinary amount of detail about sorties, targets, results, and other aspects of the war, often within hours. The public was never in the dark about what was happening. For their part, the media devoted adequate air time and page space to cover the war comprehensively. Radio and television broadcast, usually uncut, the daily briefings from the war zone and the Pentagon.

No amount of operational detail, however, seemed to satisfy some of the reporters, who demanded more and more numbers and who refused to recognize the need to hold back some kinds of information. In one instance, for example, they badgered the briefing officer for a description of the markings by which pilots recognized traffic on the ground as allied rather than enemy vehicles.

"We understand as well as anyone the urge to inform the American public fully," the Florida *Times-Union* said in an editorial, "but why does a farmer in Nebraska or a cabbie in Manhattan need to know exactly how many A-10 Thunderbolts are stationed northwest of Jubayl?"[4]

The media contingent in Saudi Arabia eventually swelled to more than 1,600.[5] Some continued to report from Baghdad,

[1] Henry Allen, "The Gulf Between the Media and the Military," Washington *Post*, Feb. 21, 1991.

[2] Walter Cronkite, "What is There to Hide?," *Newsweek*, Feb. 25, 1991.

[3] Jack Anderson and Dale Van Atta, "Government Stenographers," Washington *Post*, March 3, 1991.

[4] "Press Zeal Could Help Saddam Unless Self-Restraint is Shown," Florida *Times-Union*, Jan. 25, 1991.

[5] *Conduct of the Persian Gulf Conflict*.

and a few struck out on their own in the war zone. Still others worked the war news from the Pentagon and Washington.

Many of them were rank amateurs at defense reporting, which accounted for some of the strange questions that floated up at the press briefings. Ignorance was less forgivable when commentators expounded judgments on matters they did not understand.

Military experts, for example, were deeply impressed by the feat of a missile shooting another missile out of the sky, but when one of the Iraqi Scuds got through, a National Public Radio analyst yawned that "three out of four is not very good."[6]

Government censorship of the news was rare. Pete Williams, Assistant Secretary of Defense for Public Affairs, told a Senate committee that as of February 20, the press pool had written 820 reports. Of these, only five raised questions of censorship that could not be settled in Saudi Arabia. Four of the cases appealed to Washington led to prompt clearance of the articles, and in the fifth instance, the reporter's editor agreed that the government's security concerns were valid.[7]

Some local commanders and their public affairs officers did overstep the bounds in attempting to kill stories for reasons other than security, but that practice was not typical.

Reporters also complained that they were manipulated, especially in regard to the possibility of an amphibious landing. Part of the strategy was to make the Iraqis think the allied invasion of Kuwait would come over the beach, so maritime operations offshore were conducted with high visibility. CENTCOM did nothing to discourage media interest in this activity. Many journalists felt that they were duped intentionally as part of the deception plan.

The military-media clash heated up as Schwarzkopf began his massive redeployment to the west before the ground offensive. Press pool reports datelined "With the VII Corps in Saudi Arabia" were no problem. Reporters who wanted to file their whereabouts precisely, however, were often not allowed to do so.

Moreover, the limited size of the press pools in the field meant that most of the journalists in Saudi Arabia had to do their reporting from Riyadh. Their frustration increased when the ground war began.

The pool accompanying US ground forces into combat consisted of 142 reporters.[8] In the view of most, that number was sufficient to send back the facts of battle, but the media held that more reporters should have had the opportunity to see the action first hand, and that the government should have moved their reports faster to media outlets back in the United States.

The armed forces had their complaints, too, one of which was the matter of outright bias. The most blatant example was Colman McCarthy of the Washington *Post*, who described US airmen as "sadistic" and "fearless warriors" conducting an "aerial massacre" at little risk to themselves in "a coward's air war."[9]

That sort of thing, fortunately, was rare. The real problem, from the media's point of view, boiled down to exclusives and extras. David Lamb of the Los Angeles *Times* captured the gist of it in his complaint that "pool reporting tends to dilute individual creativity, lending a homogenized quality to the reports."[10]

It was not that the public was poorly informed about the war, or even that the reporters covering it did not have the basic story or an abundance of facts to report.

What—if anything—they were being denied was the chance to go where other reporters had not been and serve up sensational scoops that the rest of the pack did not have. ■

[6] John T. Correll, "Nitwitness News," *Air Force Magazine*, April 1991.

[7] Williams, Senate Governmental Affairs Committee, Feb. 20, 1991.

[8] Guy Gugliotta, "Pool Reporting System Flaws Show," Washington *Post*, Feb. 27, 1991.

[9] Colman McCarthy, "The Coward's Air War," Washington *Post*, Feb. 17, 1991.

[10] Debra Gersh, "Where's the Beef?" *Editor & Publisher*, Jan. 26, 1991.

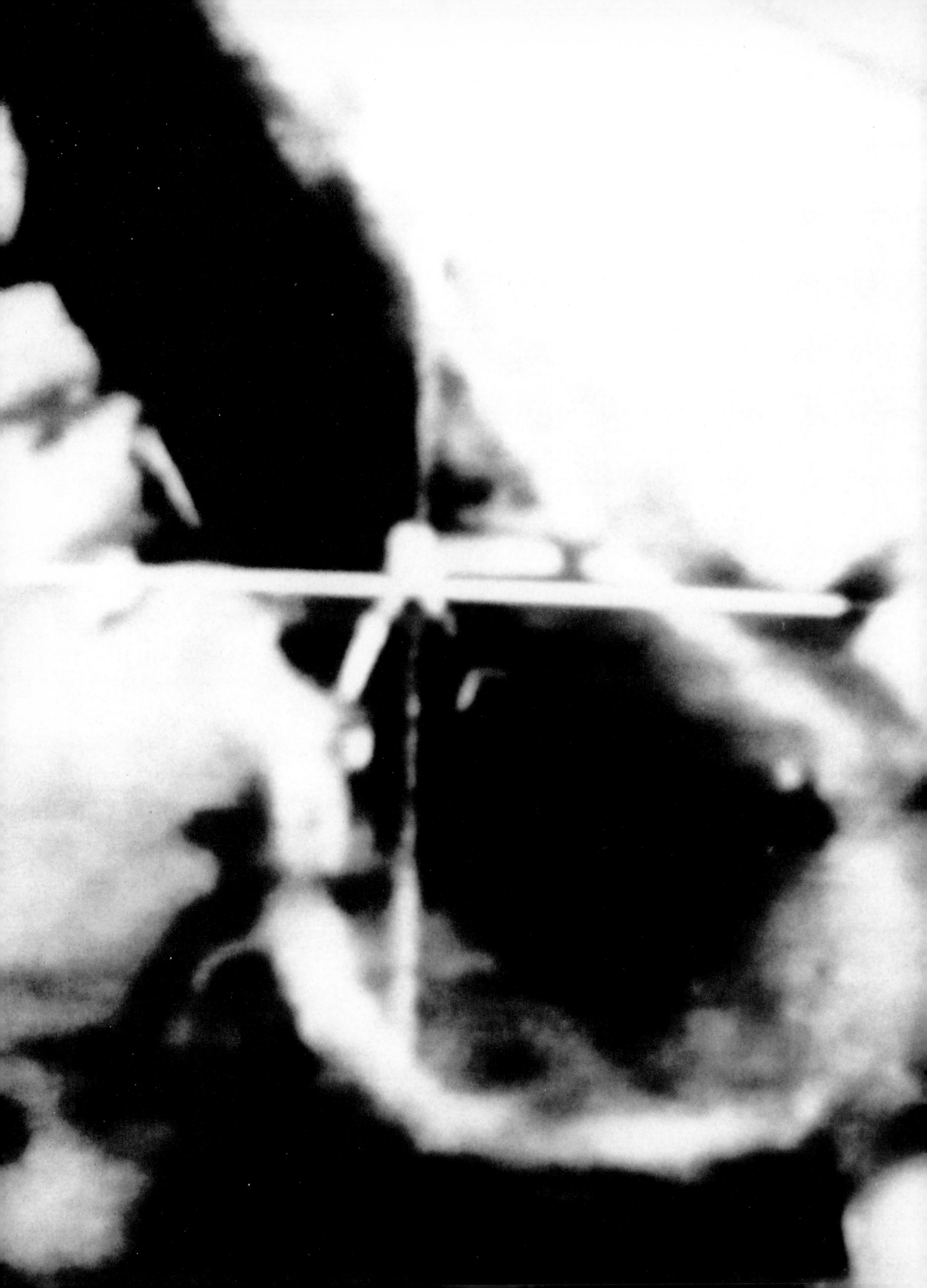

9. Technology Meets the Test

This Tu-16 Badger on a taxiway in Iraq is fixed in the crosshairs of an F-117 Stealth fighter. Scratch one Badger.

Critics said the advanced weapons would never work in combat. They were spectacularly wrong.

Overall, the Gulf War was a repudiation of critics who, for decades, had portrayed US armed forces as bunglers, staking the future on flawed and overcomplicated weapons that would never work.

Nearly all of the weapons and technologies that proved so successful in the Gulf had earlier been the subject of doubt and disdain. For example, the E-3 AWACS had been attacked as unproven and unnecessary by critics who called it "the airplane without a mission."[1]

Ten years ago, the Maverick missile—which convincingly demonstrated its worth against Iraqi armor—had been deemed a "fiasco" by the press, and the General Accounting Office doubted that US troops could ever use it effectively in combat.[2]

The high technology systems worked every bit as well as advertised, and sometimes better than advertised. Operation Desert Storm was a spectacular vindication of technology in at least six areas.

- *Stealth.* The F-117 fighter, penetrating Baghdad defenses by surprise and at will, more than lived up to claims the Air Force made before the war for "low observables" technology.
- *Precision-guided munitions.* Never before had such accuracy been seen in combat. It will be difficult now for doubters to return to their previous view that "smart bombs" are a novelty or an extravagance.
- *Electronic superiority.* A major factor in the course of the war is that coalition electronics—offensive and defensive, for surveillance, communications, and other purposes—worked superbly, whereas Saddam's didn't. Early on, General Schwarzkopf reported that the Iraqis had switched to backup command, control, and communications systems that were less secure, far less effective, and more easily targeted.[3]
- *Night-fighting capability.* Just a few years ago, US forces had to suspend many kinds of combat operations when darkness fell. No longer. "It has been this marriage of infrared sensors, terrain-following radar, and laser designators that give our fighters the ability to pierce the cover of darkness," Lt. Gen. Thomas R. Ferguson of the Aeronautical Systems Division said with the war still in progress. "We've talked about flying at Mach .85 on the deck at night. Now we're doing it in combat."[4]
- *Ballistic missile defense.* Americans watching the war on television were witnesses to the unprecedented spectacle of enemy missiles shot out of the air in their terminal phase of attack.
- *Space.* Lt. Gen. Thomas S. Moorman, Jr., commander of Air Force Space Command, calls Desert Storm "a watershed event in military space applications because, for the first time, space systems were an integral part of terrestrial conflict and were crucial to its outcome."[5]

Performance in Battle

While stealth did not make the F-117 fighter truly invisible to Saddam's air defense system, it did veil the aircraft so well on its attack missions through the thickest air defenses in history that not a single hit was scored upon it.

[1] Peter J. Ognibene, "The Plane That Would Not Die," *New Republic*, April 13, 1974.

[2] John T. Correll, "The Many Battles of Maverick," *Air Force Magazine*, March 1983.

[3] James W. Canan, "Airpower Opens the Fight," *Air Force Magazine*, March 1991.

[4] Lt. Gen. Thomas R. Ferguson, AFA Symposium, Orlando, Fla., Jan. 31–Feb. 1, 1991.

[5] James W. Canan, "A Watershed in Space," *Air Force Magazine*, August 1991.

Precision-guided munitions—"smart" bombs and missiles guided by radar or laser reflections or by television imagery—destroyed their targets with astounding accuracy, avoiding civilian casualties and minimizing collateral damage to nearby buildings and facilities.

Superaccurate navigation systems, some using state-of-the-art ring-laser gyro technology and others relying on "fixes" from satellites orbiting in space, enabled the crews of properly equipped fighters, bombers, and helicopters to know precisely, within feet, their position and altitude in relation to the earth.

Using forward-looking infrared systems to see ahead, coalition attackers were able to fly "nap of the earth," in total darkness at 200 feet (or less) above the desert terrain, at speeds of 600 knots.

Unmanned cruise missiles, launched hundreds of miles from their targets, used inertial navigation and digital mapping to follow a predetermined track along the ground to their targets.

Remotely-piloted vehicles (RPVs), guided by radio, conducted reconnaissance sweeps over high-risk areas, providing images to launching units without risk to the crews.

Satellites in space provided weather information over the battle area. Different satellites utilized side-looking radar to pinpoint enemy installations. Still other satellites watched for missile launches, reporting them by radio datalink transmitted to Air Force Space Command in Colorado. When it was determined the missile was a Scud, a launch warning, as well as the missile's predicted impact area, were flashed from Colorado to the Gulf, where the Patriot batteries were alerted.

The Patriot air defense missile, recently modified to intercept missiles as well as aircraft, knocked down most of the Scuds against which it was employed.

Stealthy Does It

Col. Alton C. Whitley, Jr.'s 37th Tactical Fighter Wing, flying the F-117A, dropped the first bombs on Baghdad. The wing's mission was to "cut off the head" of the Iraqi Integrated Air Defense System (IADS) so that direction and coordination of the system would be impossible.

The F-117A Stealth fighter was General Horner's weapon of choice for this mission. Its weapon delivery system was superbly accurate, and the aircraft itself would be nearly impossible for the Iraqi radars to pick up. The plan was for the F-117s to fly undetected into Iraq and knock out the IADS without alerting defenders.

They struck in two waves because each key Iraqi communications and air defense site, including radar facilities and command and control nodes, had been targeted at least twice to ensure that any Iraqi airfields or air defense sites remaining would be isolated and ineffective. If a pilot in the second wave found that his primary target was destroyed by the first wave, he diverted to a different target.

The 415th Tactical Fighter Squadron led the first wave. The 416th followed about thirty minutes later.

The F-117s had flown from their home base at Tonopah, Nev., to Khamis Mushait AB on August 19. Khamis Mushait is in southwest Saudi Arabia, about 900 nautical miles due south of Baghdad. Each night during the war, F-117 pilots flew more than twice the distance from New York to Chicago to employ their weapons and return.

Except for the very long distance to key Iraqi targets, Khamis Mushait—with its modern facilities, twin 12,000 foot runways, and a climate very similar to Tonopah—was ideal for the F-117A. Forty-two of the wing's fifty-six aircraft deployed to the Gulf.The 37th had been training with the stealth aircraft for years, but it had never been tested against a modern air defense system.[6]

The Lockheed F-117 is the world's first truly stealthy aircraft. The need for stealthy aircraft was recognized in the 1940s, but while designers made some progress in reducing radar signatures, it would be many years before technology caught up with the theories.

By the 1970s, however, the fabled Lockheed "Skunk Works" was ready to begin work on what would become the F-117A.

[6] Lt. Col. Barry E. Horne, interview, Nov. 26, 1991.

Improved computer capabilities enabled Lockheed engineers to calculate how a body with different shapes would reflect radar energy. They designed an aircraft with no curved surfaces at all except the leading edges of the wings and tail surfaces.

Unlike the Northrop B-2 bomber, the F-117 does not achieve its stealthiness with compound curves. Its planar surfaces, set at unusual angles, scatter incoming radar beams instead of reflecting them. The result is to dramatically reduce the aircraft's radar cross section and its "footprint" on a radarscope.[7]

Two test demonstrators were built and flown in the "Have Blue" program in 1975. The prototypes—scaled at sixty percent the size of the real thing—were equipped with electronic flight controls borrowed from the F-16. Both Have Blue aircraft crashed, but they survived long enough to prove the concept of stealth and to launch the highly successful F-117A program.

Four Sources of Stealth

Four characteristics make a modern aircraft truly stealthy. First, it must have low radar cross section (RCS). Second, the aircraft must give off little heat or infrared (IR) energy. Third, the aircraft must be relatively quiet. And last, the aircraft must be difficult to see. (Flying on dark nights solves part of this problem.) Lockheed tackled all of these features with the F-117A. Every detail about it—from hidden air intakes lined with radar-absorbent materials to cooled exhaust—is designed for stealth.

Furthermore, the edges of the airframe are angled to reflect radar energy away from the enemy emitter. The wing and tailplanes sweep back sixty-seven degrees. All surfaces are divided into small, perfectly aligned flat planes, allowing the smallest possible reflection of energy in any one direction. The smooth bottom of the fuselage and blended body also reduce RCS.

Radar-absorbent material (RAM) fills cavities in the fuselage and engine bay. "Iron ball" radar-absorbent paint further reduces the image the enemy sees on his screens. Around the cockpit area, the top FLIR has a RAM mesh around it, the cockpit and windscreen are pyramid shaped, and the high-strength windshield has a thin layer of gold or indium-tin to prevent radar waves from entering and being reflected from the cockpit.[8]

To reduce heat emissions, two General Electric F404-GE-F1D2 nonafterburning turbojets, which provide 10,800 pounds of thrust each, are buried deep in the fuselage.[9] From outside, cool air flows past the engines through a shroud, which, with the help of a low pressure compressor, injects it into the exhaust. The engine exhausts are directed above the "platypus" tail, which reduces the chances of detection by infrared seekers below. The exhausts are rectangular and have louvers to diffuse the engine jet flow, and this also tends to reduce the heat pattern of the exhaust. Heat from the avionics and environmental control system is carefully shielded from IR detectors.

The GE F404 engines, which also power the Navy/Marine F/A-18A, have a high thrust-to-weight ratio and are fuel efficient. The engine is fairly quiet, and the exhaust design reduces noise still more.

The Stealth fighter remains visible to the human eye, of course, and the solution to that problem was to make it a night attack aircraft. It is painted black, and the bright decals are removed for combat. The RAM coating and the shape of the aircraft reduce light reflections and make it very difficult to see, even with night vision aids.

How the F-117A Fights

The pilot operates a very accurate Honeywell ring-laser gyro inertial navigation system. The aircraft has two weapons bays, one for each for its primary weapons, which are 2,000-pound laser-guided bombs. The aircraft is fitted with an exceptionally accurate weapons computer. It also has a FLIR sensor that produces TV-quality images of distant objects, even on hazy nights.

A second downward-looking IR system under the aircraft is used for weapons delivery. Both IRs are steerable and can be aimed by the pilot or, automatically, by the INS. The downward-looking IR sensor is

[7] Jeffrey P. Rhodes, "The Black Jet," *Air Force Magazine*, July 1990.

[8] Bill Sweetman and James Goodall. *Lockheed F-117A*. Motorbooks, 1990.

[9] Susan H. H. Young, "Gallery of USAF Weapons," *Air Force Magazine*, May 1991.

boresighted to a laser designator to guide the LGBs.[10] It was this sensor that provided the image, widely shown on world television, of a laser-guided bomb destroying Saddam's telecommunications building in downtown Baghdad.

The pilot views FLIR imagery on a large cathode-ray tube in the center of his instrument panel. The same screen provides flight information such as attitude, altitude, airspeed, and navigation information. The pilot acquires the target on his FLIR, usually in the wide-field-of-view mode, identifies the target, and then switches to the downward-looking IR for weapons delivery through the weapons computer.

After acquiring the target, the pilot positions the cross hairs of his weapon system on the aimpoint and actuates the laser designator by depressing a button on his throttle. The computer then takes over, and when the pilot depresses the consent (or "pickle") button, releases the weapon at a point in flight from which it can home in on the laser energy reflected from the aimpoint. The pilot monitors the automatic process, or can perform it manually.[11]

Adjusting to combat in the Persian Gulf, pilots would typically wake up in the afternoon to report to briefings as early as 4 p.m. for an 8 p.m. takeoff. The next wave of pilots would report at 8 p.m. for a midnight takeoff. Although the times varied and at times takeoffs or landings were made in daylight, the combat operations were at night.[12]

At Tonopah, the average mission lasted 1.6 hours. Flying out of Khamis Mushait, the long distance from Iraqi targets pushed the average sortie time up to 5.4 hours per sortie, with some sorties lasting almost seven hours.[13]

Pilots refueled in the air before crossing into Iraq and after coming out. F-117 pilots also worked shifts in the wing's combat planning cell. After a shift, they rested for twenty-four hours. Most aircraft flew twice each night.[14]

The principal munition for the F-117 was the GBU-27, an improved 2,000-pound bomb, modified with a Paveway III laser guidance kit. The bomb was developed in the mid-1980s when US Air Force studies indicated the Warsaw Pact and other potential adversaries were hardening likely military targets against conventional attack.

The I-2000 casing is forged from high-strength steel. It is slim and bullet shaped, and in tests it was able to penetrate reinforced concrete more than six feet thick, remain intact, and then detonate reliably. It was just what the Air Force needed to destroy Saddam's 600 hardened aircraft shelters, command bunkers, and command and control facilities.

Other weapons employed by the F-117A in Operation Desert Storm were the standard 2,000-pound bomb and the 500-pound Mk 82, both with Paveway II laser guidance kits. They were deadly against all except the most hardened targets.

Precision-Guided Munitions

US pilots employed 7,400 tons of precision-guided munitions—popularly called "smart bombs"—in the Gulf War. The Air Force dropped ninety percent of all the smart bombs employed in the conflict.

Many precision-guided munitions (PGMs) are stand-off weapons, which means the aircrew can release them from a relatively safe point outside target air defenses and the weapon can guide itself, or home in, on the target. They were in development for a relatively long time.

Several PGMs were introduced in Vietnam, including the Bullpup, which the launching pilot guided with a small control stick on his cockpit console. It was not very accurate and it had a short range.

Other PGMs included electro-optical (TV guided) weapons like the Walleye and the Hobo. They were better than the Bullpup, but short on reliability, accuracy, and destructive power.

In the Vietnam War, the Air Force employed a 2,000-pound smart bomb called the Mk 84. Equipped with a Texas Instruments Paveway I guidance system, the bomb homed in on laser or television designated targets. The target illuminator, called the Pave Knife system, was carried in a pod by a fighter while another fighter released the smart bomb. It was very effective against

[10] Michael Dornheim, "F-117A Pilots Conduct Precision Bombing in High Threat Environment," *Aviation Week & Space Technology*, April 22, 1991.

[11] Horne interview.

[12] Dornheim.

[13] Capt. Donald R. Chapman, interview, Nov. 26, 1991.

[14] Dornheim.

highway and railroad bridges and other point targets in North Vietnam.

After Vietnam, the US Navy developed the Walleye II television-homing glide bomb. The new Walleye II has a 1,000-pound warhead and a glide range in excess of twenty nautical miles.[15] The Navy still uses the Walleye II. It was the most-used Navy PGM in the Gulf War.

The Navy carried out accurate strikes with the Walleye II. Watching their television displays, Navy aircrews literally guided the weapons through windows and doorways of targets while staying well outside of Iraqi defenses.

In the Gulf War, modern PGMs were used with enormous effect. For example, F-111F aircrews, using the 500-pound GBU-12 laser-guided bomb, were credited with destroying more than 1,000 Iraqi tanks and armored vehicles. As the date for the ground invasion approached, this "tank plinking" destroyed 150 pieces of armor per night.

The F-111F was equipped with a Pave Tack FLIR targeting pod, which has a swiveling seeker head that sweeps for heat emissions from tanks and vehicles.

Locating a target, the F-111 weapons system operator in the right hand seat designates it for the GBU-12 with a laser beam. The bomb homes in on the laser reflection with great accuracy. Nearly half of the smart bombs dropped in the Gulf War were GBU-12s.

Other laser-guided smart bombs were employed, too. The F-111s also used the 2,000-pound GBU-24 laser-guided bomb against hardened aircraft shelters. F-117s dropped GBU-27 2,000-pounders on heavily constructed command and control centers, communications centers, aircraft shelters, and other point targets.

F-111s and F-15Es delivered GBU-24s on bunkers in chemical, biological, and nuclear storage areas, as well as bridges and aircraft shelters. On one occasion, a single two-ship flight of F-15Es destroyed sixteen tanks with sixteen GBU-12 laser-guided 500-pound bombs.[16]

Late in the war, F-111s employed the GBU-28, a new, 4,700-pound laser-guided bomb specially designed for extremely deep penetration of underground command bunkers. At least one bunker was destroyed with a GBU-28.

The Navy introduced a new weapon in Operation Desert Storm—the McDonnell Douglas AGM-84E Standoff Land Attack Missile (SLAM). The SLAM is the land-attack version of the Navy's ship killer, the AGM-84 Harpoon. The SLAM has a range of approximately sixty nautical miles and carries a 500-pound shaped charge warhead. The weapon weighs 1,500 pounds at launch and although there are a lot of similarities between the SLAM and Harpoon, there are significant differences.

The SLAM retains the Harpoon's radar altimeter and midcourse guidance unit, but the new missile has the imaging infrared seeker developed for the Maverick antitank missile. The SLAM utilizes a Walleye television datalink so that the launching aircraft can move the seeker head to acquire targets. A receiver-processor on a Global Positioning System (GPS) satellite provides altitude and position information the missile uses as part of its internal navigation.[17]

Before launch, mission data is stored electronically in the missile system's memory. Once launched, the SLAM uses GPS to navigate to the target. In preplanned strikes, the missile's Walleye datalink and seeker become active about one minute before impact. At this point, the operator guides the missile with a joystick in the cockpit and uses datalink to select the proper target and to lock the missile onto the aimpoint.

An older Air Force PGM, the rocket-propelled Maverick, was employed in the Gulf with lethal efficiency, principally by the A-10, but also by the F-4G Wild Weasels and the F-16s.

The USAF version of the Maverick can be fitted with an imaging infrared (IIR) or an electro-optical (television) guidance package. The Marines employed a laser-guided Maverick.

The Maverick's principal targets were Iraqi tanks. One $70,000 missile could knock out one $1.5 million T-72 tank. Nearly 5,500 Mavericks were fired during

[15] Norman Friedman, *The Naval Institute Guide to World Naval Weapons Systems.* Naval Institute press, 1990.

[16] USAF white paper, September 1991.

[17] "SLAMs Hit Iraqi Target In First Combat Firing," *Aviation Week & Space Technology*, Jan. 28, 1991.

the Gulf War, ninety-nine percent of them by US Air Force aircraft. More than two-thirds of them were the IIR version. A-10 pilots, mainly using Maverick, destroyed 1,000 tanks, 2,000 other vehicles, and 1,200 artillery pieces.[18]

In the Gulf War, PGMs brought an order of magnitude improvement in bombing accuracy. During World War II, it took a force of 108 B-17s, dropping a total of 648 bombs, to guarantee two hits on a single electrical power generating plant. In the Gulf War, one F-117A with two precision-guided weapons could destroy a power generation station's transformer yards.

Put another way, for the number of bomber sorties in World War II required to disable two power stations, coalition aircraft with PGMs disabled the transformer capacity of every targeted generation facility in Iraq.[19]

Penetrating the Night

Night vision devices, principally infrared detectors, gave the coalition air forces a tremendous advantage in night fighting. FLIR-equipped aircraft and helicopters operated almost as freely at night as in the daylight and attacked Saddam's war machine twenty-four hours a day.

The 48th TFW aircrews flying F-111Fs with the Pave Tack II pod mounted in the weapons bay, capitalizing on the aircraft's long range and excellent ground mapping radar, could hit a wide range of targets. F-111Fs employed guided bombs against high-value targets such as airfield facilities and oil manifolds.[20]

The system that, more than any other, gave the US Air Force control of the night was LANTIRN. Forty-eight F-15Es from the 4th TFW, Seymour Johnson AFB, N.C., flew out of Al Kharj, Saudi Arabia, equipped with Martin Marietta LANTIRN (Low-Altitude Navigation and Targeting Infrared for Night) pods.

The LANTIRN navigation pod has terrain-following radar. The F-15E can be flown manually, or the TFR can be coupled to the F-15E autopilot. There is also a FLIR sensor which provides a wide field-of-view for the pilot's head-up display.

The targeting pod contains a FLIR tailored for target detection and lock on, as well as a target tracker, and a laser designator and range-finder. It also includes a device called a boresight correlator for employment of the AGM-65 Maverick missile.[21]

F-16C pilots also employed the LANTIRN navigation pod. The FLIR was a boon to pilots flying at night. "It was like driving down a deserted highway in the middle of West Texas at two in the morning and then all of a sudden seeing the biggest Fourth of July fireworks demonstration that you've ever seen in your life all at once." Lt. Col. Tom Rackley, commander of the 421st TFS, said. "And that's what it was.

"In fact, one of the starkest contrasts that will always stick with me is going out there and taking off, going to the tanker, and on clear nights, just sitting there and looking at the beautiful stars and having it very calm, peaceful, and relaxing.

"Then you go and get your gas and you go into Kuwait or Iraq and your whole world lights up. You're watching all those missiles go by and all the AAA going off and you're trying to find your targets, you're trying to avoid other airplanes and everything is just one thing after another.

"And then, after about twenty minutes of that, you're back in the peaceful night sky again. Coming out of there and climbing up to a very high altitude to come home, putting the autopilot on, turning all the lights off, and just sitting there and allowing yourself to calm down and relax and behold the beauty of the universe. That's what I'll always remember."[22]

LANTIRN was the key to F-15E effectiveness in night combat. For example, when Joint STARS found what it believed to be a Scud missile site, the F-15E crew, with their synthetic aperture radar, could locate the missile/launcher precisely, even if it was camouflaged, then use LANTIRN to acquire the target visually and illuminate it for the LGB.

FLIR, low-light-level TV, and night vision goggles were extremely important for Air Force Special Forces aircrews. For ex-

[18] USAF white paper, September 1991.

[19] USAF white paper, September 1991.

[20] USAF white paper, April 1991.

[21] William B. Scott, "LANTIRN Provides Breakthrough In Night-Fighting Capabilities," *Aviation Week & Space Technology,* April 25, 1988.

[22] Lt. Col. Thomas Rackley, interview, May 27, 1991.

ample, they relied on them for employing the MC-130E Combat Talon on low-level operations deep in Iraq.

The crews of AC-130H Spectre gunships, and HC-130N/P Combat Shadow inflight refueling birds, were equipped with them. Crews of MH-53J Pave Low night attack helicopters and the HH-3E Jolly Green Giant as well as Marine HH-53 Super Jolly rescue helicopters had them. Night vision goggles were also essential and effective for Army aviators and ground troops.

The ANVIS-6 night vision goggles were the newest in a series of NVGs and were issued to US aviators in Desert Storm. They amplify limited visible or infrared light reflected from the surface of an object.

Airborne Eyes and Ears

Horner pulled in every reconnaissance platform the coalition could provide. That included satellites, the high-flying TR-1/U-2R aircraft,the RF-4C for tactical information, the E-8A Joint STARS to find ground targets; the RC-135 Rivet Joint to monitor electronic emissions, remotely-piloted vehicles, and Navy F-14s equipped with TARPS.

TARPS is the acronym for the Tactical Air Reconnaissance Pod System. It transforms the F-14 into a reconnaissance platform. The pod contains three sensors and ancillary control components. The sensors include two high resolution cameras—one for forward oblique and vertical photography and the other for panoramic views—and a sophisticated infrared sensing system.[23] Although conceived as a low-to-medium altitude strike planning and battle-damage assessment system, TARPS was employed at high altitude during Desert Storm because of the heavy defenses.[24]

Lt. James Kuhn, an F-14 pilot, and Lt. Cmdr. Davis Parsons, a radar intercept officer (RIO) recounted one TARPS mission, flown off the USS *John F. Kennedy*. "I remember saying to 'Dog' [Kuhn] as we ingressed, in the first few moments, 'faster, faster,'" said Parsons, "and seeing him glance up in the mirror with his 'I am' look. You never knew just where the SAM was going to launch from. We were all eyes all of the time. The ground just wasn't moving fast enough for me.

"Once we got to that point where we were so close the jamming wasn't shielding us from the SAMs, it was just jinking and chaffing and jinking some more. It's my wing [man]'s job to watch for any smoke or dust cloud from a launch. He's our insurance policy. The cameras were on. Just like with any camera, I said to myself... ninety degrees right, then ninety degrees to the left, then check cameras running. Settle down for just a moment, make it easier on the camera, then back with a little duck to the right and slice to the left. I took one last look, checked cameras again... one potato, two potato, three potato, four—and started to use our twelve-miles-a-minute speed to get our jet out of harm's way."[25]

During Desert Shield, General Horner repeatedly sent F-15s, Tornados, and F/A-18s racing toward the Iraqi border to locate Iraqi air defenses and discern operating frequencies and types of communications. They would turn around before reaching the border but not before triggering an Iraqi response. Big RC-135 Rivet Joint electronic reconnaissance aircraft monitored the Iraqi radar and communications response, gradually building a comprehensive knowledge of Iraqi defensive systems and capabilities. As the days went on, larger and larger packages feinted toward the Iraqi border, both day and night, continuing to exercise the Iraqi IADS while running dress rehearsals for the coalition air forces.[26]

The 9th Wing deployed U-2s and TR-1As from Beale AFB, Calif., to Taif, Saudi Arabia. The TR-1A and U-2R, which have nearly identical airframes but are fitted with different electronic equipment, performed a significant operational intelligence role, both during Desert Shield and after the hot war started. The operational altitude is above 70,000 feet and the range is more than 3,000 miles. Cruising speed is 400 knots. Twelve of these aircraft worked out of Taif.[27]

The U-2R and TR-1A carry a multitude of sensors, including infrared, radar, and long-range optical systems for all-weather

[23] *The United States Navy in Desert Shield/Desert Storm*.

[24] Mark Meyer, "Going Up to Big Al," *US Naval Institute Proceedings*, June 3, 1991.

[25] Meyer, "Going Up to Big Al."

[26] Gen. Michael Dugan, "The Air War," *US News & World Report*, Feb. 11, 1991.

[27] Col. Thomas J. Keck, interview, July 17, 1991.

capability, day or night. The aircraft can be tailored for specific intelligence missions by changing the sensors in the wing pods.

Because of the high altitudes at which they fly, U-2/TR-1 pilots are laced into a tight pressure suit (cockpit altitude is usually above 30,000 feet), which they don more than an hour before takeoff time. They breathe 100 percent oxygen. Missions last nine hours or longer.

Capt. Stephen I. Feldman, a U-2/TR-1 aircraft commander, flew some missions over Iraq that lasted eleven hours. "The trip up to the border was an hour and a half from Taif. We would have specific routes to fly and specific targets to hit with our sensors.

"Sometimes, we would be called on the radio to do some spur of the moment BDA [bomb-damage assessment]. Other times, we were taking pictures to show what was out there.

"From our altitude, at night, we had a box seat to watch some of the most phenomenal light shows ever produced—the war. They were beyond description. Every night. Usually, two or more of us were up at the same time, in different areas, and we could communicate on VHF.

"Sometimes, at night, we would get a Scud launch warning. I would watch it take off, trailing flame, zoom up through my altitude, and disappear. We would report the direction it was traveling, although I think the reconnaissance satellites gave CENTCOM that information. Sometimes, it would go right over the flight path. Then, as I watched, it would come back down into the atmosphere, glowing, and, if it was going into Saudi, we could see it get intercepted by Patriot."[28]

Lower-level reconnaissance was provided by twelve RF-4Cs from the 12th TRS of the 67th TRW, Bergstrom AFB, Tex. The scarce RF-4Cs were supplemented by the 117th TRW of the Birmingham, Ala., Air National Guard. The 117th deployed to Saudi Arabia August 17 and provided six RF-4Cs equipped with the long-range oblique photograph (LOROP) camera. The squadron provided photographs of key targets while staying outside of enemy defenses. The 117th was relieved by aircrews and support personnel of the 152d TRG, Reno, Nev., in early January 1991.

Airborne Command and Control

The only two existing prototypes of the E-8A Joint Surveillance Target Attack Radar System (Joint STARS) aircraft deployed to Saudi Arabia in January 1991. Joint STARS got results beyond all expectations, providing CENTCOM real-time data on deployment and movement of Saddam's forces. Three examples illustrate the intelligence Joint STARS can, and did, provide:

Schwarzkopf used the aircraft to watch Iraqi ground reaction when he moved his troops into position for his "Hail Mary" flanking movement. The Iraqis did not react. In a second case, the aircraft detected an Iraqi armored division marshaling for an attack into Saudi Arabia. Allied air forces reacted, destroying the division's offensive capabilities. A third example was the E-8A's ability to detect suspected Scud launchers and missiles, vectoring F-15Es in to attack the sites.

Other SAR-equipped aircraft played a vital part in the Gulf War. When TR-1As could not take off due to excess winds, Army SAR-equipped OV-1Ds were called to fill in some of the intelligence gaps.[29] SAR was a vital part of tactical intelligence in the Gulf War.

The E-3B/C AWACS controlled the air-to-air war and the EC-130E ABCCC controlled the air-to-ground war. Early in the air war, AWACS coordinated the destruction of the Iraqi IADS, vectoring aircraft to and from tankers and managing the crowded airspace over the theater. AWACS coordinated the Scud hunt and provided early warning of Iraqi air attacks.

The flexible, mobile, jam resistant E-3B/C Sentry is a highly modified Boeing 707 transport. The large aircraft carries an extensive complement of mission avionics, including a computer, radar, IFF, communications, display, and navigation systems. The AWACS radar, built by Westinghouse, provides a look-down capability and can acquire and track multiple targets. The first aircraft was delivered to the US Air Force

[28] Capt. Stephen I. Feldman, interview, July 17, 1991.

[29] "'Filtering' Helped Top Military Leaders Get Proper Intelligence Information," *Aviation Week & Space Technology*, April 22, 1991.

in 1977. The Air Force has thirty-three. NATO operates eighteen, and Saudi Arabia has five. Other nations have also purchased the aircraft.

AWACS is air refuelable, which gives it unlimited range and duration. The aircraft is powered by four Pratt & Whitney TF33-PW-100/100A turbofan engines with 21,000 pounds of thrust each. There are twenty aircrew members, including sixteen AWACS mission specialists.[30]

The ABCCC is a C-130 specially modified to carry a high-tech command, control, and communications module in the cargo compartment.

The 7th Airborne Command and Control Squadron, Keesler AFB, Miss., operated two ABCCCs in the Gulf with modules that had recently been delivered by Electronic and Information Systems Group of Unisys Defense Systems, Inc. The module houses twelve consoles with graphic displays for the battle staff to control fighter-bombers on ground attack missions.

Although AWACS controlled the "big picture" and the air war, ABCCC was responsible for controlling ground attack, including interdiction missions and close air support missions. The ABCCC concept of operations was much like that used in Vietnam, except that the modern ABCCC is much more highly automated and is capable of handling many more combat flights.

The daily CENTAF tasking orders, if printed out, would be the size of a Washington, D.C., telephone book. They were loaded onto optical disks aboard the aircraft. An ABCCC controller could then call up and sort the order on his computer to find the part that applied to the fighters he was directing at the time.[31]

Inputs for the list came from many sources. In the 9th Air Force exercise, *Internal Look*, conducted in July 1990, specific targets in Iraq had been selected and wargamed. After Saddam's invasion of Kuwait, a rapid study of targets was made under Air Force Col. John A. Warden, Deputy Director of Strategy, Doctrine and Plans, Air Staff, and his *Checkmate* organization.

Warden's list contained 84 targets. The CENTCOM staff had compiled a list of 141. Many targets were on both lists. Horner's list—the "real" list—totaled 112. By war's end, the total grew to 423. It included not only tactical targets, such as air defenses and the interdiction of the Iraqi army, but also strategic targets,electrical production facilities, generating stations, and oil refineries.[32]

As Horner's CENTAF staff formed in Riyadh in the fall of 1990,targeting functions were handled by Glosson's "Black Hole" group. As the list expanded, aircraft and weapons were matched to targets, and a chronological order of attacks was determined.[33]

Space

Desert Storm became the first war the United States fought that was partially waged and supported from space. Military and CIA satellites played a heavy role in the Gulf War.

Satellite imagery, including intelligence imagery from photographic and Lacrosse-1 radar spacecraft provided important targeting and BDA information. CENTCOM also utilized the French SPOT and US Eosat/Landsat data for targeting and map updates so important to the air and ground war. Even a Soviet satellite, Meteor, was used to collect weather information. They provided mapping improvements that could be coupled with the terrain-contour matching navigation capabilities of the Tomahawk to enable the cruise missiles to accurately navigate to and hit their targets.[34]

At the peak of hostilities, military satellites were handling eighty-five percent of the communications for the force.[35] Two Defense Satellite Communications System DSCS-2 spacecraft and one DSCS-3 provided extensive support. This could only be done after Air Force Space Command controllers moved a reserve satellite from its position over the Pacific to a new geostationary orbit 22,300 miles above the Indian Ocean. This was historic—the first time ever a satellite had been repositioned to support combat operations.[36]

Scud launch warnings were provided by two Air Force Space Command Defense

[30] Young, "Gallery of USAF Weapons," *Air Force Magazine*.

[31] David Hughes, "USAF Adapts Off-the-Shelf Computer Hardware, Software in New Systems," *Aviation Week & Space Technology*, June 3, 1991.

[32] Barton Gellman, "Allied Air War Struck Broadly in Iraq," Washington *Post*, June 23, 1991.

[33] Glosson interview, May 28, 1991.

[34] Canan, "A Watershed in Space."

[35] Secretary Donald B. Rice, AFA Symposium, Oct. 24–25, 1991.

[36] Canan.

Support Program (DSP) missile-warning satellites that provided warning data on Iraqi Scud B launch plumes within two minutes after launch. As with B-52s used in the tactical role, the DSPs also switched from a strategic to a tactical role in support of the Gulf War.

Weather satellites were important, too. Meteorological conditions in the desert are nowhere near as stable as popularly imagined. "The fact is," Air Force Secretary Rice said later, "General Horner and his people had to plan attacks around unexpected cloud cover, winds aloft, thunderstorms, ice, you name it. It turned out during Desert Storm to be the worst weather in the fourteen or fifteen years of recorded weather history in that part of the world."

The Navstar Global Positioning System (GPS) was as useful to ground forces as it was to the coalition air forces. GPS and DSCS provided allied forces the extraordinary navigational accuracy needed to move and be resupplied at precise points in the desert.

In addition, GPS allowed the coalition ground forces to locate and mark Iraqi mine fields with precision, helping coalition forces to move through and around them. Although the GPS constellation is still incomplete, there were enough "balls" in orbit to provide almost full coverage.

Secretary Rice recounts one of the many GPS anecdotes to come out of the war. Maj. Mike Cook, an F-16 pilot, had been diverted from hunting Scuds for a night rescue mission. "Eight of our special operations troopers were surrounded by 200 Iraqi troops closing in on them, deep behind the lines. They radioed for extraction. With GPS manpacks, they could relay their exact position.

"Major Cook's F-16 also had GPS. He zeroed in and quickly saw that the Iraqis were too close to the friendlies to use his bombs. He climbed to 18,000 feet, then dove straight at the ground, covering them with a sonic boom. After a couple more booms of that sort, the Iraqis ran to their trucks and hightailed it out of there. Mike Cook returned to his Scud hunt, found his targets, and dropped his bombs. The next day a special forces trooper walked into Mike's tent back at his air base to say, 'thanks for saving our lives.'"[37]

Patriots and Scuds

The coalition countries were not defenseless against the Scud tactical ballistic missiles. US Army Patriot batteries had been emplaced in Saudi Arabia and Israel, but the Israeli batteries had not yet become operational. An additional US battery was rushed to Tel Aviv and began to intercept the Scuds. Of the eighty-six Scuds fired at Israel and Saudi Arabia, thirty-nine fell harmlessly into the desert or the Mediterranean Sea. Of the forty-seven Scuds that were heading for populated areas, the Patriot intercepted all but two.

(Although "Patriot" is commonly used here and elsewhere as a standard proper name for the missile, it is a US Army acronym for "Phased-Array Tracking to Intercept of Target".) The missile is the most recently developed US major air defense weapon. The system is built around a phased-array radar and fast computers.

A single Patriot battery can simultaneously track more than 100 targets and engage multiple enemy aircraft. The missile is launched and guided to the target in three phases. First, the missile's guidance system turns the Patriot toward the target as it flies into the radar beam. Next, the computer directs the missile toward its target. In the third phase, the missile becomes semiactive as its internal radar receiver guides it to the interception. Finally, a proximity fuze detonates the warhead.

Originally designed for defense against aircraft, Patriot was refined to defend against tactical ballistic missiles (TBM). In 1986, it successfully intercepted an Army Lance TBM.[38]

Industry to the Rescue

Time after time, US industry responded to urgent needs of the armed forces in the Gulf War. In one case, the Army needed a software modification to allow the Patriot missile to distinguish an incoming Scud from warhead debris. Raytheon, working completely without a contract, delivered the modification on a rush basis.

[37] Secretary Rice, AFA Symposium.

[38] David Hughes, "Success of Patriot System Shapes Debate on Future Antimissile Weapons," *Aviation Week & Space Technology*, April 22, 1991.

When seven Marines were killed by a Maverick missile launched by an A-10 at Umm Hujul in early February, the need for an "anti-fratricide" identification device became obvious. A Test Systems Incorporated (TSI) engineering technician in New Hampshire, Robert Walleston, learned about the tragedy from a CNN report on television. He sketched out an idea for a battery-powered infrared "beacon" that could be seen through night vision goggles and FLIR.

Meanwhile, Air Force Lt. Gen. Michael Carns asked the Defense Advanced Research Projects Agency to search for a solution. DARPA acquired and tested several versions of the device Walleston had sketched. TSI's product, modified several times, was judged superior to twenty-one other prototypes, and it was on its way to the war zone by February 21. TSI also worked without a formal contract.[39]

In the third case, the Air Force needed a weapon to attack super-hardened and deeply buried Iraqi command and control bunkers. A "quick reaction" team at Eglin AFB, Fla., marshaled the efforts of Lockheed Missile & Space Co. and Texas Instruments to produce it.

The bomb casing, fabricated from surplus Army eight-inch artillery barrels, was machined to the proper size, then fitted with a hardened steel nose cone and a tail plug to protect the fuze. Six hundred and fifty pounds of molten tritonal explosive were poured by a "bucket brigade."

Four of the finished bombs were shipped by air while the explosive was still hot. Two went to Nellis AFB, Nev., for testing, and the other two went to Saudi Arabia for combat use. An existing guidance system was modified by Texas Instruments.

The bomb, designated the GBU-28, was fabricated in just seventeen days. A total of thirty were produced. The formal paperwork came later.

Pointers and Pioneers

During the last week of the Gulf War, thousands of Iraqis surrendered. Virtually all units of the coalition ground forces were taking prisoners. Iraqis popped out of their bunkers, waving white cloths, when they heard helicopters approach, and the helicopters herded prisoners in groups toward collection points.

One of the most unusual surrenders took place when a Pioneer remotely-piloted vehicle droned above the battlefield, surveying potential targets. Five Iraqi soldiers waved white flags at its tiny television camera. It was the first time in history that men surrendered to a robot.

RPVs were used extensively in Desert Shield and Desert Storm, not only by the United States but also by coalition forces. Learning from Israel's clever use of RPVs in overwhelming Syrian air defenses in the 1982 Bekaa Valley operation, the US Navy, Marine Corps, and Army used basically two types of RPVs in the Gulf War, the Pointer and the more sophisticated Pioneer. Both were guided by human controllers who flew the drones by datalink, using video images transmitted back to the launch site by the drones.

The Pointer is battery-powered and weighs nine pounds. A four-member control team launches it into the air by hand. Counting the launch control equipment and the drone, total weight is about forty pounds, so ground troops pack Pointer around with ease. This inexpensive system gives a company-sized unit its own aerial reconnaissance capability, and it was employed by both the Army and Marines in the theater.[40]

The Army, Navy, and Marine Corps employed a larger and more sophisticated system, the Pioneer, developed by the Israelis and produced in the US. Pioneer has a datalink range of 100 nautical miles and a flight duration of five hours. It can carry a multitude of sensors including television and FLIR. The Navy used the Pioneer to adjust gunfire from the battleships *Wisconsin* and *Missouri* and for bomb-damage assessment. The Marines and the Army used it for reconnaissance, surveillance, and target spotting. The Army's 1st UAV [unmanned aerial vehicle] platoon from Ft. Huachuca, Ariz., supported the 82d Airborne with Pioneers in Desert Storm.

Ironies and Anomalies

As William J. Perry, former Under Sec-

[39] Michael Schrage, "War Project Shows Pentagon Procurement Can Be Fast, Flexible," Washington *Post*, June 14, 1991.

[40] Bruce D. Nordwall, "US Relies on Combination of Aircraft, Satellites, UAVs for Damage Assessment," *Aviation Week & Space Technology*, Feb. 4, 1991.

retary of Defense for Research and Development, reminds us, the impressive technology of the Gulf War was not really all that new. "With the exception of Stealth," he says, "the underlying technology of these new weapon systems as well as the components embedded in them can be found in commercial products that have been on the market for five to ten years."[41]

To that, Norman R. Augustine, chairman of Martin Marietta, adds a reminder that we were fortunate to have the technology we did have. He notes that such combat stars as Patriot, LANTIRN, Maverick, and Apache would have been killed in development if the critics had gotten their way and that "we came perilously close to not having 'invisible' airplanes, not owning the night, not having 'smart' munitions that could select the room within a building to hit, not possessing some of the spacecraft that constituted the high ground over the desert, and not having a 'bullet that could hit a bullet.'"[42]

Among the ironies and anomalies of the war were:

• *The Tactical Digital FAX.* In 1990, the Air Force had been widely criticized in the press for purchasing super-rugged facsimile machines that cost far more than the standard fax machines used by most offices and businesses.

Under harsh desert conditions, the Tactical Digital Fax (TDF) demonstrated that its difference went beyond cost.

"During the initial days, the TDFs were the only means of hard copy communications," Lt. Gen. Gordon Fornell of the Electronic Systems Division said. Later, the tough little machines provided a timely and secure way to update target folders without flying them from base to base by airborne courier.

"The extreme temperatures and blowing sand that the machine was designed to withstand were right on target," General Fornell added. "The cases on the commercial faxes we brought over literally melted on the desert runways last August."[43]

• *The Commercial GPS Substitute.* With military models of the GPS receiver in limited supply, US forces made do in many instances with commercial versions. The commercial GPS receivers, however, lack the "selective availability" feature that allows the decoding of encrypted satellite data. Highly accurate information of prime military value is normally encrypted to deny its use to the enemy.

"When we were forced into a quick buy of commercial receivers to support the desert operations, we made a conscious decision to turn [the selective availability] off and risk allowing enemy use," Gen. Donald J. Kutyna, commander in chief of US Space Command, told the Senate. "Iraq was not equipped with smart weapons which might use GPS in their guidance systems, so risk to the coalition forces was minimal. In the light of the startling success and praise heaped on GPS by the troops, this situation will not be prevalent in the future."[44] ■

[41] William J. Perry, "Desert Storm and Deterrence," *Foreign Affairs*, Fall 1991.

[42] Norman R. Augustine, "How We Almost Lost the Technological War," *Wall Street Journal*, June 14, 1991.

[43] Lt. Gen. Gordon E. Fornell, AFA Symposium, Jan. 31–Feb. 1, 1991.

[44] Gen. Donald J. Kutyna, statement to the Senate Armed Services Committee, April 23, 1991.

Air Force forward air controllers use a Navstar Global Position System receiver to navigate in the desert. GPS enabled both air and ground forces to determine their positions precisely and was among the technology success stories of the Gulf War.

USAF Photo by Sgt. Pedro Ybanez

An explosive ordnance disposal team assigned to the 4409th Combat Support Group recovers the remains of a Scud missile northwest of Riyadh. Of all Iraq's military assets, the Scud was used to best advantage, but between F-15Es and Patriot missiles, Iraqi Scuds and launchers were severely inhibited.

10. Combat Logistics and Support

Airmen from the 435th Aircraft Generation Squadron, Rhein-Main AB, Germany, change an engine on a C-130E. The Air Force expected a great effort from its support troops, but got an even greater one.

USAF Photo by MSgt. Jose Lopez

Ground crews turned the F-15s around in seventeen minutes—and that's just part of the story.

The regular standard for "hot pit" turnaround of an F-15 fighter is tough. A well-trained ground crew, making everything click just right, is supposed to refuel and reload an airplane, check it over, and return it to action in twenty to twenty-five minutes.

Support troops in the Gulf War tried hard to beat that standard, and often succeeded. Capt. Brad Gallup, in charge of a maintenance crew from the 71st Tactical Fighter Squadron, said his team always shot for a seventeen-minute turnaround so "we'll have more planes able to go back at them again and again."[1]

That kind of performance—and the attitude behind it—was typical of the support effort in Desert Shield and Desert Storm. One wing deputy commander for operations described the response of the single maintenance person available when aircraft arrived at a remote base:

"The aircraft had to be turned and put on status, so the Chief did the only thing he could do under the circumstances," he said. "He enlisted cooks, cops, and engineers, and had every aircraft ready to go inside an hour."[2]

Air Boss Horner, interviewed in the combat zone shortly after the war ended, had high praise for the people who backed him up. "If I needed an airplane loaded, it got loaded," he said. "If I needed bombs delivered, they got delivered. If I wanted to move a squadron from Base A to Base B, it happened.

"The airplanes stayed in commission. Over ninety percent of the time, they were ready to fly. A normal, reasonable number for this type of activity would be sixty or seventy percent. These guys would not allow the airplane to get broken."[3]

The success of airpower in the Gulf was a function of more than superb aircrews, operating excellent systems, and carrying out an effective plan. Day after day, Air Force effectiveness depended on the achievements, often unheralded, of its mechanics, medics, civil engineers, security policemen, and support troops in all specialties.

"Every time we'd give the logistics people a hard task, they'd succeed," Horner said after the war. "For example, I wanted to get the LANTIRN more into the Scud hunt in the southern part of Iraq, but the F-16Cs were flying out of Al Minhad, in the United Arab Emirates. That was way out on the horn of the UAE [near the Straits of Hormuz]. If I could move them up to King Fahd International Airport, I could get another hour of station time out of them.

"But there was a lot more involved than just moving airplanes. There had to be someplace to park them at the new field. We needed housing for the pilots and, just as important, for the maintenance people who take care of the airplanes. They needed workspaces, too. Was there enough support—jet fuel, and so on—at the new base? Moving a fighter outfit was a complicated undertaking.

"So, one afternoon, I turned to my logistics chief, Col. Bill Rider, and told him I wanted to move the F-16s up where the A-10s were, near Dhahran, so we could get

[1] Stewart M. Powell, "Voices From the War," *Air Force Magazine*, April 1991.

[2] USAF white paper, April 1991.

[3] Richard Mackenzie, "A Conversation With Chuck Horner," *Air Force Magazine*, June 1991.

more sorties and more time over the battlefield out of them.

"'Would you please look into it,' I said, 'and see if there are any show stoppers.' I told my Director of Operations, Jim Crigger, the same thing. The next day, at staff meeting, I said 'How's the move coming?'

"I thought they would say they were working the problem. They responded 'The F-16s are there now!' That's what these young logistics people brought to this war—tremendous enthusiasm and tremendous confidence."[4]

The logistics buildup culminated in the successful deployment, beddown and employment of 1,229 tactical fighters, tactical airlift cargo planes, and reconnaissance aircraft as well as strategic tankers and bombers at twenty-five bases.

More than $1.3 billion worth of "bare base" assets, used to create bases where only runways had existed before, were deployed to support over 55,000 US Air Force people in the Arabian peninsula, the island of Diego Garcia, and Egypt.

Air Force logistics organizations, working through the CENTAF Deputy Chief of Staff for Logistics, Col. William M. Rider, USAF, provided 138.6 million pounds of bombs, missiles, bullets, and other ordnance and 824 million gallons of fuel to support USCENTAF aircraft as they flew 66,128 combat missions. The overall aircraft mission capable rate never dropped below ninety-three percent.[5]

Throughout the war, not only mission-capable rates but also aircraft utilization rates, sortie rates, and other measures of performance were consistently higher than in peacetime.[6]

The support effort was phenomenal, both in the combat zone and at bases back in the United States. In May, the Federal Quality Institute bestowed the 1991 President's Award for Excellence on Air Force Logistics Command. The Air Force community was in full accord with that judgment.[7]

[4] Lt Gen. Charles A. Horner, interview, May 30, 1991.

[5] Col. William M. Rider, interview, Dec. 6, 1991.

[6] Colleen A. Nash, "Desert Storm Logistics," *Air Force Magazine*, May 1991.

[7] John T. Correll, "Let's Hear It for the Loggies," *Air Force Magazine*, August 1991.

Mission Capable Rates

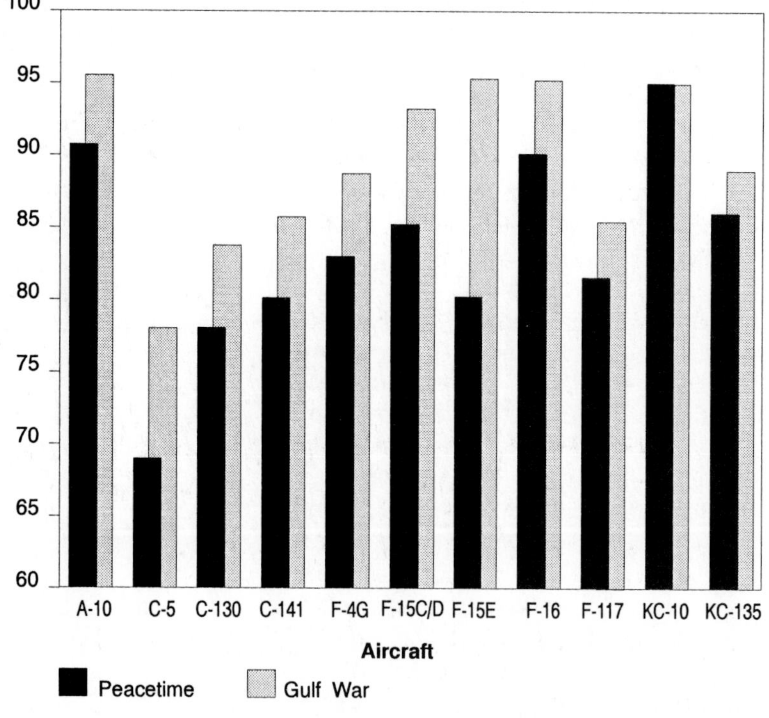

One of the great success stories of Desert Storm is that US Air Force aircraft achieved mission capable rates equal to or better than in peacetime, and did so while flying more sorties per day. Part of this is attributable to the quality of the equipment, but the main explanation is that support troops gave an incredible effort to keep the airplanes flying.

Source: US Air Force.

Delivering Stocks and Equipment

"First, we carried in the 82d Airborne," said Gen. H. T. Johnson, MAC Commander. "Then, within eight days, we had to get the Marines into Saudi to marry up with their heavy equipment, which was coming into Dhahran on the prepositioned ships out of Diego Garcia.

"That's five ships, meeting 16,000 Marines. It takes 250 C-141 loads to carry that many Marines, plus their rifles, helicopters, and other things not transported on the ships. We flew them in from Camp Pendleton, Calif., from Camp Lejeune, N.C., and also from Hawaii. And we got them there on time.

"We did just as well with the Army's 24th Infantry Division. We promised the Army we'd have their thousands of troops there within so many hours before and so many hours after each ship landed; and we did that.

"Another challenge we met was redistributing the huge stocks of equipment that we had prepositioned on the Saudi peninsula. We had to get it from the few places at which we had stored it to units all over the combat zone, and we did that with the C-130s."[8]

"Most of the prepositioned equipment was at Thumrait, in Oman," Colonel Rider, the CENTAF Director of Logistics, explained. "We moved as much of it as we could on the ground. At first, in the early days of Desert Shield, that was tough.

"Our trucks would drive from Oman into the United Arab Emirates, and then into Saudi Arabia. At the border, there might be a customs agent who was not entirely clear about what the cargo was for, and he would refuse permission to enter Saudi Arabia. Sometimes, we'd have twenty-five to thirty trucks loaded with munitions or some other important cargo held up by the customs people.

"And they might stay there for a week or so until we could get proper authority to release it. But we didn't have that problem when we flew the equipment or supplies in by C-130. They landed at military fields well inside Saudi Arabia. Much simpler."[9]

An Early Morning Start

Johnson activated his MAC Crisis Action Team (CAT) August 2. "We got the call somewhere between three and four in the morning (US Central Time)," said CAT Director Col. Daryl L. Bottjer. "The initial information was incomplete, but we formed up and stood by."[10]

The execute order came about seventy-two hours later. "What developed after that was an insatiable thirst for lift that seemed to grow exponentially as the hours went by," Colonel Bottjer said.

"General Schwarzkopf had a very difficult task. He's looking across the border at several armored divisions and mechanized infantry divisions and a very sophisticated air force, and he needs to put in a ground force that will block the Iraqis from moving into Saudi Arabia.

"But that force has to be placed there in such a manner, at specific numbers and types of equipment and with enough speed so that, if Saddam Hussein went south, that force would have a reasonable chance of surviving until they could be reinforced."

Bottjer's CAT scrambled to work an airlift flow to fit the priorities set by CINCCENT. MAC airlift teams started strategic airlift to move people and cargo from the US to Saudi Arabia. US forces were poised, waiting for permission from King Fahd to enter Saudi Arabia. Just before midnight, August 6, permission was granted.

The first MAC C-141 StarLifters departed the US on August 7. The same day, two commercial passenger aircraft took off from Pope AFB, N.C., with troops of the 82d Airborne Division. Their destination was Dhahran.

At 2:45 p.m., Greenwich Mean Time (GMT) August 7, a C-141 from the 437th Military Airlift Wing, tail number 67-0016, took off from Charleston AFB, S.C., and picked up the people and equipment of an Airlift Control Element (ALCE) from the 438th Military Airlift Wing, McGuire AFB, N.J., and flew to Torrejon AB, Spain, where the aircraft was refueled.

A fresh aircrew from the 459th Military Airlift Wing (AFRES), Andrews AFB, Md., took over and flew C-141 67-0016 into Saudi Arabia, landing in Dhahran on August 8 at 9 a.m. GMT. The first USAF aircraft into the combat zone, then, was an active duty C-141 flown by a Reserve aircrew.

It was followed within a few hours by the F-15s of the 1st Tactical Fighter Wing, Langley AFB, Va., and wing support elements in two C-141s, one flown by an Air National Guard crew, the other by an Air Force Reserve crew.

Right behind them, another MAC C-141 brought in the first USCENTCOM command elements from MacDill AFB, Fla., followed quickly by the two commercial contract airliners carrying lead elements of the 82d Airborne.[11]

Check Your MOG

From then on, aircrews of both military and civil transport fleets began to log extra

[8] Gen. H.T. Johnson, interview, Oct. 23, 1991.

[9] Rider interview.

[10] Maj. Sheila L. Tow, "Victory Began With Airlift," MAC, June 12, 1991.

[11] Military Airlift Command Chronology of the Gulf War.

long days flying from the US to Europe, Europe to Saudi Arabia, Saudi Arabia back to Europe, then back to the US.

Typical flying time from a US east coast air base to Spain or Germany was eight hours, followed by eight hours to Saudi Arabia, nine hours back to Europe, and then nine hours returning to the east coast.

"The challenge was something called MOG: Maximum on the Ground," Johnson said. "Too many airplanes in one place at the same time could slow up, or even stop, the flow. What was really important, though, was throughput. If your MOG is six, but you can get them refueled and out in an hour, then you can put an awful lot of airplanes through.

"In the end, Dhahran and King Fahd International Airport could handle sixty airplanes, big airplanes, per day. But that meant we had to unload them, fix any problems, refuel them, put on any retrograde cargo and people and get out, so there was room for follow-on aircraft.

"We couldn't park airplanes in the AOR. That meant we had to have crews to move them back out. Here's what we did. We'd fly a StarLifter or Galaxy from the United States to Torrejon or Rhein-Main. We also used Zaragosa and Ramstein.

"After refueling, a fresh crew would fly the aircraft into the AOR, stay with it during the unloading and reloading, and then fly it back to Europe. The normal crew day was sixteen hours.

"We went to twenty hours, and then, augmenting the crew with an extra pilot, twenty-four, or more. One crew had a thirty-nine hour crew day, but that was a real exception.

"The extra pilot flew between Europe and Saudi Arabia, and the crews, after resting in Europe, would fly back to the States to do it all over again."[12]

Capt. Joseph M. Jose, an aircraft commander in the 438th Military Airlift Wing, McGuire AFB, N.J., describes his first Desert Shield mission: "We flew some Marines into the AOR. We landed at Thumrait, in Oman, and then flew on to Masirah, an island off the coast of Oman, where we dropped them off.

"Then, we refueled and returned to Rhein-Main. We had a thirty-hour duty day. I was pretty excited about the whole thing, to tell the truth. It was a lot of hard work, but you are motivated because you are doing something worthwhile.

"I thought, 'hey, we're working hard but a lot of guys in this war have it worse than us.'"[13]

Capt. Tony Senci, also in the 438th MAW, flew many missions into the AOR but remembers one particularly: "It was a pitch black night. I was part of an augmented crew. We thought we had traffic coming across our flight path, not too close. It looked like a real airplane, a few blinking lights showing.

"The first pilot called out the traffic and then, it exploded. It was a Scud. We heard the radios at Riyadh and Dhahran: 'Condition Red!' 'Take Cover!' We knew we weren't in any real danger and laughed a bit because there were other C-141s on the ground and their crews probably had to scramble away and jump into a ditch. We made a little joke out of it."[14]

Call for More Airlift

Within the first few days of Desert Shield, the magnitude of the airlift requirements exceeded the ability of the active duty force to support it. "In the initial days, we got a tremendous number of volunteers from the Reserve component—both the Air Force Reserve and the Air National Guard," said Colonel Bottjer. "But even that was insufficient, so we began calling up Reserve units.

By the middle of August, ninety-five percent of MAC's C-5s and ninety percent of the C-141s were "flying the pipeline." More than 100 civilian airline missions had been contracted. It wasn't enough.

On August 17, General Johnson activated Stage I of the Civil Reserve Air Fleet (CRAF). Sixteen civilian airlines provided thirty-eight airliners (seventeen passenger and twenty-one cargo aircraft).[15]

"The enormity of this airlift struck me immediately," said Michael Carlozzi, an American Trans Air pilot. "You could have walked across the Mediterranean on the

[12] Johnson interview, Oct. 23, 1991.

[13] Capt. Joseph M. Jose, interview, Aug. 4, 1991.

[14] Capt. Tony Senci, interview, Aug. 4, 1991.

[15] Military Airlift Command Chronology of the Gulf War.

wings of C-5s, C-141s, and commercial aircraft moving across the region. The air flow was that heavy."[16]

The flow of aircraft began to clog the pipeline. "Too many were going through the system at once," said Maj. Bruce Babb. "Bases were becoming backlogged. They could not support the magnitude of the flow we were putting together.

"Sometimes, as many as twenty-eight aircraft were on the ground, trying to unload and refuel, at the same time. Once you get the system that backlogged, you have to stop the flow."

MAC and its subsidiary command, 21st Air Force, set up a system of time slots for missions to depart the staging bases, Rhein-Main AB and Ramstein AB in Germany and Torrejon AB and Zaragosa AB in Spain.

"We developed a log with the stage locations and listed separate slot times at each base," said Babb. "Every time, we scheduled a mission number by a slot time. That way, we made certain too many aircraft didn't land at any base at the same time."

Meanwhile, at the expanding number of airfields in Saudi Arabia, ramp space and servicing systems were becoming saturated by the huge volume of aircraft arriving or passing through—fighters, helicopters, as well as MAC transports.

"As new fields opened up, they enhanced our capabilities. But several of those fields didn't have fuel," said Colonel Bottjer. "So, you'd drop off your passengers and cargo and then go to a base that did have fuel.

"We got through it. It worked. It was like starting out with a hose with an eight-inch opening in the US and going down to one with a two-inch opening in Saudi Arabia."

In August alone, MAC moved more than 106 million pounds of cargo and transported more than 72,000 people 7,000 miles into the Gulf War zone.[17]

Keep Them Flying

By September 11, sustainment—keeping the forces supplied—became a main objective. Keeping the airplanes flying became tougher, too, because so many (more than 2,000 missions in August) were being flown.

The people maintaining C-130s discovered that the adverse weather and the sand in the area of operations (AOR) were increasing wear and tear on the aircraft. "The soil is a very, very fine powder and it contains a lot of salt," said Col. David C. Davis, chief of Maintenance Management Division at MAC.

MAC maintainers found a new lubricant for use in the desert environment and instituted special precautions for lubricating equipment exposed to the highly corrosive sand.

From September to January, MAC set up an aeromedical evacuation system to accommodate the projected number (still classified) of killed and wounded to be removed from the combat zone. "The plan," Colonel Bottjer said, "was to withdraw casualties from Saudi Arabia and transport them to Germany, the United Kingdom, and the United States. Medical evacuation units from the Air National Guard and Air Force Reserve were activated.

"We also created a program to carry human remains out and enhanced the mortuary facilities at Dover AFB, Del.," Bottjer said. "Fortunately, we didn't have to use either program—aeromedical or mortuary—very much."

In November, President Bush announced a doubling of forces in the AOR. MAC's projected requirements skyrocketed. "In this phase, we actually exceeded what we thought was the ability of the force to fly," said Bottjer.

"We stayed at our high rate of operations longer than anybody ever dreamed we could and longer than our textbooks tell us we can and longer than the war plans tell us we should. And we sustained that rate through all of December, January, and well into February."

By the middle of December, sixty-five aircraft a day were delivering up to 8,000 troops at sixteen different airfields. A strategic airlift transport plane was landing every twenty-two minutes. During Desert Storm, the peak would be 127 aircraft landing each day, or one every eleven minutes.[18]

[16] Tow, "Victory Began With Airlift."

[17] Tow.

[18] USAF white paper, September 1991.

Secretary of Defense Cheney declared an airlift emergency on January 17 and authorized activation of the second stage of CRAF, which provided up to sixty additional civilian passenger planes and nineteen cargo aircraft. "We didn't need passenger planes this time as much as we needed cargo capability," General Johnson said. MAC initially did not contract for the authorized number of passenger planes, but eventually used many of them for cargo.

Ultimately, a total of 158 civilian aircraft were contracted by MAC for the strategic airlift mission.[19]

"In addition," Johnson said, "we received *gratis* airlift from the Japanese, which hired US airlines to fly for them. They also hired Maarten Air, which is a Dutch carrier.

"We had help from Korean Air Lines. They would use their cargo flights returning to Korea to carry our cargo from New York to Dover AFB, Del., down to the Persian Gulf, and then continue on east back to Korea.

"Luxembourg provided cargo space for us on Cargo Lux. So we had some help from other countries that is not generally known."[20]

C-130 Herculean Effort

By the end of January, 151 MAC C-130s had been deployed to the theater of operations for tactical airlift. The "Herky-Birds" continued to haul the beans and bullets of the war, picking up supplies from major military bases in Saudi Arabia and hauling them to front-line units all along the border.

Throughout the Gulf region, the C-130 filled theater airlift requirements. By October, C-130s were lifting people and cargo into every major CENTCOM base and many remote locations. In the intratheater airlift system, "Camel" missions moved primarily cargo, "Star" missions mainly passengers. These aircraft were scheduled regularly throughout the AOR.

For Desert Shield and Desert Storm, C-130s flew almost 47,000 sorties, delivering more than 300,000 tons of cargo and 209,000 troops.[21]

In February, MAC combat controllers set up portable navigation aids and brightly colored panels to mark highway sections to be used as runways in northwest Saudi Arabia, along the Iraqi border.[22]

Thanks to US Air Force airlift, sealift, and CENTCOM's in-theater logistics system, American forces in the Gulf War were better supplied, better maintained, and better supported than any American forces in any previous war.[23]

"Eighty-five percent of the dry cargo went by sea," Johnson said. "From the States and Europe, we shipped 500,000 tons by air and 3.9 million tons by sea. In addition, an incredible 6.9 million tons of petroleum, oil and lubricants (POL) went by sea, but a lot of that came from Saudi Arabia and went directly to our forces supporting the Gulf War. Ninety-five percent of cargo went by sea if you count POL."

When coalition ground forces began to pour into Iraq and Kuwait late on the night of February 23 and early morning of February 24, a MAC combat controller team was with each Army and Marine division.

Strategic Airlift Maintenance

During the war, the strategic airlifters, C-5 Galaxies and C-141 StarLifters, flew four times as many hours as they fly in peacetime. They carried the bulk of the airlifted cargo—513,000 tons. Desert Storm cargo missions took seventy-five percent of the C-5s and eighty percent of the C-141s in the fleet. This brought unprecedented demands on the maintenance people.[24]

Depot maintenance was accelerated on seventy airlifters and fighters (twelve C-5s, forty-one C-141s, and seventeen fighters) to provide the commands operating them nearly 1,000 extra flying days.

The movement of many Air Force units to southwest Asia increased the demand for parts to fill the war readiness spares kits that accompany deploying units. The kits contain enough spare parts to keep a squadron (up to twenty-four aircraft) flying for thirty days, or until a permanent supply line can be established.

Some kits are large enough to fill a half

[19] MAC Chronology of the Gulf War.

[20] Johnson interview.

[21] USAF white paper, September 1991.

[22] Tow, "Victory Began With Airlift."

[23] USAF white paper, September 1991.

[24] "AFLC Operations in Desert Storm," Air Force Logistics Command white paper, July 1991.

dozen tractor trailers. But many of these kits were not fully equipped. To fill them out, AFLC expedited maintenance on more than 90,000 critical parts. In addition, maintaining routine support for the accelerated Desert Storm flying meant providing 60,000 more parts per month than in peacetime.

To meet critical wartime requirements, engines were rebuilt twenty to sixty days faster than in peacetime. The Air Logistics Centers at Oklahoma City, Okla., and San Antonio, Tex., overhaul the majority of the thousands of engines in the Air Force. Oklahoma City accelerated repair on 221 engines, and San Antonio did another forty-five, plus 559 major engine sections.

Parts From the Boneyard

B-52s flew 1,624 missions and delivered more than 25,700 tons of munitions on area targets in the AOR.[25] The Aircraft Maintenance and Regeneration Center at Davis Monthan AFB, Ariz., yielded 424 parts for B-52s, saving both time and money over new purchases. Older model B-52s, stored at the Center because they are too valuable to scrap, become donors of expensive or no longer available parts.

More than 1,700 Air Force Logistics Command people deployed, both in the US and overseas, during Desert Storm. Some 810 reservists were mobilized to augment AFLC units; fifty-five deployed to the Gulf.

A number were Air National Guard or Air Force Reserve medical people who filled in at AFLC hospitals when their active duty counterparts were deployed overseas. Others included intelligence specialists, trans-portation people, security police, chaplains, and explosive ordnance disposal personnel.

Building Cities

More than 120 AFLC civil engineers, in addition to erecting tents and dining halls, literally helped to build cities in the desert to house the thousands of Air Force people coming into the combat zone. To accommodate a new fighter wing at Al Kharj, for example, they helped local engineering people build roads and construct water and sewage facilities, install generators and string electric lines for a base population of more than 5,000 people.

In two weeks, they also constructed a storage area complete with roads, concrete storage pads, and hardened bunkers to hold five and a half million pounds of munitions.[26]

"In twenty-six days," Colonel Rider said, "we had a base for 125 fighters, about eighteen C-130s and a ramp for unloading the strategic airlifters, the C-141s, and the C-5s."

Col. Hal Hornburg, commander of the 4th Wing (Provisional) commented, "when we got there, the tallest things on the base were the two-inch high taxiway lights. What a difference a few weeks made."[27]

Throughout Saudi Arabia, Air Force civil engineers erected more than 5,000 tents, most of them air-conditioned, constructed more than 300,000 square feet of buildings, and laid more than 500,000 square meters of concrete and asphalt foundations, ramps, roads, and walkways. Community support specialists, among other things, served more than 20 million meals.

A typical base, erected by "Red Horse" and "Prime Beef" engineering teams and Saudi contractors, consisted of 380 tents, four field kitchens, a fifty-bed hospital, tactical field laundry, nineteen latrine and shower facilities, and a tactical field exchange. US engineers supplied their own electrical power at these bases.[28]

Repairing Battle Damage

Aircraft battle damage repair teams take charge of an aircraft damaged in combat, inspect it and decide whether it can be returned to combat or used as a source of parts to repair other aircraft. Their motto is "One More Flight."

The first team deployed with the F-15s out of Langley AFB, Va. Depending on the aircraft and team members' specialties, teams range from five to thirty-four persons. A total of forty-two teams, each of which included an aeronautical engineer, engine specialists and airframe experts, were deployed during Desert Storm.[29]

The teams operate in the field with wing

[25] USAF white paper, April 1991.

[26] AFLC white paper.

[27] Col. Hal Hornburg, interview, May 31, 1991.

[28] USAF white paper, April 1991.

[29] AFLC white paper.

battle damage experts like TSgt. Richard W. Somerfeldt, a structural repair technician with the 511th TFW, RAF Alconbury, in the United Kingdom. He was deployed to King Fahd International Airport. "We operated out of a trailer that really was a mobile machine shop," explained Sergeant Somerfeldt.

"Each trailer was fitted out for the aircraft we were supporting, with generators, compressors, soldering irons, and whatever else we needed. We worked twelve-hour shifts.

"The first battle damage we had was caused by a bullet. An A-10 actually ran into the bullet, which was on its downward trajectory. It came in through the top of the wing leading edge. It only pierced the primary, outer, skin of the wing and slightly dented the secondary structure inside, and it rattled around in there.

"We recovered the bullet in almost perfect condition and gave it to the pilot as a souvenir. He didn't know he'd been hit. We had the aircraft fully mission capable and ready to go in less than nine hours."

"Right after the A-10," Sergeant Somerfeldt recalled, "we had a transient F-16. He'd been nicked pretty well by a SAM just as he was pulling off his target. He had come into King Fahd because it was the closest base.

"He had sporadic damage under the engine intake, but some of the shrapnel had penetrated right through the intake and came up under the cockpit floor. It took out a couple environmental lines, too.

"Farther back, he had some small shrapnel holes in the skin, but there wasn't much electrical or hydraulic damage. The major worry was a hole through his left wing. He was losing fuel out of it. We conferred with the engineers and the McClellan ALC people about the damage.

"They performed a generic repair right out of the Aircraft Battle Damage Manual, did a few other temporary fixes, and the pilot flew the bird back to his home base."[30]

[30] TSgt. Richard W. Somerfeldt, interview, Aug. 8, 1991.

The A-10, operating at low level against tanks and in close support of ground forces, took more damage than any other aircraft in the war. The severity of it sometimes necessitated repairs that normally would be performed at Stateside depot repair facilities, 8,000 miles away.

One A-10 returned from a mission with 380 shrapnel and bullet holes. It was patched up and returned to full combat readiness. Two others had most of their tail sections shot away, while another lost most of its right wing. They were quickly repaired and flew missions again.

Another aircraft returned with its center wing section too badly damaged for repair. It had to be replaced. This is a complicated depot-level job, not performed at an operational base, not even in the United States. In this case, the wing was removed on the ramp in Saudi Arabia, and replaced with a wing from a trainer in the States—in eight days.

At another base, F-15 maintenance people reported cracks in the leading edges of vertical stabilizers (rudders). An F-15 AFLC battle damage repair team notified Warner Robins ALC, and within a week, repair kits had been assembled and shipped to Saudi. The team, with wing maintenance people, repaired the cracks on more than fifteen aircraft. Battle damage repair teams returned thirty aircraft to service, including A-10s, F-15s, F-16s, B-52s, and C-130s. They also repaired one Army UH-60 helicopter.

Since 1984, AFLC's Aerospace Guidance and Metrology Center at Newark AFB, Ohio, had been developing a portable calibration lab for ensuring the accuracy of "smart" weapon guidance systems. During Desert Shield, in September 1990, the first portable lab deployed.

Through the war, technicians in this lab calibrated aircraft and missile systems along with myriad other instruments that ordinarily would have been returned to home base or a stateside depot. They even calibrated guidance systems of the Army's Patriot missiles, sustaining their accuracy.

The first E-3 Sentry Airborne Warning and Control System (AWACS) deployed on the first day of Desert Shield, and controlled the air war. Tinker AFB, Okla., is not only the home base for the AWACS unit but also the air logistics center that manages the aircraft. A single office, "Sentry Control Point," tracked more than 600 critical parts, ensuring that no E-3s were grounded for parts during Desert Shield/ Storm.[31]

Heads on the Horizon

Parts and components required special packaging so they could be shipped back to depots for repairs, and large incoming shipments had to be broken down and repackaged for shipment to individual requesting units. This work was performed by people like Sgt. Pamela Fripp, who deployed to Al Kharj, Saudi Arabia, from Bitburg AB, Germany.

"We performed the same job we did at Bitburg, but there was more urgency to it because we were in the war zone," Fripp said.[32] "We had to be prepared for anything. We worked hard to expedite shipments coming in or going out. Parts being shipped out for repair were always moved on an urgent basis."

"When we first got there, we worked twelve hours a day, seven days a week," she said. "At first, we had to scrounge plywood, two by fours, and other materials, to get our packaging done. We had hammers, nails, things like that. Then, in a very short time, we began to get all the reusable containers and other shipping materials we needed. We kept stuff moving in and out as fast it could be moved."

Being in the supply business meant doing any job that needed doing. "The second day of the war,I got temporarily augmented to the Security Police," said SSgt. Edward W. Kirk, Jr., a stock control and requisitions NCO from Bitburg.

"I found myself sitting in a bunker with a reservist from Syracuse, N.Y., way out on the end of the Al Kharj flight line. He had an M-16 and one clip with thirty rounds in it.

"Suddenly, on the horizon, we could see heads bobbing up and down. We didn't know what it was, but it was a long line, with maybe thirty heads moving up and down. It looked like something was going to happen.

"The reservist, who was in charge, called for backup and the cops came down and they set up a perimeter with their Humvees and their M-16s and their grenade launchers and everything else. They were all pretty excited, watching that line of heads bobbing toward us, and I was scared.

"It turned out to be a herd of camels wandering by. It was the second day of the war. We expected an attack at any moment."[33]

Fuel, Radios, and Other Solutions

The rapid fighter deployment to the Gulf, the massive airlift, and the operational tempo of the war were critically dependent on aerial refueling tankers provided by Strategic Air Command.

SAC deployed 256 KC-135s and forty-six KC-10s to the war zone. During the Desert Shield buildup, these tankers refueled 14,588 receivers, including Navy and Marine Corps aircraft. During the six weeks of Desert Storm, they refueled 45,955.

[31] AFLC white paper.

[32] Sgt. Pamela Fripp, interview, Aug. 6, 1991.

[33] SSgt. Edward W. Kirk, Jr., interview, Aug. 6, 1991.

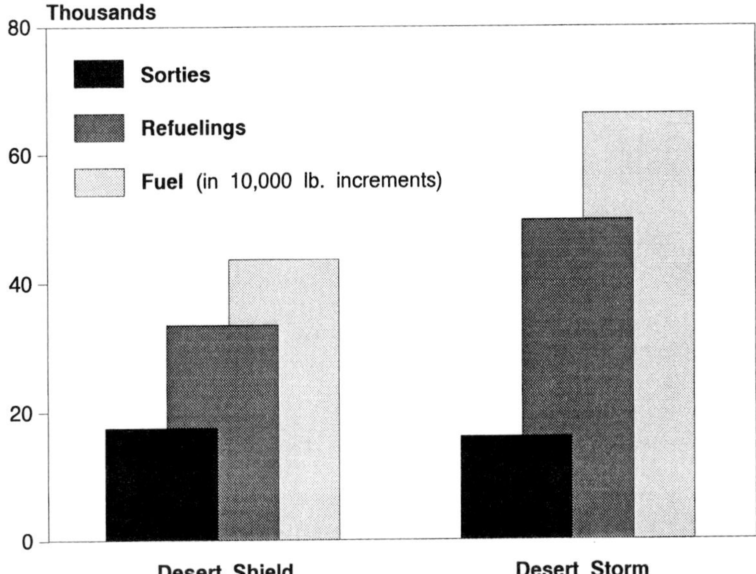

Air Force tankers refueled USAF, Navy, and Marine aircraft. One pilot said "there was more gas in the sky over Saudi than in the ground below."

As one F-15 pilot said about tanker accessibility, "there was more gas in the sky over Saudi than in the ground below."[34]

Forty percent of the aircraft refueling from the tankers were Tactical Air Command fighters and AWACS. In presenting his command's 1991 Spaatz trophy to the tankers who flew that extraordinary "air bridge," Gen. John M. Loh, commander of TAC, noted that the fact that it was done completely without incident had been a remarkable feat of airmanship.

"When I was the SAC IG [Inspector General], I looked at every single tanker outfit in the command and the fact that they always got 1.0, absolutely perfect scores, used to bother me," said Gen. George L. Butler, SAC commander. "I said, we cannot be doing this right. Our criteria are not tough enough. But you know, when the right test came—combat—they were 1.0."[35]

"Hardly a shooter in the AOR could get to the target and back without inflight refueling," said Col. Richard W. Salisbury, who commanded ten tankers which were part of his 1700th Strategic Wing (Provisional) at Riyadh.[36] Other tankers were based at King Khalid International Airport at Jiddah, on the Red Sea, and a half dozen other locations.

"In the forty-three days of the air war, the ten aircraft of the 1700th wing flew 480 successful refueling flights," Salisbury said. "That is a tremendous utilization rate."

At the beginning of Operation Desert Storm, more than 230 KC-135 Stratotankers and KC-10 Extenders were based in the combat zone. Eventually, some 300 tankers, half the total possessed by the Air Force, were involved in Gulf War operations.[37]

Refueling in the combat zone was always done under complete radio silence, said TSgt. Mark E. Sletten, a boom operator in the 350th Air Refueling Squadron, based at Riyadh. "This made it really exciting, especially on nights when we were doing post strike refueling of the F-117s. They flew long missions, which took a lot of gas. When they came back out, they wanted that fuel right away.

"We had a small floodlight on top of the tail. The F-117 was a black plane and it would come at you out of the black night. Suddenly, one would just be there, visible out my rear window in the dim glow of the floodlight. I'd signal him into proper position by flashing the pilot director lights and then fly the boom down to his inflight refueling receptacle.

"Once the boom made contact in the receptacle, I could talk to the pilot on intercom. Usually, he'd say he was glad to see my tanker. He'd get his gas and the boom would automatically disconnect. By that time, his wingman would have arrived, and I'd fill him up, too. They always sounded relieved to get that gas. I was proud to pump it to them."[38]

In the early going, however, the supporters needed some support themselves. When the crisis began, the KC-135s did not have radios that enabled them to talk to many of the aircraft of allied countries.

This made inflight refueling difficult and, to a degree, dangerous. In less than a month, logistics people located a suitable radio. The radios were installed in 120 KC-135s already operating in Saudi Arabia. The radio installation team then moved to Moron AB, Spain, and installed radios on all KC-135s en route to the Gulf.

To a downed pilot, a hand-held emergency radio is the ticket to rescue. With it, the pilot can guide rescue aircraft to his location.

When the first allied pilots were shot down over Iraq, it became apparent that the Iraqis were able to monitor the few fixed frequencies of US survival radios and determine the location of downed coalition aircrews. On at least one occasion, they got to the allied pilot before rescue forces arrived.

Sacramento ALC quickly developed and fielded a modification for 1,000 survival radios to give them a variable frequency capability, foiling the Iraqis' attempts to reach the downed pilots ahead of coalition rescuers.

It is difficult enough to repair aircraft when the temperature on a Saudi Arabian ramp is 120 degrees. Add a rubber chemical warfare suit with gas mask, and heat stroke becomes a real danger.

[34] USAF white paper, April 1991.

[35] Gen. John M. Loh and Gen. George L. Butler, AFA symposium, Jan. 31, 1992.

[36] Col. Richard W. Salisbury, interview, July 17, 1991.

[37] Gen. Merrill A. McPeak, Pentagon news briefing, March 15, 1991.

[38] TSgt. Mark E. Sletten, interview, July 17, 1991.

Air Force Systems Command's Human Resources Laboratory designed a cooling system built around a standard aircraft ground air conditioning unit. It allowed up to ten persons to connect an adaptor vest, worn under their chemical warfare suits, to a hose that provided cooled, filtered air. After cooling off near their aircraft, they could return to work. The San Antonio Air Logistics Center, working with the Human Resources Lab and using an innovative new contracting program, brought the complete system from prototype to deployment in less than four months.

By the end of December, 370 cooling units and 13,000 vests, enough for everyone working around American aircraft, had been shipped to the AOR.

All over the AOR, blowing sand scratched soft plastic canopies and windshields. Scratches create glare spots, and glare can hide enemy aircraft—with fatal results.

Soft cloth protective covers simply trapped blowing sand between the cover and the plastic. Within two weeks, Sacramento ALC designed a rigid fiberglass cover for the F-15E that fits over the canopy and windshield without touching the plastic.

In addition to providing the needed protection from scratches, there was a bonus—the cover kept the cockpits relatively cool as the aircraft sat on the ramp in the hot sun between missions.

As the forces grew, so did the need for vehicles. At the beginning of the war, some 3,400 vehicles were already prepositioned in theater. AFLC located and redistributed another 2,100 from Air Force locations worldwide. These included refuelers, materials handling equipment, base maintenance and construction vehicles, fire trucks and others.

A majority of additional vehicles came from prepositioned War Reserve stocks in Europe. Units in the Gulf leased some vehicles locally. At the beginning of Desert Storm, there were more than 9,000 US Air Force vehicles in the theater of operations.[39]

Expediting the Supply Line

As the air war intensified in January, port facilities were strained. Some munitions stored aboard ships could not be unloaded fast enough to keep up with demand. This threatened a sudden critical shortage of some types of bombs.

The Ogden, Utah, Air Logistic Center prepared munitions shipments, and MAC airlifted more than 11,000 bombs (3,600 tons) into Saudi Arabia. The airlift continued round-the-clock for three weeks. No other operation in Air Force history moved more munitions further or faster in such a short period.

San Antonio ALC was the collection and departure point for other critically needed munitions that were delivered direct from the factory. Many civilian contract aircraft, not primarily configured to carry cargo, were employed to carry the munitions.

This meant many of the standard shipping packages had to be modified to fit these aircraft. The packages were modified without delaying a single shipment. In all, AFLC pipelined 577,000 tons of additional munitions and components to the theater to supplement supplies that had been prepositioned in the years before the war.[40]

Once Air Force bases had been established, a ground transportation system between them was needed to augment the airlift. Ground transportation of freight was supposed to be provided by the Army, but it never materialized.

"I remembered hearing about the Red Ball Express the US Army ran in World War Two," Colonel Rider said. "Hundreds of dedicated trucks rushed spare parts and equipment wherever they were needed in a hurry." He decided to duplicate the operation in Saudi Arabia.

"Since this was to be an Air Force operation, I decided to call it the Blue Ball Express," he said. Colonel Rider rented 100 Saudi trucks and requested 200 drivers from the States.

The drivers were obtained through the command post of "CENTAF Rear," who was Maj. Gen. Michael E. Ryan, Tactical Air Command's Deputy Chief of Staff for Operations, at Langley AFB, Va.

[39] AFLC white paper.

[40] AFLC white paper.

Ryan's staff identified 200 volunteer drivers in less than a week. The drivers were deployed to Saudi Arabia.

"They moved everything from equipment to fuel to water to munitions," Colonel Rider said. "About forty percent of the material moved between Air Force bases in Saudi Arabia after November 1990, traveled on the Blue Ball Express," he estimated.[41]

The cargo pallet, a simple device, almost became a critical problem. For military air shipment, everything not on its own wheels is packed onto standard size military pallets and tied down with webbed cargo nets.

Cargo-handling machinery is designed to handle loads on pallets, so the number of pallets proliferated along with the expansion of Desert Storm logistics. Thousands of pallets, laden with cargo and equipment, were arriving in the Gulf. Some remained there, and others could not be sent back to the US right away because the material on them was awaiting delivery to other points in the AOR. More pallets were coming in than were going out.

A pallet shortage soon loomed in the United States. "I spent a lot of time worrying about pallets and nets, that is, the things we load onto aircraft that carry our supplies and equipment," Gen. Charles C. McDonald, commander of Air Force Logistics Command, said later. "We were managing those things on a day-to-day, even hour-to-hour basis, because we were short, and we were especially short because we weren't getting them back from the theater as rapidly as we should have."[42]

Logisticians in the AOR took aggressive action to locate pallets and ship them back to the States. Additional pallets were borrowed from allied forces and units not directly participating in the war, and damaged pallets, when possible, were quickly repaired. More than 40,000 new pallets and nets were purchased under contract. The combined result was that no shortage developed.[43]

At Ogden ALC, the security police squadron serviced and packed 2,400 weapons for deployment in twelve days. Several "bare base" kits of portable buildings, utilities and their accessories, everything needed for a 1,200-person air base except runways—were shipped from Warner Robins ALC.

Knowing the location of the part ordered was a big problem in the beginning. Commanders cannot plan operations unless they know when and how much of their equipment is available. In less than five weeks after the first deployments, drawing from reports on transportation and parts supply status, AFLC people developed a computerized tracking system to monitor individual parts from the time they were ordered until they were delivered to the combat unit that needed them.

A single database was formed. It could be accessed by anyone—provider, transporter, or recipient—with a desktop computer and a phone line connection. Parts could also be diverted to a different recipient if priorities changed.

Extra airlift support was needed to move all the parts and equipment from origination points in the US to ports and aerial ports for shipment overseas. AFLC contracted 488 extra missions on its Logistics Airlift (LOGAIR), its civilian contract airlift operation, which normally operates cargo routes between fifty-six locations in CONUS. An additional twenty-one locations were added during Desert Shield. More than half the extra missions moved war reserve materiel (WRM) directly to Army and Air Force units preparing to deploy from their home stations to the war zone.[44]

The materiel flow strained aerial port facilities almost to the breaking point. New equipment was procured for four major aerial ports: Dover AFB, Del., Tinker AFB, Okla., Travis AFB, Calif., and McGuire AFB, N.J.

Dover needed it because outbound tonnage jumped from 200 tons per day to 750 tons per day, and the original equipment could handle only 450 tons per day.

McGuire's cargo operations surged from forty tons a day to more than 135 tons, much of it mail for the troops in the theater.[45]

Several of the coalition forces use American equipment. An International Logistics

[41] Rider interview.

[42] McDonald, AFA symposium, Jan. 31, 1992.

[43] AFLC white paper.

[44] AFLC white paper.

[45] AFLC white paper.

Center expedited deliveries of spare parts and equipment to those coalition armed services. More than a billion dollars worth of spares, support equipment, and munitions was provided, principally to Saudi Arabia, Bahrain, Oman, United Arab Emirates, Canada, Germany, and the United Kingdom.

"Desert Express"

At first, even critically needed parts took sixteen days to get from the United States to units in Saudi Arabia.

On October 30, MAC launched the first daily "Desert Express" mission out of Charleston AFB, S.C. "Desert Express was conjured up," General Johnson said, "because we were having difficulty getting critical spare parts into the AOR. We decided we ought to have some way to provide those parts very quickly and with tremendous reliability.

"We decided to use organic [MAC-owned, as opposed to contracted] air, the C-141, and to operate out of a base that had civilian as well as military service. We chose Charleston AFB, S.C.

"The result was Desert Express, which guaranteed that priority cargo delivered to MAC at Charleston by 10:30 a.m. would be placed on a C-141 that would take off at 12:30 p.m., refuel in Spain, and land in Dhahran, Saudi Arabia, seventeen and a half hours later."

During the Gulf War, only two flights were not completed, one because of bad weather and another because of a ban on incoming flights at the start of Desert Storm. No "Desert Express" shipment was late. More than 25,000 shipments of critical parts traveled on time via Desert Express.[46]

On December 8, reflecting the increased tempo of the buildup, MAC initiated the first "European Desert Express" mission out of Rhein-Main AB, Germany, providing daily delivery of high priority items to Saudi Arabia in eight hours.

By January 16, the day before Desert Storm was unleashed, MAC strategic airlift had flown more than 10,600 missions in the AOR, delivering more than 397,000 passengers and more than 366,000 tons of cargo.

Rapid airlift became important in yet another way when Saddam Hussein began lobbing Scud missiles into Tel Aviv and Haifa. The Israelis did not have an operational defense in place. At 1:15 a.m. GMT, January 19, MAC was ordered to transport, as expeditiously as possible, Patriot missiles to Israel to intercept the Iraqi Scuds.

Sixteen missiles already aboard a C-141 on the way to Saudi Arabia were diverted to Israel in eleven hours, and another eight were flown in from Europe, to provide a full-up operational Patriot missile in Israel by 9:45 p.m., GMT the same day.

By February 28, when the shooting war officially ended, MAC had flown more than 15,000 strategic airlift missions, transporting more than 483,000 passengers and more than 521,000 tons of cargo.[47]

The Store in the Desert

Throughout the Saudi desert, from the summer of 1990 through the early spring of 1991, the Army and Air Force Exchange Service (AAFES) set up exchanges to support the men and women serving in Desert Shield and Desert Storm. Servicemen and women were able to buy consumer goods from AAFES exchanges set up in tents.

Within fifteen days of the start of Desert Shield, AAFES set up thirty field exchanges in Saudi to support Army, Air Force, and Marine units deployed there. At the peak, there were 152 unit exchanges, which were run by exchange people from the home bases of the units in the States. In addition, AAFES ran seventeen direct operations in Saudi Arabia, staffed by fifty-nine AAFES civilians.

The first unit exchange arrived in Saudi in early September, shortly after the 354th Tactical Fighter Wing, from Myrtle Beach AFB, S.C., deployed. AAFES workers brought BX merchandise with them.

A typical unit exchange was the BX "Dhahran Express," a tactical field exchange operated by the Air Force Commissary Service for members of the Air National Guard's 136th Tactical Airlift Wing, from Hensley Field, near Dallas, Tex.

The BX was housed in an ordinary US military desert tent. Inside were handmade

[46] AFLC white paper.

[47] MAC Chronology of the Gulf War.

plywood shelves and tables filled with an assortment of pudding, crackers, chips, cookies, T-shirts, innersoles, shampoo, toothpaste and toiletries. In the back were stacked cases of cold soda.

By the end of February 1991, a full-fledged distribution center was in place, handling 1,006 different items, with an inventory worth $162 million. Soldiers who could not visit one of the exchanges could order goods electronically by laptop computer.[48]

Medics and Hospitals

"We thought we would need a lot of aeromedical evacuation people," said MAC's General Johnson. "Ninety-two percent of the aeromedical people are in the reserve forces. We put out a call for members to report to McGuire AFB, N.J. We were oversubscribed. They literally had to draw straws at McGuire to see who got the honor of living in the sand for ninety days."

In a very short time, the largest collection of medical people in American history was assembled in the Gulf. The first of fifteen Air Transportable Hospitals, with fifty beds, was set up in Saudi Arabia, ready to receive patients, less than two weeks after Saddam's invasion of Kuwait. These hospitals, together with a 250-bed contingency hospital, provided the primary Air Force medical support in the AOR.[49]

More than 6,200 active-duty medical people and 5,500 from the Air Reserve Components deployed to Europe or to the AOR. The Reserve forces also provided more than 6,600 people to augment military medical facilities in the United States. During Desert Shield and Desert Storm, medical facilities in the AOR handled 130,000 outpatient visits and 3,500 admissions.

The only contingency hospitals outside the AOR for Desert Shield/Desert Storm were those of the US Air Forces in Europe. In August, USAFE was tasked to provide 3,740 hospital beds.

The USAFE Command Surgeon met the requirement by expanding four peacetime treatment facilities and activating four USAFE "mothballed" contingency hospitals at RAF Bicester, RAF Little Rissington, and RAF Nocton Hall in the United Kingdom and at Zweibrücken, Germany.

By November 14, Bicester, Little Rissington, and Zweibrücken were functionally ready to receive patients, although they did not at that time have medical staffs assigned. Nocton Hall was ready by November 30. With its activation, RAF Little Rissington, with 1,500 beds, became the largest medical center in the US Air Force. USAFE became the largest medical command in the Air Force.

By January 12, contingency hospital staff were arriving at the European hospitals. Medical deployments continued throughout the air campaign. Two weeks before the ground war began, USAFE met its total commitment and had 3,740 beds available. Nearly 4,350 medical people from the United States were deployed to staff the hospitals.

On February 6, the first war zone patients were admitted to the Air Force contingency hospitals at Bicester and Little Rissington. Throughout the war and follow-on operations through November 1991, nearly 11,000 patients were evacuated from the AOR to the medical facilities in Europe. Another 7,400 patients were airlifted from Europe to the United States from August 1990 to May 1991.[50]

Competence and Compassion

US medical people carried their competence with them in the field under all conditions.

"I flew on a US Air Force C-130 medical evacuation flight," reported Dr. Robert Arnot, CBS News Medical Commentator. "We departed Jubail AB in Saudi Arabia and flew north.

We landed, not at an air base, in fact, there wasn't even a runway ... we just landed on the desert sand ... near a battlefield ... next to a mobile Army surgical hospital.

It was nighttime ... it was raining ... and the winds were gusty ... certainly not an easy task for the pilots.

"The job for those in the back of the plane was no less difficult. They loaded on

[48] Amy D. Griswold, "The Store in the Desert," *Air Force Magazine*, June 1991.

[49] USAF white paper, April 1991.

[50] USAFE Chronology of the Gulf War.

fifty wounded soldiers ... some in critical condition. One had just come from brain surgery ... another was unable to breathe on his own ... a technician had to manually blow air into his lungs for the entire flight back.

"All of the doctors, nurses, and technicians performed heroically. Many of the wounded would not have survived had it not been for their professional care and courage.

"Here they were, flying into a battle area in terrible weather, landing on nothing more than hard packed sand ... risking their lives to save others.

"Perhaps the most amazing aspect of all, however, was that all fifty wounded soldiers were Iraqis. As I stood back and watched ... I realized that America is not only a powerful nation ... it is also a good nation."[51] ■

[51] Television News report by Dr. Robert Arnot, CBS News Medical Commentator, Feb. 25, 1991.

11. Total Force

Capt. Robert Swain of the 706th TFS, Air Force Reserve achieved the first-ever A-10 air-to-air victory when he shot down an Iraqi helicopter over central Kuwait.

Guard and Reserve participation began the first hour of the first day.

Desert Storm was the first war of the Total Force era. In August 1970, Secretary of Defense Melvin Laird directed that a "Total Force" concept be applied in all assumptions of planning, programming, manning, equipping, and employing the Guard and Reserve Force.

The Guard and Reserve were no longer to be regarded as "weekend warriors," equipped with hand-me-down weapons from the active forces. As Laird envisioned it, they were to be serious partners in the national defense posture and take over some missions previously assigned to active-duty forces.

Three years later, Secretary of Defense James R. Schlesinger announced that Total Force was no longer just a concept. "It's now a policy that integrates active, Guard, and Reserve units into a homogenous whole," he said.[1]

The services took to the new concept with varying degrees of enthusiasm and commitment. As Sen. Sam Nunn (D-Ga.), Chairman of the Senate Armed Services Committee, remarked in his broad review of defense planning in 1990, the Air Force was a clear leader in using its reserve components effectively.[2]

The Air Force was soon relying on the Guard and Reserve for large portions of the airpower it put on the line. By the 1980s, these forces were flying modern aircraft and their rosters were filled with experienced veterans. They frequently bested their active-duty counterparts in weapons meets and other competition.

The new active-reserve mix worked very well. "The only difference in a Guard or Reserve tactical fighter unit today is twenty-four hours," Gen. Robert D. Russ, commander of Tactical Air Command, said seven months before the gulf crisis. "We give the Guard and Reserve twenty-four hours to get started so they can recall their people."[3]

When the Desert Storm buildup began, there was no doubt that the Air Guard and Reserve would be part of it, and it came as no surprise when they responded with effectiveness and style.

"The very first day, the first hour, I asked for all the C-5s and C-141s owned by the Guard and Reserves," Gen. H. T. Johnson of Military Airlift Command recalled. "I had no right to do that [the Guard and Reserve had not been mobilized at that point] but they gave them to me.

"I also asked for all their crews, and we were oversubscribed in crews. Volunteer. I was musing one day and said, 'We need some 130s, but we cannot call up individual crews in 130s. Why don't we set up a provisional unit?' I was only thinking [but] I thought in the presence of my Guard and Reserve advisors. Within two hours, they came back and said, 'The two lead units, the Reserve is from Dobbins in Georgia and the Guard is from Charleston in West Virginia. Each of them will have four airplanes, six crews, and the rest of them come from other units. When do you want them to move?'"[4]

When Iraq invaded Kuwait, Maj. Gen. Philip G. Killey, Director of the Air National Guard, and Maj. Gen. Roger P. Scheer, Chief of the Air Force Reserve, alerted their troops to get ready.

[1] Capt. Napoleon B. Byars, "Manpower, Missions, and Muscle," *Air Force Magazine*, September 1986.

[2] Sen. Sam Nunn, "A New Military Strategy," speech to US Senate, April 19, 1990.

[3] Gen. Robert D. Russ, AFA Symposium, Feb. 1–2, 1990.

[4] Gen. H. T. Johnson, AFA Symposium, Oct. 25, 1991.

Guard and Reserve Call-up

By State, as of February 15, 1991

State	ArmyNG	USAR	USNR	USMCR	ANG	AFRES	USCGR	Total
Alabama	4,366	2,222	393	651	179	205	8	8,024
Alaska	8	16	20	68	21	7	----	140
Arizona	1,200	861	190	428	275	456	----	3,410
Arkansas	2,789	1,079	87	279	175	69	----	4,478
California	1,221	3,329	3,206	3,919	461	3,306	106	15,548
Colorado	501	1,229	322	120	149	678	3	3,002
Connecticut	557	483	82	298	70	303	----	1,793
Delaware	128	153	54	38	253	529	2	1,157
District of Columbia	569	205	46	83	9	53	----	965
Florida	1,439	3,726	1,380	1,245	112	1,314	42	9,258
Georgia	4,627	3,388	353	809	149	496	9	9,831
Hawaii	1	39	104	50	----	26	1	221
Idaho	18	261	46	138	56	40	----	559
Illinois	812	2,617	487	1,297	524	640	23	6,400
Indiana	266	2,450	166	460	117	464	8	3,931
Iowa	1,612	827	152	318	144	25	1	3,079
Kansas	205	1,328	160	143	427	62	2	2,327
Kentucky	1,132	2,280	75	334	113	28	4	3,966
Louisiana	5,974	1,894	297	782	24	626	8	9,605
Maine	231	481	103	115	201	15	----	1,146
Maryland	599	1,598	551	654	227	639	17	4,285
Massachusetts	606	681	224	797	108	1,149	2	3,567
Michigan	1,501	2,433	466	1,129	247	364	7	6,147
Minnesota	359	1,614	179	361	154	147	6	2,820
Mississippi	4,939	1,245	122	306	370	84	----	7,066
Missouri	940	1,932	590	546	355	373	2	4,738
Montana	19	506	53	68	66	8	----	720
Nebraska	144	1,052	195	64	9	135	1	1,600
Nevada	101	203	78	123	140	70	----	715
New Hampshire	175	176	74	142	115	78	1	761
New Jersey	280	1,349	314	753	279	1,006	14	3,995
New Mexico	219	615	50	138	61	106	----	1,189
New York	1,185	4,197	679	1,860	975	1,222	23	10,141
North Carolina	2,035	2,732	724	567	186	640	79	6,963
North Dakota	448	322	41	10	68	8	----	897
Ohio	916	4,367	446	979	634	929	76	8,347
Oklahoma	1,377	1,272	114	401	244	229	3	3,640
Oregon	260	442	155	255	69	149	3	1,333
Pennsylvania	586	3,986	776	1,403	807	1,211	23	8,792
Rhode Island	344	133	36	157	138	26	1	835
South Carolina	1,597	1,594	402	596	740	948	6	5,883
South Dakota	572	339	17	22	42	5	----	997
Tennessee	2,418	2,626	345	706	552	64	14	6,725
Texas	1,718	5,454	1,165	1,776	528	2,193	48	12,882
Utah	1,314	907	258	207	207	240	5	3,138
Vermont	308	80	25	38	44	24	----	519
Virginia	755	1,765	1,353	1,237	103	617	54	5,884
Washington	158	1,343	388	526	301	931	16	3,663
West Virginia	645	848	105	120	404	20	2	2,144
Wisconsin	1,028	2,495	220	435	413	248	6	4,845
Wyoming	112	54	17	13	87	10	----	293
American Samoa	----	2	----	----	----	----	----	2
Guam	28	32	----	----	----	3	----	63
Puerto Rico	253	1,026	29	----	37	5	----	1,350
US Virgin Islands	----	2	----	----	----	1	----	3
Overseas	----	193	43	----	----	6	----	242
Unknown	----	195	194	430	6	17	5	847
Totals:	**55,595**	**78,678**	**18,151**	**28,394**	**12,175**	**23,247**	**631**	**216,871**

The number of Guardsmen and Reservists on active duty changed continuously during the operation, but the Department of Defense says that these call-up totals on February 15, midway through the fighting, are illustrative of the participation.

Source: Department of Defense.

Flying and support units ran telephone checks to determine how many aircrews would be willing to volunteer. By the time the operational commands officially asked for help, volunteers were lined up in Guard and Reserve outfits across the country. In fact, there were more than the Air Force could process, assign, and use. The initial call was for 6,000 volunteers. By the third week in August, all 6,000 were on active duty, and more were standing by. In the first seventy-two hours after the call for volunteers, 15,000 Guardsmen and Reservists had stepped forward.[5]

Note: The Department of Defense uses the terms "Air Reserve Forces" (ARF) and "Air Reserve Components" (ARC) to refer to the Guard-Reserve combination. Many Guardsmen take issue with these terms, believing it obscures their presence in the force mix. They are likely to present a pocket "ARF card," suggesting different practice, to those who use the official acronyms.

A Volunteer Tradition

In previous crises, on a voluntary basis only, without the necessity of Presidential mobilization, the Guard and Reserve responded in strength. The 1973 Yom Kippur War in the Middle East and the 1975 capture of the *Mayaguez* are examples.

Reserve component volunteers also turned out for the 1983 conflict in Grenada. They had only a few hours to respond, and, because of national security considerations, could not be told where they were going or for how long. Security considerations also kept a secret shroud around the "Eldorado Canyon" operation against Libya in 1986, but again, Guardsmen and Reservists responded within twenty-four hours.

In 1987 and 1988, during the war between Iran and Iraq, reservists joined active-duty forces and flew escort missions for oil tankers that had been placed under US protection in the Persian Gulf.

During Operation Just Cause in Panama in 1989, reservists flew combat missions in fighters and AC-130A Spectre gunships. Many were involved in support functions.

As the Persian Gulf crisis approached, most of the US strategic and tactical airlift capability was in the Air reserve components. Some fifty-five percent of the crews who operate strategic airlifters (C-5s and C-141s) are in the reserves. Almost sixty percent of the tactical airlift (C-130s) capability is in the Guard and Reserve.

Furthermore, nineteen air refueling squadrons, about half of SAC's total capability, are in the reserve forces. These squadrons provide the country's wartime air refueling surge capability. Sixteen of them were ultimately activated during the Gulf War.[6]

Under the Total Force Policy, fifty-seven percent of the aerial port units, sixty-seven percent of aeromedical evacuation units, and forty-six percent of tactical reconnaissance assets were in Air Force reserve components when Saddam invaded Kuwait.

Reservists and Guardsmen came from all walks of life. 2d Lt. Becky Armendariz, for example, worked in the personnel office at the White House. She was also a member of 60th Aeromedical Evacuation Squadron (AES) at Andrews AFB, Md., near Washington.

"I arrived in Dhahran, Saudi Arabia on November 7," she said. "I had, at first, expected to spend thirty days on active duty, but it turned out to be ninety days." When President and Mrs. Bush visited the war zone later that month, they paid a call on Armendariz's unit.

"I was wearing one of the chocolate-chip floppy hats that morning and they [the President's advance team] took the hat for the President to wear that day," she remembers. "I went around the rest of the day without a hat." She retrieved her headgear when she shook the President's hand at the end of the presidential visit.[7]

The Call-up

For Operation Desert Shield, Guardsmen and Reservists were called to active duty under two provisions of federal law.[8]

For volunteer service, Title 10 of the US Code authorizes the Secretary of Defense to order individual members of the reserve components to active duty *with their consent* and (for National Guard personnel) that of their state governors. Another sec-

[5] Desert Storm Point Paper, Air Force Reserve, May 30, 1991.

[6] Total Force Policy Study Group Report.

[7] Timothy N. Miller, "Employer Support Starts with the Boss," *Citizen Airman*, August 1991.

[8] *Air National Guard Lessons Learned: Operation Desert Shield*. Vol. I. NSA, Inc. March 8, 1991.

tion of Title 10 authorizes the President to call to active duty units of the Selected Reserve, up to a total of 200,000 people for not more than ninety days, with one ninety-day extension possible.

When enacting the Fiscal Year 1991 defense budget, Congress specifically authorized the President to extend the duration of the Desert Shield call-up for combat units to 180 days, with a 180-day extension.

Mobilized or volunteer reservists often face special problems. For many, active service in the Gulf War meant large pay cuts, since military compensation did not match their civilian salaries. Others had to repay bonuses they had gotten from their employers. Some were even furloughed or released. Although the law provides protection, practically speaking, getting a job back often means lost time and money, even if the individual is successful.[9]

Most employers—like President Bush and the White House Personnel office—supported their employees called to active duty, but some did not.

Another problem was that Guard and Reserve members had to leave their families suddenly and unexpectedly.

Maximum Effort

By August 3, the Air Reserve components were prepared to augment the active-duty Air Force with complete units or small packages of people with individual, specialized, skills. As General Johnson said, MAC put aircraft and aircrews into the airlift pipeline immediately. The Air Guard, for example, provided six C-141s and fourteen augmented crews from the 172d Military Airlift Group, Jackson ANG Base, Miss., and two C-5s and three crews from the 105th MAG, Stewart ANGB, N.Y. The Reserve responded with similar numbers.

MSgt. William R. Cary, a flight engineer with the 701st MAS, was one of the early C-141 crewmen to volunteer. The first flight told him this was a maximum effort. "We normally flew at a max weight of 275,000 pounds in the C-141," said Cary. "Now, we were operating at 375,000 pounds."[10]

By August 6, when the United States began to move a war machine manned by 250,000 people as far as 8,000 miles, ANG KC-135 inflight refueling outfits were assigned to tanker task force locations at Bangor ANGB, Me.; Pease ANGB, N.H.; Phoenix Sky Harbor International Airport, Ariz.; and Forbes Field, Kan.[11]

ANG and AFRES C-5 and C-141 aircraft and crews were incorporated into the MAC system on August 7. By then, aircraft maintenance and support volunteers from the Air Reserve Components were also working full time.

Air Reserve Component Tactical Airlift Squadrons (Provisional) were formed from volunteers. The AFRES 94th TAS(P) was composed of eight C-130Hs and crews, four each from the 94th Tactical Airlift Wing, Dobbins AFB, Ga., and the 908th Tactical Airlift Group, Maxwell AFB, Ala.

The Guard provided the 130th Tactical Airlift Squadron (Provisional) with eight C-130Hs, four from the 130th Tactical Airlift Group, Charleston, W.Va., and four from the 136th Tactical Airlift Wing, Dallas, Tex.

The two provisional squadrons were destined to operate out of Al Kharj airfield, Saudi Arabia, but at first, there were no facilities there for transport aircrews and ground personnel, so the squadrons operated out of the United Kingdom, flying between Al Kharj and the UK for several weeks while temporary facilities were constructed.[12]

Contingency Support Staffs

On August 7, when the first air and ground elements began to arrive in Saudi Arabia, the Guard activated its Contingency Support Staff at Andrews AFB. The Reserve manned a CSS at its headquarters at Robins AFB, Ga. The Air Force activated a central Contingency Support Staff at the Pentagon on August 8.

The 172th MAG, Jackson, Miss., provided the first Guard airlift sortie in support of Operation Desert Shield, airlifting troops and equipment of the 82d Airborne Division.

Right behind them was the Guard's 169th Electronic Support Squadron, Salt Lake

[9] "Desert Shield—Getting Ready." *TIG Brief, AFRP 11-1*. The Air Force Inspection and Safety Center, November 1990.

[10] MSgt. William R. Cary, interview, Sept. 8, 1991.

[11] *Air National Guard Lessons Learned*, NSA, Inc.

[12] Lt. Col. William F. Spitzer, interview, July 25, 1991.

City, Utah, which deployed three Arabic-speaking people as part of its 41st Electronic Control Squadron.[13]

On August 9, Joint Communications Support Equipment (JCSE) from the 224th Joint Communication Support Squadron (ANG), Brunswick, Ga., deployed to MacDill AFB, Fla., from where it later deployed to the Gulf.

The next day, the 190th Air Refueling Group, Topeka, Kan., deployed volunteer crews and six KC-135E aircraft to Jiddah, Saudi Arabia, on the Red Sea.

Led by Col. Michael Baier, the 190th joined active duty and reserve tankers to form a provisional wing. Colonel Baier was appointed commander.[14] The AFRES deployed twelve KC-135E tankers and volunteer crews from two squadrons, the 336th Air Refueling Squadron (AFRES), March AFB, Calif.; and the 314th, Mather AFB, Calif.

Overall, four Air Force Reserve refueling squadrons were mobilized for Desert Storm. One squadron was equipped with the KC-10 Extender and the other three with the KC-135 Stratotanker.

During the Gulf War, the reserve force tankers refueled more than 8,000 warplanes, dispensing more than eighteen million gallons of fuel.[15]

On August 11, aeromedical units began deploying. ANG and AFRES volunteer medical professionals were sent directly to the Gulf region and also reported Stateside as replacements for active-duty medics sent to the war zone.

Since AFRES aeromedical evacuation units provided seventy-one percent of MAC's medical crews, volunteers were essential to meet anticipated needs.[16]

President Bush issued an executive order August 22, calling up units of the Selected Reserve for ninety days. More call-ups came August 24. Orders were cut for the 183d Military Airlift Squadron (C-141), Jackson, Miss.; 137th MAS (C-5), Stewart ANGB, N.Y.; and the 136th Military Aerial Port Support Squadron (MAPS), Naval Air Station Dallas, Tex.

In addition, the 117th Tactical Reconnaissance Wing (TRW), Birmingham, Ala., deployed six RF-4C aircraft to the Persian Gulf, joining RF-4Cs deployed by the 67th Tactical Reconnaissance Wing, Bergstrom AFB, Tex.

When the 183d MAS was activated, the unit used home-station volunteers to turn Allen C. Thompson Field, at Jackson, into a round-the-clock operating base to support maintenance and rapid repair of C-130 transports placed on active duty.

AFRES units called up were: The 756th MAS (C-141), Andrews AFB, Md.; 732d MAS (C-141 Assoc.), McGuire AFB, N.J.; and the 337th MAS (C-5), Westover AFB, Mass.

Near the end of August, the 193d Special Operations Group, Harrisburg International Airport, Middletown, Pa., deployed four EC-130E Volant Solo II psychological operations aircraft to the Gulf.[17]

Guard and Reserve Airlift

On August 29, a C-5A Galaxy transport, flown by a volunteer Reserve crew, carrying active-duty passengers and cargo to Saudi Arabia, crashed shortly after takeoff from Ramstein AB, Germany, killing all but four of the seventeen people aboard.

The only aircrew member to survive, SSgt. Lorenzo Galvan, Jr., a loadmaster from the 68th MAS, Kelly AFB, Tex., later received the Airman's Medal for risking his life while evacuating passengers.[18]

The 68th MAS, Kelly AFB, Tex., the 301st MAS (Assoc.), Travis AFB, Calif., and the 326th MAS (Assoc.), Dover AFB, Del., all equipped with C-5s, were called up.

By the end of August, the Guard and Reserve were flying forty-two percent of the strategic airlift and thirty-three percent of the aerial refueling missions.[19]

Concurrently, the Guard deployed sixteen C-130H tactical airlifters to the Gulf. The C-130H, the newest version of the Lockheed Hercules, has powerful T56-A-15 turboprop engines, a redesigned and strengthened outer wing, updated avionics, and improved cargo-handling capabilities.[20]

During the second week of September, the 335th MAS (Assoc.), McGuire AFB, N.J., and the 701st MAS (Assoc.), Charleston AFB, S.C., equipped with big C-141B StarLifters, were activated.

[13] *Air National Guard Lessons Learned.*

[14] Maj. Gen. Philip Killey, interview, June 6, 1991.

[15] Air Force Reserve Desert Storm point paper, Nov. 25, 1991.

[16] "Air Force Reserve," USAF fact sheet 89-25.

[17] Susan H.H. Young, "Gallery of USAF Weapons," *Air Force Magazine*, May 1991.

[18] "Air Force Reserve," *Air Force Magazine, May 1991.*

[19] *Conduct of the Persian Gulf Conflict.*

[20] *Conduct of the Persian Gulf Conflict.*

[21] "Air Force Reserve Participation in Desert Shield/Desert Storm," AFRES fact sheet.

[22] AFRES fact sheet.

[23] Bob Woodward. *The Commanders*. 1991.

[24] Lt. Gen. Charles A. Horner, interview, May 30, 1991.

[25] AFRES fact sheet.

Call-ups were issued for the 708th MAS (Assoc.) Travis AFB, Calif., and the 97th MAS (Assoc.), McChord AFB, Wash.[21] These units also were equipped with StarLifters.

By September 20, as MAC expected, wartime sortie rates, made possible by the addition of activated Guard and Reserve aircraft and aircrews, resulted in a huge surge in flying hours. This created a need for greater aircraft maintenance capabilities.

As planned, MAC issued a call for more maintenance people from the Guard and Reserve. Individual maintenance personnel from the ANG and AFRES began to be recalled and put in the MAC infrastructure.

On October 10, the 63d TAS, Selfridge ANGB, Mich.; and the 328th TAS, Niagara Falls International Airport, N.Y., equipped with C-130Es, were activated and deployed to Saudi Arabia, along with their maintenance support organizations.

More medical people were activated in October, including the 37th Aeromedical Evacuation Group, aerial port squadrons at Dover, McChord, Charleston, and Tinker AFBs in addition to Youngstown, Ohio, and Wyoming City, Pa.[22]

By October, the White House came to the conclusion that economic sanctions would not force Saddam to withdraw. Only offensive military operations would push the Iraqi army out of Kuwait and stabilize the region's balance of power. The President wanted to know what it would take to do the job.

Doubling the Forces

General Schwarzkopf, through Gen. Colin Powell, Chairman of the Joint Chiefs of Staff, informed President Bush that he needed an additional 200,000 troops to go on the offensive.

Some would come from bases and reserve components in the United States, but with the cold war in Europe ending, the Army could move its crack VII Corps from the continent without significant risk.[23] In November, President Bush ordered 200,000 more troops for the Gulf.

"The decision was made that we needed a ground campaign," recalled General Horner, "and the army requested a second corps, so they sent a corps from Europe. Then the Navy said they would increase the number of carriers in the area to six.

"If we were to get a second Army corps, that meant we had doubled the requirement for full service support. I looked at each of our airfields to see what additional forces we could accommodate, so we built our air force support up about half again as much."[24] More reserve and active duty units were ordered up.

The President issued another executive order, extending active duty for those originally called up for an additional ninety days. It was clear by now that the crisis would not be over quickly. When General Powell had visited the war zone in October, the troops asked repeatedly when they were going home. He told them he did not know.

In December, more Guardsmen and Reservists were called up. Among them were firefighters from Reserve civil engineering squadrons, medical personnel from the 913th Medical Squadron, Willow Grove, Pa., and the 42d Aeromedical Patient Staging Squadron and the 35th Aerial Port Squadron, both from Norton AFB, Calif., aircrews from the 336th Air Refueling Squadron, and maintenance and support personnel from the 435th Air Refueling Wing and the 916th Air Refueling Group.[25]

Calling Up the Fighters

Call-up of Guard and Reserve fighter units began December 3. The F-16s of the 169th TFG, McEntire ANGB, Eastover, S.C., were alerted. So were the F/A-16s of the 174th TFW, Hancock Field, Syracuse, N.Y. Reconnaissance aircrews and support personnel from the 152d TRG, Reno, Nev., replaced the 117th TRW, Birmingham, Ala., which had been in the initial call-up.

From the Air Force Reserve, the 926th Tactical Fighter Group, New Orleans, La., with A-10 Thunderbolt II close air support fighters, was alerted.

These units were carefully selected. The 169th TFG had won the 1989 Gunsmoke competition, which pits the best Air Force fighter teams from commands around the world.

The 174th TFW has Tactical Air Command's only F/A-16A fighters. The F/A-16, an enhanced variant of the basic multirole fighter, is a prime asset in air-to-ground operations.

The 926th TFG, equipped with A-10s, was ideal for helping to fill the increased close air support requirements that went along with the new influx of ground troops.

During the Gulf War, the Thunderbolt II and the 926th performed well. Based not far from the Kuwaiti border at King Fahd International Airport, Saudi Arabia, with Air Force A-10 outfits, the 926th was almost on the front lines of the ground war.

"The single, most recognizable, and feared aircraft at low level was the Thunderbolt II. This black-colored jet was seen as deadly accurate, and rarely missed its target," said a captured Iraqi captain. "Conducting bombing raids three or four times a day, the A-10 was a ubiquitous threat. The actual bomb run was terrifying, but the aircraft's loitering around the target area prior to hitting the target caused as much, if not more, anxiety, since the Iraqi soldiers were unsure of the chosen target."[26]

The Reserve A-10s flew 1,300 combat sorties and logged over 3,000 combat hours.[27]

In addition, the 439th Military Airlift Wing, Westover AFB, Mass., was activated December 3 to augment airlift operations from the US to the war area.[28] The 439th kept Westover AFB open on a twenty-four-hour basis, finally closing shop on July 31, 1991.

The 152d TRG deployed its RF-4Cs to Saudi Arabia on December 5. The RF-4C proved a vital reconnaissance asset during the Gulf War. Tactical intelligence was hard to come by and relied on overhead satellite imagery as well as high flying TR-1As, and U-2Rs.

It was difficult to get up-to-date tactical intelligence, General Schwarzkopf reported. Besides a delay in getting the information to the field, weather and oil smoke interfered with bomb-damage assessment and new target intelligence. The flexibility and responsiveness of the RF-4C helped reduce the scarcity of real-time intelligence.

Just before Christmas, Air National Guard KC-135E tanker outfits were alerted for activation. The call-up finally included twelve of the thirteen ANG tanker units. The units, with a total strength of sixty-two tankers, were quickly deployed with maintenance support to Saudi Arabia,[29] where the tempo of training operations was revving up.

Between Christmas and New Year's, the flow of Guard and Reserve people toward the Gulf continued. Security police from the 301st Security Police Flight (SPF), Carswell AFB, Tex., 924th SPF, Bergstrom AFB, Tex., and medical personnel from the 32d Aeromedical Evacuation Group, Kelly AFB, Tex., were called to active duty.[30]

The 913th Tactical Airlift Group, with C-130E transports, Willow Grove, Pa., the 706th TFS (A-10s), and the 406th Combat Logistics Support Squadron, McClellan AFB, Calif., were called up.

On December 29, the 169th TFG, first Guard fighter unit to deploy, launched twenty-four F-16As to Al Kharj AB, Saudi Arabia. More than 700 support people deployed in transports.

On January 2, the 174th TFW deployed eighteen F/A-16 aircraft to Al Kharj AB and, along with the 169th TFG, was incorporated into the 4th Tactical Fighter Wing (Provisional). Together, the 169th and the 174th flew more than 3,000 sorties during the war.[31]

Capt. Grich Goodwin, an F-16 pilot with the 174th, had spent ten years flying A-10s in the active force before joining the New York Air Guard in 1990. "I finally got a job with American Airlines and two days into training, I got the call," Goodwin said. "It was December 29 and they called me at lunch." Goodwin would fly thirty-eight combat missions in the Gulf, and notes wryly that his former active duty A-10 colleagues had not deployed.

Guardsmen and Reservists served on all fronts. Back at the 174th's home station, Hancock Field, the workday for CMSgt. Marshall B. Carter, chief enlisted mainte-

[26] "Operation Desert Storm," 23d TFW(P) and 354th TFW(P) briefing, King Fahd International Airport, Saudi Arabia.

[27] Desert Storm point paper, AFRES.

[28] "Operation Desert Storm" briefing, 23d TFW (P) and 345th TFW (P).

[29] Killey interview.

[30] AFRES fact sheet.

[31] "F-16As Prove Usefulness in Attack Role Against Iraqi Targets in Desert Storm," *Aviation Week & Space Technology*, April 22, 1991.

nance superintendent, started at 4 a.m. and often went into the night. "I asked to go to Saudi Arabia, but they needed me here," he said.[32]

An A-10 Victory

On February 6, Capt. Robert Swain, of the 706th TFS, in the first-ever A-10 air-to-air victory, shot down an Iraqi helicopter over central Kuwait.

"As I was leaving the target area—after dropping six 500-pound bombs and firing my two Maverick missiles at tanks—I noticed two black dots running across the desert. They weren't putting up any dust and, yet, they were moving fast over the ground."

They were helicopters. On the radio, he told the forward air controller, flying nearby in an OA-10, about the two choppers. The helicopters split up, one heading north, the other south. The OA-10 pilot moved in close to the helicopter flying south, established it was Iraqi, and began to fire marking rockets along its path. Swain was "cleared in, hot."

Diving in, he lined up his target. "On the first pass, I tried to shoot an AIM-9 heat-seeking missile, but I couldn't get it to lock on [the target]" he said. "So, on the second pass, I fired a long burst of 30-mm from the cannon and the helicopter looked like it had been hit with a bomb. We tried to identify the type of [helicopter] after we were finished, but it was just a bunch of pieces."[33]

The 100-hour ground war began February 24. A Reserve C-130E from the 1650th TAW (Provisional), composed of the 914th and 927th TAGs, flew the first aeromedical evacuation flight of the ground campaign. The 1650th evacuated wounded US Marines from the southern Kuwait battlefield to hospitals in Saudi Arabia.[34]

Cease-Fire and Victory

When President Bush declared the cease-fire,12,098—or twenty-two percent—of the 54,706 Air Force people in the Gulf theater were Guardsmen or Reservists.[35]

On July 31, Congress mandated that all reservists called to active duty be demobilized. Many air reserve component people volunteered for active duty, returning equipment and people to home bases.

Reservists took pride in serving their country in wartime, but the Air Force policy of first in, first out, which sounded fair on the surface, in reality caused them problems. Many Reservists came on board late in Desert Shield. They had to wait to be demobilized.

With financial and professional difficulties mounting back home, many felt they should have been released sooner.

Capt. Buddy Young, a South Carolina F-16 fighter pilot, for example, had built up an ambulance and tour bus business that employed fifty people. It was a family-owned business, and, without his management, it almost went under during the months that he was gone.[36]

SSgt. Lanty Mimnaugh, a loadmaster with the 701st MAS, lost his construction business while on active duty. Both Young and Mimnaugh say they would go again if called, but feel that the first in, first out policy is a tough burden that reservists and employers should not have to bear.

Most employers kept the reservists' jobs open for them. Some made up the difference between military and civilian pay. Many gave special aid and support to the families of Guardsmen and Reservists.

That support was recognized and appreciated. On October 6, 1991, for example, the 166th Tactical Airlift Group (ANG) of Wilmington, Del., held "Appreciation Day" for companies and individuals that stood behind them during the Gulf War by preserving their jobs and by helping their families. One employer had given $40,000 to families hard pressed financially. Employers saluted at Wilmington ranged from a small family bakery to the giant du Pont Company.[37]

In another example, the Topeka *Capital Journal* selected as its Kansans of the Year for 1991 Col. Charles M. Baier and the unit he commanded in the Gulf, the 190th Air Refueling Group of the Kansas Air National Guard.[38]

[32] Maj. Jean Marie Beall, "Air Guard Fighters: Training Prepared Them Well for Combat," *National Guard*, June 1991.

[33] Becky Colaw, "Thunderbolt Hits Iraqi Chopper," *Citizen Airman*, February 1991.

[34] AFRES fact sheet.

[35] Lt. Col. Fred Baker, AF/REO.

[36] Interview with pilots of the 169th TFG, Sept. 6, 1991.

[37] "Employer Appreciation Day," Greater Wilmington Airport, Wilmington, Del., Oct. 6, 1991.

[38] Gene Smith, "1991 Kansans of the Year," Topeka *Capital-Journal*, Jan. 5, 1992.

Sour Notes in Perspective

The Total Force image suffered somewhat in the early going when a few National Guard roundout brigades were judged not in shape to deploy when they were called up. Secretary of Defense Dick Cheney said that the problem was confined to three Army Guard units and that those who read it as a broader indictment of Guard and Reserve forces were wrong.[39]

After the war, Cheney recounted an anecdote that, in his view, put the Reserve component performance in better perspective. B Company of the Fourth Marine Tank Battalion was activated in December and went into battle with their Abrams tanks February 24.

"Before dawn the next day, moving north inside Kuwait, Company B spied a large formation of Iraqi tanks," Cheney said. "They were the Iraqi army's top-of-the-line T-72s. Dug in behind them was another group of Iraqi armor.

"All told, there were thirty-five enemy tanks. The odds didn't stop them. During the engagement, the thirteen tanks of Company B destroyed or stopped thirty-four of the enemy. In fact, in a total of four engagements, Company B stopped fifty-nine Iraqi tanks, thirty of them T-72s.

"What makes it all the more impressive is that Company B had never used those high-tech Abrams tanks before being called up for duty in the Gulf. Before getting to Saudi Arabia, they had just twenty-three days of training on the Abrams at camp in California. At home, they normally trained with older model M-60s."[40]

Overall, the reserve components performed with distinction in the Gulf War, and if anyone was surprised by the effectiveness of the Air Guard and Reserve, it certainly was not the US Air Force, which had known the caliber of these units all along. ■

[39] Cheney, remarks to Association of Former Members of Congress, April 17, 1991.

[40] Cheney, address to National Committee for Employer Support of Guard and Reserve conference, April 19, 1991.

12. Command and Control

One of the star performers of Desert Storm was the E-3 AWACS, employed to control the air war. The Air Force is now looking at ways to combine the capabilities of AWACS and Joint STARS, a standout in air-to-ground surveillance, into a single radar.

In the electronic age, information and communications are powerful weapons.

Before the age of electronics and aerospace technology, command and control—in the modern sense of the term—was a comparatively minor element in warfare.

Field commanders used information about the enemy when they could get it, of course, but communications and the means to exploit intelligence were limited. To win their battles, commanders relied mainly on firepower and maneuver.

By the time of the Gulf War, that had changed. Technology had given military commanders the capability to perceive the battle area quickly and in considerable detail, allowing them to adjust tactics and make decisions based on hard information. They could also direct their forces with communications of unprecedented quality.

Command and control (in extended jargon, "command, control, communications, and intelligence," or C^3I) is no longer peripheral to strategy. Information and the means to use it well are among the most effective of modern military weapons.

A military C^3 systems loop includes five elements: a sensor—often radar—to collect data, computers to sort and analyze it, communications to pass the information back and forth, a means of imagery and interpretation so that humans can use the data, and command posts or other facilities enabling them to plug into the system.

Command and control also refers to the command arrangements for using these assets and data.

Desert Storm showcased the role of C^3I in modern warfare. There were many innovations both in the systems and the process, and airborne and spaceborne sensors were employed with stunning effect.

Shortly after Saddam instigated the Gulf crisis, Lt. Gen. Chuck Horner, temporarily operating as "CINCCENT Forward," set up headquarters in Riyadh, Saudi Arabia. Among his first tasks was to get the C^3I arrangements in place.

"My job was to receive forces. Then, figure out where to put them and how we would use them if Saddam attacked," Horner said.[1] Saddam Hussein already had an efficient, well-oiled C^3I system of his own, which had been installed by the Soviets and the French. Stripping him of it was a prime objective of the coalition.

"As Desert Storm began, our commanders emphasized again and again that targeting Saddam Hussein's command and control network is a number one priority," said Lt. Gen. Gordon E. Fornell of the Air Force's Electronic Systems Division.[2]

The Chain of Command

In establishing their own command and control arrangements, Schwarzkopf and Horner had some advantages not enjoyed by field commanders in previous wars. The Goldwater-Nichols Department of Defense Reorganization Act of 1986 had strengthened and delineated a field CINC's authority and his relationships with the individual military service departments as well as with the President.

Just as important, the act ensured a geographical commander-in-chief the authority to carry out his responsibilities.

[1] Lt. Gen. Charles A. Horner, interview, May 30, 1991.

[2] Lt. Gen. Gordon E. Fornell, AFA symposium, Jan. 31–Feb. 1, 1991.

For Operation Desert Shield/Storm, CINCCENTCOM—or Schwarzkopf—was the designated "supported CINC," to be provided whatever assistance and forces he required from other CINCs and the services, who assumed supporting roles. Goldwater-Nichols prescribed that.[3]

Schwarzkopf reported directly through the Secretary of Defense to the President. The Army and the other services were not in the chain of command, even though they provided the forces Schwarzkopf and Horner commanded.

McPeak, the Air Force Chief of Staff, understood this very well. "You may have inquiries or advice directly from the Air Staff," he told Horner. "Ignore them if you want to. If I need to know or say anything, I'll go to the Joint Chiefs of Staff, the JCS will go to CENTCOM, and CENTCOM will pass it on to you."[4]

Goldwater-Nichols escalated the level of attention devoted to strategy and contingency planning, ensuring a role for Department of Defense civilian officials. Previously, commanders developed operations plans to carry out missions assigned them in the national military strategy. Most of this work took place below the level of the Office of the Secretary of Defense.

The legislation also increased civilian oversight of the operational planning process by requiring the Under Secretary of Defense for Policy to review war plans. Formerly, this was not done above the uniformed service level.

The Defense Planning Guidance thus prepared and issued by the Secretary of Defense is one of the Department's primary tools for linking strategy and resource planning.

The guidance prepared in the fall of 1989 called for additional emphasis on the defense of the Arabian Peninsula against strong threats developing in the Middle East and southwest Asia. This shift in focus reflected the weaker Soviet threat to the region and the growing power of Saddam Hussein.

Almost a year before the Gulf crisis, Schwarzkopf had invited Horner, who headed the command's air component, CENTAF, to his headquarters at MacDill AFB, Fla., where they discussed the more probable forms of conflict that might occur in the Middle East and southwest Asia.

By the time Saddam attacked, they had prepared a concept for the defense of the Arabian Peninsula. That concept was the basis for the defensive operations plan developed after the Iraqi invasion of Kuwait.[5]

Of great command and control significance in the Gulf War was the "hands off operations" policy followed by the President and the Secretary of Defense. Unlike Vietnam, operational decisions were left to the operational commander.

Under President Bush, Secretary of Defense Cheney, Chairman of the Joint Chiefs of Staff Gen. Colin Powell, and National Security Advisor Brent Scowcroft (a retired Air Force lieutenant general) all had a close working relationship.

The plan, the multiservice coordination, the execution, and the C^3I were almost textbook perfect.

Working Together

When Horner arrived in Saudi Arabia in August 1990, there was little to be seen of a C^3 organization anywhere in the region. Although there were a surprising number of well developed ports and airfields (which were not always equipped with adequate housing and support structures), C^3I had to be formed as coalition troops arrived.

The force deployed in the Persian Gulf region consisted of more than 800,000 troops from thirty-six nations, equipped with all manner of western and Soviet weapon systems. US forces alone had a wide diversity of weapons, communications, and support equipment spread among the Army, Navy, Marine Corps, Coast Guard, and Air Force.

Command and control arrangements could have been very cumbersome, but surprisingly, those adopted worked very well.

Islamic forces of the allied coalition were organized into a Joint Forces Theater of Operations Command structure under Saudi Lt. Gen. Khalid bin Sultan bin Abdul-Aziz.

The non-Islamic forces of the coalition were commanded by General Schwarzkopf. There was, in fact, no single overall com-

[3] *Conduct of the Persian Gulf Conflict.*

[4] Horner interview.

[5] *Conduct of the Persian Gulf Conflict.*

mander. This seemingly awkward arrangement worked well, partly because of the close personal working relationship between Schwarzkopf and the Saudi general.

Together, they created the Coalition Coordination, Communications, and Integration Center (C^3IC) and, under it, a number of combined planning teams that drew members from both Islamic and non-Islamic forces. These organizations smoothed command and control functions between the Islamic and non-Islamic forces.

The separate, parallel lines of communication and authority had little impact on coordinating operations because of the spirit of teamwork and the carefully constructed coordination teams. Yet, if the ground war had lasted much more than 100 hours, there is little doubt the "fog and friction of war" would have created significant problems for this command arrangement.

As it was, the only awkward part of the command arrangement surfaced several days into the ground war, when Generals Khalid and Schwarzkopf conducted a press conference. General Schwarzkopf kept prompting the Saudi General to answer questions more cautiously. Schwarzkopf interjected answers of his own several times while General Khalid was speaking, to both generals' embarrassment.

Running the Air War

Horner had fewer command problems. He was the Joint Forces Air Component Commander (JFACC).

"The trait that made the JFACC work was that Adm. Stan Arthur, the Navy aviator, Gen. Walt Boomer, the Marine, Gen. John Yeosock, the Army leader, and myself were all team players," Horner said. "We had the deepest respect for one another.

"If we had a difference of opinion, we talked about it civilly and bent over backwards to accommodate each other."

After the November buildup, Horner had enough combat aircraft under his command to fight the first three phases of the air war simultaneously.

This gave him the luxury of permitting the Army, Navy, Air Force, Marines, and the air forces of allied nations—within the bounds of reason—to choose the kind of targets they wished to attack and the areas in which they wanted to fight the air war. There were plenty of targets to pick from.

For example, the Kuwaiti air force, equipped with A-4KU attack fighters, chose to attack Iraqis in Kuwait. The British, carrying JP-233 airfield denial weapons on their Tornado fighter-bombers, chose airfields as their primary targets.

At first, the French decided not to operate over Iraq and grounded their Mirage F1s because the Iraqi Air Force was flying the same type of fighter. Saddam had purchased the Mirage from France. The French feared coalition fighters might shoot down their F1s by mistake.

The US Marines initially declared the intention to withhold their strike aircraft from daily flying operations so that they would be available to support Marine ground elements preparing for battle, as Marine Corps doctrine dictates. Horner, concerned by this impending holdback of air assets as the coordinated campaign got underway, persuaded the Marine Corps to stay in the unified air war.[6]

Within a week after the shooting air war began on January 17, coordination and unity were working smoothly. Considering the lethality of enemy air defenses, Horner called for attacks to be made from medium altitude, keeping some distance from the most concentrated antiaircraft artillery. At that point, six RAF Tornados had been lost on low-altitude missions.

The French decided to attack targets in Iraq and also decided it was safe to fly their Mirage F1s because NATO-style Identification, Friend or Foe (IFF) procedures and equipment would differentiate them from the Iraqis.

While there was no supreme commander of the coalition overall, General Horner was, in fact, the single air commander.

The "Air Boss" Issue

Most analysts of the war agree that having a single "air boss" in control and all coalition aircraft operating from a single air tasking order was a good approach. The

[6] Horner interview.

US Air Force, which has campaigned since World War II for unified control of airpower in combat, certainly thought it was a good approach.

"There are doctrinal disagreements about how to employ air in a theater of operations," General McPeak said. "We feel, I think correctly so, that whoever brings the most airpower to the tactical theater ought to have the overall tasking authority for everything in the theater.

"It doesn't always have to be the Air Force. In some contingencies, we may not be there, or we may be there in very small numbers."

Sometimes, he said, it might be the senior naval aviator who puts out the air tasking order. "What we're saying is that the right way to do this is to have one guy run it."[7]

In fact, had it been further along, an Air Force reorganization that McPeak began in 1990 would have given Horner even greater control of USAF assets than he had in Desert Storm. Under McPeak's plan, the Air Force will be largely restructured into composite wings and fighting units that own, rather than call upon, many of the assets they need for combat.

The arrangement in the Gulf War worked in great part because of Horner's leadership and the cooperation he received, McPeak said, but "he had actual command of only some of his fighters and electronic warfare assets, those from the 9th Air Force that went with him to the theater. He did not have actual command of the other fighters, for instance Bitburg's F-15s or Lakenheath's F-111s. He had operational control, or OPCON, of them, but not actual command." Likewise, Horner had OPCON but not command of the airlifters, tankers, and bombers.[8]

On the other hand, there were those who disliked the single air boss approach and the concept of a centralized ATO and who thought Horner should have had less control, not more.

"The Navy had never subscribed to the ATO system," Norman Friedman wrote in a history of the Gulf War published by the US Naval Institute.[9] "War at sea, or even against a coast, is just too unpredictable to brook so rigid a planning technique."

He acknowledged that there are benefits of coordination, but added that "the Navy and the Marines saw matters very differently from the Air Force; they were much more willing to accept inefficiency as the cost of operational flexibility."

The ATO, according to Friedman, "was well suited to a relatively static phase of the air war [but] was not well-suited to the naval war, which was always much more dynamic."

Furthermore, Friedman charged, coalition command and control, "as exemplified by the ATO, sometimes had too slow a decision cycle. A more aggressive and determined enemy might have done much better by exploiting its inherent lags."

The Air Force, which has heard similar arguments for years, prefers to point to the Gulf War as supporting evidence for what it has been saying all along.

[7] Gen. Merrill A. McPeak, AFA Symposium, Jan. 30, 1992.

[8] McPeak, "Tomorrow's Air Force: Reshaping the Future," USAF videotape, Nov. 18, 1991.

[9] Norman Friedman, *Desert Victory: the War for Kuwait*. Naval Institute Press, 1991.

The Air Tasking Order

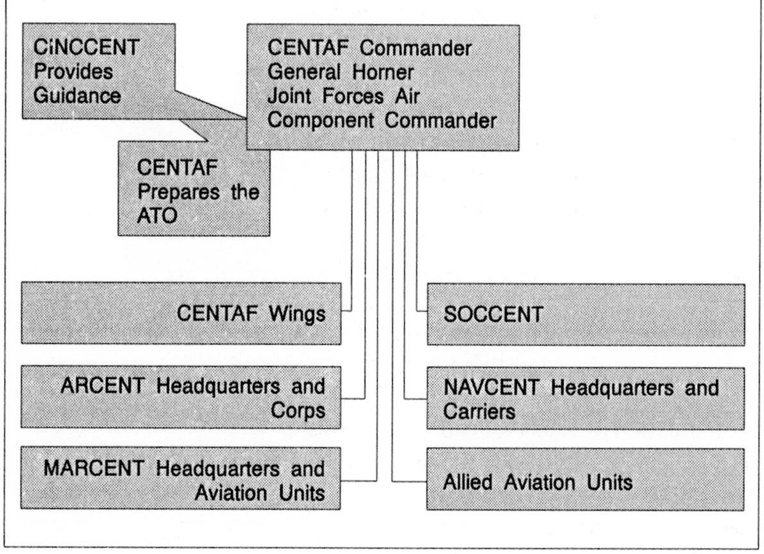

The ATO incorporated the latest guidance from Schwarzkopf. Horner used his CENTAF staff to prepare the ATO daily and issue it. Units with CAFMS got the order that way, and relayed it to nearby allied forces without the computerized system. The ATO was put on computer disk and flown to naval units, which did not have CAFMS.

Sorties by the Thousands

The Air Tasking Order carried all the detail necessary to plan and coordinate more than 1,000 sorties per day (rising eventually to more than 3,000 sorties a day). Among other things, the ATO included flight call signs, radio frequencies, takeoff times, inflight refueling times, locations, tracks, and altitudes, targets to be hit, the kind and number of munitions to be employed, mission numbers, and much more.

In addition, all the other support details such as Wild Weasel and other electronic defense suppression forces, and search and rescue efforts had to be coordinated. With computer support, this system worked very well.

The daily air tasking order was the size of a metropolitan area telephone book and required about two hours for transmission to all units. The Air Force Computer-Aided Force Management System used to produce the daily "frag"[10] was not compatible with Navy computers.

The lack of a common transmission and computer system to send and receive the ATO between the Air Force and Navy terminals created difficulties. During Desert Shield, the Navy utilized normal DoD message transmission service to receive daily training frag orders. During Desert Storm, however, because of the sheer volume of information to be transmitted, this couldn't work.

The Air Force offered the Navy five CAFMS terminals, but lack of on-board super high frequency transmission facilities precluded the Navy from using them. For Operation Desert Storm, the Navy had to resort to ferrying the ATO on floppy diskette each night from Riyadh to the command aircraft carriers in the Red Sea and Persian Gulf.

From the command ships, the ATO was carried by helicopter to other carriers and ships. This system was time-consuming and awkward, but it was the best arrangement available for coordination of the air war.[11]

A year after the war, Gen. Jimmie V. Adams (USAF Deputy Chief of Staff for Plans & Operations at the time of Desert Storm) said that tactical battle management was "a major headache" because in 1991, not all of the tactical commands in the Air Force were standardized on CAFMS, and the Army, Navy, and Marine Corps use yet other systems.

Now, he said, all of the Air Force operational commands and the Navy have agreed to adopt CAFMS, and the Navy has begun installing the system on its carriers.[12]

Communicating

As Schwarzkopf's forces grew, so did the command and control challenge, especially in communications. That problem rested on the shoulders of Air Force Brig. Gen. Roscoe M. Cougill, who was CENTCOM's Director of C^4 Systems (the fourth C stands for computers).

"On August 2, 1990," Cougill said, "we had no voice or message switching capability in the theater of operations. We did have three small communications centers, but as the coalition forces began to pour into the area of responsibility, they were quickly overwhelmed.

"There was one satellite communications terminal in Bahrain and one in Riyadh. There was one terrestrial communications link, between Bahrain and Dhahran, Saudi Arabia."[13]

During the war, he said, terrestrial systems carried much of the communications within the theater of operations. Supported by the services and the Defense Communications Agency, Cougill deployed the assets available.

"At the peak of the operations," he said, "we had 118 Ground Mobile Force Satellite terminals working off four satellites—the East Atlantic, the Indian Ocean, the Indian Ocean Reserve (which was moved to the theater during the operation), and the United Kingdom Skynet satellite." CENTCOM also utilized twelve high-capacity commercial satellite terminals.

By the time the air war began, Cougill had installed sixty-six voice switches and sixty-six message switches in the war zone. Each switch supported twenty terminals located with military units.

"At the onset of hostilities," he said, "we had 324 automated voice 'trunks' connecting with European and stateside switches. Thirty data 'trunks' to European and stateside switches supported 186 com-

[10] Fragmentary order, a breakout from the ATO assigned to particular operational units for execution.

[11] *Conduct of the Persian Gulf Conflict.*

[12] Gen. Jimmie V. Adams, AFA Symposium, Jan. 30, 1992.

[13] Brig. Gen. Roscoe M. Cougill, Armed Forces Communications and Electronics Association, June 4, 1991.

munications centers. We provided over 700,000 telephone connections per day and processed over 150,000 messages daily."

There had been no plan ahead of time for such a communications buildup. "It is true that, conceptually, we had identified most of the combat forces, but we had not taken the next step, which is developing all the plan annexes," Cougill said. "We were building our communications annex [which describes the network] as the forces deployed. We built, modified and remodified on a daily basis."

Satellite terminals were constantly moved to accommodate the needs of the force, he said. "More than thirty terminals, with associated voice and message centers, moved each day during the period January 1 to March 31, 1991."

Cougill credits centralized control of communications people, equipment, procedures, and policy with the coalition success in the war. CENTCOM validated requests for all communications resources, he said, with support from Washington by Air Force Lt. Gen. James Cassity, the Joint Staff Director of Command, Control, and Communications.

Even radio frequencies were centrally controlled and apportioned, Cougill explained. Without Cassity's work in Washington, Cougill declared, "early deploying forces would have consumed most available resources during the initial deployments. It was vital to conserve some resources for follow-on deployments."

Joint use of communications was the watchword. "At the height of the operation, over 2,500 'joint circuits' were being shared by two or more services," Cougill said.

"We also knew the ground war would provide us a whole new set of challenges—how to maintain communications with huge forces moving rapidly over vast distances," he said. The answer was "the multichannel satellite terminal and, because of its mobility, the eight-foot transmission/receiving dish." By the end of the ground war, Cougill had deployed thirty-three of the terminals in Iraq and Kuwait.

It was particularly difficult to maintain communications over long distances between units in the field. They were connected by ultrahigh frequency (UHF) "point-to-point" radios that often did not transmit far enough across the desert.

It was necessary to augment them with UHF tactical satellite terminals, and it required "Herculean efforts" to support the new equipment.

Cougill is proud of the communications linkup that was eventually established among the headquarters and field forces in eight countries throughout the CENTCOM area of responsibility.

"Our equipment was fully interoperable with the USA mobile subscriber equipment [MSE], British Ptarmigan equipment, and the French RITA system," he pointed out.

The command and control assigned to the CINC by Goldwaters-Nichols could not have been supported without interoperable communications.

"Overall, the communications system established in support of Desert Shield and Desert Storm was unparalleled in the history of military warfare," Cougill said.[14]

[14] Cougill.

The I in C³I

The efficacy of intelligence gathering, analysis, and dissemination has long been a bone of contention between intelligence agencies and operations people in the armed forces.

The Goldwater-Nichols Act did not resolve the issue completely, but it did redirect the flow of critical information. Previously, intelligence had been routed mainly through the individual services or retained at the national level. The field commander drew from these sources the intelligence information he needed to plan and operate.

As a result of Goldwater-Nichols, Schwarzkopf got his data much faster than the old process would have disseminated it. No previous commander or coalition of forces ever had so complete a picture of the adversary or a comparable intelligence capability. Overall, intelligence support for operations in Desert Storm must be rated as effective and successful.

Nevertheless, there were problems—gaps in coverage, outdated data and imagery, and, of particular concern, shortcomings in bomb-damage assessment. Ironically, part of the problem lay with unanticipated complexities created by Goldwater-Nichols. Schwarzkopf's staff was neither large enough or properly equipped to handle the volume of raw and finished intelligence data coming in. Nor were they well prepared to manage the intelligence collection assets.[15] Trying to get a grip on this, Schwarzkopf quadrupled the size of his intelligence staff during the five-month Desert Shield buildup.

Bomb-damage assessment analysts in Washington often underestimated bombing effectiveness. In some cases, pilots flew restrike sorties against targets that had already been knocked out.

It was a matter of perception. To the analyst, a hardened aircraft shelter with a hole punched in the roof by a laser-guided 2,000-pound bomb did not look as if it had taken much damage. Yet, when the people fighting the ground war reached such a shelter, they often found everything inside—aircraft, support equipment, armament, even concrete floors—wrecked or completely disabled.

In other instances, DIA analysts rated the damage to certain Iraqi hangars at ten percent. Troops arriving on the scene discovered them to have been almost totally destroyed.

A basic problem was a lack of fast, tactical post-strike target intelligence, despite the data brought back by Air Force RF-4Cs, Navy F-14s, and Army, Navy, and Marine Corps unmanned aerial vehicles.

Furthermore, Schwarzkopf told the Senate Armed Services Committee after the war, battlefield analyses from intelligence agencies were "caveated, disagreed with, footnoted, and watered down."[16] CENTCOM, the Defense Intelligence Agency, the National Security Agency, and the CIA disagreed frequently about bombing results. Schwarzkopf said the bomb-damage assessment by the intelligence agencies was poor.

"There were many people [not in the combat zone] who felt they were in a better position to judge battle damage rather than allowing the theater commander, who is the person that really has to make the ultimate assessment, to apply good military judgment to what he is seeing," he said.

Schwarzkopf said CIA and DIA provided unrealistically conservative estimates of the damage inflicted upon Iraqi forces, arms, and infrastructure. More important, he added, intelligence was not provided to senior ground commanders fast enough, or in a useful form.

"The intelligence community should be asked to come up with a system that will, in fact, be capable of delivering a real-time product to a theater commander when he requests that," Schwarzkopf advised.

General Corder, CENTAF Director of Operations, cited a "high-level problem of 'what is the status of the enemy?' The question was important because General Schwarzkopf wanted fifty percent destruction of enemy forces before he would attack on the ground."

The problem was not so much in gathering intelligence but in verifying it, analyzing it, and understanding what it meant. Before making assessments on target damage, DIA and CIA "wanted photographs of everything, I understood—every truck, every tank, every foxhole, every troop," Corder said. "That's impossible.

"How do you take a photograph of an enemy division that's spread out over miles of desert? How do you photograph a troop concentration or supply area being hit at night?

"I would say that ninety to ninety-five percent of the time a photo was possible—bridges knocked down or tanks destroyed, for example—a photo was supplied [by military intelligence]."

A photo of a bunker with one bomb hole in the roof did not always convince the analysts that it was seriously damaged. "When a bunker sheltering an Iraqi aircraft was knocked out," Corder said, "the Intelligence people would say it wasn't destroyed because it could be repaired or rebuilt in a certain number of weeks.

[15] *Conduct of the Persian Gulf Conflict.*

[16] Schwarzkopf, Senate Armed Services Committee, June 12, 1991.

"They couldn't seem to realize that we had a lot of aircraft out there, and *nothing* was going to get rebuilt during that war, I could guarantee it."[17]

There were also complaints that new target information collected by "national assets"—satellites, TR-1/U-2s and, other, classified, systems—that reported directly to intelligence agencies outside the war area, took too long to get to the commanders.

Joint STARS provided virtually the only "real-time" intelligence available to the tactical commanders. It linked directly with Army and Air Force data centers in Riyadh. Joint STARS sounded the alarm when the Iraqis suddenly attacked Khafji, and when they attempted to retreat out of Kuwait City toward Basra (the "Highway of Death").[18]

"I knew we would have some deficiencies in intelligence, just as we have had in all wars," Horner said. "Getting current targeting materials, such as photographs, to the aircrews was a problem. We didn't have the production facilities we needed.

"Nevertheless," he said emphatically, "we had far more information than any commanders have ever had in any previous war. The bottom line is, Saddam couldn't turn a wheel without us knowing about it."[19]

Beating the Bottlenecks

Because the Navy's computer systems were incompatible with the Air Force's, Schwarzkopf told the Senate committee, much intelligence data could not be speedily provided to ships, compounding intelligence problems.[20]

Operators and intelligence specialists found ways to work around some of the bottlenecks. Daily, Rear Adm. Michael McConnell, Director for Joint Staff Intelligence, spoke by secure telephone with Brig. Gen. Buster C. Glosson, Horner's Director of Campaign Plans, and imparted critical targeting information.

"This was extremely helpful," Horner said. "We would know what weapons we needed to hit these new targets. We would already have the strike aircraft properly configured when the imagery would come in via satellite.

"We actually had cases in which we could hand a datafax photo to a pilot in the cockpit just before takeoff and he would take his flight to Target A rather than Target B."[21]

In the Pentagon, the Air Staff's strategic planning and analysis group, *Checkmate*, became a round-the-clock information clearing and dissemination center for fast battlefield intelligence. During Desert Storm, Lt. Col. Bernard E. Harvey, Chief of the Strategic Assessments Section, convened a small group from DIA, CIA, NSA, and the Air Staff to analyze target intelligence gathered by "national assets"—highly-classified satellites and sensing systems.

This intelligence was transmitted by the satellites to Washington, not to CENTCOM. Often, there was a delay of hours, and occasionally days, before intelligence agencies in Washington could analyze the data, process it, and transmit it to the Gulf. Sometimes, lucrative targets were long gone before strike aircraft could reach their reported positions.

Checkmate quickly analyzed the raw intelligence and sent, sometimes within minutes, target locations and descriptions by secure telephone or telefax to the planning and operations cell at CENTAF, allowing attack of many mobile and fleeting targets that might have escaped had the information relay awaited normal, slower channels.[22] Glosson received much of the same information by telephone from Admiral McConnell.

The postwar conclusion was that the Department of Defense and the entire national intelligence community must develop a better process for delivering to the commander in chief in the field the intelligence he needs, when he needs it, and in the right amounts.[23]

Command and Control Aircraft

Horner controlled the entire air effort. He operated three types of command and control aircraft. They were central to the success of the air and ground war during Desert Storm. These were the E-3B Sentry Airborne Warning and Control System (AWACS), the E-8A Joint STARS, and the

[17] Corder interview, July 8, 1991.

[18] *Conduct of the Persian Gulf Conflict.*

[19] Horner interview, May 30, 1991.

[20] Molly Moore, "Schwarzkopf: War Intelligence Flawed," Washington *Post*, June 13, 1991.

[21] Horner Interview.

[22] Lt. Col. Bernard E. Harvey, interview, May 9, 1991.

[23] *Conduct of the Persian Gulf Conflict.*

EC-130E Airborne Battlefield Command and Control Center (ABCCC).

The big AWACS birds operated out of Riyadh and flew over Saudi Arabia. As the hot war loomed, Air Force Systems Command provided special communications equipment to enable the Saudi AWACS to communicate with the US fleet despite enemy jamming.[24]

For purposes of coverage and control, Gulf war airspace was divided into three zones—east, central, and west—along the Saudi border with Iraq and Kuwait. One AWACS controlled the air battle in each zone. An additional E-3 was always airborne as a spare or to fill in when one of the primary aircraft left its orbit for inflight refueling.[25]

The AWACS battle staff did its work well, controlling pre- and post-strike refuelings, tankers, reconnaissance aircraft, and other support aircraft as well as the air-to-air and air-to-ground fighters.

The rotating domes atop the E-3s contained not only deep-looking radar but also Identification, Friend or Foe (IFF) systems. In the early going, AWACS performed the valuable function of sorting out coalition aircraft from the Iraqi force. This task eventually vanished because the only aircraft in the sky were those flown by the coalition forces.

AWACS controlled "packages" of fighter aircraft as they entered and exited air-to-ground battle areas. The flying command post identified and contacted post-strike fighter-bombers on their way home, obtained bomb-damage assessment and other strike information, and, if necessary, coordinated additional attacks. The two Air Force E-8A Joint STARS aircraft, with their remarkably discriminating air-to-ground radar, proved adept at detecting enemy ground formations as they formed up or moved across Iraq and Kuwait. Early in the ground war, Joint STARS picked up an Iraqi armored division marshaling for a night attack and sounded the alarm. Coalition air attacks destroyed the enemy formation, so the Iraqi attack never materialized.

The E-8As frequently spotted Iraqi mobile Scud launchers as they moved into position and set up for night launches. They relayed the location coordinates to strike aircraft in orbit over known Scud launch areas. The fighters on orbit were usually F-15E Strike Eagles, equipped with LANTIRN night attack systems, and thus cued, they made short work of numerous Scuds.

The prime Joint STARS job is to report where and how enemy traffic is moving, but the flip side of this information also turned out to be extremely useful. Ground commanders, for example, said it was enormously valuable to know where the Iraqis were *not* moving.

Early in the war, Joint STARS told the coalition defenders in the border town of Khafji that the Iraqis attacking them were not backed up by reinforcements. With that information, the allies launched an immediate and successful counterattack.[26]

In another "flip side" application, tapes from the E-8A radar tracking were played backwards—with the result that sequential blips on the screen pointed directly to the places where the enemy vehicles had begun their trips. If that point of origin turned out to be a supply dump or some other concentration of Iraqi assets, an air strike would soon be on the way.

"We will not ever again want to fight any kind of combat without a Joint STARS kind of system," Air Force Chief of Staff McPeak declared part way through Desert Storm.[27]

EC-130E ABCCCs, less famous than their more elaborate AWACS and Joint STARS cousins, controlled the air-to-ground attacks. In the cargo hold of each EC-130E deploying to the Gulf was a new computerized module with fifteen console positions. At these, controllers and communicators scanned nineteen-inch cathode-ray tubes, calling up maps, imagery, and air tasking order information to use as they employed attack aircraft over the battle area.[28]

Coping With Friction and Fog

All in all, C^3I in the Desert Storm went far, far beyond anything seen in previous wars. The technology, the training, and the systems worked. So did the chain of command and tasking, and coalition forces found

[24] Lt. Gen. Gordon E. Fornell, AFA Symposium, Jan. 31, 1991.

[25] Jeffrey M. Lenorovitz, "AWACS Fleet Supplied Surveillance Data Crucial to Allies'Desert Storm Victory," *Aviation Week & Space Technology*, June 22, 1991.

[26] Peter Grier, "Joint STARS Does Its Stuff," *Air Force Magazine*, June 1991.

[27] Gen. Merrill A. McPeak, AFA Symposium, Jan. 31-Feb. 1, 1991.

[28] Fornell.

ways to overcome or work around most of the problems they encountered.

Clausewitz's *friction and fog of war* weighed heavily. Saddam's Soviet-style command and control system, dependent upon centralized direction from Baghdad, was rendered virtually useless. Allied air attacks destroyed the coordination and effectiveness in the first twenty-four hours of the war.

Individual command nodes, radar, surface-to-air missile sites, and antiaircraft batteries could not function efficiently in isolation from the command and control system.[29]

For the coalition it was different. Talk of "battle management," Gen. Ronald W. Yates of Air Force Systems Command noted early in the campaign, "implies a kind of calm, boardroom style of warfighting. What commanders in the Gulf are really dealing with are dispersed forces in an environment where the fog and friction of war exacerbate every problem. The job of C^3 is to pierce the fog and minimize the friction."[30]

The strength of coalition C^3I, plus the fact that Saddam's had been essentially destroyed, was important up to the end of the Gulf War.

"The allied coalition was able to covertly reposition forces immediately before the ground combat phase began because the Iraqis did not have an aerial surveillance capability," said Gen. Donald J. Kutyna of US Space Command. "This move allowed General Schwarzkopf to completely surprise Iraqi ground forces and minimize allied casualties."[31] ■

[29] Bruce D. Nordwall, "Electronic Warfare Played Greater Role in Desert Storm Than Any Conflict," *Aviation Week & Space Technology*, April 22, 1991.

[30] James W. Canan, "How to Command and Control a War," *Air Force Magazine*, April 1991.

[31] Gen. Donald J. Kutyna, Senate Armed Services Committee, April 23, 1991.

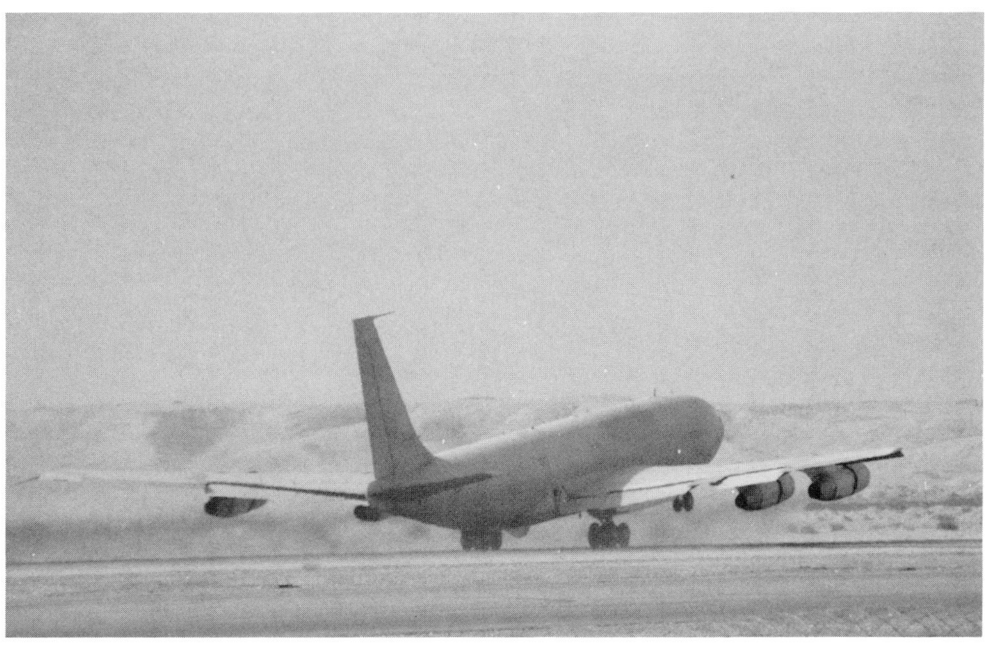

Six years before its official deployment date, the E-8A Joint STARS made a spectacular combat debut in the Gulf War. Every night, one of the Air Force's two E-8As flew a wide-area surveillance and targeting mission lasting ten to twelve hours.

Meeting within the "Black Hole" are General Glosson (second from left), Col. Tony Tolin (standing), and Lt. Col. David Deptula (far right). While they discuss the Jan. 30, 1991, attack plan, Maj. Ernie Norsworthy (left) works on an F-16 issue.

13. The Last 100 Hours

A 101st Airborne trooper gets ready for his part in the war. Coalition airpower stepped up its emphasis on support of ground forces in the last days of the conflict. Air Force leaders express deep respect for the Marines and Army troops who pushed forward into Iraq and Kuwait.

His air force gone, Saddam was blind to Schwarzkopf's massive shift to the west.

In a bombastic radio speech January 20, Saddam predicted that the Iraqi "banner will flutter with great victory in the Mother of All Battles" when his ground forces engaged the enemy.[1]

As the war entered its sixth week, though, the Iraqi field army was still hunkered in its defensive positions. The punishing assault from coalition airpower and artillery intensified as G-Day—the beginning of the ground campaign—drew closer.

In classic military terms, the artillery barrage before an infantry charge is a "battlefield preparation." Coalition airmen figured that they were achieving that, and then some.

"We are not *preparing* the battlefield," declared a sign in the Black Hole. "We are *destroying* it."[2]

The Iraqi communications and supply lines had been cut to shreds. About half of Saddam's armor had been destroyed. Divisions along the border had lost more than half of their troops.

The Iraqis knew the coalition ground offensive was coming, but they expected it to be a frontal and amphibious assault. They were dug in behind minefields, barbed wire, and trenches filled with oil, which they planned to set afire when the coalition attacked.

The strength of their defenses was on the Kuwaiti coastline to the east and along the border with Saudi Arabia to the south. They had chosen this deployment to defend their key locations, Kuwait City and Basra, and also to provide forward defense of Iraq.[3]

Saddam had his poorest troops in front, where they would bear the first brunt of the coalition charge. His best forces, the Republican Guard units, were positioned in the rear echelon as a theater reserve. The strategy was to let the attackers expend their momentum against the mines, the wire, and the weakened forward defenses, then draw them north in increments where the elite Iraqi forces would counterattack.

That was not at all the way it happened when Schwarzkopf launched his ground offensive at 4 a.m. on February 24.

Hail Mary

Throughout the air campaign, Schwarzkopf kept his ground forces deployed opposite the strength of the Iraqi defensive positions. "We made a deliberate decision to align our forces within the boundary looking north towards Kuwait [so] it looked like they were aligned directly on the Iraqi positions," he said.[4]

The actions of Naval and Marine forces in the Gulf suggested that a massive amphibious assault was coming. Schwarzkopf insisted that this maneuvering, including a showy exercise called *Imminent Thunder*, was more than a deception.

"We had every intention of conducting amphibious operations if they were necessary," he said. In any event, the Iraqis were convinced, and tied up six full divisions guarding the Kuwaiti coastline.

Schwarzkopf's main blow, however, was forming up far beyond the Iraqi right flank. "Very early on," he said, "we took out the Iraqi air force. We knew that [Saddam] had

[1] Saddam Hussein, speech on Radio Baghdad, Jan. 20, 1991, reprinted in Sifry and Cerf, *The Gulf War Reader*, Random House, 1991.

[2] USAF white paper, September 1991.

[3] Bruce Watson et. al. *Military Lessons of the Gulf War*. Presidio Press, 1991.

[4] Schwarzkopf, CENTCOM news briefing, Feb. 27, 1991.

USAF Photo by Sgt. Prentes Tramble

very, very limited reconnaissance means. Therefore, when we took out his air force, for all intents and purposes, we took out his ability to see what we were doing down here in Saudi Arabia.

"Once we had taken out his eyes, we did what could best be described as the 'Hail Mary' play in football.... When we knew that he couldn't see us any more, we did a massive movement of troops all the way out to the west, to the extreme west, because at that time, we knew that he was still fixed in this area [the Kuwaiti front] with the vast majority of his forces."

Schwarzkopf said he could not recall a comparable flanking maneuver from any point in military history.

"Not only did we move the troops out there, but we literally moved thousands and thousands of tons of fuel, of ammunition, of spare parts, of water, and of food out here in this area, because we wanted to have enough supplies on hand so [if] we got into a slugfest battle, which we very easily could have gotten into, we'd have enough supplies to last for sixty days."

Schwarzkopf had shifted two entire corps of ground forces, totaling 200,000 troops, and 65,000 vehicles. The coalition's XVIII Airborne Corps moved 250 miles west; the VII Corps moved 150 miles. An observer standing at a given spot during the shift would have seen eighteen trucks pass in any given minute, hour after hour.

The logistics effort moved 5,000 tons of ammunition, 555,000 gallons of fuel, 300,000 gallons of water, and 80,000 meals to points in the west. The number of troops and amount of equipment in the Hail Mary exceeded the scope of Patton's movement to attack the German flank in the Battle of the Bulge during World War II.[5]

Air Force C-130 transports, supporting the ground force redeployment, flew almost 1,200 missions, delivering 14,000 people and more than 9,000 tons of equipment. At the height of the airlift, a C-130 landed every ten minutes, a surge pace that required some units to fly at twice their normal wartime mission rates. The C-130s flew into Logistics Base Charlie, where a mile-long strip of the Trans-Arabian Pipeline road had been marked off as a runway.[6]

As additional cover for the Hail Mary, the Marine Corps exercised visibly in the east, and the CENTCOM staff dropped broad hints to news reporters about the "necessity" of an amphibious invasion. Dummy tanks were set up in positions vacated by the forces that had redeployed, and the remaining tanks and vehicles drove back and forth repeatedly along the border. Powerful loudspeakers broadcast the sounds of tank and troop activity.

As G-Day approached, the coalition ground forces were arrayed in five major formations.[7]

The easternmost, under Saudi command, was positioned inland from Khafji, poised to attack straight north. This formation included the Saudi National Guard and forces of Kuwait, Qatar, and Morocco.

The next formation inland was US Marines, facing northeast toward Ahmed Al Jaber air base and Kuwait City. On their left flank, still along the Kuwaiti border, was the third formation, with Egyptian, Syrian, and more Saudi forces.

The other two formations, hundreds of miles to the west, would deliver the main blow. The huge VII Corps consisted of US infantry, cavalry, and armored divisions, and two British armored divisions. On its left flank, the XVIII Corps included units of the 82d and 101st Airborne Divisions, a mechanized division, an armored cavalry regiment, aviation brigades, and the French 6th Light Armored Division.

Coalition forces of the far flank were to punch into western Iraq. Most would then wheel and dash eastward, attacking the Republican Guard and cutting off its escape routes.

The Battle Begins

In the final days before the ground offensive, concentrated air and artillery strikes destroyed much of the Iraqi artillery that had survived the weeks of air attack. Attack helicopters knocked out army command posts, air defense sites, and gun positions with Hellfire missiles.[8]

[5] *Conduct of the Persian Gulf Conflict.*

[6] USAF white paper, September 1991.

[7] *Conduct of the Persian Gulf Conflict.*

[8] USAF white paper, September 1991.

The 1st Marine Expeditionary Force began the assault at 4 a.m. on February 24, punching through the defenses and driving toward Ahmed Al Jaber airfield in southern Kuwait. Strong firepower prevented the Iraqi forces from maneuvering, and when they attempted to move to safer territory, they were struck by air, artillery, and tank fire.

As the attack unfolded, the coalition got a break from the weather. For months, the prevailing winds had been out of the northwest, blowing toward the US Marine positions in Saudi Arabia. Now they shifted, blowing out of the southeast, pushing the smoke from the burning oil fires back toward the Iraqis and adding to their problems.[9]

In the west, the VII and XVIII Corps advanced rapidly. In less than eight hours, they were positioned to threaten the entire Tigris and Euphrates Valley. The 24th Mechanized Infantry began its end-run that eventually hooked around for more than 250 miles, ending up twenty-seven miles west of Basra, on the coast.[10]

By afternoon, Schwarzkopf could report, "Ten hours into this ground offensive, more than 5,500 prisoners have been captured. We've received reports of many hundreds more north of our positions with white surrender flags. Friendly casualties have been...remarkably light."[11]

Mobs of Iraqi soldiers ("ridden down by bombing," as one British spokesman described them), surrendered in the first hour. The 8,000 Iraqi prisoners in custody by the end of the first day would eventually be joined by 78,000 more.

Many of the troops that remained in position were intimidated or ineffective. The bombing had left the Iraqis with only primitive means of collecting and using battlefield target intelligence. Moreover, some artillerymen refused to man their guns, fearful that they would attract air strikes if they fired.[12]

The coalition advance on the ground was supported strongly by strike and special-function aircraft. The E-8A Joint STARS, for example, detected a blocking force of Iraqis forming up to confront the 3d Egyptian Mechanized Division, whose northward push was impeded by the fire trenches. Joint STARS directed air attacks against the Iraqis and broke up their counterattack.[13]

Throughout the day, Radio Baghdad broadcast messages from Saddam Hussein to his troops at the front, directing them to "show no mercy" to the coalition forces. His remarks were interspersed with messages from Muslim religious leaders, who assured soldiers a place in paradise if they died in battle.[14]

With the French

CENTCOM had assigned US liaison officers, most of them from the Special Operations forces, to non-American units of the coalition. Capt. Walter D. Givhan, an Air Force F-15 pilot and a forward air controller, was with the French. He spoke French fluently, and had previously served as a liaison officer with the French during several operations when he was assigned to US Air Forces in Europe.[15]

Forward air controllers went forward in battle to spot targets and direct strike aircraft onto them. The French did not have FACs, nor did they have ground attack aircraft in Desert Storm. They were vitally interested, however, in aerial firepower.

"We were under the XVIII Airborne Corps and were to have an important end-run mission," Givhan said. "They [the French] would need priority close air support during the first days of the ground war. The French were very concerned about the kind of support they were to get and how it was going to be employed."

On February 23, the day before the ground war began officially, Givhan and his FACs moved into Iraq with the French division. On G-Day, they began calling in ground-support sorties. For the first three days, until the American forces completed their turn toward the east, the French received priority from the attack aircraft.

"We were running against the Iraqi 45th Infantry Division," Givhan said. "It was protecting the city of As Salman, its military airfield, and other positions. During those first three days, my teams controlled or coordinated forty-six close air support

[9] Robert F. Dorr, *Desert Storm Air War*. Motorbooks, 1991.

[10] USAF white paper, September 1991.

[11] Schwarzkopf briefing, Feb. 24, 1991.

[12] Watson et al. *Military Lessons of the Gulf War*.

[13] USAF white paper, September 1991.

[14] Nora Boustany, "'Show No Mercy,' Saddam Tells His Troops," Washington *Post*, Feb. 25, 1991.

[15] Jim I. Swinson, Jr. "French Connection-Pilot Fights War From Ground," Eglin (AFB), *Eagle*, Aug. 2, 1991.

strikes." The strikes were flown in flights of two or four.

"The French were pretty impressed with the continuous flow of F-16s and A-10s," he said. "By the time we got to the enemy positions, the Iraqis were offering little opposition. They had been hit pretty hard."

The first day, coalition air forces flew more than 3,000 sorties. Of these, 700 were in support of ground operations.[16]

The AirLand Battle concept, the basis for much of the Army and Air Force joint planning in the 1980s, was not employed to any real extent in the Gulf War. The air campaign had so devastated the Iraqi field army that not much close air support was required.

There were some pitched battles, but they were fought by artillery and armored forces, and the opposing sides were frequently miles away from each other during the exchange.

Mobile ground units of the coalition met pockets of determined resistance, but little large-scale opposition. They moved forward so rapidly that the classic situation for close air support—troops in contact with the enemy—rarely developed.

Fighter bombers and helicopter gunships mostly moved ahead of the advancing ground troops, clearing the way with massive firepower.

C-130 airlifters supplied the coalition advance with airdrops of food, water, and ammunition. The C-130s also evacuated wounded and non-battle casualties as well as more than 600 wounded Iraqi wounded prisoners who required immediate medical attention.

With the Army

"We were out west with the 'Hail Mary' troops," said Air Force Capt. Phillip D. Tau, an air liaison officer with the 2d Brigade of the 1st Armored Division. "Because the Army, Navy, and Marines were doing so well in Kuwait, we jumped off into Iraq eighteen hours ahead of plan. We just kept rolling along. We got to our objective, Al Busyah, where the Iraqis had a huge supply depot, much earlier than we expected.

"We stopped outside the town. There was some fighting, and some Iraqis were running around, waving anything white to surrender. There were some troops in the town who were firing at us, and you could hear the AK-47 rounds pinging off the vehicles.

"The PsyOps people began to harangue them with loudspeakers: 'You'd better surrender, or it's all over.' They didn't want to surrender at first. But then, they saw the tanks, and began to surrender in groups. I didn't have to call for close air support because the tactical situation didn't warrant it.

"Pretty soon, we were moving forward and were literally surrounded by starving, surrendering Iraqis. All we could do was toss them some MREs [Meals Ready to Eat field rations] and tell them to sit down. The military police would be along to accept their surrender. We just kept rolling."[17]

Air Force SSgt. William J. Burns was an air control specialist with the 2d Armored Cavalry Regiment. His unit headed straight north, toward the Republican Guard in Kuwait.

The mission was battlefield interdiction and according to Burns, consisted of "backing up tanks and APCs fighting Iraqi armor, both during the day and at night."

"The Army would run into groups of tanks out there, and we'd put aircraft in to attack them. At night, you could see the artillery rounds arcing up and coming down, and the sabot rounds from the tank guns shooting out in straight lines. Mostly, we employed A-10s."[18]

"It wasn't close combat," Tau said. "It was more like a search and destroy mission. Go out in the general area and find some enemy armor and destroy it. By the time the Army rolled in, we could see by the wreckage that something had been there. There was lots of ground fighting, but it always seemed to be a long range type thing between tanks, APCs and artillery. I didn't see any close air support, in the classic sense."

The Rout

The Iraqi III Corps, desperately trying to escape the 1st Marine Expeditionary Force approaching from the southwest and the Saudi-led Arab formation coming from

[16] Brig. Gen. Richard I. Neal, CENTCOM News Briefing, Feb. 25, 1991.

[17] Capt. Phillip D. Tau, interview, Aug. 7, 1991.

[18] SSgt. William Burns, interview, Aug. 7, 1991.

the south, broke and fell back into the city, where they became entangled with Iraqi occupation forces.[19]

"Monday night, February 25, I got a phone call from the Kuwaiti Resistance," Glosson said.[20] "This communication lash up came through the Saudi Air Force. The caller said, 'It looks like the Iraqis are putting their stuff together and getting ready to leave.' In the TACC, we checked the Joint STARS downlink display. It showed a few vehicles on the roads, but nothing to confirm a mass withdrawal. The vehicles had not yet begun to leave the city. We tasked Joint STARS to watch the area north of the city very closely."

Inside the city, the troops were panicky, but not too panicky to load stolen goods into whatever kind of vehicles they could find. Every kind of vehicle imaginable, tanks, trucks, school buses, ambulances, and Mercedes sedans—many of them piled high with TV sets, refrigerators, clothing, jewelry, computers, and other property—was soon clogging the highway to Basra.

On the Joint STARS radar screen, a moving vehicle on the ground shows up as a small cross. The traffic fleeing north from Kuwait City was so heavy that the individual crosses on the Joint STARS display merged into thick lines.

"The weather was lousy, in some places as low as 200 feet overcast," said Glosson. "The Scud hunters attacked, but, with the weather, they couldn't stop the vehicles moving north up Highway Six.

"It was no picnic. The people in the convoy were firing back with antiaircraft guns, small arms, and shoulder mounted infrared missiles. I realized the only thing that could stop the convoy was the F-15E.

"The Strike Eagle crews could do that, at night, under bad weather, because they had something nobody else had—the LANTIRN system along with the LANTIRN targeting pods, and an aircraft optimized for that kind of operations.

"So, I called Hal Hornburg, the 4th Provisional Wing Commander at Al Kharj, where the F-15Es were based. He had gone to his tent, ready to go to bed. He and his aircrews had been flying that night, since 5 p.m. the previous afternoon. Most of his aircrews had flown missions as long as five or six hours. The maintenance people and the armorers had been up most of the night, too, of course."

Glosson recalls telling Hornburg, "Hal, I hate to do this to you and your people. I know you've just finished a hard night's flying, but I've got a job for you. This may be painful, but I want you to put your guys back in their aircraft, fly over to Kuwait, and stop a convoy.

"I explained the importance of these troops not getting their equipment back to Iraq, where it could be used to fight again. I also explained that among the Iraqis in the convoy were those who had occupied Kuwait and committed unspeakable atrocities. 'Stop them at all costs,' I said."

"I talked to my squadron commanders," Hornburg said. "They decided who was to fly those missions. It didn't matter how much these guys had already flown that night. This was important. If we could stop the Iraqi retreat, it could have a significant impact on the war.[21]

"I told the squadron commanders to look each pilot and weapon system officer in the eye. If you get a firm look back, put him in the cockpit. If you get 'a thousand yard stare,' send him back to bed."

They had no trouble getting enough aircrews.

"We launched six flights, each with two aircraft." Glosson said. "They flew the mission and they stopped the convoy. We didn't lose anybody.

"In less than ninety minutes, the first Strike Eagles were off the ground. Joint STARS briefed them in the air on target locations. They hit the front of the convoy near Iraq, just before it got to Mutla Pass, which became a chokepoint. The whole column of trucks was stopped dead. Then, the F-15Es hit the rear of the convoy so they couldn't get back into Kuwait City. Twelve F-15Es stopped the convoy cold."

The F-15Es then hit the vehicles caught in the road congestion. Coming in unseen out of the night, relying on their LANTIRN pods to find their targets, they struck repeatedly with cluster bombs, precision-

[19] USAF white paper, September 1991.

[20] Brig. Gen. Buster C. Glosson, interview, May 28, 1991.

[21] Col. Hal Hornburg, interview, Jan. 21, 1992.

guided munitions, and general-purpose bombs.[22]

"By morning," Glosson said, "the weather had cleared, and we hit the trapped Iraqi column with hundreds of Air Force and Navy attack sorties. Everything—trucks, buses, tankers, armored personnel carriers, stolen civilian vehicles—everything was blasted."

Other roads leading to Iraq were also under attack. By the afternoon of the next day, US Army tanks joined in the destruction.

More than 1,000 Iraqi tanks, trucks, and other vehicles were trapped. When the road jams became too great, many Iraqis ran off into the desert.

There was a short letup in the road attacks, between the last F-15E strikes of the night and the time other attack aircraft arrived after sunup.

"It is unfortunate that a significant number of Iraqis who had been riding in convoy vehicles were able to escape into Iraq on foot [during that interval]," Glosson said. "They should have been made to pay for their atrocities in Kuwait."

"Later," Hornburg said, "we heard about the Highway of Death, but that night, as far as we were concerned, it was just normal Strike Eagle business, hitting targets in the dark."

During the air war, the F-15Es had concentrated on airfield installations, the Iraqi electric power system, aircraft shelters and bridges. They had carried a large share of the load in the great Scud hunt. In the last days of the war, they had stunning success against still other kinds of targets. The 335th TFS, for example, destroyed 478 pieces of artillery, according to its commander, Lt. Col. Stephen Pingel.[23]

The End and the Aftermath

Not all of the Iraqi guns had been silenced. The coalition lost four aircraft to ground fire February 25 and another on February 27. US armor engaged the Republican Guard February 27 in the largest tank battle since 1943. Some Iraqi units were still fighting as late as March 2.

One of the last Scud missiles fired during the war struck a US billeting facility in Dhahran February 25, killing twenty-eight troops and wounding 100. The Iraqis had more than 600 fires burning in Kuwait, 517 of them at oil wellheads. Coalition forces would soon discover the extent of the depredations they had committed before they pulled back.

Nevertheless, the rout was so complete that it generated some sympathy for Saddam Hussein and his battered armed forces. Later, a reporter asked Gen. Merrill A. McPeak, Air Force Chief of Staff, if the "excessive use of violence" had not been "sort of like clubbing baby seals."

In his measured reply, McPeak pointed out that "the alternative is that we should never attack a disorganized enemy. We should wait until he is stopped, dug in, and prepared to receive the attack."[24] Another reporter remarked on how easy it all looked. He asked Schwarzkopf if the speed of the coalition advance into Kuwait did not indicate that the minefields and fire trenches had been "overrated in the first place?"

Schwarzkopf riveted the reporter with a stare and asked: "Have you ever been in a minefield?"

The reporter had not. Schwarzkopf—who had—said that "one of the toughest things that anybody ever has to do is go up there and walk into something like that and go through it."[25]

After the war, Schwarzkopf said that when he launched the ground attack on the morning of February 24, he expected that it would take three weeks. Instead, it took 100 hours.[26]

As Schwarzkopf told reporters, the coalition could have destroyed Iraq if that had been its purpose. "We were 150 miles away from Baghdad, and there was nobody between us and Baghdad," he said. His forces could have moved into the Iraq capital "unopposed, for all intents and purposes."

Between February 24 and February 27, the US Air Force flew 3,000 sorties in conjunction with ground operations. Of these, four percent were counterair, thirty-five percent were support of ground operations, and sixty-one percent were interdiction.

[22] USAF white paper, September 1991.

[23] Lt. Col. Stephen Pingel, interview, May 31, 1991.

[24] Gen. Merrill A. McPeak, Pentagon news conference, March 15, 1991.

[25] Schwarzkopf, CENTCOM news briefing, Feb. 27, 1991.

[26] USAF white paper, September 1991.

Over the four days, the Air Force flew 1,050 sorties in support of ground operations, and US Marine aircraft provided an additional 750.[27] Army aircraft operated day and night. Attack and observation helicopters flew in teams, locating Iraqi artillery positions and command posts and destroying them with Hellfire missiles.[28]

Iraq agreed to a cease fire on February 28, and although sporadic fighting continued for a few more days, the war was effectively over.

Air Boss Horner credits Schwarzkopf with having been "right on target in using airpower to maintain the initiative and fight the war on our terms rather than on Saddam Hussein's terms.

"Saddam Hussein," Horner said, "wanted to attack us. He didn't care if he lost a quarter of a million men so long as he could inflict seven to ten thousand casualties on us and say he defeated the Americans. His whole strategic point was to inflict casualties, and we were able to withhold that from him by using airpower to maintain the initiative."[29]

The self-styled field marshal, who had spent a third of his gross national product for ten years to build an enormous army and air force, had seen them cut to shreds, mainly by airpower.

It has been suggested, in the popular news media and elsewhere, that the coalition armed forces prosecuted the Gulf War in the spirit of a game or a blood sport. That is not the conclusion that emerges from discussions with those who actually fought the war. Their attitude is reflected more accurately by this segment from the 48th TFW's unofficial history of the war, written primarily for circulation within the unit:

"After the war, there were no parties, no raucous celebrations, and no gloating about what we had done. The same quiet professionalism and low-key determination that had sustained the unit through the war would do just as well here."[30] ■

[27] CENTCOM Situation Report, March 14, 1991.

[28] *Conduct of the Persian Gulf Conflict.*

[29] James W. Canan, "Lesson Number One," *Air Force Magazine*, October 1991.

[30] Operation Desert Storm. Unofficial history of the 48th TFW, Taif, Saudi Arabia, 1991.

14. Global Reach—Global Power

A B-52G takes on fuel from a California Air Guard KC-10 tanker in Desert Storm. On the opening night of the war, the aging B-52 demonstrated the Global Reach concept by striking targets in Iraq on a round-trip mission launched from Louisiana.

The Gulf War set a new standard: to win quickly, decisively, with overwhelming advantage, and with few casualties.

As with all wars, the analysis and commentary continued long after the shooting had stopped. A year after Operation Desert Storm, the Department of Defense was still sifting the "lessons learned." Strategists, politicians, journalists, and others, in and out of government, were still arguing about the conclusions to be drawn.

Most Americans would probably agree with President George Bush. "Gulf Lesson One is the value of airpower," he said emphatically in his May 1991 speech to the graduating class at the US Air Force Academy.[1]

Citizens by the hundreds of thousands, lining parade routes in Washington and New York and flocking to celebrations all over the nation, clearly seemed to think the armed forces had achieved something impressive in the Gulf.

Journalist James Kitfield dug out a copy of a white paper, *Global Reach—Global Power*, that the Air Force had published in June 1990, and noted how closely it tracked with actual operations and results in Desert Storm.[2]

On the first anniversary of Saddam's invasion of Kuwait, CBS news analyst Harry Smith echoed the theme of President Bush's Academy commencement speech. "The Iraqi military machine folded under the pressure of allied smart bombs and airpower," Mr. Smith declared.[3]

Others, however, took a different view. The Air Force's constant critic, Dr. Jeffrey Record, complained that airpower had again not been decisive. *[See "The Airpower Controversy," p. 40.]* He found it remarkable that airpower had left some targets undestroyed and deemed it "a failure and an embarrassment" to the Air Force that Saddam Hussein survived the war. He pointed out that airpower had missed some of the Scuds and did not get all of the Iraqi nuclear, biological, and chemical weapons facilities.[4]

"Airpower did not obliterate Baghdad or destroy Iraq," *Air Force Magazine* responded in an editorial. "That was not the objective. Had it been, a ruthless air campaign could have done an adequately awesome job of it."[5]

The Testimony of Results

It is impossible to dispute logically that airpower was *a* decisive factor in the Gulf War. Furthermore, there are strong grounds for arguing that it was *the* decisive factor.

The air campaign followed Air Force doctrine faithfully and was a convincing vindication of it.

Coalition air forces first gained air superiority, then waged a successful strategic air campaign against Iraq's military resources and infrastructure. Concurrently, they chewed up Saddam Hussein's armies in Kuwait and Iraq. Finally, coalition ground forces muscled their way across the battlefield and drove the Iraqis from Kuwait.

Allied air forces achieved air superiority in a very short time by destroying or suppressing most of Saddam Hussein's SAM and AAA sites, shooting down thirty-five Iraqi aircraft while losing none in air-to-air fighting, knocking out 375 aircraft shelters, and destroying more than 200 air-

[1] Weekly Compilation of Presidential Documents, June 3, 1991.

[2] James Kitfield, "The Drive for 'Global Reach'," *Government Executive*, December 1991.

[3] Commentary, Harry Smith, CBS, Aug. 2, 1991.

[4] Jeffrey Record, "The Air War Missed Its Biggest Target," Baltimore *Sun*, Nov. 21, 1991.

[5] John T. Correll, "Airpower, One Year Later," *Air Force Magazine*, February 1992.

craft on the ground. All this precipitated an aerial rout in which more than 120 of Saddam's aircraft fled to Iran, where they were confiscated.

Airpower set back his nuclear research, development, and production capability eight to ten years, reduced his chemical research, development, and production capability by seventy-five percent, and destroyed 100 percent of his identified biological research, development and production facilities. His ability to produce offensive missiles, aircraft, armor, and artillery was destroyed or severely damaged.[6]

Saddam's military communications were virtually destroyed. He could not talk to his commanders or control his troops effectively, nor could he collect much information about his own forces, much less those of the enemy.

His air force and most of his armor were gone. His remaining forces were primarily infantry, useful for facing down citizen mobs but inadequate against modern military forces of other nations or for carrying out Saddam's expansionist dreams. (Most of the helicopters, which were never specifically targeted, survived and Saddam later used them to put down Iraqi and Kurdish uprisings.)

In discussing the effects of the air campaign on Iraqi fighting forces, Air Boss Horner likes to quote an exchange from the interrogation of an Iraqi prisoner:

Interrogator: "Why did your men give up?"

Iraqi Division Commander: "You know."

Interrogator: "I don't know. Why?"

Division Commander: "It was the airplanes."[7]

That summed up the effect on Saddam's soldiers, as they listened to the almost continuous roar of coalition warplanes overhead, day and night, and were subjected to the concussions and destruction of aerial weapons throughout the five weeks of the air campaign and the four days of ground operations.

"During the Iran war, my tank was my friend because I could sleep in it and know I was safe," an Iraqi general said. "During this war, my tank became my enemy. None of my troops would get near a tank at night because they just kept blowing up."[8]

The effect of airpower on Iraq was apparent from the first day of the air campaign, five weeks before the ground war started. This was recognized by Secretary of Defense Cheney, who remarked flatly, after the war, "The air campaign was decisive."[9]

On another occasion, Cheney said, "I think it set the stage for the very enormous success that we enjoyed once the ground operation started."[10] Later, he added that Iraq could not fight back "because the air war turned out to be absolutely devastating."[11]

In fact, the success of Operation Desert Storm was so spectacular that it may have changed the standard for performance of US forces in armed conflict.

According to Gen. John M. Loh, who relayed Schwarzkopf's initial requirements for the air campaign *(see p. 43)* and who later moved on to head Tactical Air Command, the new standard is "to win quickly, decisively, with overwhelming advantage, and with few casualties."

Congress and the public now expect US forces to prevail by "99-1, not 55-54 in double overtime," Loh said.[12]

The "Exceptional" Setting

Air Force leaders acknowledge that circumstances and conditions in the Gulf theater were almost ideal for an air war.

Modern air bases on the Arabian peninsula and in Turkey could receive thousands of coalition aircraft. At some bases, fast construction of housing and other structures was required. A few bases were built practically from scratch. At most locations, however, the basic airfield facilities were already in place.

Although the weather over the Arabian peninsula was often poor, it was still better than what US forces might have encountered at other crisis spots around the world.

Against the desert terrain, with little vegetation and few features, targets stood out clearly for air-to-ground radars and attacking aircrews.

There were also military disadvantages, including the thick, ubiquitous, local Iraqi

[6] Lt. Gen. Charles A. Horner, "Reflections on Desert Storm," May 1991.

[7] Horner briefing.

[8] USAF white paper, September 1991.

[9] Cheney, "Meet the Press," April 14, 1991.

[10] Cheney, quoted in Horner Briefing.

[11] Cheney, interview by Harry Smith, CBS, Aug. 2, 1991.

[12] Loh, AFA symposium, Jan. 31, 1992.

air defenses, the long flying hours, the extended distances over which supplies and equipment had to be transported, and the harshness of the climate and the geography.

Much has been made of the fact that the challenges of the Gulf War were unique, that the nature of the enemy and the setting make it impossible to draw any conclusions from this experience that would be relevant to other conflicts.

A commentary by the bipartisan Aspen Strategy Group puts that observation in perspective: "The first lesson of the Gulf War is clear: the Gulf War was exceptional. But here's the rub: there is no rule to which a war may be an exception. All wars are extraordinary."[13]

The Gulf War, which rates as a "major regional contingency" in current US defense strategy, may be fairly typical of conflicts that the armed forces are most likely to face in the years ahead. Iraq had a large and capable military force, even if Saddam Hussein and his generals did not use it well.

Furthermore, as Loh points out, victory in the Gulf took a third more fighter forces than the strategy estimated for such a contingency and required most of the US Air Force's best aircraft and the largest coalition air fleet to see combat since World War II.[14]

Desert One and Desert Storm

Rep. Les Aspin (D-Wis.), chairman of the House Armed Services Committee, drew a comparison between the Gulf War and "Desert One," the disastrous attempt in 1980 to rescue Americans held hostage in Tehran. That mission was a total failure, aborted after an airplane crash and the death of eight members of the rescue team short of their intended destination.

"The US military was not as bad as it looked at Desert One, and it is probably not as good as it looks after Desert Storm," Aspin declared.[15]

In his opinion, success in the Gulf War was leveraged by four factors: the extraordinary caliber of the troops, improved organization—for which he specifically credits the Goldwater-Nichols Act—more realistic thinking in US strategy, and the quality of the military technology.

"Basically," Aspin said, "high technology was vindicated in Desert Storm. There was a school that argued that the US was going in for too much high tech in its military equipment. They said we should develop simpler, more reliable equipment.

"They reasoned that we needed simpler and more reliable equipment because the high tech would not work in the grit, grime, and hard knocks of warfare, and that it was too complicated for soldiers with a high school education to operate and repair.

"My view is that Desert Storm proved the worst fears of this school to be unfounded. The equipment did not suffer breakdowns just getting to the battlefield as some feared. It did stand up to the rigors of war, and it could be operated by high school graduates.

"My second tentative conclusion about high tech is that we know how to orchestrate its use in a way that makes the sum bigger than the parts."

Stars of the Show

Various forces, systems, and capabilities proved outstanding in the Gulf War. Almost every military commander one talks to remarks on the incredible performance of the airlifters and the logisticians.

To airmen down behind enemy lines, the search and recovery crews rate high on the hero list. The maintenance people set new records for keeping aircraft in the air. It is virtually impossible to heap too much praise on the combat crews.

There were also standouts among the weapons and systems. The Patriot missile, shooting Scuds out of the sky, was certainly impressive. The deep-looking radars on AWACS and Joint STARS provided the coalition an unprecedented grasp of a war in progress. After January and February 1991, few are likely to ever again think of precision-guided weapons as overly-expensive novelties.

The system superstar of Desert Storm, however, was probably the F-117 Stealth fighter. The Air Force declares emphatically that stealth technology will be a fea-

[13] Bobby R. Inman *et al*, "Lessons From the Gulf War," *Washington Quarterly*, Winter 1992.

[14] Loh, AFA Symposium, Jan. 31, 1992.

[15] Aspin, "Desert One to Desert Storm," Center for Strategic and International Studies, June 20, 1991.

ture of any new combat airplanes it buys from here on, and in view of operations in the Gulf, there isn't likely to be too much objection from anyone on that point.

The commander in chief was among the believers.

Speaking shortly after the war, President Bush said that "the F-117 proved itself by doing more, doing it better, doing it for less, and targeting soldiers, not civilians. [It] carried a revolution in warfare on its wings."[16]

Even in comparison with other coalition aircraft—some of which were quite impressive themselves—the F-117's performance was astounding.

For example, on one attack against one airfield, eight attack aircraft striking the airfield were protected by four Wild Weasels, five radar jammers, and twenty-one fighters carrying radar-guided missiles.

This package of thirty-eight aircraft (with a crew total of sixty-five) was needed to ensure that eight aircraft could hit one target with a good expectation of success and survival. The ratio of support aircraft to strike aircraft was almost five to one, with an aircraft to target ratio of thirty-eight to one.

At the same time twenty-one F-117s were striking thirty-seven targets by themselves.[17]

The Air Force's commitment to stealth rests not only on such results in the Gulf War but also on the knowledge that the F-117 is almost ten years old and that current stealth technology, developed for the B-2 bomber, is several generations more advanced.

Moreover, whereas the F-117 can carry two precision-guided weapons, the B-2 carries sixteen, and has far greater range. A popular "what if" discourse in the Air Force these days examines what might have been possible in the Gulf had the B-2 been available there.

For example, the F-117s flew fifty sorties against a complex of hardened chemical munitions bunkers in an area where the defenses were judged too lethal to send any other aircraft. Two stealthy bombers with precision weapons could have done the same job.

Before big-payload B-52s could bomb a particular storage and maintenance complex north of Baghdad, the F-117s had to go in first to knock out the Iraqi air defenses so B-52s could destroy it. A single stealthy bomber, even without precision-guided munitions, would have been plenty for the whole task.

The "what if" discussions point to indirect support to the F-117 that could have been eliminated by the larger platform. On one mission, the Stealth fighters went against Iraqi nuclear research and development sites, bunkers, and aircraft shelters at Kirkuk, Qayyarah, and Mosul. They did not need cover and protection themselves, but it was a long trip, and they did require fuel.

That meant that both air superiority fighters and electronic warfare aircraft had to go along for the protection of the tankers flying deep in Iraqi airspace.

The Commanders and the Troops

Over and over, military commanders remarked that the performance of US forces in the Gulf was an outcome of Red Flag operations at Nellis AFB, Nev., joint exercises at the National Training Center at Fort Irwin, Calif., and the general quality of training carried out day after day, year after year.

The troops did perform well, and so did their equipment, but the outcome also owed much to the most effective command arrangement—starting at the top—seen in any war in recent times.

Unlike some of his predecessors, President Bush left field decisions to field commanders, and gave the armed forces the flexibility they needed to fight the war.

As Schwarzkopf said, "I'm very thankful for the fact that the President of the United States has allowed the United States military and the coalition military to fight this war exactly as it should have been fought, and the President in every case has taken our guidance and our recommendations to heart, and has acted superbly as the Commander-in-Chief."[18]

Schwarzkopf meant every word of it, and other military leaders concurred wholeheartedly.

Air Force officers further remarked on how well Schwarzkopf, an Army officer,

[16] Weekly Compilation of Presidential Documents, June 3, 1991.

[17] USAF white paper, September 1991.

[18] Schwarzkopf, news briefing, Feb. 27, 1991.

understood airpower, and they appreciated the opportunity to demonstrate what airpower, properly employed, could do.

The Gulf War "confirmed what we've known since 1942," Lt. Gen. Michael A. Nelson, USAF deputy chief of staff for Plans and Operations said. "Airpower must be highly integrated and used very efficiently and. . .the only way to do that is to have an airpower expert running the show with all the air assets in his grasp. Chuck Horner proved that that is indeed the way to do business."[19]

Some disagreement notwithstanding *(see Chapter 12, "Command and Control")*, the Gulf War validated the centralized control of air assets by a single "air boss" and a coordinated air tasking order for all aircraft flying in the Kuwait theater of operations.

Fleet defense aircraft, flying over the Persian Gulf but not in Iraqi or KTO airspace, were controlled directly by the Navy, but the ATO covered the operations of all coalition air forces, special operations Forces, most naval and Marine air, TLAMs, and part of the Army Tactical Missile System capability.[20]

The results were a classic demonstration of the Air Force's belief that airpower is best employed as a unified, theater asset rather than broken out locally into penny packets.

Reaching deep and striking hard, airpower in the Gulf destroyed nearly all of Saddam's air force and much of his ground forces before they could be brought to bear on the coalition.

General McPeak, the Air Force Chief of Staff, says that no American soldier has been killed by an enemy airplane since 1953. In the Korean war and in more recent conflicts, he said, "we conducted the air fight in the other guy's airspace. We fought the air battle over the Yalu, or over Hanoi, or over Baghdad."[21]

Airpower and Casualties

Airpower, as Horner applied it, yielded a swift and decisive victory for the coalition. Airpower was also the reason American casualties were far lower than in any previous conflict.

Thirty-five US troops were killed and seventy-three wounded by accidental friendly fire. Of the 108 US friendly fire casualties, airpower was responsible for eleven killed and fifteen wounded.

"In two separate instances, the United States Air Force attacked friendly vehicles," McPeak said. "We destroyed both of those vehicles, and we killed thirteen of our own people—Marines in one case and Brits in another.

"That's two separate mistakes we made. We attacked probably something on the order of 10,000 vehicles. These mistakes were made in the fog of combat, heavy fighting on the ground. They were both done at night. It's a very difficult problem, to do this kind of thing at night.

"We certainly deeply regret this kind of thing. It's a problem we work on all the time. I feel badly about it. My only consolation is that by the grace of God and dint of hard work, perhaps we saved a few who might otherwise have been claimed."[22]

The casualties sustained by the United States in the Gulf War would have been vastly higher had Saddam Hussein's forces been in good physical condition, well supplied, intact, and in place, awaiting the ground invasion.

Instead, they were poorly equipped, starving, ill-housed, lice-infested, confused, dispersed out of unit areas, and out of touch with their commanders. Their condition was attributable primarily to the air campaign.[23]

"The air war, obviously, was very, very effective," Schwarzkopf said ". . .In the earlier phases we made great progress in the air war. In the latter stages, . . .the enemy had burrowed down in the ground as a result of the air war. That, of course, made the air war a little bit tougher, but when you dig your tanks in and bury them, they're no longer tanks. They're now pillboxes. That makes a difference....So the air campaign was very, very successful and contributed a great deal.[24]

"Airpower found, fixed, fought, and finished the Iraqi military," a postwar USAF analysis said.[25] Airpower not only reduced the risk to American forces from the enemy but also kept

[19] Canan, "Lesson Number One."

[20] Horner briefing.

[21] McPeak, USAF news conference, Orlando, Fla., Jan. 31, 1992.

[22] McPeak, Pentagon news briefing, March 15, 1991.

[23] USAF white paper, September 1991.

[24] Schwarzkopf, CENTCOM news briefing, Feb. 27, 1991.

[25] USAF white paper, September 1991.

resistance from forming to pose a significant threat.

The total number of Iraqi troops killed in the Kuwait theater of operations is not known. The Pentagon has avoided Vietnam-style "body counts" of enemy dead, and Saddam's announcements about Iraqi casualties have been based more on propaganda goals than on actual counting.

US estimates of Iraqi soldiers killed are reported to range from 20,000 to 100,000.[26] Given the initial size of the Iraqi force and the intensity of the bombing, either of those casualty estimates is indicative of air campaign that emphasized precise use of weapons and sought victory at the lowest cost possible in human lives.

Airpower Decisive—But Not Alone

"Our work in Desert Storm speaks for itself," McPeak said a year after the conflict, "but it doesn't help to act as though we made the only contribution.

"Those Marines that went through the wire and raced into Kuwait, they did something. Our Army guys, this generation of Army officers, have got maneuver in their blood.

"The Navy and the maritime forces slapped on an embargo in August....It has been leakproof...It has been a magnificent, highly professional job about which not much has been said.

"And, of course, all of the services made contributions to the airpower part of the equation."[27]

The Gulf War was not fought by airplanes alone, nor was the air campaign conducted solely by the US Air Force alone.

The war constituted "the whole picture of what airpower is all about: space assets, intelligence gathering and reconnaissance, command and control, electronic combat, the shooters, the SEAD [suppression of enemy air defenses] campaign," Nelson said. It was a textbook example of "the totality" of US airpower—"Air Force air and space, Navy air, Marine air, and Army air with helicopters."[28]

Corder, the CENTCOM Director of Operations, agrees that "the Air Force didn't do it alone. Somebody had to walk in on the ground and plant the flag."[29]

As Horner said, Desert Shield and Desert Storm "emphasized the role of airpower because of the strategy and the environment—the nature of the war. It did not make airpower the only element or the supreme element, but it did emphasize the contribution of airpower."[30]

The Air Force's concept in *Global Reach—Global Power* anticipated quite accurately the air operation and campaign to come. That document had even identified Iraq, on the first page, as a potential adversary.

It cited the inherent characteristics of airpower: speed, range, flexibility, precision, and lethality.

The Air Force, it said, could project power rapidly over great distances, employ airlift for reinforcement and resupply, use airborne and spaceborne platforms for command, control, communications, and intelligence, hit critical targets in the first hours of conflict, establish control of the air, reduce the enemy's forces and his means to make war, and ultimately ensure a favorable ratio for the ground forces at the point of contact.[31]

This is a fair description of what happened in Operations Desert Shield and Desert Storm.

General McPeak summed it up this way: "The US Air Force can go anywhere in the world very quickly, and it can have tremendous destructive effect when ordered to do that by the President."[32] ■

[26] "Strategic Campaign Focused on Targets and Cut Casualties, Pentagon Maintains," *Aviation Week & Space Technology*, Jan. 27, 1992.

[27] McPeak, AFA symposium, Jan. 30, 1992.

[28] Canan, "Lesson Number One."

[29] Corder interview, July 8, 1991.

[30] Canan, "Lesson Number One."

[31] *The US Air Force and National Security: Global Reach—Global Power*, USAF white paper, June 1990.

[32] McPeak, Pentagon news briefing, March 15, 1991.

USAF Photo by MSgt. Timothy Hadryck

This photo was snapped January 21, moments after Sgt. Ben Pennington, Air Force PJ, leaped from an MH-53J rescue helicopter to pick up Navy Lt. Devon Jones, who had been shot down the night before. *(see p. 104.)*

Photo by William Campbell/Time

Air Force Secretary Donald B. Rice and other dignitaries were on hand to welcome the 1st Tactical Fighter Wing back home to Langley AFB, Va., after Operation Desert Storm—but the welcome that the pilots and support personnel had most looked forward to was from their families.

Maj. Gregory A. Feest (left), flying an F-117 Stealth fighter, dropped the first bomb of the war in the early morning hours of January 17. Capt. John K. Kelk (right) shot down a MiG-29 near Mudaysis January 17. It was the first Iraqi fighter to fall in Operation Desert Storm.

USAF Photo by MSgt. Thomas Leigue, Jr.

Gen. Colin Powell, chairman of the Joint Chiefs of Staff, and Secretary of Defense Dick Cheney meet with General Schwarzkopf (right) to discuss Desert Storm operations.

Chronology of the Air War

July 17, 1990 In televised speech, Saddam Hussein warns he will attack Kuwait if his demands are not met regarding an old border dispute, a decrease in Kuwaiti oil production, and a reduction in Kuwait's share of oil from the Rumalia oil field, which extends under the Iraq-Kuwait border.

July 18 Kuwaiti forces placed on alert. • US Ambassador to Iraq April Glaspie tells Iraqi Foreign Ministry that United States insists all disputes in Middle East be settled peacefully.

July 19 Gen. Colin Powell, Chairman, Joint Chiefs of Staff, telephones Gen. H. Norman Schwarzkopf, Commander in Chief, Central Command, to discuss contingency planning for defense of Kuwait and Saudi Arabia against attack by Iraq. • Brig. Gen. Buster C. Glosson, USAF, en route to new post as Deputy Commander of Joint Task Force Middle East, pays courtesy call on Schwarzkopf. Schwarzkopf instructs Glosson to be prepared to oversee combined Exercise *Ivory Justice*, in which Mirage fighters of United Arab Emirates will spend two weeks practicing extensive in-flight refueling operations with USAF aerial tankers.

July 20 Iraqi newspapers report deployments of Iraqi troops to border with Kuwait. • CIA reports 30,000 Iraqi troops deployed.

Last two weeks of July At Eglin AFB, Fla., Lt. Gen. Charles Horner, Commander in Chief, US Central Air Forces (CENTAF) conducts Exercise *Internal Look*, a command post exercise postulating invasion of Saudi Arabia by "a country to the north." • Considerable exercise time spent determining where US reinforcements would be deployed in Saudi Arabia in such a contingency. Exercisers place great value on immediate availability of $1 billion worth of USAF equipment already prepositioned in Gulf area.

July 21 Glosson begins *Ivory Justice.* Order of battle for exercise includes AWACS aircraft. • US installs mobile tactical air control center at Abu Dhabi, capital of UAE.

July 24 US and UAE announce they are conducting joint exercise.

July 25 Ambassador Glaspie summoned to meet with Saddam Hussein. He correctly interprets US participation in *Ivory Justice* as demonstration of support for Kuwait, says he is dismayed and disturbed. As separate matter, he states he will not resolve dispute with Kuwait by force.

July 26 Kuwait agrees to cut oil production to levels demanded by Iraq.

July 30 CIA reports 100,000 Iraqi troops and more than 300 tanks massed on Kuwait border. • Iraqi, Kuwaiti, and Saudi representatives meet in Jiddah, Saudi Arabia, to reconcile differences. The talks fail. • Saddam reassures President Mubarak of Egypt and Saudi King Fahd that he will not attack Kuwait.

August 2 At 1 a.m., local time, Iraq invades Kuwait, using land, air, and naval forces. • President Bush issues executive orders 12722 and 12723, declaring a National Emergency, addressing threat to national security and implications for foreign policy. • Kuwaiti and Iraqi assets in US frozen. Trade and financial relations with Iraq stopped. • Joint Staff reviews military options, including Central Command Operations Plan 1002-90, a Top Secret contingency plan to move ground troops and supporting air and naval forces to region over three to four months. • CENTCOM staff starts formulating air campaign for defense of Saudi Arabia. • *Ivory Justice* terminated, but US KC-135s in UAE for exercise are retained there.

August 3 Additional US naval forces deploy to Gulf. General Powell confers with service chiefs on options. No decisions made by President, nor do Joint Chiefs recommend any. • Horner meets with Schwarzkopf at MacDill AFB, Fla. They finalize concept for CENTCOM defensive air campaign for briefing to President.

August 4 At Camp David, President, Secretary of Defense Cheney, and General Powell briefed by Schwarzkopf on concept for ground war and by Horner on concept for air campaign. • USS *Dwight D. Eisenhower* carrier battle group dispatched from Mediterranean to Red Sea; carrier USS *Independence* and eight escort ships in Indian Ocean head for North Arabian Sea.

August 6 At direction of the President, Cheney, Schwarzkopf, and Horner go to Saudi Arabia to confer with King Fahd Ibn Abdul Aziz and his inner circle. • US proposes Operation Plan 1002-90, which would place 250,000 American soldiers, sailors, and airmen in Gulf region within three months. King's approval is required. He invites US and allied forces to enter kingdom. • Cheney and Schwarzkopf return to Washington. Horner stays in Riyadh, Saudi Arabia, as "CINCCENT Forward." • President Bush orders F-15 fighters from Langley AFB, Va., 82d Airborne Division, and maritime prepositioning ships from Diego Garcia and Guam to deploy to the Gulf.

August 7 F-15s depart Langley for Saudi Arabia. • USS *Independence* carrier battle group arrives in Gulf of Oman, just south of Persian Gulf.

August 8 C-141 carrying Airlift Control Element (ALCE) lands in Dhahran, first USAF aircraft into the crisis zone. • F-15s from 1st TFW, Langley AFB, Va., and elements of 82d Airborne Division, Fort Bragg, N.C., arrive in Saudi Arabia. • US AWACS aircraft augment Saudi AWACS orbiting over Saudi Arabia. • Iraq annexes Kuwait. • Headquarters USAF activates Contingency Support Staff at the Pentagon. • General Schwarzkopf asks Lt. Gen. John M. Loh, USAF Vice Chief of Staff, for help in drawing up a strategic air campaign. • *Checkmate*, Air Staff planning group under Col. John Warden in Directorate of Plans (XOX), starts development of basic plan for the strategic air war that will eventually open Operation Desert Storm.

August 10 Pentagon announces name of operation as "Desert Shield." • Warden and staff brief concept plan to Schwarzkopf at MacDill. He approves. • Air Force, Navy, and Army units now arriving in Gulf theater in large numbers, stretching available facilities. F-16 fighters from Shaw AFB, S.C., C-130 transports from Pope AFB, N.C., arrive. • At Riyadh, Horner draws up contingency plan for coalition forces to fall back to Bahrain, Qatar, and United Arab Emirates if Hussein attacks Saudi Arabia before sufficient defensive forces are in place.

August 11 Military Airlift Command rapidly increases capabilities with Air Reserve Component (ARC) volunteers and aircraft. • Strategic Air Command calls for ARC volunteers to man KC-135 inflight refueling tankers. • Warden briefs plan to Powell, who directs expanding it to ensure Iraqis cannot escape Kuwait before their tank force is destroyed. Powell suggests adding Navy and Marine aviators to Warden's group. (During August planning, twenty-five percent of group membership will be Navy and Marine aviators.)

August 12 Thirty-two KC-135 tankers deploy to Saudi Arabia, the vanguard of a tanker force that will in time total more than 300 KC-10s and KC-135s. • MH-53J Pave Low helicopters from 1st Special Operations Wing arrive in Dhahran. • News media pool deploys to Saudi Arabia.

August 14 Soviets join US and allies in naval quarantine of Iraq. • Pentagon announces presence of KC-10 and KC-135 tankers, RC-135s, and E-3 AWACS in Gulf region.

August 15 F-117 Stealth fighters from Tonopah, Nev., and F-4Gs from George AFB, Calif., deploy to Gulf.

August 16 A-10s from Myrtle Beach AFB, S.C., deploy.

August 17 Saddam Hussein's forces in Kuwait, heavily reinforced, prepare massive defensive positions along Kuwaiti-Saudi border, signaling intent to stay. • Warden briefs revised concept plan to Schwarzkopf and CENTCOM staff at MacDill. Schwarzkopf directs Warden to take plan to Saudi Arabia and brief it to Horner. • Stage I of Civil Reserve Air Fleet (CRAF) activated for first time in its thirty-eight-year history. Sixteen civilian carriers provide eighteen long-range international passenger aircraft and crews and twenty-one LRI cargo aircraft and crews. • Air Force Space Command establishes DSCS satellite communications links for Desert Shield. • First Afloat Prepositioned Ships begin offloading in Saudi Arabia. • Speaker of Iraqi parliament announces that citizens of "aggressive" nations will be held until crisis ends and threatens their use as "human shields."

August 18 USS *John F. Kennedy* carrier battle group deploys to Gulf region.

August 19 F-117A Stealth fighters deploy from Tonopah, Nev., to Gulf.

August 20 More US troops, including 82d and 101st Airborne Divisions and 24th Mechanized Infantry Division, arrive. Horner concludes that air and ground strength now sufficient to defend Saudi Arabia against an Iraqi invasion. • Warden and his group brief concept plan to Horner in Riyadh.

August 21 USAF presence in Gulf now includes additional F-15s, F-16s, F-15Es, F-4G Wild Weasels, F-117A Stealth fighters, A-10 attack aircraft, AWACs, RC-135 reconnaissance aircraft, KC-135 and KC-10 tankers, and C-130 transports. • Air Force Reserve has 6,000 volunteers, enough to meet the initial requirement, on active duty, but 15,000 volunteer and mobilize within seventy-two hours of the call. • Cheney announces Saudi Arabia can now be successfully defended against an attack by Iraq.

August 22 President Bush issues executive order 12727, invoking 10 USC 673b, his authority to call up to 200,000 troops and units of Selected Reserve for duration of ninety days. • A second executive order, 12728 (10 USC 673c) suspends legal provisions relating to promotion, retirement, or separation of members of the armed forces. This is a "stop loss" action to stabilize the American military forces for duration of crisis.

August 23 Secretary Cheney issues memorandum implementing Presidential call-up of Reserve forces, setting maximum numbers to be called: Army, 25,000; Navy, 6,300; Marine Corps, 3,000; Air Force, 14,500. • C-130 transports from US Air Forces in Europe deploy to the Gulf.

August 24 117th Tactical Reconnaissance Wing, Birmingham, Ala., deploys six RF-4C aircraft to Gulf, joining RF-4Cs deployed by 67th Tactical Reconnaissance Wing, Bergstrom AFB, Tex.

August 25 USAF F-111 fighters from RAF Lakenheath in United Kingdom deploy to the Gulf.

August 27 First sealift forces arrive in Saudi Arabia.

August 28 193d Special Operations Group, Harrisburg International Airport, Middletown, Pa., deploys four EC-130E Volant Solo II psychological operations (PSYOP) aircraft. • Iraq declares Kuwait its nineteenth province.

August 29 C-5A transport, flown by volunteer AFRES crew, carrying active-duty passengers and cargo to Saudi Arabia, crashes shortly after takeoff from Ramstein AB, Germany, killing all but four of seventeen people on board.

August 30 President Bush urges nations around the world to help pay costs and contribute personnel and equipment for Operation Desert Shield. • USAF F-16 fighters from Torrejon AB, Spain, deploy to Qatar.

August 31 A massive number of aircraft, coalition as well as US Air Force and US Navy, have streamed into the Gulf region. At this point, ANG and AFRES volunteers have flown forty-two percent of the strategic airlift missions and thirty-three percent of the aerial refueling missions to support Operation Desert Shield.

September 4-5 Idea of "second front" in Turkey briefed by Gen. Robert C. Oaks, CINCUSAFE, to Gen. John R. Galvin, CINNCEUR, who in turn discusses it with General Powell.

September 5 Five ANG units begin deployment of C-130H, newest version of the tactical airlifter, to Gulf.

September 8 AC-130H gunships from the 16th Special Operations Squadron arrive in the Gulf.

September 13 Schwarzkopf and Powell briefed in Riyadh by Glosson on the now-complete operational air war plan. Powell asks when Air Force would be able to execute plan. Glosson says "within twenty-four hours."

September 17 Secretary Cheney fires Gen. Michael J. Dugan, Air Force Chief of Staff.

September 20 ANG and AFRES maintenance personnel called from their units and assigned to MAC structure to cover surge to wartime sortie rates. • Iraq's Revolutionary Command Council (of which Saddam is head) declares there will be no retreat and says the "mother of all battles" is inevitable.

September 23 Saddam threatens to destroy regional oil fields and draw Israel into war.

September 25 SAC tanker force in AOR totals 100.

September 28 Desert Shield sealift reaches peak with ninety ships at sea: sixty-nine en route to the Middle East, twenty-one on way back for more cargo.

October 2 USS *Independence* enters Persian Gulf, first carrier in that waterway since 1974.

October 4 USS *Independence* exits Persian Gulf.

October 10 Air Force fighter units arriving in AOR fly local training sorties to better prepare for the type of desert warfare they will soon be fighting. Combat air patrols by F-15Cs now routine. • Back in US, a small antiwar movement emerges. Relatives of some troops deployed to Gulf participate in Capitol Hill protest against Operation Desert Shield.

October 30 MAC launches first "Desert Express" mission, overnight airlift of critical items to Gulf.

November 8 President Bush orders 200,000 more US troops to Gulf. (In October, Schwarzkopf had told Powell he would need such an addition to carry out successful ground offensive in Kuwait.)

November 9 Pentagon announces deployment of three carriers, *Roosevelt*, *America*, and *Ranger*, to Gulf region.

November 13 President Bush issues executive order 12733, extending active duty for those called up under 10 USC 673b for additional ninety days.

November 14 Hospitals at RAF Bicester and RAF Little Rissington in UK, Zweibrücken AB, Germany, ready to receive wounded if war begins. With its activation, RAF Little Rissington becomes largest medical center in USAF with 1,500 beds.

November 17 Defense Communications Agency repositions DCS II satellite over the Indian Ocean to improve support for Desert Shield.

November 21 OA-10s from Davis-Monthan AFB, Ariz., deploy.

November 22 President Bush spends Thanksgiving with troops in the Gulf. • EC-130 psychological operations aircraft broadcast "Voice of America" into Kuwaiti theater of operations.

November 29 UN Security Council passes Resolution 678, authorizing use of force to expel Iraq from Kuwait. Resolution allows Iraq "one final opportunity" to comply with previous resolutions.

November 30 Saddam Hussein rejects President Bush's offer to send Secretary of State James A. Baker III to Baghdad for talks. • Hospital at RAF Nocton Hall ready to receive wounded.

December 1 Department of Defense enacts "stop loss" authority contained in August 22 executive order to keep military personnel with critical skills from retiring or separating from service while Desert Shield is under way.

December 2 More F-117 Stealth fighters deploy.

December 3 Three ANG units alerted for call-up: F-16A-equipped 169th TFG, McEntire ANGB, Eastover, S.C.; the F/A-16A-equipped 174th TFW, Hancock Field, Syracuse, N.Y.; and aircrews and support personnel from the 152d TRG, Reno, Nev., to replace the 117 TRW, Birmingham, Ala., personnel. AFRES A-10 Thunderbolt II-equipped 926 TFG, New Orleans, also alerted.

December 5 152d TRG, Reno, Nev., with RF-4Cs, deploys to Saudi Arabia to replace 117th TRW.

December 6 Saddam Hussein announces he will release all civilian hostages held since beginning of crisis.

December 8 First "European Desert Express" mission. Based on overnight delivery of critical items from US to Gulf, European express speeds similar items to AOR in less than eight hours.

December 20 Air Guard KC-135E units alerted. Call-up finally includes twelve of the thirteen ANG tanker units, with total strength of sixty-two tankers, which are deployed with maintenance support to Saudi Arabia. By December 26, SAC has 200 tankers in the Gulf.

December 21 USAF EF-111s deploy to the Gulf.

December 22 Bob Hope and entourage arrive in Middle East for Christmas shows.

December 29 169th TFG deploys twenty-four F-16As to Al Kharj AB, Saudi Arabia. This is first ANG fighter unit to deploy.

January 2 174th TFW deploys eighteen F/A-16 aircraft to Al Kharj, and along with 169th TFG, is incorporated into the 4th TFW (Provisional). • CENTCOM announces US troop strength in Gulf is more than 325,000.

January 8 Pentagon announces US troop strength in Gulf has topped 360,000. • Analysts estimate Saddam has 540,000 Iraqi troops in or near Kuwaiti Theater of Operations.

January 9 Secretary of State Baker meets with Iraqi Foreign Minister Tariq Aziz in Geneva. Peace talks fail.

January 12 Congress approves use of military force against Iraq.

January 13 UN Secretary General Javier Perez de Cuellar meets with Saddam Hussein, concludes there is little hope for peace.

January 15 Deadline for Iraq's withdrawal from Kuwait passes. • Pentagon announces that US has 415,000 troops in Gulf area, opposed by 545,000 Iraqi troops.

January 16 CENTCOM announces 425,000 US troops in theater, supported by ground forces of nineteen nations and naval efforts of fourteen nations. • First elements of USAFE Joint Task Force headquarters deploy from Ramstein AB, Germany, to Incirlik AB, Turkey, and prepare to establish USAF's first wartime composite wing.

January 17 Coalition air forces under Lieutenant General Horner initiate Operation Desert Storm at 3 a.m. Baghdad time (January 16, 7 p.m. Eastern Standard Time). Phase I of the air war, which is to gain air superiority, destroy Iraq's strategic capability, and disrupt command and control, begins. • Capt. Jon K. Kelk of the 33d TFW, Eglin AFB, Fla., draws first air-to-air blood, shooting down an Iraqi MiG-29 at 3:10 a.m. • Capt. Robert E. Graeter, 33d TFW, downs two Iraqi Mirage F1s at 3:54 a.m. • Coalition forces fly more than 750 attack sorties from land bases during the early morning and day. • US Navy launches 228 combat sorties from six carriers in Red Sea and Arabian Gulf. • Combat sorties flown by A-6s, A-7s, AV-8Bs, A-10s, B-52s, EA-6Bs, EF-111s, F-4s, F-14s, F-15s, F-16s, F/A-18s, F-111s, F-117As, AH-64s, Saudi and British Tornados, French Jaguars, and Kuwaiti A-4s, under the control of USAF AWACS and US Navy E-2Cs. • Turkish Parliament approves USAF use of Incirlik Air Base and Turkish airspace to carry out UN Security Council resolutions. USAFE immediately deploys fighters and other aircraft to Turkey.

January 18 Early in the morning, Iraq launches Scud missiles against Israel and Saudi Arabia, firing seven at Tel Aviv and Haifa. One aimed at Dhahran misses by 1.5 miles. • Secretary Cheney activates Stage II of Civil Reserve Air Fleet, raising total draw from airlines to seventy-nine passenger aircraft and 108 civilian cargo aircraft. • Navy Lt. Jeffrey Zaun captured after his A-6E is shot down. • 2,250 attack sorties flown by allied forces.

January 19 Flying out of Doha AB, Qatar, two F-16Cs from 614th TFS, Torrejon AB, Spain, shot down by SAMs; both pilots are taken prisoner by Iraqis. • Three more Scuds hit Tel Aviv, injuring ten people. • In violation of Geneva Convention, Iraq parades seven allied airmen on television. • President Bush signs order allowing extension of duty for 160,000 reservists. • Coalition flies 1,700 attack sorties.

January 20 First Purple Heart of war awarded to Navy corpsman hit by shrapnel January 17 while on a Marine patrol near Kuwaiti border. • USAF fighter-bombers attack Iraqi nuclear facilities, air defense complexes, and Scud missile launchers. • Allies fly 2,300 attack sorties.

January 21 Air Force MH-53J Pave Low helicopter rescues a Navy F-14 Tomcat pilot more than 100 miles inside Iraq. A-10 Thunderbolt IIs destroy Iraqi army truck heading toward Navy pilot. • Patriot missiles intercept nine Scuds fired at Dhahran and Riyadh. A tenth missile falls harmlessly into Persian Gulf. • Refugees crossing into Jordan from Iraq say they saw heavy bombing of Republican Guard in southern Iraqi city of Basra. • Allies fly 1,100 attack sorties.

January 22 After a brief bombing letup caused by bad weather, heavy air attacks strike in and around Basra, the supply gateway to Kuwait, and against Republican Guard positions along Iraqi-Kuwaiti border. • E-8A Joint STARS, orbiting over Saudi Arabia, detects large convoy moving toward Kuwait, vectors AC-130 gunship and two A-10s to attack. They destroy fifty-eight of seventy-one vehicles in convoy. • Navy A-6Es sink Iraqi patrol boat, seriously damage a minelayer and another enemy ship in Persian Gulf. Two other Iraqi ships flee. • A Scud hits Tel Aviv, destroying twenty buildings. Three killed and ninety-six injured. • Four Scuds blown out of sky by Patriots over Dhahran. • US complains to UN Security Council about abuse of allied POWs. • Allies fly 1,900 attack sorties.

January 23 After almost a week of coalition bombing, only five Iraqi air bases appear functional. Iraqi sorties are down to forty or fewer per day (prewar, Iraqis flew up to 235 a day). • Allies capture tiny Gulf island of Qaruh, which Iraqis had used as forward observation post. • Iraqis begin dumping huge volumes of Kuwaiti oil into Persian Gulf, begin setting fire to Kuwaiti oil well heads and related facilities. • US Navy destroys Iraqi Silkworm missile site. • Twenty-four mines floating in Gulf destroyed. • Allies fly 2,000 attack sorties.

January 24 Saudi pilot flying F-15C shoots down two Iraqi F1 Mirages attempting to attack allied ships with Exocet missiles. • Saudi naval forces use Harpoon missile to sink Iraqi mine-laying ship in northern Persian Gulf. • Iraq withdraws troops and boats from Qaruh Island, about 35 miles off Kuwait's southern coast. US Navy seizes island, killing three Iraqis and capturing fifty-one. • Allies fly 2,570 attack sorties, for a total of 14,750 during first eight days of war.

January 25 Air Force F-15Cs shoot down three Iraqi MiG-23s. Allies destroy three Iraqi bombers on ground. • Major attacks on Iraqi hardened aircraft shelters begin. US Air Force, using new I-2000 superhard bomb, has spectacular success. • Another British airman captured. Iraq announces it no longer will broadcast interviews of prisoners of war. • Intelligence reports execution of commanders of Iraq's air force and antiaircraft defenses. • Five Scuds strike central and northern Israel, killing one and wounding forty. • Iraq sabotages Kuwait's main supertanker loading pier, dumping millions of gallons of crude oil into Gulf; blames allied bombing for spill.

January 26 Phase II of air war complete. Phase I, hampered by bad weather, continues. Phase III, which shifts emphasis to Iraqi field army in Kuwait, begins. • Iraqi aircraft begin flight to Iran (by war's end, 122 had fled). • F-15Cs shoot down three MiG 23s over central Iraq. • Patriot missiles intercept Scuds fired at Saudi Arabia. • Marines fire 155-mm howitzers at Iraqi troops six miles inside Kuwait.

January 27 Two pilots from 53d Tactical Fighter Squadron, 36th TFW, Bitburg AB, Germany, flying F-15Cs, down four Iraqi fighters. • F-111Fs, using GBU-15 guided bombs, destroy oil-pumping manifold at Kuwaiti terminal, drastically reducing flow of oil into Gulf. • Schwarzkopf announces air supremacy. • F-16 "Killer Scout" program begins.

January 28 Marine Harrier jet fighters attack Iraqi convoy just inside Kuwait's border at night, destroy twenty-four tanks, armored personnel carriers, and trucks. • Baghdad radio announces at least one captured Allied pilot killed and other captured pilots hurt in allied bombing raids. • One Scud intercepted over Riyadh. Seventh Scud attack on Israel hits Arab villages on occupied West Bank.

January 29 US and USSR declare cease-fire possible if Iraq makes "unequivocal commitment" to withdraw all troops from Kuwait and takes "concrete steps" in that direction. • Joint STARS aircraft detects column of fifty Iraqi tanks moving toward Saudi Arabia from inside Kuwait. • US Navy A-6Es and British Lynx helicopters sink five Iraqi boats. • US Marines recapture Umm Al Maradim, a Kuwaiti island.

January 30 Using deception (tanks advancing with guns pointed to the rear, as if surrendering), 1,500 Iraqi troops in three battalions attack Khafji and Umm Hujul in Saudi Arabia. • Heavy allied air attacks by Air Force A-10s, Marine A-6Es and AH-1 Cobra helicopters. For first time, allied ground forces counterattack. Elements of 1st Marine Division engage with anti-tank and automatic weapons. • Eleven US Marines killed, the first ground troops to die in battle. Marines lose three armored vehicles in the battle for Khafji while Iraqis lose twenty-four tanks, thirteen armored vehicles. • British Lynx helicopters attack and sink three Iraqi patrol boats in northern Gulf. • USAF fighter-bombers destroy pipes and manifolds, stopping the oil spill—now biggest in history—into Gulf.

January 31 AC-130H Spectre gunship, supporting Marines around Khafji, shot down by Iraqi infrared surface-to-air missile. Fourteen crew members killed. • Two US soldiers, one of them a woman, from Army transportation unit captured by Iraqi soldiers at Iraqi-Saudi border. • Saudi troops, assisted by Qatari forces, US Marines, and heavy air support, recapture Khafji. Thirty Iraqis killed, thirty-three wounded, 500 taken prisoner. • Coalition aircraft attack and disrupt two Iraqi divisions assembling north of Khafji for attack. Iraqis routed before they can join battle.

February 1 Iraqi force, estimated at 60,000, masses for attack near Kuwaiti town of Al Wafra. (Air strikes subsequently drive Iraqis into defensive positions.)

February 2 Six-month anniversary of invasion of Kuwait. • B-52 bomber goes down in Indian Ocean, returning to Diego Garcia after mission over Kuwait. Three crew members rescued, three lost. • CENTCOM reports an USAF A-10 and Navy A-6E shot down. • Marine AH-1 Cobra attack helicopter crashes in Saudi Arabia while on escort mission, killing both pilots.

February 3 CENTCOM declares Iraqi Navy no longer exists as effective fighting force. • Iraq withdraws troops from Khafji area. • Qatari forces engage five Iraqi tanks. • French fighter-bombers attack Iraqi artillery positions in Kuwait. • Marine UH-1 utility helicopter crashes in eastern Saudi Arabia, killing crew.

February 4 USS *Missouri* uses sixteen-inch guns against Iraqi concrete bunkers in Kuwait as part of plan to deceive Iraqis into expecting an amphibious invasion by US Marines. • RAF Tornados and Buccaneers attack bridges and barracks in Iraq and Silkworm missile site in Kuwait. • Four Marine AV-8B Harriers knock out twenty-five Iraqi tanks. • Air Force fighter bombers attack major targets (military bases, suspected C^3 sites) at Tikrit, Hussein's home town, ninety miles north of Baghdad. • Cluster bomb dropped by mistake on US Marine position, killing one. • US Marine artillery attacks Iraqi ground radar and infantry positions. • Allies fly 2,566 sorties, for a total of 43,566 in first nineteen days of war.

February 5 Iranian President Ali Akbar Hashemi Rafsanjani offers to mediate between Iraq and US. • Air Force fighter bombers attack Scud missiles and launchers. B-52s and allied aircraft hit Republican Guard positions. • US Navy F-14 Tomcats shoot down Iraqi helicopter. • USS *Missouri* knocks out two artillery emplacements, damages four others. *Missouri's* sixteen-inch guns destroy radar site and surface-to-air missile position along Kuwait coast.

February 6 Capt. Robert Swain, 706th TFG (AFRES) shoots down Iraqi helicopter over central Kuwait in first-ever aerial victory by A-10. • Air Force F-15Cs shoot down two MiG-21s and two Su-25 Frogfoot fighter-bombers fleeing to Iran. • RAF knocks out key bridge across Tigris in Baghdad.

February 7 Secretary Cheney and General Powell head for the Gulf to meet with Schwarzkopf, discuss air offensive and pending ground offensive. • F-15Cs shoot down two Iraqi planes fleeing to Iran. • US Army helicopter crashes in Saudi Arabia, killing one and injuring four. • Navy F/A-18, returning to its carrier after mission in northern Gulf, is lost. • Sixteen-inch guns of battleship *Wisconsin* knock out Iraqi artillery in southern Kuwait. • Terrorists claim responsibility for killing retired Air Force master sergeant who worked at Incirlik AB, Turkey.

February 8 British Navy Lynx helicopter from HMS *Cardiff* fires two Sea Skua missiles at Iraqi Zhuk fast patrol boat, leaving it floundering. Boat later sunk by US Navy aircraft. • As oil slick drifts down the gulf, Saudi desalination plant at Safaniya stops operation as precautionary measure.

February 9 Scud hits Tel Aviv, injuring twenty-six. • Cheney and General Powell meet for more than eight hours with Schwarzkopf. • Marine Harrier shot down over southern Kuwait. • Navy A-6Es attack two Iraqi patrol boats in northern Gulf. • "Tank plinking" begins.

February 11 Allies fly 2,900 attack sorties, for a total of 61,862 in twenty-six days of air war.

February 12 Three downtown Baghdad bridges—Martyr's Bridge, Republic Bridge, and July 14 Bridge—destroyed.

February 13 Two F-117As attack hardened bunker in Baghdad that intelligence had identified as important Iraqi command center. More than 100 civilians killed. • Iraqi armored division caught moving during night and destroyed by airpower. • RAF, attacking bridge near Falujah, kills and wounds civilians with laser-guided bomb that does not guide properly. • Saudi F-5 lost over Iraq. • Kuwaiti air force pilots, employing French-built Gazelle helicopters, attack Iraqi tanks, damaging two.

February 14 RAF Tornado shot down by a missile over Baghdad. • Two USAF crewmen killed when EF-111A Raven lost in Saudi Arabia after mission over Iraq. • Back in US, antiwar demonstrators splash blood and oil on a Pentagon doorway.

February 15 Saddam Hussein's five-man Revolutionary Command Council announces that Iraq is ready "to deal" with UN resolution requiring withdrawal from Kuwait. • Navy A6-E intruder lost in a crash landing aboard carrier *America*. Both crewmen rescued. • Capt. Tim Bennett in F-15E drops laser-guided bomb on hovering Iraqi helicopter, the first aerial victory ever with a bomb.

February 16 Two A-10 Thunderbolt IIs shot down while attacking Iraqi Republican Guard positions in northwester • Kuwait. • US Army Apaches make nighttime strike on Iraqi positions. • Two Scuds hit southern Israel.

February 17 Heavy bombing of Iraqi army in Kuwait has increased. By this date, 1,300 of Iraq's 4,280 tanks and 1,100 of the 3,110 artillery pieces in Kuwait are destroyed. • AH-64 Apache helicopter mistakenly fires Hellfire missiles at US soldiers in Bradley infantry fighting vehicle and M113 armored personnel carrier, killing two and wounding six. • Apache helicopters destroy Iraqi mortar position and two bunkers, taking twenty Iraqi soldiers prisoners. • Iraq's foreign minister, Tariq Aziz, arrives in Moscow for talks with Soviet President Mikhail Gorbachev.

February 18 Two US Navy vessels, amphibious assault ship *Tripoli* and guided missile cruiser *Princeton*, strike mines in Gulf, take significant damage. Several seamen seriously injured. • Tariq Aziz returns to Baghdad with peace proposal from Gorbachev.

February 19 President Bush declares Soviet peace proposal inadequate. • Four US senators meeting with Israeli Defense Minister Moshe Arens experience Scud attack. • Mixed force of F-4G Wild Weasels and F-16s from composite wing in Turkey launch daylight attack on Baghdad from north. • Troops from 1st Infantry Division and 2d Marine Division skirmish with Iraqi troops. • Coalition navies destroy at least eighty mines in Gulf, but at least eighty more estimated to be still afloat. • Allies fly a record 3,000 attack sorties; total for thirty-four days of air war rises to 83,000.

February 20 US Army engages Iraqi reconnaissance unit, destroying five tanks and twenty artillery pieces. One US soldier killed, six wounded. • Allied attack sorties again reach 3,000 in one day.

February 21 Patriots intercept three Scuds launched toward King Khalid Military City. • Army OH-58 helicopter crashes during night combat operations, killing both crew members. • F-16 engine fails and the aircraft crashes; pilot ejects safely.

February 22 It is announced that 33d Tactical Fighter Wing, Eglin AFB, Fla., employing F-15Cs, has topped all other coalition air force units by downing fifteen Iraqi aircraft and running another Iraqi aircraft into the ground during pursuit. • Army UH-60 med-evac helicopter crashes on training mission, killing all seven aboard. • Four Scuds fired into Saudi Arabia are successfully intercepted.

February 23 B-52s pound Iraqi positions. Helicopter gunships sweep Iraqi defensive positions, striking war machines with rockets and machine guns. • Iraqis set 100 more Kuwaiti oil wells on fire. • Two Scuds, one fired at Israel, the other at Saudi Arabia, break up in flight. • Total allied attack sorties flown during air war reach 94,000. • Schwarzkopf determines that attrition of Iraqi combat effectiveness is sufficient to make success of coalition ground offensive with low casualties probable.

February 24 G-Day. Coalition forces begin the 100-hour ground war. • Tanks equipped with bulldozer blades punch openings through sand berms Iraqis built as defensive walls in front of their trenches. Tanks then wheel around and bury Iraqi troops in trenches. • Air war enters fourth and final phase—support for coalition ground forces attacking in Iraq and Kuwait. • Schwarzkopf throws more than 100,000 troops into "Hail Mary" attack on Kuwait. Iraqi defenders surrender in large numbers. • Fierce fighting continues in isolated armor battles. • Allied attack sorties again reach the 3,000 level, bringing total flown in war to 97,000.

February 25 Scud missile hits warehouse in Dhahran used as barracks, killing twenty-eight and wounding more than 100 Army Reservists who had just arrived in Saudi Arabia. • Baghdad Radio airs message from Saddam Hussein, telling Iraqi armed forces to withdraw from Kuwait. • At least 517 oil wells now on fire. • Four US aircraft—two Harriers, one A-10, one AH-64 Apache—shot down by ground fire. • Coalition forces again fly more than 3,000 sorties.

February 26 The "Mother of All Retreats" is in progress. In early morning hours, Iraqi soldiers attempt to escape coalition envelopment of Kuwait. Thousands of military and civilian vehicles, loaded with looted goods, clog four-lane highway out of Kuwait City. Repeated air attacks destroy much of panicked army's equipment. • About 590 oil wells and many tank farms on fire in Kuwait. Scores of oil facilities, including refineries, destroyed by Iraqis.

February 27 As coalition forces liberate Kuwait City and envelop Iraqi forces in northern Kuwait and southern Iraq, President Bush calls for cease-fire to take effect at 8 a.m. Kuwait time Wednesday, February 28. • Largest tank battle since Soviet-German combat at Kursk in 1943 rages. Some 800 US tanks of 101st Airborne, 24th Mechanized Infantry, and 3d Armored Division attack about 300 tanks of Revolutionary Guard's Medina and Hammurabi armored divisions and decimate them. • Two specially made 4,700 pound-GBU-28 LGBs destroy hardened, "impregnable" command bunker at Al Taji Air Base. • Pilot from 10th TFS, 50th Tactical Fighter Wing, Hahn AB, Germany, shot down and captured. • Allied attack sorties reach a new record of 3,500 for the day.

February 28 The fighting stops Iraq agrees to cease-fire and to participate in military-to-military talks on cessation of hostilities. • During the air war, thirty-eight Iraqi aircraft, including helicopters, were shot down. In addition, 234 Iraqi aircraft confirmed destroyed on the ground. • At end of hostilities, coalition air forces had lost seventy-five aircraft (sixty-three US, twelve allied). Of US losses, twenty-eight were fixed aircraft lost in noncombat mishaps, five were helicopters lost in combat, and eighteen were helicopters lost in noncombat operations. • Allied air forces again fly a daily 3,500 sorties, for a total of 110,000 attack sorties flown during Desert Storm.

March 2 Sporadic fighting continues. 140 Iraqi tanks and other vehicles run into US troops and begin shooting. Apparently, some Iraqi units did not get word of cease-fire or chose to ignore it. Supported by airpower, US forces counterattack, destroy sixty Iraqi tanks, and capture the remainder. • Coalition ground forces occupy southeast corner of Iraq. • Coalition air forces maintain "air occupation" of Iraq, including Baghdad.

March 3 Schwarzkopf meets with Iraqi Lt. Gen. Al-Jabburi to implement cease-fire. Talks held at Safwan, site of an Iraqi air base some five miles northwest of the Kuwait frontier. Schwarzkopf chose the location to emphasize to world that coalition forces had penetrated Iraq. • Out of 54,706 Air Force personnel in the Gulf theater, 12,098 were ANG or AFRES. On this day, twenty-two percent of Air Force personnel in theater are from Air Reserve Components.

March 8 1st Tactical Fighter Wing returns in victory to Langley AFB, Va. Other early returning units include 42d Bomb Wing, Loring AFB, Me., and the 55th and 9th Special Operations Squadrons, Eglin AFB, Fla.

March 10 Twenty-one former US prisoners of war—including eight members of the Air Force—met at Andrews AFB, Md., by Secretary Cheney, General Powell, and several thousand spectators.

March 19 Redeployment of 545,000 American troops stationed in Persian Gulf officially begins, with tempo of operations matching the deployment. Some troops will remain in theater for many months after war, but most will return rapidly.

April 11 Iraq agrees to accept all terms of UN cease-fire resolution. The Persian Gulf War officially ends April 11, 1991, at 10:00, New York time.

May 2 Total of 61, 597 enemy prisoners of war (EPWs) and 5,848 civilian internees held by US. France and UK transfer an additional 5,849 EPWs to US custody. Other coalition forces hold 17,300 EPWs. All were treated humanely and within guidelines of Geneva Convention.

Flight Operations Summary Up to the cease-fire, in addition to 110,000 attack sorties summarized in chronology above, B-52s flew 1,624 combat missions and dropped more than 72,000 bombs for total of 25,700 tons. • Special Operations C-130s flew 830 missions. • Transport C-130s flew 46,500 sorties during Desert Shield and Desert Storm. • KC-135 and KC-10 aerial tankers flew 15,434 sorties, refueling 45,955 receivers. ■

Sources Include: CENTCOM Chronology of Significant Events, 1991. *Conduct of the Persian Gulf Conflict: an Interim Report to Congress* (Department of Defense). Military Airlift Command. Strategic Air Command. Air Force Special Operations Command. Air Force Space Command. Pacific Air Forces. Tactical Air Command. US Air Forces in Europe. Gen. Merrill A. McPeak, Pentagon press conference, March 15, 1991. USAF white papers, April 1991 and September 1991. Lt. Gen. Charles A. Horner, USAF. Maj. Gen. Buster C. Glosson, USAF. Maj. Gen. John A. Corder, USAF. Col. John Warden, USAF. Pentagon Working Document, United States Aircraft Losses, June 7, 1991.

USAF Photo by MSgt. Bill Thompson

A Marine Corps F/A-18 returns from a bombing mission flown during the third week of the war.

USAF Photo by TSgt. Marvin Lynchard

An active duty F-16C from the 388th TFW, Hill AFB, Utah, fills its tank from a KC-135, courtesy of the 171st Air Refueling Wing, Air Force Reserve.

Bibliography

1. Interviews

ADKINS, Maj. Bruce, AFRES. [C-141B Pilot, 701st MAS (Assoc.), Charleston AFB, S.C.] *Charleston, Sept. 8, 1991.*

ALFONSON, MSgt. Charles, USAF. [Superintendent, Security Police Administration Spangdahlem AB, Germany, deployed to Batman AB, Turkey.] *Spangdahlem, Aug. 6, 1991.*

ALLEN, Lt. Col. William A., USAF. [Asst. Dep. Cmdr., Resources Mgt., 52d TFW, Spangdahlem AB, Germany, deployed to Sheikesa AB, Bahrain.] *Spangdahlem, Aug. 6, 1991.*

ARKIN, William M., Military Analyst, *Greenpeace*, Washington, D.C., Jan. 15, 1992.

ARNOLD, Col. Larry, ANG. [National Guard Bureau Assistant Director for Readiness, ANG Support Center, Andrews AFB, Md.] *Pentagon, June 17, 1991.*

ATERBURN, Ernest Ray. [AFRES Deputy Director of Personnel Plans and Data Systems, Hq. AFRES, Robins AFB, Ga.] *Robins, Aug. 9, 1991.*

BAILEY, Col. Gregory P., USAF. [Vice Commander, 20th TFW (F-111E), RAF Upper Heyford, UK, deployed to Incirlik AB, Turkey.] *Upper Heyford, Aug. 9, 1991.*

BATTLE, SSgt. Kelvin D., AFRES. [C-141B flight engineer, 701st MAS (Assoc.), Charleston AFB, S.C.] *Charleston, Sept. 8, 1991.*

BELDING, TSgt. Gerald W., AFRES. [Technician, 38th Aerial Port Squadron AFRES, Charleston AFB, S.C., deployed to Dhahran AB, Saudi Arabia.] *Charleston, Sept. 7, 1991.*

BELL, MSgt. Edward J., USAF. [Chief, Munitions Ops. Div., 36th TFW, Bitburg AB, Germany. Did not deploy.] *Bitburg, Aug. 6, 1991.*

BELLINGER, Maj. John N., [F-16A fighter pilot and Squadron Weapons Officer, 169th TFG, McEntire ANGB, S.C., deployed to Al Kharj AB, Saudi Arabia.] *McEntire, Sept. 6, 1991.*

BENNETT, Lt. Col. Keith A., USAF. [Squadron Commander, 511th TFS (A-10), 10th TFW, RAF Alconbury, UK, deployed to King Fahd International Airport, Saudi Arabia.] RAF *Alconbury, Aug. 8, 1991.*

BAKER, Lt. Col. Fred L., USAF. [Operations, Readiness Plans Div., Office of Air Force Reserve.] *Pentagon, June 5, 1991.*

BENNETT, Capt. Tim, USAF. [F-15E pilot, Seymour Johnson AFB, N.C.] Interviewed by Frank Oliveri, *AIR FORCE Magazine*, at *Nellis AFB, Nev., Oct. 11, 1991.*

BERG, Col. Walter R., USAF. [Asst. D.O. 48th TFW (F-111F), RAF Lakenheath, UK, deployed to Taif, Saudi Arabia.] *Lakenheath, Aug. 8, 1991.*

BOOHER, Ist Lt. Aaron, USAF. [F-16C pilot, 10th TFW, 50th TFW, Hahn AB, Germany, deployed to Al Dhafra AB, United Arab Emirates.] *Hahn, Aug. 5, 1991.*

BOWERS, Maj. Cary, USAF. [Asst. Ops. Officer, 561st TFS (F-4G WW), 35th TFW, George AFB, Calif., to Sheikesa AB, Bahrain.] *George, July 18, 1991.*

BOYD, Maj. Jon, USAF. [F-117A pilot, 37th TFW, Nellis AFB, Nev., deployed to Khamis Mushait, Saudi Arabia.] *Andrews AFB, Md., May 10, 1991.*

BRANDNER, Capt. Brian S., USAF. [F-111E pilot and Chief, Weapons and Training, 79th TFS, 20th TFW, RAF Upper Heyford, UK, deployed to Incirlik AB, Turkey.] *Upper Heyford, Aug. 9, 1991.*

BURAK, Capt. Paul, USAF. [F-15C fighter pilot, 71st TFS, 1st TFW, Langley AFB, Va., deployed to Dhahran AB, Saudi Arabia.] *Langley, June 3, 1991.*

BURGESON, Capt. Erik, USAF. [F-16C pilot, 10th TFW, 50th TFW, Hahn AB, Germany, deployed to Al Dhafra AB, United Arab Emirates.] *Hahn, Aug. 5, 1991.*

BURNS, SSgt. William J., USAF. [Brigade, Air Liaison Officer, 2d Brig., 2d Armored Cav. Reg., Ramstein AB, Germany, deployed to Saudi Arabia and fought in Iraq attached to the 1st Armored Division.] *Ramstein, Aug. 7, 1991.*

CALL, MSgt. Ralph G., USAF. [Propulsion Branch Production Supervisor, 36th TFW Bitburg AB, Germany, deployed to the AOR.] *Bitburg, Aug. 6, 1991.*

CANTWELL, TSgt. Paul A., USAF. [F-16C Maintenance Crew Chief, 10th AMU, 50th TFW, 50th TFW, Hahn AB, Germany, deployed to Al Dhafra AB, United Arab Emirates.] *Hahn, Aug. 5, 1991.*

CAREL, SSgt. Morris W., USAF. [Security Police, 36th TFW, Bitburg AB, Germany, deployed to Silopi, Turkey.] *Bitburg, Aug. 6, 1991.*

CARNOT, TSgt. Fernando L., USAF. [Jet Engine Maint. Supervisor, 36th TFW, Bitburg AB, Germany. Did not deploy.] *Bitburg, Aug. 6, 1991.*

CARUANA, Brig. Gen. Patrick P., USAF. [Commander, 42d Air Division, Grand Forks AFB, N.D. Deployed as Director, Strategic Forces, CENTAF, Riyadh, Saudi Arabia.] *Via telephone, Offutt AFB, Neb., Oct. 30, 1991.*

CARY, MSgt. William R., AFRES. [C-141B flight engineer, 701st MAS (Assoc.), Charleston AFB, S.C.] *Charleston, Sept. 8, 1991.*

CHAPMAN, Capt. Donald R., USAF. [F-117 pilot, 417th Tactical Fighter Training Squadron, deployed to Khamis Mushait, Saudi Arabia.] *Via telephone, Nov. 26, 1991.*

CHARTIER, MSgt. John D., USAF. [NCOIC, 81st Specialty Flight, Spangdahlem AB, Germany, deployed to Sheikesa AB, Bahrain.] *Spangdahlem, Aug. 6, 1991.*

CLAYTON, MSgt. John, AFRES. [C-130H flight engineer, 94th TAW, Dobbins AFB, Ga., deployed to Sharja, United Arab Emirates.] *Dobbins, Aug. 11, 1991.*

CLEARY, Lt. Col. Bill, AFRES. [Staff member, AFRES Lessons Learned Study.] *Pentagon, June 12, 1991.*

CLOSNER, Maj. Gen. John J. III, AFRES. [Chief of the Air Force Reserve.] *Pentagon, May 31, 1991.*

CONAWAY, Lt. Gen. John B., ANG. [Chief, National Guard Bureau.] *Pentagon, June 27, 1991.*

CORDER, Maj. Gen. John A., USAF. [CENTAF Director of Operations, Riyadh AB, Saudi Arabia. Commander of TAWC, Eglin AFB, Fla.] *Eglin, July 8, 1991.*

COUSINS, SSgt. Lee R. Jr., USAF. [Food Services Specialist, 48th TFW , RAF Lakenheath, UK, deployed to Taif AB, Saudi Arabia.] *Lakenheath, Aug. 8, 1991.*

CUTCHIN, SSgt. Jerry O., USAF. [Engine Technician, 81st TFS, 52d TFW, Spangdahlem AB, Germany, deployed to Sheikesa AB, Bahrain.] *Spangdahlem, Aug. 6, 1991.*

DANIELS, Capt. Darren R., USAF. [OIC, Prime Beef Team, 36th TFW, Bitburg AB, Germany, deployed to Batman AB, Turkey.] *Bitburg, Aug. 6, 1991.*

DEMUTH, Capt. Paula J., USAF. [Assistant JAG, Spangdahlem AB, Germany, deployed to Incirlik AB, Turkey.] *Spangdahlem, Aug. 6, 1991.*

DEPTULA, Lt. Col. David A., USAF. [Chief Planner, JFACC Special Planning Cell (Desert Shield); Director, Iraq/Strategic Planning Cell (Desert Storm), Riyadh, Saudi Arabia. SecAF Staff Group.] *Pentagon, and via telephone Jan. 8, 1992, Nov. 22, 1991, June 27, 1991, and May 2, 1991.*

DIETZ, Capt. Thomas N., USAF. [F-15C fighter pilot, 53d TFS, 36th TFW, Bitburg AB, Germany, deployed to Al Kharj AB, Saudi Arabia.] *Bitburg, Aug. 6, 1991.*

DITTMER, Maj. Kurt B., USAF. [F-16 pilot, 23d TFS, Spandahlem AB, Germany, deployed to Incirlik AB, Turkey.] *Pentagon, Jan. 13, 1992.*

DOWNER, Brig. Gen. Lee A., USAF. [Director of Plans, Hq. USAFE, Ramstein AB, Germany, deployed as the Commander, 7440th Wing (Provisional), Incirlik AB, Turkey.] *Ramstein, Aug. 5, 1991.*

DRIGGERS, Col. William B.,USAF (Ret.). [Texas Instrument employee.] *Via telephone, May 2, 1991.*

DRUMMOND, Lt. Col. Jan, USA. [Patriot Battery Commander.] *Springfield, Va., May 15, 1991.*

DUTHIE, Col. Dana, USAF. [Deputy Chief of Operations, 50th TFW, Hahn AB, Germany, did not deploy.] *Hahn, Aug. 5, 1991.*

EASTER, CMSgt. Donald K., USAF. [NCOIC, 10th AMU, 50th TFW, Hahn AB, Germany, deployed to Al Dhafra AB, United Arab Emirates.] *Hahn, Aug. 5, 1991.*

ESKRIDGE, Maj. Robert D., USAF. [F-117 pilot, 415th TFS, 37th TFW, Tonopah Test Range, Nev., deployed to Khamis Mushait, and Riyadh, Saudi Arabia.] *Pentagon, Dec. 20, 1991.*

ESLICK, Lt. Col. Thomas J., USAF. [Administrator, Aeromedical Staging Facility RAF Upper Heyford, UK, deployed to Incirlik AB, Turkey.] *Upper Heyford, Aug. 9, 1991.*

FEEST, Maj. Gregory A., USAF. [F-117 pilot, 415th TFS, 37th TFW, Tonopah Test Range, Nev., deployed to Khamis Mushait, Saudi Arabia.] *Via telephone, Dec. 17, 1991.*

FELDMAN, Capt. Stephen I., USAF. [U-2/TR-1 pilot, 9th Strategic Wing, Beale AFB, Calif., deployed to Taif, Saudi Arabia.] *Beale, July 17, 1991.*

FERRELL, SSgt. John H., USAF. [Fuel Specialist, 52d Support Squadron, 52d TFW, Spangdahlem AB, Germany, deployed to Sheikesa AB, Turkey.] *Spangdahlem, Aug. 6, 1991.*

FINK, Capt. Merrill P., USAF. [F-16C fighter pilot, 52d TFW, Spangdahlem AB, Germany, deployed to Incirlik AB, Turkey.] *Spangdahlem, Aug. 6, 1991.*

Fox, SSgt. John F., USAF. [Budget Technician, 52d TFW, Spangdahlem AB, Germany, deployed to Batman AB, Turkey.] *Spangdahlem, Aug. 6, 1991.*

Fripp, Sgt. Pamela, USAF. [Freight and Packaging Specialist, 36th TFW, Bitburg AB, Germany, deployed to Incirlik AB Turkey.] *Bitburg, Aug. 6, 1991.*

Garan, Capt. Ronald, USAF. [F-16C Weapons Officer, 17th TFS, 363d TFW, Shaw AFB, S.C., deployed to Al Dhafra, United Arab Emirates.] *Shaw, May 30, 1991.*

Garno, Capt. Edward A., USAF. [Asst. Ops. Officer, 561st TFS (Wild Weasel), 35th TFW, George AFB, Calif., deployed to Sheikesa AB, Bahrain.] *George, July 18, 1991.*

Glosson, Brig. Gen. [subsequently Maj. Gen.] Buster, USAF. [Director of Air Campaign Plans and Commander, 14th Air Division, CENTAF, Riyadh, Saudi Arabia. Chief, Secretary of the Air Force Office of Legislative Liaison.] *Pentagon, May 28, 1991, Jan. 19, 1992, and March 5, 1992.*

Godber, TSgt. Joel, USAF. [Shift Supervisor, Manual Electronic Warfare Shop, 36th TFW, Bitburg AB, Germany, did not deploy.] *Bitburg, Aug. 6, 1991.*

Graeter, Maj. Robert E., USAF. [F-15C fighter pilot, 58th TFS, 33d TFW, Eglin AFB, Fla., deployed to Tebuk AB, Saudi Arabia.] *Eglin, July 8, 1991.*

Green, MSgt. Larry D., USAF. [Security Police, 36th TFW, Bitburg AB, Germany, did not deploy.] *Bitburg, Aug. 6, 1991.*

Griffith, Maj. Michael W., AFRES. [C-141 pilot, 701 MAS (Assoc.), Charleston AFB, S.C.] *Charleston, Sept. 8, 1991.*

Guzowski, Lt. Col. Paul T., USAF. [Assistant Operations Officer, 561st TFS (Wild Weasel) and EWO, 35th TFW, George AFB, Calif., deployed to Sheikesa AB, Bahrain.] *George, July 18, 1991.*

Hallman, Capt. Chris, AFRES. [C-130H navigator, 94th TAW, Dobbins AFB, Ga., deployed to Sharja, United Arab Emirates.] *Dobbins, Aug. 11, 1991.*

Hanf, Maj. Linda, AFRES. [Nurse, 31st Air Evacuation Squadron (AFRES), Charleston AFB, S.C., deployed to Dhahran AB, Saudi Arabia.] *Charleston, Sept. 7, 1991.*

Harris, MSgt. Sherman J., USAF. [Chief, Munitions Maint. Div., 36th TFW, Bitburg AB, Germany. Did not deploy.] *Bitburg, Aug. 6, 1991.*

Harvey, Lt. Col. Bernard E., USAF. [Chief, Strategic Assessments Section, Checkmate, Air Staff; special assistant, Director of Campaign Plans, Riyadh, Saudi Arabia.] *Pentagon, May 9 and June 27, 1991 and via telephone Jan. 16, 1992.*

Hehemann, 1st Lt. Robert W., USAF. [F-15C fighter pilot, 53d TFS, 36th TFW, Bitburg AB, Germany, deployed to Al Kharj AB, Saudi Arabia.] *Bitburg, Aug. 6, 1991.*

Hendix, TSgt. Michael F., AFRES. [C-141B flight engineer, 701st MAS (Assoc.), Charleston AFB, S.C.] *Charleston, Sept. 8, 1991.*

Hills, Capt. Larry C., USAF. [F-111F pilot, 492d TFS, 48th TFW, RAF Lakenheath, UK, deployed to Taif AB, Saudi Arabia.] *Lakenheath, Aug. 8, 1991.*

Hoffman, TSgt. Carole B., AFRES. [Technician with the 38th Aerial Port Squadron, Charleston AFB, S.C., deployed to Dhahran AB, Saudi Arabia.] *Charleston, Sept. 7, 1991.*

Hogan, Capt. Thomas J., USAF. [EF-111 pilot, 42d ECS, 20th TFW, RAF Upper Heyford, UK, deployed to Taif AB, Saudi Arabia.] *Upper Heyford, Aug. 9, 1991.*

Hoover, TSgt. Richard E., USAF. [NCOIC Missile Maint. Div., 36th TFW, Bitburg AB, Germany deployed to Al Kharj AB, Saudi Arabia.] *Bitburg, Aug. 6, 1991.*

Hornburg, Col. Hal, USAF. [Commander, 4th TFW, Seymour Johnson AFB, N.C., deployed to Al Kharj AB, Saudi Arabia as Commander, 4th TFW (Provisional). *Seymour Johnson, May 31, 1991, and via telephone, Jan. 21, 1992.*

Horne, Lt. Col. Barry E., USAF. [Commander, 417th Tactical Fighter Training Squadron (F-117), Tonopah Test Range, Nev. Deployed as Operations Officer, 415th TFS, Khamis Mushait, Saudi Arabia.] *Via telephone, Tonopah, Nov. 26, 1991.*

Horner, Lt. Gen. Charles A., USAF. [Commander, CENTAF, Riyadh AB, Saudi Arabia. Commander 9th AF and CENTAF, Shaw AFB, S.C.] *Shaw, May 30, 1991, and Jan. 3, 1992.*

Hunneycutt, Lt. Col. Bobby T., USAF. [Assistant Deputy for Operations (F-15Cs) 36th TFW, Bitburg AB, Germany, deployed as 4th TFW (Provisional). ADO for F-15Cs, Al Kharj AB, Saudi Arabia.] *Langley AFB, Va., Aug. 2, 1991.*

Jackson, SSgt. Mark Scott, USAF. [Explosive Ordnance and Disposal Technician, 52d TFW, Spangdahlem AB, Germany, deployed to Incirlik AB, Turkey, then to Zako, Iraq.] *Spangdahlem, Aug. 6, 1991.*

JERNIGAN, Lt. Col. George, ANG. [F-16A fighter pilot, 169th TFG, McEntire ANGB, S.C., deployed to Al Kharj AB, Saudi Arabia.] *McEntire, Sept. 6, 1991.*

JOHNSON, Gen. H. T., USAF. [CinC MAC and CinC USTRANSCOM.] *Pentagon, Oct. 23, 1991.*

JORDAN, CMSgt. Pete, AFRES. [Senior Enlisted Advisor, 94th TAW, Dobbins AFB, Ga., deployed to Sharja, United Arab Emirates.] *Dobbins, Aug. 9, 1991.*

JOSE, Capt. Joseph M., USAF. [C-141 aircraft commander, 438th MAW, McGuire AFB, N.J.] *Rhein-Main AB, Germany, Aug. 4, 1991.*

KALNOSKE, SrA. Thomas J., USAF. [F-15C radar technician, 53d AMU, 36th TFW, Bitburg AB, Germany deployed to Al Kharj AB, Saudi Arabia.] *Bitburg, Aug. 6, 1991.*

KAMPS, Maj. Daniel K., USAF. [F-16C Flight Commander, 17th TFS, 363d TFW, Shaw AFB, S.C., deployed to Al Dhafra AB, United Arab Emirates.] *Shaw, May 30, 1991.*

KECK, Col. Thomas, USAF. [Commander, 9th Strategic Reconnaissance Wing, Beale AFB, Calif. Did not deploy.] *Beale, July 17, 1991.*

KEITH, Chaplain (Maj.) Lawrence J., USAF. [Senior Protestant Chaplain, 10th TFW, RAF Alconbury, UK, deployed to King Fahd International Airport, Saudi Arabia.] *Alconbury, Aug. 8, 1991.*

KELLY, 1st Lt. Jeffrey W., USAF. [WSO, F-111F, 492d TFS, 48th TFW, RAF Lakenheath UK, deployed to Taif AB, Saudi Arabia.] *Lakenheath, Aug. 8, 1991.*

KIERSTEAD, SrA. Christopher L., AFRES. [C-141 loadmaster, 701st MAS (Assoc.), Charleston AFB, S.C.] *Charleston, Sept. 8, 1991.*

KILLEY, Maj. Gen. Philip G., ANG. [Director, Air National Guard.] *Pentagon and via telephone, June 6 and June 17, 1991.*

KING, Maj. Chris, AFRES. [Public Affairs, 315th MAW (Assoc.), Charleston AFB, S.C.] *Charleston, Sept. 7, 1991.*

KIRK, SSgt. Edward W. Jr., USAF. [NCOIC, Stock Control and Requisitions, 36th TFW, Bitburg AB, Germany, deployed to Incirlik AB, Turkey.] *Bitburg, Aug. 6, 1991.*

KLEBER, Sgt. Chris, AFRES. [Public Affairs Office, 315th MAW (Assoc.), Charleston AFB, S.C.] *Charleston, Sept. 7, 1991.*

KLEBER, SSgt. Mark, AFRES. [C-141B loadmaster, 701st MAS (Assoc.), Charleston AFB, S.C.] *Charleston, Sept. 8, 1991.*

KOHNEN, Sgt. Joseph M., USAF. [81st TFS F-4G crew chief, 52d TFW Spangdahlem AB, Germany, deployed to Sheikesa AB, Bahrain.] *Spangdahlem, Aug. 6, 1991.*

LAMY, Chaplain (Capt.) Raymond J., USAF. [Chaplain, 48th TFW, RAF Lakenheath, UK, deployed to Taif AB, Saudi Arabia.] *Lakenheath, Aug. 8, 1991.*

LAVOYE, Capt. Steven G., USAF. [OIC, 10th AMU, 50th TFW, Hahn AB, Germany, deployed to Al Dhafra AB, United Arab Emirates.] *Hahn, Aug. 5, 1991.*

LENNON, Col. Thomas, USAF. [Commander, 48th TFW, RAF Lakenheath, UK, deployed to Taif AB, Saudi Arabia.] *Via telephone, Lakenheath, April 22, 1991.*

LING, Capt. Christopher M., USAF. [F-111F WSO, 492d TFS, 48th TFW, RAF Lakenheath, UK, deployed to Taif AB, Saudi Arabia.] *Lakenheath, Aug. 8, 1991.*

McCALLUM, SrA. Timothy S., USAF. [Crew Chief, 81st TFS, 52d TFW, Spangdahlem AB, Germany, deployed to Sheikesa AB, Bahrain.] *Spangdahlem, Aug. 6, 1991.*

McELROY, Capt. Kevin J., USAF. [EF-111 EWO, 42d ECS, 20th TFW, RAF Upper Heyford, UK, deployed to Taif AB, Saudi Arabia.] *Upper Heyford, Aug. 9, 1991.*

McGOVERN, Capt. James J., USAF. [F-111F pilot, 492d TFS, 48th TFW, RAF Lakenheath, UK, deployed to Taif AB Saudi Arabia.] *Lakenheath, Aug. 8, 1991.*

McINTYRE, Col. James H., USAF.[Deputy Chief of Maintenance, 50th TFW, Hahn AB, Germany. Did not deploy.] *Hahn, Aug. 5, 1991.*

MADDUX, MSgt. Robert A., USAF. [NCOIC, Security Police, RAF Mildenhall, UK, deployed to Al Dhafra AB, United Arab Emirates.] *Mildenhall, Aug. 8, 1991.*

MARLOW, Capt. Dan, AFRES. [C-130H pilot, 94th TAW, Dobbins AFB, Ga., deployed to Sharja, United Arab Emirates.] *Dobbins, Aug. 11, 1991.*

MARSHALL, Lt. Col. John, ANG. [F-16A Squadron Commander, 157th TFS, 169th TFG , McEntire ANGB, S.C., deployed to Al Kharj AB, Saudi Arabia.] *McEntire, Sept. 6, 1991.*

MAXWELL, Capt. Ronald B., USAF. [F-111E WSO, 55 TFS, 20th TFW, RAF Upper Heyford, UK, deployed to Incirlik AB, Turkey.] *Upper Heyford, Aug. 9, 1991.*

Meir, Capt. Michael R., USAF. [A-10 pilot and flight commander, 511th TFS, 10th TFW, RAF Alconbury, UK, deployed to King Fahd International Airport, Saudi Arabia.] *Alconbury, Aug. 8, 1991.*

Merton, MSgt. Bill, AFRES. [Public Affairs Office, 315th MAW (Assoc.), Charleston AFB, S.C.] *Charleston, Sept. 7, 1991.*

Midkiff, SSgt. Stephen J., USAF. [Packing and Crating, Traffic Management, 52d TFW, Spangdahlem AB, Germany, deployed to Al Kharj, Saudi Arabia.] *Spangdahlem, Aug. 6, 1991.*

Mimnaugh, SSgt. Lanty, AFRES. [C-141B loadmaster, 701st MAS (Assoc.), Charleston AFB, S.C.] *Charleston, Sept. 8, 1991.*

Moffitt, Lt. Col. Jack, USAF. [Tactical Air Command LANTIRN Project Office]. *Langley, April 17, 1991.*

Moore, Capt. Douglas, USAF. [F-15C fighter pilot, 71st TFS, 1st TFW, Langley AFB, Va., deployed to Dhahran AB, Saudi Arabia.] *Langley, June 3, 1991.*

Moore, MSgt. Ralph G., USAF. [NCOIC, Electronic Warfare Shop, 36th TFW, Bitburg AB, Germany, deployed to Incirlik AB, Turkey.] *Bitburg, Aug. 6, 1991.*

Morey, Lt. Col. John B., USAF. [Administrator, 20th TFW Hospital, RAF Upper Heyford, UK, deployed to Incirlik AB, Turkey.] *Upper Heyford, Aug. 9, 1991.*

Mosher, Col. (Dr.) John E., AFRES. [AFRES Command Surgeon, Pentagon, Washington, D.C.] *Pentagon, March 13, 1991.*

Murchison, SSgt. William T., AFRES. [Maintenance technician, 94th CAMS, 94th TAW, Dobbins AFB, Ga., deployed to Sharja, United Arab Emirates.] *Dobbins, Aug. 10, 1991.*

Murphy, MSgt. John, AFRES. [94th Aerial Port Squadron NCOIC, Robins AFB, Ga. Did not deploy.] *Robins, Aug. 9, 1991.*

Murray, 1st Lt. Vince, AFRES. [C-141B pilot, 701st MAS (Assoc.), Charleston AFB, S.C.] *Charleston, Sept. 8, 1991.*

Myers, TSgt. William F., USAF. [F-16C crew chief, 401st TFW, Torrejon AB, Spain, deployed to Incirlik AB, Turkey.] *Via telephone, Torrejon, Aug. 7, 1991.*

Nelson, Col. Jerry L., USAF. [Commander, 401st TFW, Torrejon AB, Spain, deployed to Doha AB, Qatar as the 401st TFW Spain.] *Via telephone, Torrejon, Aug. 7, 1991.*

Nottoli, 1st Lt. Scott, ANG. [F-16A pilot, 169th TFG , McEntire ANGB, S.C., deployed to Al Kharj AB, Saudi Arabia.] *McEntire, Sept. 6, 1991.*

Oaks, Gen. Robert C., [Commander-in-Chief, US Air Forces in Europe.] *Telephone interview, Jan. 15, 1992.*

O'Conner, Charles. [AFRES Historian, Hq. AFRES, Robins AFB, Ga.] *Robins, Aug. 9, 1991.*

Padden, Capt. Pollyanna A., USAF. [C-141 aircraft commander,437th Airlift Wing, Charleston AFB, S.C.] *Charleston, Dec. 13, 1991.*

Payne, 1st Lt, Robert Doyle, AFRES. [C-130H co-pilot, 94th TAW, Dobbins AFB, Ga., deployed to Sharja, United Arab Emirates.] *Dobbins, Aug. 11, 1991.*

Peck, Col. William A., USAF. [Dep. Cmdr. Operations, 20th TFW, RAF Upper Heyford, UK, deployed to Incirlik AB, Turkey.] *Upper Heyford, Aug. 9, 1991.*

Pfister, Capt. Susan J., USAF. [OIC, 511th AMU, 10th TFW RAF Alconbury, UK, deployed to King Fahd International Airport, Saudi Arabia.] *Alconbury, Aug. 8, 1991.*

Phair, MSgt. Carlos D., USAF. [Production Supervisor, 79th AMU 20th TFW, RAF Upper Heyford, UK, deployed to Incirlik AB, Turkey.] *Upper Heyford, Aug. 9, 1991.*

Pilots of 169th TFG, (ANG) McEntire ANGB, S.C., Sept. 6, 1991.

Pingel, Lt. Col. Stephen, USAF. [Operations Officer, 336th TFS (F-15E), 4th TFW, Seymour Johnson AFB, N.C., deployed to Al Kharj AB, Saudi Arabia. Squadron Commander, 335th TFS, Seymour Johnson.] *Seymour Johnson, May 31, 1991.*

Pischer, A1C Robert B., USAF. [Aerospace Med. Tech., 48th TFW Hospital, RAF Lakenheath, UK, deployed to Taif AB, Saudi Arabia.] *Lakenheath, Aug. 8, 1991.*

Pope, Lt. Col. Howard, USAF. [Commander, 71st TFS, 1st TFW, Langley AFB, Va., deployed to Dhahran AB, Saudi Arabia.] *Langley, June 3, 1991.*

Rackley, Lt. Col. Thomas, USAF. [Squadron Commander, 421st TFS (F-16Cs), 388th TFW, Hill AFB, Utah, deployed to Doha AB, Qatar.] *Via telephone, Hill, May 27, 1991.*

Ragan, MSgt. Jerry M., USAF. [Supt., Resource Plans, LGX, 36th TFW Bitburg AB, Germany, deployed to Incirlik AB, Turkey.] *Bitburg, Aug. 6, 1991.*

RICHARDSON, MSgt. Edward, USAF. [NCOIC, Automatic Test Station Shop, 36th TFW, Bitburg AB, Germany. Did not deploy.] *Bitburg, Aug. 6, 1991.*

RICHEY, 1st Lt. Michael W., USAF. [F-111E pilot, 55 TFS, 20th TFW, RAF Upper Heyford, UK, deployed to Incirlik AB, Turkey.] *Upper Heyford, Aug. 9, 1991.*

RIDER, Col. William M., USAF. [Deputy Chief of Staff/Logistics, 9th Air Force, and CENTAF/LG, deployed to Riyadh, Saudi Arabia.] Via telephone, Dec. 6, 1991.

ROBERTS, SSgt. John R., USAF. [Fuel Dispatcher, 513th Supply Sqdn., RAF Mildenhall, UK. Did not deploy.] *Mildenhall, Aug. 8, 1991.*

ROBINSON, Capt. Charles M., USAF. [F-15E fighter pilot, 336th TFS, 4th TFW, Seymour Johnson AFB, N.C., deployed to Al Kharj AB, Saudi Arabia. Currently 334th TFS pilot, Seymour Johnson.] *Seymour Johnson, May 31, 1991.*

ROGERS, Maj. Mark B., USAF. [F-16 pilot, Chief, Force Planning and Integration Branch, Checkmate. Deployed as Deputy Director, Special Planning Group, Desert Shield, and Deputy Director, Strategic Campaign Targets, CENTAF, Riyadh, Saudi Arabia.] *Pentagon, Jan. 7, 1992.*

RUSH, Maj. Tim, ANG. [F-16A fighter pilot, 169th TFG, McEntire ANGB, S.C., deployed to Al Kharj AB, Saudi Arabia.] *McEntire, Sept. 6, 1991.*

RYAN, Maj. Gen. Mike, USAF. ["CENTAF Rear," MacDill AFB, Fla. Currently TAC/XP, Langley AFB, Va.] *Langley, June 3, 1991.*

SALISBURY, Col. Richard W., USAF. [Commander, 1700 Strategic Wing (Provisional), deployed to Riyadh AB, Saudi Arabia. Vice Wing Commander, 9th Strategic Reconnaissance Wing, Beale AFB, Calif.] *Beale, July 17, 1991.*

SCHAPIRO, Capt. David B., USAF. [F-111E WSO and flight commander, 55th TFS, 20th TFW, RAF Upper Heyford, UK, deployed to Incirlik AB, Turkey.] *Upper Heyford, Aug. 9, 1991.*

SCHEER, Maj. Gen. Roger P., AFRES (Ret.). [Chief, Air Force Reserve. Deputy Assistant Secretary for Reserve Affairs.] *Pentagon, June 7, 1991.*

SCHIAVI, Capt. Anthony E., USAF. [F-15C fighter pilot, 58th TFS, 33d TFW, Eglin AFB, Fla., deployed to Tebuk AB, Saudi Arabia.] *Eglin, July 8, 1991.*

SCHMITT, Maj. Tom, AFRES. [C-141B pilot, 701st MAS (Assoc.), Charleston AFB, S.C.] *Charleston, Sept. 8, 1991.*

SCHRECK, SSgt. Margaret A., AFRES. [Technician, 38th Aerial Port Squadron, Charleston AFB, S.C., deployed to Dhahran AB, Saudi Arabia.] *Charleston, Sept. 7, 1991.*

SENSI, Capt. Tony, USAF. [C-141 co-pilot, 428th MAW, McGuire AFB, N.J.] *Rhein-Main AB, Germany, Aug. 4, 1991.*

SIMPSON, Lt. Col. Terry L. [Commander, 55th TFS (F-111E), 20th TFW, RAF Upper Heyford, UK, deployed to Incirlik, AB Turkey.] *Upper Heyford, Aug. 9, 1991.*

SKILLMAN, TSgt. Thomas M., AFRES. [Technician, 38th Aerial Port Squadron, Charleston AFB, S.C., deployed to Dhahran AB, Saudi Arabia.] *Charleston, Sept. 7, 1991.*

SKOVINSKI, CMSgt. Wesley J., USAF. [NCOIC 53d AMU, 36th TFW, Bitburg AB, Germany, deployed to Al Kharj, Saudi Arabia.] *Bitburg, Aug. 6, 1991.*

SLETTEN, TSgt Mark E., USAF. [KC-135Q inflight refueling systems operator, 9th Strategic Wing, Beale AFB, Calif., deployed to Riyadh, Saudi Arabia.] *Beale, July 17, 1991.*

SOKOLY, Capt. Steven B., USAF. [F-4G EWO, 81st TFS, 52d TFW, Spangdahlem AB, Germany, deployed to Sheikesa AB, Bahrain.] *Spangdahlem, Aug. 6, 1991.*

SOMERFELDT, TSgt. Richard W., USAF. [Structural repair technician, 511th ATS, 10th TFW, RAF Alconbury, UK, deployed to King Fahd International Airport, Saudi Arabia.] *Alconbury, Aug. 8, 1991.*

SPITZER, Lt. Col. William F., USAF. [Hq. 21st AF, McGuire AFB, N.J., deployed as Deputy Commander for Airlift Forces, Riyadh, Saudi Arabia.] *Via telephone, McGuire, July 25, 1991.*

SPRATT, Maj. Thomas Bruce, ANG. [F-16A fighter pilot, 169th TFG , McEntire ANGB, deployed to Al Kharj AB, Saudi Arabia.] *McEntire, Sept. 6, 1991.*

STEPHENS, Lt. Col. Dennis E., AFRES. [Air Staff, Reserve Requirements, Pentagon, Washington, D.C.] *Pentagon, July 25, 1991.*

STEPHENS, Capt. Larry F., USAF [Operations Officer, 5th Mobile Aerial Port Squadron, 313th TAG, RAF Mildenhall, UK, deployed to Dhahran AB, Saudi Arabia.] *Mildenhall, Aug. 8, 1991.*

SUTER, Col. Richard, USAF (Ret.). [Consultant, Fort Worth, Tex.] *Pentagon, June 7, 1991.*

SWAIN, Maj. Daniel, USAF. [Commander, 625th Aerial Port Squadron, Torrejon AB, Spain. Did not deploy.] *Via telephone, Torrejon, Aug. 7, 1991.*

Tau, Capt. Phillip D., USAF. [Air Liaison Officer, 2d Brig., 2d Armored Cav. Reg., Ramstein AB, Germany, deployed to Saudi Arabia and fought in Iraq attached to the 1st Armored Division.] *Ramstein, Aug. 7, 1991.*

Tennyson, Maj. June E., USAF. [Assistant Chief Nurse, 20th TFW Hospital , RAF Upper Heyford, UK, deployed to Incirlik AB, Turkey.] *Upper Heyford, Aug. 9, 1991.*

Tice, Maj. Jeffery S., USAF. [F-16C pilot and Flight Commander, 612th TFS, 401st TFW, Torrejon AB, Spain, deployed to Incirlik AB, Turkey.] *Via telephone, Torrejon, Aug. 7, 1991.*

Travis, Maj. Joe, AFRES. [C-141B pilot, 701st MAS (Assoc.), Charleston AFB, S.C.] *Charleston, Sept. 8, 1991.*

Ustick, Capt. John C., USAF. [F-4G pilot and Flight Commander, 81st TFS, 52d TFW, Spangdahlem AB, Germany, deployed to Sheikesa AB, Bahrain.] *Spangdahlem, Aug. 6, 1991.*

Viccellio, Lt. Gen. Henry, USAF. [DCS/Logistics, Air Staff, Pentagon.] *Pentagon, May 15, 1991.*

Wagner, TSgt. Alan L., USAF. [NCOIC Load Planning, 5th Mobile Aerial Port Squadron, 313th TAG, RAF Mildenhall, UK, deployed to Dhahran AB, Saudi Arabia.] *Mildenhall, Aug. 8, 1991.*

Walton, Lt. Col. George W., USAF. [Squadron Commander, 561st TFS (Wild Weasel), 35th TFW, George AFB, Calif., deployed to Sheikesa AB, Bahrain.] *George, July 18, 1991.*

Warden, Col. John A., USAF. [Deputy Director for Warfighting Concepts, Directorate of Plans, Hq. USAF, Pentagon.] *Pentagon, April 16 and May 17, 1991.*

Waters, Maj. Charlie L., AFRES. [C-130H navigator, 94th TAW, Dobbins AFB, Ga., deployed to Sharja, United Arab Emirates.] *Dobbins, Aug. 11, 1991.*

Wetzel, Capt. Mark, USAF. [F-15E fighter pilot, 336th TFS, 4th TFW, Seymour Johnson AFB, N.C., deployed to Al Kharj AB, Saudi Arabia. Currently 334th TFS pilot.] *Seymour Johnson, May 31, 1991.*

Whiting, Capt. Gregory S., USAF. [Mobility Officer and F-16C fighter pilot, 612th TFS, 401st TFW, Torrejon AB, Spain, deployed to Incirlik AB, Turkey.] *Via telephone, Torrejon, Aug. 7, 1991.*

Whitmire, 1st Lt. Bradley J., USAF. [A-10 pilot, 511th TFS, 10th TFW, RAF Alconbury, UK, deployed to King Fahd International Airport, Saudi Arabia.] *Alconbury, Aug. 8, 1991.*

Williams, Col. Phil, USAF. [Director, Operations and Contingency Plans, AFLC.] Interviewed by Colleen Nash, *Air Force Magazine, March 14, 1991.*

Williams, MSgt. Steven M., USAF. [NCOIC, Avionics Test Station, 10th CRS, 10th TFW, RAF Alconbury, UK, deployed to King Fahd International Airport, Saudi Arabia.] *Alconbury, Aug. 8, 1991.*

Wolf, MSgt. Michael S., USAF. [Production Superintendent, 42d AMU 20th TFW, Upper Heyford, UK, deployed to Incirlik AB, Turkey.] *Upper Heyford, Aug. 9, 1991.*

Wood, Lt. Col. Steve, USAF. [Operations Officer (F-16C), 10th TFS, 50th TFW, Hahn AB, Germany, deployed to Al Dhafra AB, United Arab Emirates.] *Hahn, Aug. 5, 1991.*

2. Documents, Statements, and Reports

4th Tactical Fighter Wing History. Dec. 1, 1989.

"The 4th TFW (Provisional), Al Kharj AB, Saudi Arabia." A paper on Desert Storm operations. Undated.

"The 10th TFW Unofficial History of the Gulf War." RAF Alconbury, UK. May 11, 1991.

20th Tactical Fighter Wing History. Undated.

"The 26th Tactical Reconnaissance Wing History of the Gulf War." Zweibrücken AB, Germany. Undated.

"The 32d TFS Unofficial Gulf War History." 32d TFS, Soesterberg, Netherlands. Undated.

33d TFW Aerial Victories. Undated.

39th Tactical Group. Incirlik Air Base, Germany. Challenges Overcome During Operations Desert Storm and Provide Comfort. Undated.

52d TFW Unofficial History, Spanghdalem AB, Germany, 1991.

71st SOS Message: "Desert Storm Lessons Learned." May 17, 1991.

"The 322d Airlift Division Unoffical Gulf War History." 322d Airlift Division, Ramstein AB, Germany. Undated.

"The 401st TFW Unofficial History of the Gulf War," Torrejon AB, Spain 1991.

"The 406th TFW Unofficial Gulf War History." The 406th TFW, Zaragoza AB, Spain. Undated.

The 601st TCW Participation in the Gulf War. 601st TCW, Sembach AB, Germany. Undated.

The 7440th Composite Wing in Action. 7440th Composite Wing, Incirlik AB, Turkey. Undated.

Adams, Gen. Jimmie V., remarks at Air Force Association Symposium, Orlando, Fla., Jan. 30, 1992.

"AFLC Operations in Desert Storm," Air Force Logistics Command white paper, July 1991.

AH-64 Apache. McDonnell Douglas Helicopter Co. March 1991.

The Air Force and US National Security: Global Reach—Global Power, USAF White Paper, June 1990.

Air Force Association. *Lifeline Adrift: The Defense Industrial Base in the 1990s.* Aerospace Education Foundation. September 1991.

"Air Force Cross Recipients," TAC news release, Jan. 27, 1992.

"Air Force Logistics Command: the Pillar of Desert Storm Airpower," AFLC, June 5, 1991.

Air Force Performance in Desert Storm, USAF white paper. April 1991.

"Air Force Reserve," undated USAF fact sheet.

Air Force Reserve USAF fact sheet, 89-25, September 1990.

Air Force Reserve Desert Storm point paper, Nov. 25, 1991.

"Air Force Reserve Participation in Desert Shield/ Storm." Hq. AFRES fact sheet. Not dated.

"Airlift and US National Security: The Case For the C-17. An Air Force Perspective." Secretary of the Air Force, 1991.

Air National Guard Lessons Learned: Operation Desert Shield. Vol. I. NSA, Inc. March 8, 1991.

Air National Guard Long Range Plan. Air National Guard Bureau. May 1991.

Apache: After Desert Storm. McDonnell Douglas Corp. October 1991.

Arkin, William M., Damian Durrant, and Marianne Cherni, *Modern Warfare and the Environment, A Case Study of the Gulf War,* A Greenpeace Study, London, May 1991.

Arnot, Dr. Robert, CBS News Medical Correspondent, News Report, Feb. 25, 1991.

Aspin, Rep. Les, Chairman House Armed Services Committee, *The Aspin Paper: Sanctions, Diplomacy, and War in the Persian Gulf,* The Center for Strategic and International Studies, Washington, D.C., 1991.

___,"Assessing the War in the Gulf: Looking for the Answers in the Right Places," speech to Reserve Officers Association, Jan. 23, 1991.

___, "Desert One to Desert Storm," remarks to Center for Strategic and International Studies, June 20, 1991.

___, "The Military Option: The Conduct and Consequences of War In the Persian Gulf," white paper, Jan. 8, 1991.

___, "National Security in the 1990s: Defining a New Basis for US Military Forces," remarks to Atlantic Council of the United States, Jan. 6, 1992.

___, Press conference text, House Radio and TV Gallery, Aug. 17, 1990.

___, "The Role of Sanctions in Security US Interests in the Persian Gulf," white paper, December 1990.

___,"Swift, Phased Military Campaign Designed For Gulf," news release, Jan. 8, 1991.

"Aspin Grades International Performance in the Mideast," news release, Nov. 16, 1990.

B-2 Stealth Bomber. Global Reach-Global Power for the 21st Century. USAF briefing.

Berteau, David J., Deputy Assistant Secretary of Defense for Production and Logistics, Testimony to House Banking Subcommittee on Economic Stabilization. June 4, 1991.

British Ministry of Defence. Briefing Transcript. April 19, 1991.

Bush, Pres. George, remarks at Air University, Maxwell AFB, Ala., April 13, 1991.

___, "The Ultimatum." (Statement of Feb. 22, 1991).

Butler, Gen. George L., Air Force Association Symposium, Orlando, Fla., Jan. 31, 1992.

___, "The Desert Storm Strategic Air Campaign: What We Did and Why We Did It." Undated briefing.

___, "The Other Strategic Air Command: Desert Shield, Desert Storm and SAC's Conventional Role." Unpublished and undated monograph.

Bryand, Capt. Leah M. "Eglin Acquisition Community Contributes to Desert Storm Success." Eglin AFB, Fla. May 10, 1991.

"The C-17 In Desert Shield/Desert Storm: Impact." MAC briefing. April 13, 1991.

Carter, Capt. John, 511th TFS, written statement, May 1991.

CENTCOM Chronology of Significant Events, 1991.

CENTCOM Situation Report, Riyadh, Saudi Arabia, March 14, 1991.

Center for Strategic & International Studies. *The Gulf War: Military Lessons Learned*. July 1991.

Cheney, Secretary of Defense Dick, address to the Association of Former Members of Congress, April 17, 1991.

___, address to the Executive Club of Chicago, Nov. 7, 1991.

___, address to National Committee for Employer Support of Guard and Reserve conference, April 19, 1991.

___, Pentagon news conference, Sept. 17, 1990.

___, Gen. Colin Powell and Pete Williams, Assistant Secretary of Defense (Public Affairs), news briefings, Jan. 17–23, 1991.

Closner, Maj. Gen. John J., Chief of Air Force Reserve, statement to Senate Appropriations Subcommittee on Defense, April 1991.

Conduct of the Persian Gulf Conflict: An Interim Report to Congress. Department of Defense. July 1991.

Cougill, Brig. Gen. Roscoe M., CENTCOM Director of C^4, briefing to Armed Forces Communications and Electronics Association, June 4, 1991.

Crowe, Adm. William J., USN (Ret.), "Give Sanctions a Chance," testimony to the Senate Armed Services Committee, Nov. 28, 1990.

Davis, Paul K. and John Arquilla, "Deterring or Coercing Opponents in Crisis: Lessons from the War with Saddam Hussein," RAND report R-4111-JS, 1991.

Delaware Air National Guard Employer Appreciation Day. Greater Wilmington Airport, Wilmington, Del. Oct. 6, 1991.

"Desert Shield/Desert Storm/Proven Force." Maj. Gen. Philip L. Metzler, Jr., Hq. USAFE LG. Undated.

"Desert Shield—Getting Ready." *TIG Brief, AFRP 11-1*. The Air Force Inspection and Safety Center, November 1990.

"Desert Storm Aircraft Losses," Department of Defense Working Paper, March 20, 1991.

Desert Storm C41 Panel. AFCEA's 45th International Convention and Exposition. June 4, 1991.

"Desert Storm Casualty Reports Numbers 64, 70 and 74." Assistant Secretary of Defense (Public Affairs). March 3, 5, and 9, 1991.

"Desert Storm Communications." CENTCOM Briefing. Undated.

Desert Storm Point Paper, Air Force Reserve/REL, May 30, 1991.

Donnelly, Gen. Charles L., Jr., USAF (Ret.), Testimony to House Armed Services Committee, Dec. 13, 1990.

Donnelly, Dr. Chris. Lecture at USAF Checkmate. Nov. 25, 1983.

Dougherty, Gen. Russell E., USAF (Ret.), Testimony to House Armed Services Committee, Dec. 13, 1990.

Dunleavy, Vice Adm. Richard M., Assistant Chief of Naval Operations (Air Warfare), statement to Senate Armed Services Committee, May 9, 1991.

"F-15C and F-15E Performance in Operation Desert Storm," fact sheets, McDonnell Douglas Corp., Nov. 14, 1991.

"F/A-18 Performance in Operation Desert Storm," fact sheets and performance data. McDonnell Douglas Corp.

"F-117 Revolutionizes Warfare." Tactical Air Command news release. May 1, 1991.

Ferguson, Lt. Gen. Thomas R., Commander, USAF Aeronautical Systems Division, Air Force Association Symposium, Orlando, Fla., Jan. 31–Feb. 1, 1991.

Fitzwater, Marlin, "Criteria for Withdrawal," statement Feb. 22, 1991.

Fornell, Lt. Gen. Gordon E., Commander, USAF Electronic Systems Division, Air Force Association Symposium, Orlando, Fla., Jan. 31–Feb. 1, 1991.

Fries, Capt. Douglas R., letter, Dec. 3, 1991.

Gallagher, Lt. Col. Mike, USAF. CENTCOM Briefing. Riyadh, Saudi Arabia. Jan. 20, 1991.

Galvin, Gen. John R., Commander in Chief, US European Command, statement to Senate Armed Services Committee, March 7, 1991.

General Accounting Office, "Operation Desert Storm: the Services' Efforts to Provide Logistics Support for Selected Weapon Systems," GAO report NSIAD 91-321, September 1991.

___, "Operation Desert Storm: Transportation and Distribution fo Equipment and Supplies in Southwest Asia," GAO report NSIAD 92-20, December 1991.

Global Positioning System, information provided by Litton Electron Devices Division.

"GPS Success in Desert Storm," Air Force Space Command, August 1991.

The Gulf War: The 36th TFW Story. Bitburg AB, Germany. 1991

Harkin, Sen. Tom (D-Iowa), "The Obligation to Debate," speech, Jan. 14, 1991.

A Historical Perspective, 1947–1990: The United States Air Force and US National Security. USAF, 1991.

"History of Desert Shield/Storm, 50th Tactical Fighter Wing," 1991.

Horner, Lt. Gen. Charles A., USAF, CENTCOM Briefing, Riyadh, Saudi Arabia. Jan. 18, 1991.

___, "Reflections on Desert Storm: The Air Campaign," May 1991.

___, remarks to Business Executives for National Security Education Fund. Washington, D.C., May 8, 1991.

___, Senate Armed Services Committee, May 21, 1991.

House Armed Services Committee hearings on the Persian Gulf Crisis, Dec. 13, 1990.

"HQ USAFE Logistics (LG) History." Hq. USAF/LGX. Undated.

Hussein, Saddam, "The Mother of All Battles," Speech on Baghdad radio, Jan. 20, 1991, reprinted in Michal L. Sifry and Christopher Cerf, ed., *The Gulf War Reader*, Random House, 1991.

Jehn, Christopher, Assistant Secretary of Defense for Force Management and Personnel, statement to Senate Armed Services Subcommittee on Manpower and Personnel, April 17, 1991.

Johnson, Gen. H. T., Commander in Chief, Military Airlift Command, Air Force Association Symposium, Los Angeles, Oct. 25–26, 1991.

___, Pentagon press conference, Aug. 21, 1990.

___, speech to St. Louis Club. April 9, 1991.

___, speech to Wings Club. June 12, 1991.

Johnson, Maj. Gen. Robert B., USMC, news briefings, Riyadh, Saudi Arabia. Jan. 19–Feb. 2, 1991.

Joint Arab Forces Command Daily News Briefing. Briefers: Col. Ahmed Al-Robayan and Col. Ayed Al-Jeaid. Riyadh, Saudi Arabia. Feb. 14, 1991.

Kelly, Gen. Thomas (USA) DoD news briefing, Feb. 28, 1991.

Kemp, Capt. Dar, "A Minute Too Late—No SAR Required," unpublished statement, 511th TFS, 1991.

Killey, Maj. Gen. Philip, Director, Air National Guard, statement to Senate Appropriations Subcommittee on Defense, April 1991.

Kissinger, Henry A., "How To Cut Iraq Down to Size," testimony to Senate Armed Services Committee, Nov. 28, 1991.

Kutyna, Gen. Donald J., Commander in Chief, US Space Command, statement to Senate Armed Services Committee, April 23, 1991.

"Lift and the Future," MAC, June 10, 1991.

Loh, Gen. John M., Commander, Tactical Air Command, Air Force Association Symposium, Orlando, Fla., Jan. 31, 1992.

McDonald, Gen. Charles, Commander, Air Force Logistics Command, Air Force Association Symposium, Orlando, Fla., Jan. 31, 1992.

___, statement to Senate Armed Services Subcommittee on Readiness, Sustainability, and Support, April 17, 1991.

McPeak, Gen. Merrill A., Chief of Staff, USAF, Air Force Association Symposium, Orlando, Fla., Jan. 31–Feb. 1, 1991.

___, AFA Symposium, Orlando, Fla., Jan. 30, 1992.

___, Pentagon press conference, March 15, 1991.

___, "Reflections on Desert Storm." Undated Briefing.

___, "Tomorrow's Air Force: Reshaping the Future," USAF videotape, Nov. 18, 1991.

___, USAF news conference, Orlando, Fla., Jan. 31, 1992.

Mead, Paco and Sheik Nacke. *Tiger Tracks to Iraq.* 36th TFW.

Milhollin, Gary, "How Close Is Iraq to the Bomb?" testimony to Senate Armed Services Committee, Nov. 30, 1990.

"Military Airlift Command." Undated MAC fact sheet.

"Military Airlift Command Chronology of the Gulf War, MAC, Nov. 21, 1991.

"Military Forces in Transition," Department of Defense, October 1991.

Moore, Maj. Gen. Burton, USAF, news briefing, Riyadh, Saudi Arabia, Jan. 21, 1991.

Moynihan, Sen. Daniel Patrick, "Authorization for Use of Military Force," Joint Congressional Resolution, Jan. 12, 1991.

Neal, Brig. Gen. Richard I., USMC, CENTCOM briefings, Riyadh, Saudi Arabia, Feb. 6–12, 1991.

"Night Vision," Information provided by the Air National Guard Test Center, Tucson, Ariz.

Nunn, Sen. Sam, "A New Military Strategy," speech to US Senate, April 19, 1990.

Operation Desert Shield/Storm: Use of Navy and Marine Corps Reserves, GAO report, June 1991.

"Operation Desert Storm," A-10 Briefing at King Fahd International Airport, Saudi Arabia. Spring 1991.

"Operation Desert Storm" briefing, 23d TFW (P) and 345th TFW (P) King Fahd International Airport, Saudi Arabia, Spring 1991.

Operation Desert Storm. Unoffical history of the 48th TFW at Taif, Saudi Arabia. 48th TFW, RAF Lakenheath, UK. Undated.

"Operation Granby," RAF Fact Sheet. Aug. 19, 1991.

Patriot Fact Sheet, Raytheon, Jan. 9, 1992.

"Patriot Missile System," information and documents provided by US Army and Ratheon Missile Systems Division.

Pepin, Lt. Col. Greg, USA, CENTCOM Briefing, Riyadh, Saudi Arabia, Jan. 20 and 24, 1991.

___, and Rear Admiral Conrad C. Lautenbacher, Jr., USN, CENTCOM briefing, Riyadh, Saudi Arabia, Jan. 22, 1991.

Performance of MCAIR Combat Aircraft in Operation Desert Storm. McDonnell Douglas Corp. Undated.

Powell, Gen. Colin L., Pentagon press brieifing, Jan. 23, 1991.

___, remarks to Armed Forces Communications and Electronics Association, Washington, D.C., June 5, 1991.

Press Conference on Friendly Fire Casualties in Gulf War, Department of Defense Public Affairs, the Pentagon, Aug. 13, 1991.

Reaching Globally, Reaching Powerfully: The United States Air Force in the Gulf War. USAF white paper. September 1991.

Reserve Component Programs. Report of the Reserve Policy Board. Department of Defense. 1990.

Rice, Secretary of the Air Force Donald B., "From Desert Storm to Nuclear Drawdown," remarks at Air Force Association Symposium, Los Angeles, Calif., Oct. 24–25, 1991.

Rosamond, John B., Assistant Secretary of Defense for Reserve Affairs (Material and Facilities). Statement Subcommittee on Military Construction, House Appropriations Committee. March 13, 1991.

Russ, Gen. Robert D., remarks at Air Force Association Tactical Warfare Symposium, Orlando, Fla., Feb. 1–2, 1990.

"SAC Participation in the Persian Gulf War." Briefing by Hq. SAC. Undated.

Schwarzkopf, Gen. H. Norman, CENTCOM briefings, Riyadh, Saudi Arabia, Jan. 18–27, 1991.

___, CENTCOM briefing, Riyadh, Saudi Arabia, Feb. 27, 1991.

___, "Mother of All Briefings," CENTCOM briefing, Riyadh, Saudi Arabia, Feb. 24, 1991.

___, remarks to Cadets at West Point. May 15, 1991.

___, remarks to Midshipmen of the US Naval Academy. May 29, 1991.

___, testimony to Senate Armed Services Committee Hearing on the Conduct of the Gulf War. June 12, 1991.

Scott, Lt. Col. Mike, USAF, CENTCOM briefing, Riyadh, Saudi Arabia, Jan. 23, 1991.

"A 'Seamless' Airlift System," Military Airlift Command. July 23, 1991.

Silberman, Robert S., Principal Deputy Assistant Secretary of Defense for Force Management and Personnel, "DoD's Readjustment of Persian Gulf Veterans," Senate Veterans Affairs Committee, July 16, 1991.

Smith, Harry, CBS, "This Morning," New York, Aug. 2, 1991.

Solarz, Rep. Stephen J. "The Case for Intervention," speech, Jan. 10, 1991.

Stein, Robert M., "Patriot ATBM Experience in the Gulf War," Raytheon, Jan. 7, 1992.

Stevens, Brig. Gen. Pata IV, USA, CENTCOM briefing, Riyadh, Saudi Arabia, Feb. 1, 1991.

Support to Desert Shield and Desert Storm, General Dynamics report to Defense Logistics Agency, April 15, 1991.

"Tactical Air Forces: Needs for the 1990s," Proceedings of Air Force Association Symposium, Orlando, Fla., Jan. 31–Feb. 1, 1991. *Foundation Forum*, Aerospace Education Foundation, 1991.

The Tip of the Sword. Hq. USAFE Engineering, Services, and Air Base Operability. (ES&ABO). Undated.

Total Force Policy Study Group Report. Office of the Secretary of Defense. Dec. 31, 1990.

"United States Central Command." Fact sheet. Undated.

The United States Navy in Desert Shield/Desert Storm, Department of the Navy, May 15, 1991.

"USAFE Comptroller Contingency Operations," undated.

"USAFE Intelligence in Desert Storm," undated. Hq. USAFE.

"USAFE Medical Service Support to Operation Desert Storm/Proven Force," Hq. USAFE, undated.

"US Air Forces in Europe Chronology of the Gulf War," USAFE, Nov. 21, 1991.

"The US Air Force Today and Tomorrow," Proceedings of Air Force Association Symposium, Los Angeles, Calif., Oct. 25–26, 1990. *Foundation Forum*, Aerospace Education Foundation, 1990.

US Department of Defense Pool Reports, Riyadh, Saudi Arabia, Jan. 17–April 5, 1991.

US Navy TARPS publication #:B119173. Undated.

Williams, Pete, Assistant Secretary of Defense for Public Affairs, testimony to Senate Governmental Affairs Committee, Feb. 20, 1991.

___, news briefings. Jan. 20, 1991, Jan. 16, 1992.

___, Maj. Gen. Martin L. Brandtner, USA, and Capt. David L. Herrington, USN, DoD news briefing, Jan. 24, 1991.

___, Maj. Gen. Martin L. Brandtner, USA, and Rear Adm. Mike McConnell, USN. DoD news briefing. Jan. 26, 1991.

___, Lt. Gen. Thomas Kelly, USA, and Rear Adm. John McConnell,USN. DoD news briefings. Jan. 19–Feb. 1, 1991.

Ziemke, Carolyn F., "Promises Fulfilled? The Prophets of Airpower and Desert Storm," Institute for Defense Analyses, January 1992.

3. Articles, Books, and Other Sources

Achenback, Joel, "The Experts, In Retreat," Washington *Post,* Feb. 28, 1991.

"AH-64A Apache Attack Helicopter," *Army,* April 1991.

"Air Force Eyes Emerging Weapons For Possible Use In Mideast," *Aviation Week & Space Technology,* Sept. 3, 1990.

"Air Force Facsimile Machine Proves Worth In Desert Shield," *Aerospace Daily,* Dec. 13, 1990.

"Air Force Reserve," *Air Force Magazine,* May 1991.

"Air Force Roughs It More Comfortably," Washington *Post,* Jan. 28, 1991.

"Air Force Space Command," *Aviation Week & Space Technology,* Jan. 28, 1991.

"Airlifters For A New Age," *Interavia*, March 1991.

"Air National Guard," *Air Force Magazine*, May 1991.

Air Strike. Time-Life Books, 1991.

Albright, Joseph, "As War Looms, Pilot Makes Peace With Death," *Atlanta Constitution,* Jan. 16, 1991.

___, "Navy Pilots Stress Safety After Air Force Crashes," *Atlanta Constitution,* Oct. 13, 1990.

Alderson, Andrew and Grace Bradberry, "Captured Airmen Reveal Full Horror of Gulf War Torture," *London Sunday Times*, Dec. 29, 1991.

Al-Khalil, Samir. *Republic of Fear*. Pantheon Books, 1990.

Allen, Henry, "The Gulf Between the Media and the Military," Washington *Post,* Feb. 21, 1991.

Allen, Thomas B., F. Clifton Berry, Jr., and Norman Polmar. *War in the Gulf.* CNN/ Turner, 1991.

"Allied Units Surge Through Kuwait; Troops Confront Elite Force In Iraq; Bush Spurns Hussein's Pullout Move," *New York Times,* Feb. 27, 1991.

Anderson, Casey, "F/A-16, A-10 Slug It Out For Top CAS Billing," *Air Force Times,* Jan. 14, 1991.

Anderson, Jack and Dale Van Atta, "Government Stenographers," Washington *Post,* March 3, 1991.

Apple, R.W., Jr., "Allies, Aided By Weather, Intensify Bombing of Iraq; Hussein Restates Defiance" *New York Times,* Jan. 25, 1991.

___, "Allied Aides Scaling Back Claims To Have Achieved Air Superiority," *New York Times,* Jan. 22, 1991.

___, "Allies Step Up Gulf Air Offensive; Strikes Focus on Iraqis in Kuwait," *New York Times,* Feb. 12, 1991.

___, "Foe's Sea Threat Gone, Allies Say; 2 US Jets Downed," *New York Times,* Feb. 3, 1991.

___, "Invading Iraqis Seize Kuwait and Its Oil; US Condemns Attack, Urges United Action" *New York Times,* Aug. 3, 1990.

___, "Iran Promises Iraqi Planes Won't Rejoin the Fighting; Bush Says US Is Prevailing," *New York Times,* Jan. 30, 1991.

Armitage, Michael, "After the Gulf War," *NATO's Sixteen Nations,* February 1991.

Atkinson, Rick, "Allies to Intensify Bombing to Prepare for Ground War," Washington *Post,* Feb. 8, 1991.

___, "Gulf Ground War Not Felt Imminent," Washington *Post,* Feb. 7, 1991.

___, "More Stockpiles Needed, Three Marine Generals Say," Washington *Post,* Nov. 9, 1990.

___, "US Raids in Kuwait Intensify; POWs Taken," Washington *Post,* Feb. 21, 1991.

___, "US to Rely on Air Strikes if War Erupts," Washington *Post,* Sept. 16, 1990.

___, "War's Course Depends on Air Power," Washington *Post,* Jan. 17, 1991.

___ and Dan Balz, "Bomb Strike Kills Scores of Civilians in Building Called Military Bunker By US, Shelter By Iraq," Washington *Post,* Feb. 14, 1991.

___ and Ann Devroy, "Bush: No Immediate Plan to Start Ground War," Washington *Post,* Feb. 12, 1991.

___ and Ann Devroy, "Bush 'Skeptical' Air Power Can Prevail Alone in Gulf," The Washington *Post,* Feb. 6, 1991.

___ and Barton Gellman, "US Confirms 'Friendly Fire' Killed 7 Marines," Washington *Post,* Feb. 4, 1991.

___ and Molly Moore, "Pentagon's Prodigious Supply Line," Washington *Post,* Aug. 22, 1990.

___ and George C. Wilson, "Land War: Centerpiece of Strategy," Washington *Post,* Dec. 8, 1990.

Auerbach, Stuart, "US Relied on Foreign-Made Parts for Weapons," Washington *Post,* March 25, 1991.

___, "Wielding the Weapons For a New Kind of War," Washington *Post,* Jan. 28, 1991.

Augustine, Norman R., "How We Almost Lost the Technological War," *Wall Street Journal*, June 14, 1991.

Bath, Lt. Col. Ronald J., "Air Guard Covers Skies Over Desert Storm," *National Guard*, May 1991.

Bayles, Fred, "Saudi Pilot Says Downing Two Mirages 'Was Easy'," Washington *Post,* Jan. 25, 1991.

Beall, Maj. Jean Marie, "Air Guard Fighters: Training Prepared Them Well for Combat," *National Guard*, June 1991.

Bedard, Paul, "US Worries Israel Will Hit Iraq First," *Washington Times,* Jan. 11, 1991.

Beecher, William, "Use of Civilian Shields Starts A New Front In War Of Words," *The Minneapolis Star-Tribune,* Feb. 14, 1991.

Bird, Julie, "1st TFW Eagle Might Claim 1st Air Kill in War," *Air Force Times*, Jan. 28, 1991.

___, "AF Leaders Foresee Fewer, Costlier Weapons," *Air Force Times,* March 11, 1991.

___, "Weasels: Endangered Species Played Key War Role," *Air Force Times,* May 13, 1991.

Blackwell, James. *Thunder in The Desert.* Bantam Books, 1991.

Boatman, John, "Who Will Run The War?" *Jane's Defence Weekly,* Dec. 8, 1990.

Boyd, Lt. Gen. Charles G. and Lt. Col. Charles M. Westenhoff, "Request Unrestricted Climb," *Airpower Journal*, Fall 1991.

Boyle, Patrick, "B-52s Still In Fight And More Than Holding their Own," *Washington Times,* Jan. 18, 1991.

Braknis, Greg, "Reservists' Jobs Not Guaranteed in All Situations," *Washington Times,* Feb. 25, 1991.

Broder, John M., "Disquiet Grows in US Military Over Buildup," *Los Angeles Times,* Dec. 5, 1990.

___, "With Its Hostages Out, US The Revises List of Iraqi Targets," *Los Angeles Times,* Dec. 13, 1990.

___ and Melissa Healy, "Decision on More Troops Could Mean Long Standoff," *Los Angeles Times,* Oct. 27, 1990.

___ and Robin Wright, "Strategic Pause Would Follow Bombardment," *Los Angeles Times,* Jan. 16, 1991.

Boustany, Nora, "Iraq Charges High Civilian Toll in Air Raids," Washington *Post,* Feb. 7, 1991.

___, "Much of Baghdad's Population Fled Before Bombing Started," Washington *Post,* Jan. 17, 1991.

___, "'Show No Mercy,' Saddam Tells His Troops," Washington *Post,* Feb. 25, 1991.

Buchanan, Patrick, "Back in the Desert as Time Goes By," *Washington Times,* Oct. 15, 1990.

___, "Defeating The Foe's Strategy," *Washington Times,* Feb. 13, 1991.

Budro, Jessica Eve, "Desert Shield Plagued By Incorrect Deliveries, Inadequate Intratheater Airlift," *Inside the Pentagon,* Sept. 6, 1990.

Bush, President George, "Why We Are in the Gulf," *Newsweek,* Nov. 26, 1990.

Byars, Capt. Napoleon B., "Manpower, Missions, and Muscle," *Air Force Magazine*, September 1986.

Campen, Col. Alan D., USAF (Ret.), "Gulf War's Silent Warriors Bind US Units Via Space," *Signal,* August 1991.

Canan, James W., "Airpower Opens the Fight," *Air Force Magazine,* March 1991.

___, "The Electronic Storm," *Air Force Magazine,* June 1991.

___, "Global Power From American Shores," *Air Force Magazine*, October 1989.

___, "How to Command and Control a War," *Air Force Magazine,* April 1991.

___, "Lesson Number One," *Air Force Magazine*, October 1991.

___, "A Line in the Sand,"*Air Force Magazine,* November 1990.

___, "A Watershed in Space," *Air Force Magazine,* August 1991.

Capaccio, Tony, "Air Force's Eyes In The Sky Alerted Marines At Khafji, Target Convoys," *Defense Week,* March 18, 1991.

___, "War College Report Says Air Power Alone Won't Dislodge Saddam's Forces," *Defense Week,* Jan. 15, 1991.

Carnegy, Hugh, "Israeli Air Force Strains At Retaliation Leash," *London Financial Times,* Jan. 23, 1991.

Carus, W. Seth, "Missiles in the Third World: The 1991 Gulf War," *Orbis.* Spring 1991.

Charen, Mona, "US And Syria: Coalitions Make Strange Bedfellows," *The Chicago Tribune,* Feb. 11, 1991.

Chua-Eoan, Howard, "Defeat and Fight," *Time,* April 15, 1991.

"Claiming Nearly Half Air-to-Air Kills Beyond Visual Range, USAF Bucks Trend," *Inside the Air Force*, Aug. 30, 1991,

Clausewitz, Carl von. *On War* (1832). Edited and translated by Michael Howard and Peter Paret. Princeton University Press, 1976.

Clawson, Patrick and W. Seth Carus, "Iraq's Economic And Military Vulnerabilities," *Policy Focus,* October 1990.

Cody, Edward, "Iraq Shuts Down Air-Defense Radar," The Washington *Post,* Oct. 15, 1990.

Cohen, Roger and Claudio Gatti, "Stormin' Into The Gulf," *Sunday Times,* June 23, 1991.

Colaw, Becky, "Thunderbolt Hits Iraqi Chopper," *Citizen Airman,* February 1991.

Colimore, Edward, "With Troops Massed, War Is Hard To Avoid," *Philadelphia Inquirer,* Dec. 23, 1990.

Congressional Quarterly. *The Middle East.* 7th edition, 1991.

Cook, Nick, "Iraq-Air Power," *Jane's Soviet Intelligence Review,* October 1990.

Corddry, Charles W., "Should The US Announce Bomb Targets In Advance?" *Baltimore Sun,* Feb. 17, 1991.

Cordesman, Anthony H. and Abraham R. Wagner. *The Lessons of Modern War*. Vol II: the Iran-Iraq War. Westview Press, 1990.

Correll, John T., "Airpower, One Year Later," *Air Force Magazine*, February 1992.

___, "The Decision to Fight," *Air Force Magazine*, May 1991.

___, "The First Thirty Days," *Air Force Magazine*, October 1990.

___, "The Force at War," *Air Force Magazine*, March 1991.

___, "How Far Is Down?" *Air Force Magazine*, October 1990.

___, "The Indictment of Airpower," *Air Force Magazine*, January 1991.

___, "Let's Hear It for the Loggies," *Air Force Magazine*, August 1991.

___, "The Many Battles of Maverick," *Air Force Magazine*, March 1983.

___, "Nitwitness News," *Air Force Magazine*, April 1991.

Cowell, Alan, "Iraq's Military Reported Hurt but Not Halted In 5 Days' Raids; Vows Captives Will Be Shields," *New York Times*, Jan. 22, 1991.

Coyne, James P., "Bombology," *Air Force Magazine*, June 1990.

___, "Electronics for the Shooting War," *Air Force Magazine*, June 1985.

___, "Standing Up for Airpower," *Air Force Magazine*, September 1986.

___, *Strike Eagles.* Avon Books, 1990.

___, "Twos," *Air Force Magazine*, April 1986.

Cronkite, Walter, "What is There to Hide? Military Arrogance Keeps Public in the Dark," *Newsweek*, Feb. 25, 1991.

Cullen, Jane and Donna Haseley, "Defense Intel- Iraqis Have Soviet MiG-23s, BMP-2 Fighting Vehicles, T-72M1 Tanks," *Inside the Army*, Oct. 29, 1990.

Cullen, Tony and Christopher Foss, *Land-Based Air Defence, 1990-91*. Bofors Aerotronics, Lidingo, Sweden.

Cushman, Lt. Gen. John H., USA (Ret.), "Command and Control In the Coalition," *Proceedings, US Naval Institute*, May 1991.

Cutshaw, Charles Q., "Lessons From The Gulf—A Time For Caution," *Jane's Intelligence Review*, July 1991.

Daly, Kieran, "USAF Gulf Tactics Dictated by Integration," *Flight International*, May 8–14, 1991.

"Death In Baghdad: Grief, Not Guilt," *New York Daily News*, Feb. 15, 1991.

"Declassified Photos Show 'Have Blue' F-117A Predecessor," *Aviation Week & Space Technology*, April 22, 1991.

Defense 91 Almanac (Special Desert Storm Section). Department of Defense, September–October 1991.

Delmonte, Paul et. al., "Group of Fighter Pilots Opposes Having Women In The Ranks," *Air Force Times*, June 17, 1991.

"Desert Shield Becomes Desert Storm," *Defense & Foreign Affairs*, January–February 1991.

"Desert Storm Highlighted Sidewinder's Vulnerability to Soviet Threat," *Inside Defense Electronics*, Sept. 27, 1991.

Diehl, Jackson and William Claiborne, "Israel Sees Scuds Failing In Purpose," Washington *Post*, Jan. 25, 1991.

___, "Patriot Battery in Israel Intercepts Iraqi Missile," Washington *Post*, Jan. 24, 1991.

Donkin, Richard, "Three Arrested Over Alleged Iraq Exports," *London Financial Times*, Oct. 17, 1991.

Dornheim, Michael A., "F-117A Pilots Conduct Precision Bombing in High Threat Environment," *Aviation Week & Space Technology*, April 22, 1991.

Dorr, Robert F. *Desert Storm Air War*. Motorbooks, 1991.

Douhet, Giulio. *The Command of the Air* (1921). Reprinted by Office of Air Force History, 1983.

Dowd, Maureen, "US Weighs Timing Of Attack Against Iraq As Deadline Arrives And Diplomacy Fails," *New York Times*, Jan. 16, 1991.

Downer, Brig. Gen. Lee A., "The Composite Wing in Combat," *Airpower Journal*, Winter 1991.

Duffy, Michael, Dean Fischer, and Ron Ben-Yishai, "The 100 Hours," *Time*, March 18, 1991.

Duffy, Thomas, "Air Force Developing High Resolution SAR as One Method To Find Mobile Targets," *Inside Defense Electronics*, May 10, 1991.

Dugan, Gen. Michael, USAF (Ret.), "The Air War," *US News & World Report,* Feb. 11, 1991.

Dunn, Dr. Michael Collins, "The Iraqi Army: How Good Is It Really?" *The Estimate*, Jan. 17, 1991.

Dupuy, Col. Trevor N., USA (Ret.), "The Soviet Second Echelon: Is This a Red Herring?" *Armed Forces Journal International*, August 1982.

"Eagles over the Gulf," Desert Storm: the Pilots' Stories, Audio Renaissance Tapes, 1991.

Ehrmann, Eric and Christopher Barton, "Iraq's Deadly Arms Network," *Journal of Commerce,* Feb. 20, 1991.

Elgood, Giles, "Air Forces Could Win It Alone, British Military Says," *Washington Times,* Dec. 26, 1990.

Epstein, Keith C., "US Sent Arms to Iraq Despite Fears of Pentagon," *Cleveland Plain Dealer,* Oct. 7, 1990.

Evans, David, "American Pilots Deal With Stress of Combat," *Chicago Tribune,* Jan. 17, 1991.

__, "Desert's Sand Grinding Down American Aircraft," *Chicago Tribune,* Dec. 8, 1990.

__, "US 'AirLand' Plan: Smash Enemy Rear," *Chicago Tribune,* Feb. 10, 1991.

Evans, Cmdr. Frank, "Senior Aircrew Share Much More Than Memories," *Airman*, June 1991.

Evans, Michael, "How The SAS Took Out The Scuds—By Major," *London Times,* May 15, 1991.

Ewers, Col. Norman G., USMC (Ret.), "A Conversation with Lt. Gen. Royal N. Moore, Jr.," *Marine Corps Gazette,* October 1991.

"F-16As Prove Usefulness in Attack Role Against Iraqi Targets in Desert Storm," *Aviation Week & Space Technology*, April 22, 1991.

"F-117s In Saudi Arabia Not Vulnerable—DoD," *Defense Daily,* Sept. 21, 1990.

Fahad, Abdulaziz H., "In Defense Of Saudi Arabia," Washington *Post,* Feb. 12, 1991.

"'Filtering' Helped Top Military Leaders Get Proper Intelligence Information," *Aviation Week & Space Technology*, April 22, 1991.

"First Kill," Air Force News Service, Sept. 6, 1991.

Fishel, Edwin C., "The Mythology of Civil War Intelligence," in John T. Hubbell ed. *Battles Lost and Won*. Greenwood Press, 1975.

Fisher, Mark, "Crash of Gulf-Bound Jet Revives German Fears," Washington *Post,* Aug. 30, 1990.

Fisk, Robert, "Marching Orders For The Media," *Los Angeles Times,* Feb. 11, 1991.

Fitchett, Joseph, "US Gulf Lesson: Toxic Arms Devalued," *International Herald Tribune,* May 15, 1991.

Flanagan, E.M., Jr., "Before the Battle," *Army*, November 1991.

"The Forces of Desert Storm," *Air Force Magazine*, March 1991.

Frantz, Douglas, "Military Gets to the Gulf 'Fastest With the Mostest,' " *Los Angeles Times,* Dec. 30, 1990.

Frederick, Otto, ed. *Desert Storm: the War in the Persian Gulf* by the Editors of *Time*. Little, Brown. 1991.

Freedman, Lawerence and Effraim Karsh, "How Kuwait Was Won: Strategy in the Gulf War," *International Security*, Fall 1991.

Friedman, Norman, *Desert Victory: the War for Kuwait.* Naval Institute Press, 1991.

__, *The Naval Institute Guide to World Naval Weapons Systems.* Naval Institute Press, 1990.

"Friendly Fire: Killed By Error," *Norfolk Virginian-Pilot,* Feb. 5, 1991.

"Fuel Air Explosive Weapon In Iraqi Hands Is 'Serious Problem'," *Aerospace Daily,* Jan. 25, 1991.

Fulghum, David A., "USAF Nears Completion of 30 GBU-28s, Plans Advanced Penetrating Bomb," *Aviation Week & Space Technology*, May 20, 1991.

Gaffney, Frank, Jr., "Cease-Fire Pressures," *Washington Times,* Feb. 14, 1991.

Gaines, Mike, "Paper Tigers?" *Flight International,* Jan. 15, 1991.

Garrett, Lawrence III, Secretary of the Navy, Adm. Frank B. Kelso, Chief of Naval Operations, and Gen. A. M. Gray, Commandant of the Marine Corps, "The Way Ahead," *US Naval Institute Proceedings*, April 1991.

Gellman, Barton, "Air Strike Against Saddam Foiled by Storm," Washington *Post,* Jan. 25, 1991.

__, "Allied Air War Struck Broadly in Iraq," Washington *Post,* June 23, 1991.

__, "Gulf War's Friendly Fire Tally Triples," Washington *Post,* Aug. 4, 1991.

___, "Saddam's Waiting Game: Keeping Might In Reserve," Washington *Post,* Jan. 23, 1991.

Gersh, Debra, "Where's the Beef?" Editor & Publisher, Jan. 26, 1991.

Gershanoff, Hal, "EC in the Gulf War," *Journal of Electronic Defense,* May 1991.

Gertz, Bill, "US Breathes Easier as it Spots Iraq's Jamming Gear," *Washington Times,* Oct. 9, 1990.

___, "Webster: US Intelligence Played Crucial Role in War," *Washington Times,* May 23, 1991.

Geyer, Georgie Anne, "Simpson Vs. Arnett," *Washington Times,* Feb. 14, 1991.

Gibbs, Nancy, "Life on the Line," *Time,* Feb. 25, 1991.

Gillert, SMSgt. Douglas J., "The Incirlik File," *Airman*, July 1991.

___, "On the Homefront: A Nation Says Thanks," *Airman*, August 1991.

"Give Patriot Credit Where Due," *Aviation Week & Space Technology,* May 13, 1991.

Goodman, Ellen, "Nuketalk: Discussing The Undiscussable Is A Brutalizing Effect of War," *Chicago Tribune,* Feb. 17, 1991.

Goodrich, Lawrence J., "Air Force Was 'Ready' for Gulf," *Christian Science Monitor,* Oct. 12, 1990.

Gordon, Michael R., "Bases Used in Spain," *New York Times,* Feb. 1, 1991.

___, "Cheney Returning to Washington With the Call for More Bombing," *New York Times,* Feb. 11, 1991.

___, "Pentagon, Disputing Moscow, Says 500 to 1,000 Soviet Advisers Are in Iraq," *New York Times,* Sept. 26, 1990.

___, "Raids, on a Huge Scale, Seek to Destroy Scud Missiles," *New York Times,* Jan. 17, 1991.

___, "US Officials Conclude Air Power Is Not Enough to Defeat Hussein," *New York Times,* Jan. 27, 1991.

Graham, CMSgt. Vickie M., "Desert Rescue: a Tale of Two PJs," *Airman*, August 1991.

Grant, Gregory M., "Want to Demoralize The Enemy? Air Power Alone Isn't Enough," *Los Angeles Times,* Sept. 23, 1990.

Greeley, SSgt. Hope, "Desert Shield Air Force Demonstrates Global Reach, Global Power," *Desert Defender,* Oct. 5, 1990.

Greenway, H.D.S., "A Time For The US To Restate Its Aims In The Gulf War," *Boston Globe,* Feb. 15, 1991.

___, "The Case For Air Power," *Boston Globe,* Dec. 16, 1990.

Greiner, John, "Governors Want Current Level of Guards to Remain," *Daily Oklahoman,* Aug. 22, 1991.

Grier, Peter, "Joint STARS Does Its Stuff," *Air Force Magazine,* June 1991.

Griswold, Amy D., "The Store in the Desert," *Air Force Magazine,* June 1991.

Gross, Richard C., "Strategy Puzzles Experts," *Washington Times,* Jan. 31, 1991.

Grossman, Elaine M., "USAF Sent F-16s To Gulf Without Software To Aid 30-mm Gun Targeting," *Inside Defense Electronics,* Aug. 2, 1991.

Grossman, Larry, "McPeak Piqued Over Post Story," *Defense Week,* April 15, 1991.

Gugliotta, Guy, "Pool Reporting System Flaws Show," Washington *Post*, Feb. 27, 1991.

___ and Caryle Murphy, "Jets Roar Off in Darkness At Start of 'Desert Storm,' " Washington *Post,* Jan. 17, 1991.

"A Guide To Gulf Weapons," *Flight International,* Feb. 19, 1991.

"Gulf Lesson: Bolster Carrier Aviation," *Aviation Week & Space Technology*, April 22, 1991.

"Gulfspeak," *US News & World Report,* Feb. 18, 1991.

"Gulf Standoff Highlights Need For Speed as Well as Power," *Congressional Quarterly Weekly Report,* Aug. 11, 1990.

"Gunsmoke: TAC's Fighter Gunnery Competition," *Air Force Magazine,* May 1991.

Halberstadt, Hal. *Desert Storm Ground War*. Motorbooks, 1991.

Hammer, Joshua, "Will Israel Hit Back?" *Newsweek*, Feb. 11, 1991.

___ and Douglas Waller, "Special Ops: the Top-Secret War," *Newsweek*, March 18, 1991.

Hampton, Capt. Dan, USAF, "The Weasels at War," *Air Force Magazine*, July 1991.

Hanne, Col. William G., *AirLand Battle and the Operational Maneuver Group*, Strategic Studies Institute: US Army War College, May 16, 1983.

Hanners, David, "B-1B Bomber Missing From Gulf War Action," *Dallas Morning News,* Jan. 19, 1991.

Harvey, David S., "Col. Billy Mitchell and Army Aviation," *Rotor and Wing International,* December 1990.

Healy, Melissa, "Navy Riding Out Storm of Criticism of Gulf War Role," *Los Angeles Times,* April 28, 1991.

___, "Pentagon to Send Stealth to Mideast," *Los Angeles Times,* Aug. 16, 1990.

___, "US Orders Pilots to Try to Avoid Civilian Casualties," *Los Angeles Times,* Jan. 17, 1991.

___ and Mark Fineman, "US Forced to Defend Basic Targeting Goals," *Los Angeles Times,* Feb. 14, 1991.

Hedges, Michael, "Iraq No Match For US In Sky," *Washington Times,* Jan. 3, 1991.

Hehir, J. Bryan, "Baghdad As Target?" *Commonwealth,* Oct. 26, 1991.

Hehs, Eric, "Ordeal in the Desert," General Dynamics *Code One*, October 1991.

Henderson, Breck, "Rescue From Above," *Air & Space*, February-March 1992.

Henderson, Simon. *Instant Empire: Saddam Hussein's Ambition for Iraq*. Mercury House, 1991.

Hennessy, Juliette A. *The United States Army Air Arm.* Office of Air Force History: 1986.

Henry, William A. III, "Fencing in the Messengers," *Time,* Jan. 14, 1991.

___, "Sorting Out the Mixed Signals," *Time,* Feb. 18, 1991.

"High Success Brings Remainder of F-117s To Gulf Operations," *Aerospace Daily,* Jan. 28, 1991.

Hittle, Brig. Gen. James D., "US Needs Continued Support Of USSR In Gulf," *Navy Times,* Feb. 18, 1991.

Hoagland, Jim, "Grinding Down Saddam," Washington *Post,* July 14, 1991.

Hochbrueckner, Rep. George (D-N.Y.), "Naval Aviation is at Crisis Point," *Defense News*, Oct. 28, 1991.

Hoffman, David, "State Dept., Panel Spar Over Envoy," Washington *Post,* July 13, 1991.

___, "US Misjudgment of Saddam Seen," Washington *Post,* Aug. 8, 1990.

Hogan, Rear Adm. E. J., Jr., USN (Ret.), "TacAir = Naval Air + Marine Air," *US Naval Institute Proceedings*, November 1991.

Holder, Lt. Col. L. D., "Maneuver in the Deep Battle," *Military Review*, May 1982.

"Hollow Victory," *US News & World Report*, Jan. 20, 1992.

Holzer, Robert and Neil Munro, "War Pressure Inspires New Tactics, Weapon Use," *Defense News,* Feb. 18, 1991.

Hood, TSgt. Sarah L., "Home Away From Home: Making a Bare Base Operational in Saudi Arabia," *Airman*, March 1991.

Hopgood, Brig. Gen. M. T., Jr., USMC, "Experience: Handle With Care," *Proceedings,* US Naval Institute, October 1991.

Hopkins, A.D., "They Built Launch Pad For Stealth Fighters," *Las Vegas Review-Journal,* May 10, 1991.

Hopkins, Robert S. III, "Ears of the Storm," *Air Force Magazine*, February 1992.

"Horner: Manned And Unmanned Recce Needed In Next War," *Aerospace Daily,* July 1991.

Horrock, Nicholas M., "Mines Offer Hidden Challenge," *Chicago Tribune,* Feb. 15, 1991.

Housman, Damian, "High-Tech Weapons Prove Worth in Gulf," *Federal Computer Week,* Jan. 28, 1991.

Hoversten, Paul, "US Jets Keep Eyes on Iraq," *USA Today,* Aug. 17, 1990.

"How Iraq Uses Clouds to Hide its Missile Launchers," *New York Times,* Jan. 25, 1991.

Huey, John and Nancy J. Perry, " 'The Skunk Works' Specialty: Stealth," *Fortune,* Feb. 25, 1991.

Hughes, David, "Canadian Air Task Group CF-18s Train With Qatari Mirage F-1s," *Aviation Week & Space Technology*, Nov. 26, 1990.

___, "Success of Patriot System Shapes Debate on Future Antimissile Weapons," *Aviation Week & Space Technology*, April 22, 1991.

___, "USAF Adapts Off-the-Shelf Computer Hardware, Software in New Systems," *Aviation Week & Space Technology*, June 3, 1991.

Inman, Bobby R., Joseph Nye, Jr., William J. Perry and Roger K. Smith, "Lessons From the Gulf War," *Washington Quarterly*, Winter 1992.

"Intelligence Goofs," *Newsweek*, March 18, 1991.

"Iraq (Military Balance)," *International Institute For Strategic Studies* Annual 1990–1991.

"Iraqi Dead, Wounded Estimated at 50,000," *Baltimore Sun*, Feb. 19, 1991.

"Iraqi Vessel Steams Ahead Despite 40 Warning Shots," *Baltimore Sun*, Oct. 22, 1990.

"Iraq's Armed Forces Equipment," *Jane's Soviet Intelligence Review*, October 1990.

"Iraq's Secret Weapons," Washington *Post*, Aug. 16, 1991.

Isa, Miriam, "Saudis Said To Lose More Than They Gain From Crisis," *Washington Times*, Dec. 28, 1990.

Jackson, Robert. *Aerial Combat*. Galahad Books, 1976.

Jane's Air-Launched Weapons. Jane's Information Group, 1990.

"Japan's Checkbook War," *Christian Science Monitor*, Feb. 19, 1991.

Jehl, Douglas, "With The 1st Armored Division: Turning Into A Lean, Mean Fighting Machine," *Los Angeles Times*, Feb. 10, 1991.

___ and Melissa Healy, "Casualties Top 50% As GIs Stage Mock Frontal Attack," *Los Angeles Times*, Jan. 11, 1991.

Jolidon, Laurence, "Engineers 'Prepare' The Battleground," *USA Today*, Feb. 19, 1991.

___, "Support Unit's Key To Success: Mobility," *USA Today*, Jan. 17, 1991.

Jones, John P., "Luck, Not Skill, Helped Sealift," *Journal of Commerce*, May 20, 1991.

Kamen, Al, "Accounts Differ on Role of Bombed Iraqi Factory," Washington *Post*, Feb. 8, 1991.

Kane, Capt. Pamela A., "The Air National Guard is First to Answer Desert Shield," *National Guard*, January 1991.

Kaplan, Fred, "Pentagon Infighting Hinders Show of Force," *Boston Globe*, Sept. 1, 1990.

Keegan, John, "The Lessons of the Gulf War," *Los Angeles Times Magazine*, April 7, 1991.

"Keeping The Bomb From Saddam," *Business Week*, Jan. 14, 1991.

Kempster, Norman, "The Most Advanced—and Expensive—US Bomber Sits Out the War," *Los Angeles Times*, Jan. 26, 1991.

Kiernan, Vincent, "Air Force Alters GPS Signals To Aid Troops," *Space News*, Sept. 24–30, 1990.

Kifner, John, "Iraq Sets Oil Refineries Afire As Allies Step Up Air Attacks; Missile Pierces Tel Aviv Shield," *New York Times*, Jan. 23, 1991.

Killey, Maj. Gen. Philip, "Why is the Air Force the Leader in Total Force?" *National Guard*, January 1992.

"King Hussein's Mistake," *Baltimore Sun*, Feb. 13, 1991.

Kirk, Don, "Turkey Won't Attack Unless Iraq Hits First," *USA Today*, Feb. 11, 1991.

Kitfield, James, "Conventional Wisdom Revisited," *Government Executive*, August 1991.

___, "The Drive for 'Global Reach,'" *Government Executive*, December 1991.

Kolcum, Edward H., "Gulf War Training Deficiencies to Dictate Future of Simulation," *Aviation Week & Space Technology*, Dec. 16, 1991.

___, "Military Leaders Say GPS Success in Gulf Assures Tactical Role for Satellites," *Aviation Week & Space Technology*, May 13, 1991.

Krauthammer, Charles, "Bombing Baghdad: No Cause for Guilt," Washington *Post*, Feb. 14, 1991.

___, "The Ground War: Hold It Off," Washington *Post*, Feb. 1, 1991.

Kritz, Francesca L., "When Breadwinners Go Off To Fight," *US News & World Report*, Feb. 25, 1991.

Lamb, David, "US Missile Unit Confident Against Iraq Threat," *Los Angeles Times*, Dec. 8, 1990.

Lawrence, William P., "Lift Barriers for Women in Military," *San Diego Union*, July 22, 1991.

LeMoyne, James, "Meshing The Parts Of The Unwieldy War Machine In The Persian Gulf," *New York Times*, Oct. 21, 1990.

Lennox, Duncan, "Iraq-Anti-Ship Capability" *Jane's Soviet Intelligence Review,* Oct. 1990.

___, "Iraq-Ballistic Missiles," *Jane's Soviet Intelligence Review,* Oct. 1990.

Lenorovitz, Jeffrey M., "Air Crew Training, Avionics Credited For F-15E's High Target Hit Rates," *Aviation Week & Space Technology,* April 22, 1991.

___, "AWACS Fleet Supplied Surveillance Data Crucial to Allies' Desert Storm Victory," *Aviation Week & Space Technology*, June 22, 1991.

___, "US F-15s Log High Flight Rates In Saudi Arabian Deployment," *Aviation Week & Space Technology*, Sept. 10, 1990.

Leonard, Sgt. Michael C., "Former POW Talks About Confinement," *Capitol Flyer*, Andrews AFB, Md., March 22, 1991.

Lewis, Jac, "Aircraft Line Up For Turkish Bases," *Jane's Defence Weekly,* Jan. 12, 1991.

"Linked Systems Eyed As Solution To Friendly Fire Problem," *Aerospace Daily,* May 23, 1991.

Lippman, Thomas W., "Overnight, Iraq Is OPEC's Most Important Member," Washington *Post,* Aug. 3, 1990.

Lupo, Alan, "Iraq's Arsenal Well Stocked by the US and Its Allies," *Boston Globe,* Feb. 12, 1991.

Luttwak, Edward N., "Victory Through Air Power," *Commentary,* August 1991.

MacKenzie, Colin, "Desertions, Understaffed Units Eroded the Threat of Iraqi Army," *Toronto Globe & Mail,* May 19, 1991.

Mackenzie, Richard, "Apache Attack," *Air Force Magazine,* October 1991.

___, "A Conversation With Chuck Horner," *Air Force Magazine,* June 1991.

Macleod, Scott, "With His Country in Ruins, How Long Can Saddam Hang On?" *Time,* March 11, 1991.

McCain, Sen. John, "Weapons Proliferation in The Middle East," *Military Engineer,* September–October 1990.

McCarthy, Colman, "The Coward's Air War," Washington *Post,* Feb. 17, 1991.

McManus, Doyle and John M. Broder, "Attack Timed to Military and Political Needs," *Los Angeles Times,* Jan. 17, 1991.

McPeak, Gen. Merrill A., "The Laurels of Excellence," *Sea Power,* April 1991.

Maize, Kennedy, "12.5 Kilos of Highly Enriched Uranium Nets Saddam A Down and Dirty A-Bomb," *Defense Week,* Aug. 20, 1990.

"Major Air-to-Air Missile Systems," *Armada International,* December/January 1990–1991.

Malthaner, TSgt. John, NYANG, "Crew Brings 60 Children Through Scud Attack," *Airman,* August 1991.

"Marines Deny Allegations Harrier Performed Poorly in Gulf War," *Inside the Navy,* May 6, 1991.

Marr, Phebe. *The Modern History of Iraq*. Westview Press, 1990.

Matthews, Tom, "The Secret History of the War," *Newsweek*, March 18, 1991.

Maugh, Thomas H. II, "US Technology Has Worked In Air, Will It Work on the Ground?" *Los Angeles Times,* Jan. 22, 1991.

Mayer, Jane and Geraldine Brooks, "How Saddam Hussein Courted Mideast Press With Cars and Cash," *Wall Street Journal,* Feb. 15, 1991.

Maze, Rick, "Task Force Ordered To Tone Down Pro-Reserve Study," *Air Force Times,* June 17, 1991.

Meyer, Mark, "Going Up to Big Al," *US Naval Institute Proceedings,* June 3, 1991.

"Military Airlift Command," *Air Force Magazine*, May 1991.

Miller, Judith, "In An Island Playground In the Gulf, The G.I.'s Let Down Their Guard," *New York Times,* Dec. 28, 1990.

___, and Laurie Mylroie, "The Rise of Saddam Hussein," in Sifry and Cerf ed., *The Gulf War Reader*, 1991.

Miller, Timothy N., "Employer Support Starts With the Boss," *Citizen Airman*, August 1991.

Mitchell, Henry, "The Ideological Winds of Desert Storm," Washington *Post,* Feb. 15, 1991.

Mitchell, William. *Winged Defense*. G.P. Putman's Sons, 1925.

Mondey, David. *The International Encyclopedia of Aviation.* Crown, 1977.

Moore, Molly, "Air Force Bans Gulf Training Flight," Washington *Post,* Oct. 12, 1990.

___, "Allies Readjusting Tactics To Counter Iraqi Shifts," Washington *Post,* Jan. 24, 1991.

___, "Jet Crash Kills 2 More US Pilots in Gulf Region," Washington *Post,* Oct. 11, 1990.

___, "Pentagon Plans to Rotate Mideast Forces," Washington *Post,* Oct. 19, 1990.

___, "Reservists: Painful Adaption in Gulf," Washington *Post,* Dec. 28, 1990.

___, "Schwarzkopf: War Intelligence Flawed," Washington *Post,* June 13, 1991.

___, "US Jets Hit Iraqi Tank Convoy In Sight of Kuwaiti-Saudi Border," Washington *Post,* Jan. 30, 1991.

___ and Barton Gellman, "Pentagon's Quick War Plan Seen Facing Pitfalls," Washington *Post,* Jan. 13, 1991.

___ and Guy Gugliotta, "Clouds and Fog Over Gulf Region Knock Allied Air Raids Off Stride," Washington *Post,* Jan. 22, 1991.

___ and Guy Gugliotta, "US Pilots Warned on Complacency," Washington *Post,* Jan. 18, 1991.

Moore, Lt. Gen. Royal N., Jr., USMC, "Marine Air: There When Needed," *US Naval Institute Proceedings*, November 1991.

Morgan, Maj. Daniel K., "Behind The Scenes-Today-In War," *Air Force Journal of Logistics.* Summer 1990.

Morrocco, John D., "Allied Strategists Altered Battle Plans To Compensate for Dugan's Comments," *Aviation Week & Space Technology,* June 22, 1991.

___, "From Vietnam to Desert Storm," *Air Force Magazine*, January 1992.

___, "Looming Budget Cuts Threaten Future of Key High-Tech Weapons," *Aviation Week & Space Technology*, April 22, 1991.

___, "US War Plan: Air Strikes To Topple Hussein Regime," *Aviation Week & Space Technology,* Sept. 24, 1990.

"MSC Ship To Load Up For 3rd Trip To Mideast," *Journal of Commerce,* Oct. 24, 1990.

Muir, Jim, "Gulf War Masks Bitter Conflict Between Arabs," *Christian Science Monitor,* Feb. 11, 1991.

Munson, Kenneth, Paul Jackson, and Bill Gunston, "Gallery of US Navy, Marine Corps, and Army Aircraft," *Air Force Magazine*, July 1990.

Murphy, Caryle, "Iraq's War Defeat, Civil Strife Causing Crisis in Baath Party," Washington *Post,* July 16, 1991.

___, "US Military Victory Could Incite Political Backlash In Arab World," Washington *Post,* Jan. 15, 1991.

___ and Molly Moore, "Iraqi Border Attacks Kill 12 US Marines; Tanks, Troops Enter Saudi Arabia at 4 Sites," Washington *Post,* Jan. 31, 1991.

Nash, Colleen A., "Desert Storm Logistics," *The Chart Page, Air Force Magazine*, May 1991.

___, "Desert Storm's First Day," *The Chart Page, Air Force Magazine*, November 1991.

___, "GPS Success in Desert Storm," *The Chart Page, Air Force Magazine*, August 1991.

Neuffer, Elizabeth, "Taking Kuwait No Cinch, Pilots Say," *Boston Globe,* Feb. 21, 1991.

New, Maj. Terry, "Airpower Enters Decisive Era," *Defense News,* May 6, 1991.

Nickerson, Colin, "From a Patch of Dust to Pride of the Air Force," *Boston Globe,* Jan. 12, 1991.

Nordheimer, Jon, "At US Military Bases, Schools Help Children Deal With Gulf Crisis," *New York Times,* Sept. 19, 1990.

Nordwall, Bruce D., "Electronic Warfare Played Greater Role in Desert Storm Than Any Conflict," *Aviation Week & Space Technology,* April 22, 1991.

___, "US Relies on Combination of Aircraft, Satellites, UAVs for Damage Assessment," *Aviation Week & Space Technology,* Feb. 4, 1991.

North, Oliver, "High Tech Proves Itself on the Battlefield," *Wall Street Journal,* Jan. 23, 1991.

"Nuclear Attack On Iraq Urged By Ex-Governor," Washington *Post,* Jan. 1, 1991.

O'Connor Phillip, "Air Reserve Boss Hails Support," *Chicago Sun-Times,* Dec. 12, 1990.

Ognibene, Peter J., "The Plane That Would Not Die," *New Republic*, April 13, 1974.

Oliveri, Frank, "When the Airlines Went to War," *Air Force Magazine*, October 1991.

Opall, Barbara, "Official Urges Navy, AF to Further Blend Air Efforts," *Defense News,* April 1, 1991.

"OSD 'Lessons Learned' Questions USAF Claims of F-117, PGMs, F-16 CAS Success," *Inside the Air Force*, Nov. 8, 1991.

Osterlund, Peter, "Congress Closes Ranks Behind War Effort," *Baltimore Sun,* Jan. 17, 1991.

Ott, James, "Desert Shield Deployment Tests CRAF'S Viability," *Aviation Week & Space Technology,* Dec. 10, 1990.

Ottaway, David B., "Separate Commands Established for Arab, US Troops in Saudi Arabia," Washington *Post,* Aug. 29, 1990.

Owens, Mackubin Thomas, "Desert Storm and the Renaissance In Military Doctrine," *The Strategic Review.* Spring 1991.

Pasternak, Douglas, "Technology's Other Payoff," *US News & World Report,* Feb. 11, 1991.

Pasztor, Andy, "In Wake of Gulf War, New Military Fight Looms Over Use of Reservists and Women in Combat," *Wall Street Journal*, April 5, 1991.

___,"US Fighter Pilots Become Subdued As They Await Call To First Combat," *Wall Street Journal,* Jan. 16, 1991.

"Pentagon: Technology 'Not Here Yet' to Avoid Fratricide," *Aerospace Daily*, Dec. 13, 1991.

Perle, Richard, "A Ground War is Foolish," *US News & World Report,* Feb. 18, 1991.

Perret, Geoffrey. *A Country Made By War*. Random House, 1989.

Perry, William J., "Desert Storm and Deterrence," *Foreign Affairs,* Fall 1991.

"Persian Gulf War: Defense-Policy Implications for Congress," *Congressional Research Service*, May 15, 1991.

Pfister, Capt. Sue, "A Day in the Life," *The Vulture: Desert Dispatches,* Jan. 6, 1991.

Phillips, Don, "Blasting Pilots Out Of Harm's Way," Washington *Post,* Jan. 24, 1991.

Piccoli, Sean, "Decoy: Sophisticated Fakes Draw Enemy Fire," *Washington Times,* Jan. 25, 1991.

Pinkerton James P., "General Schwarzkopf's New Paradigm," *Policy Review.* Summer 1991.

Porteous, Holly and Joris Janssen Lok, "Gulf Crisis Hitting F-16 Training," *Jane's Defence Weekly,* Oct. 6, 1990.

Powell, Stewart M., "Desert Duty," *Air Force Magazine,* February 1991.

___, "Friendly Fire," *Air Force Magazine*, December 1991.

___, "More Voices From the War," *Air Force Magazine,* June 1991.

___, "They Deliver," *Air Force Magazine*, August 1991.

___, "Voices From the War," *Air Force Magazine,* April 1991.

"Press Zeal Could Help Saddam Unless Self-Restraint is Shown," Florida *Times-Union,* Jan. 25, 1991.

Price, Joyce, "Military Volunteers Cry, 'We Don't Believe In War,' " Washington *Times,* Dec. 14, 1990.

Priest, Dana, "Hostages Pour Out From Iraq, Kuwait," Washington *Post,* Dec. 10, 1990.

Primakov, Yevgeni, "The Inside Story of Moscow's Quest for a Deal" *Time,* March 4, 1991.

___, "My Final Visit With Saddam Hussein" *Time,* March 11, 1991.

"Procurement Can Be Fast, Flexible," Washington *Post,* June 14, 1991.

Ramdsdell, Capt. Steven, USN, "Impressions of the Desert Storm Carriers," *Naval Aviation News,* May/June 1991.

Record, Jeffrey, "AF's Future Bright After Gulf War Showing," *Air Force Times*, March 11, 1991.

___, "The Air War Missed Its Biggest Target," *Baltimore Sun,* Nov. 21, 1991.

___, "Gulf War's Misread Lessons," *Baltimore Sun,* July 9, 1991.

___, "Into the Wild Blue Yonder: Should We Abolish the Air Force?" Heritage Foundation, *Policy Review.* Spring 1990.

___, "The Seductive Charms of Air Power," *Baltimore Sun*, Jan. 30, 1991.

___, "The US Air Force in the Post Cold War Era," *Strategic Review.*, Spring 1991.

Reno, Robert, "General's Rosy Damage Reports Way Off Target," *Long Island Newsday,* Oct. 9, 1991.

Renton, Alex, "How RAF Tornados Were Lost in the Gulf," *The Independent*, London, England, May 24, 1991.

Rhodes, Jeffrey P., "The Black Jet," *Air Force Magazine*, July 1990.

Richardson, Doug. *Stealth*. Orion, 1989.

Riley, Michael, "War's Real Cost," *Time*, Feb. 18, 1991.

Rosenberg, Eric, "Navy Touts Its Many Roles And Contributions In The Gulf War," *Defense Week*, April 29, 1991.

Roth, Margaret and Sean D. Naylor, "End Game: To Win Must We Go to Baghdad? And What Then?" *Army Times*, Feb. 18, 1991.

Rountree, MSgt. Rick, "Don't Be Alarmed," *The Vulture: Desert Dispatches*, Feb. 27, 1991.

Rufford, Nick and David Leppard, "UK Firms Helped Iraqis To Build Long-Range Scud," *London Sunday Times*, Jan. 27, 1991.

Samuelson, Robert J., "Losing The Peace," Washington *Post*, Feb. 20, 1991.

"SAS Troops Steal a Missile In Kuwait," *London Times*, Jan. 13, 1991.

Sawyer, Kathy, "US Planners Rely Heavily on Sophisticated But Limited Electronic Spy Systems," Washington *Post*, Feb. 19, 1991.

Scarborough, Rowan, "Air Force Reports Almost Complete Gulf Deployment," *Washington Times*, Sept. 11, 1990.

___, "Bombing Numbs Iraq's Intelligence," *Washington Times*, Feb. 8, 1991.

___, "Dugan Ignored Advice," *Washington Times*, Sept. 19, 1990.

___, "Iraq's Million-Man Army Built During War of '80s," *Washington Times*, Aug. 9, 1990.

___ and Michael Hedges, "Jets Kill Iraqi Tanks; 'Mighty Mo' Attacks," *Washington Times*, Feb. 5, 1991.

Schell, Jonathan, "Victory Just Isn't What It Used To Be," *Long Island Newsday*, Feb. 10, 1991.

Schemmer, Benjamin F., "Six Navy Carriers Launch only 17% of Attack Missions in Desert Storm," *Armed Forces Journal International, January 1992.*

Schmitt, Eric, "Pentagon Seeks to Diminish Effects of Officer's Remarks," *New York Times*, Dec. 21, 1990.

___, "Persian Gulf Buildup Disrupts Medical Care Back in the US," *New York Times*, Dec. 19, 1990.

___ and Michael R. Gordon, "Unforseen Problems in Air War Forced Allies to Improvise Tactics," *New York Times*, Dec. 21, 1990.

Schrage, Michael, "War Project Shows Pentagon Procurement Can Be Fast, Flexible," Washington *Post*, June 14, 1991.

Schweizer, Peter, "Moscow's Hidden Gulf Agenda," *New York Times*, Feb. 18, 1991.

Scott, William B., "LANTIRN Provides Breakthrough In Night-Fighting Capabilities," *Aviation Week & Space Technology*, April 25, 1988.

___, "Triangular Recon Aircraft May Be Supporting F-117A," *Aviation Week & Space Technology*, June 10, 1991.

"Senate Appropriations Prohibits Guard Force Structure Reductions," *National Guard*, November 1991.

"Several Aircraft Accidents Have Occurred During US Military Activities in Mideast," *Aviation Week & Space Technology*, Sept. 17, 1990.

Sheliner, Capt. Earl, "Middle East Air Campaign Report," An Interview with Lt. Gen. Charles A. Horner, *Airman*, April 1991.

Shenon, Philip, "US Bombs Kuwait Oil Stations, Seeking to Cut Flow Into Gulf; More Iraqi Planes Fly to Iran," *New York Times*, Jan. 28, 1991.

"Should Mothers Go To War?" The Washington *Post*, Feb. 14, 1991.

Sia, Richard H. P., "In An Instant, Scud Transforms Troop Haven Into Hell," *Baltimore Sun*, Feb. 26, 1991.

Sifry, Micah L., and Christopher Cerf, ed. *The Gulf War Reader.* Times Books, Random House, 1991.

Sisler, Peter F., "Kuwaiti Refugees Bring Out New Wave Of Horror Stories," *Washington Times*, Oct. 19, 1990.

___, "Saddam's Country Hideout Ready If Shooting Starts," *Washington Times*, Jan. 9, 1991.

Skanchy, Col. Thomas, USAF (Ret.), "How Events May Have Unfolded," *Air Force Times*, Aug. 27, 1990.

___, "Scorecard For the Air War Is Basically Inaccurate," *Air Force Times*, Feb. 25, 1991.

"SLAMs Hit Iraqi Target In First Combat Firing," *Aviation Week & Space Technology*, Jan. 28, 1991.

Smart, Tim, Seth Payne, John Carey, and Eric Schine, "Smart Weapons: The Next Generation," *Business Week*, Feb. 18, 1991.

Smith, Berry D., "Stealth And Surprise: Training In The 1550th," *Rotor & Wing,* October 1990.

Smith, Bruce A., "Pentagon Weighs Key Reconnaissance Issues Highlighted by Gulf War," *Aviation Week & Space Technology*, April 22, 1991.

Smith, Gene, "1991 Kansans of the Year," Topeka *Capital-Journal*, Jan. 5, 1992.

Smolowe, Jill, "After the Euphoria, a Letdown," *Time,* March 25, 1991.

___, "Iraq's Horror Picture Show," *Time,* Feb. 4, 1991.

Solarz, Rep. Stephen J., "The Stakes In The Gulf," *The New Republic,* Jan. 7 and 14, 1991.

"Spacecraft Played Vital Role in Gulf War Victory," *Aviation Week & Space Technology*, April 22, 1991.

Spinney, Franklin C., "How Effective Was The Bombing of Iraq?" *Long Island Newsday,* March 25, 1991.

"SPOT Helped Bombs Find Iraqi Targets," *Military Space,* July 29, 1991.

Starry, Gen. Donn A., "Extending the Battlefield," *Military Review.* March 1981.

Steigman, Davis S., "Gator Navy Could Rain Attack On Shore," *Navy Times,* Feb. 25, 1991.

___, "Iraq Posed Anti-Air Threat Twice Warsaw Pact's," *Navy Times*, May 3, 1991.

Stone, M. P. W. (Secretary of the Army), "Apache: Swift, Sure and Deadly," *Wall Street Journal,* May 8, 1991.

"Strategic Campaign Focused on Targets and Cut Casualties, Pentagon Maintains," *Aviation Week & Space Technology*, Jan. 27, 1992.

"Success Behind the 'Storm' Front," *Jane's Defence Weekly,* May 11, 1991.

Summers, Harry Jr., "AirLand Battle Doctrine" *Washington Times,* Feb. 13, 1991.

___, "US—Stung In Vietnam—Is Determined to Complete the Equation of War In Gulf," *Los Angeles Times,* Feb. 13, 1991.

___, "War Beginnings And Endings," *Washington Times,* Jan. 10, 1991.

___, "What Can Go Wrong?" *Washington Times,* Jan. 25, 1991.

Sweetman, Bill and James Goodall. *Lockheed F-117A.* Motorbooks International, 1990.

Swinson, Jim I. Jr., "French Connection-Pilot Fights War From Ground," Eglin (AFB) *Eagle*, Aug. 2, 1991.

"Targeting Iraq's Worst Weapons," Washington *Post,* Jan. 22, 1991.

Taylor, John W. R., "Gallery of Soviet Aerospace Weapons," *Air Force Magazine*, March 1991.

___ and Paul Jackson, "Gallery of West European Airpower," *Air Force Magazine*, August 1990.

Taylor, Ronald A., "Iraq Sabotage Leaves Deep Scar," *Washington Times,* June 11, 1991.

"Technology Allowed Rapid Retargeting of Air Assets: Gen. Horner," *Aerospace Daily,* May 22, 1991.

"Technology On Target: Operation Desert Storm," *Leading Edge,* Air Force Systems Command, June 1991.

Thomas, Capt. Vincent C., Jr., USN (Ret.), "The Sea Services' Role in Desert Shield/Storm," *Sea Power,* September 1991.

"Tornado Pilots Upset By Lack of Gulf Medals for Navigators," *Daily Telegraph,* July 10, 1991.

Tow, Maj. Sheila L. "Victory Began With Airlift." MAC, June 12, 1991.

Trainor, Lt. Gen. Bernard E., USMC (Ret.), "The Persian Gulf in Reflection of The Iran-Iraq War," DACS Seminar, Nov. 30, 1991.

Trost, Adm. Carlisle A. H., "Maritime Strategy for the 1990s," *US Naval Institute Proceedings*, May 1990.

Turque, Bill, "Rethinking the Lessons of Desert Storm," *Newsweek*, Jan. 20, 1992.

Tyler, Patrick E., "Bush Orders Efforts Aimed at Toppling Saddam; Defense Secretary Dispatched to Saudi Arabia," Washington *Post,* Aug. 6, 1991.

___, "The Powell Cheney Relationship: Blunt Give-and-Take," Washington *Post,* Feb. 16, 1991.

"USAF, Lockheed: Jammers Flew During F-117 Missions, but Support Not Needed," *Inside Defense Electronics*, Dec. 6, 1991.

US News & World Report. *Triumph Without Victory: the Unreported History of the Persian Gulf War.* Random House, 1992.

"US Photo Satellites Can't Cover Gulf Full Time, Expert Says," *Aerospace Daily,* Jan. 3, 1991.

"US Says Iraq Has Devastating Fuel-Air Explosive," *Baltimore Sun,* Oct. 5, 1990.

"Viewing The Captured Pilots," Washington *Post,* Jan. 22, 1991.

Viorst, Milton, "Report From Baghdad," *The New Yorker,* June 24, 1991.

Vogel, Steve, "Soldiers Say Continue War Despite Iraqi Offer," *Army Times,* Feb. 25, 1991.

Vuono, Gen. Carl E., US Army Chief of Staff, "Desert Storm and the Future of Conventional Forces," *Foreign Affairs*, April 1991.

Walker, Paul F. and Eric Stambler, "...And the Dirty Little Weapons," *The Bulletin of the Atomic Scientists,* May 1991.

Waller, Douglas, "Armed for Action: High Tech Gizmos," *Newsweek*, June 17, 1991.

Walte, Juan J., "Air Battle Only Way to Win, Experts Say," *USA Today,* Aug. 8, 1990.

___, "US and Allies' Buildup Shifts to the Offensive," *USA Today,* Oct. 1, 1990.

Warden, Col. John A. III, USAF. *The Air Campaign: Planning for Combat.* Published originally by National Defense University Press, 1988, Pergamon-Brassey's 1989.

Warrick, Joby, "Downed AC-130 Found," *Air Force Times*, March 18, 1991.

___, "F-15 Eagles Officially Credited With 34 Kills," *Air Force Times,* April 29, 1991.

Watkins, Steven, "Schwarzkopf Rails Against GAO Visit to Persian Gulf to Examine Army's AH-64s," *Inside the Pentagon,* July 25, 1991.

Watson, Bruce W., Bruce George, Peter Tsouras and B.L. Cyr. *Military Lessons of the Gulf War*. Presidio Press, 1991.

Watts, Lt. Col. Barry D., USAF. *The Foundations of US Air Doctrine.* Air University Press, Alabama, 1984.

Weiner, Tim, "Waging a War of Deception," *Philadelphia Inquirer,* June 30, 1991.

Weiser, Benjamin, "Success of Ground War Tied to US Logistics," Washington *Post,* Feb. 24, 1991.

While, David, "RAF 'turned down two Gulf targets,'" *London Financial Times,* May 23, 1991.

Wicker, Tom, "The War In Arab Eyes," *New York Times,* Feb. 16, 1991.

Wickham, Gen. John A., USA (Ret.), "The Intelligence Role in Desert Storm," *Signal,* April 1991.

Wielawski, Irene, "Threat of Germ Warfare Brings a New, Frightening Equation to the Gulf Crisis," *Los Angeles Times,* Dec. 29, 1990.

Wild, James and Altun Kupri, "Six Days with the Kurds," *Time,* April 15, 1991.

Wines, Michael, "US Says Bush Was Surprised by the Iraqi Strike," *New York Times,* Aug. 5, 1990.

Winston, Emanuel A., "Only Smashing Iraq Can End The Gulf War," *USA Today,* Feb. 25, 1991.

Woodward, Bob. *The Commanders*. Simon & Schuster, 1991.

___, "Key Iraqi Assets Said to Survive 10-Day Air War," Washington *Post,* Jan. 28, 1991.

Woodward, Paul, "Operation Desert Storm," *Washington Times,* Jan. 18, 1991.

World *Defense Almanac*, Vol. 15, Issue 1, 1991.

The World's Missile Systems. 8th ed. General Dynamics, August 1988.

"Yates: War Showed Need For All-Weather Precision Guided Munitions," *Aerospace Daily*, May 16, 1991.

Young, Susan H. H., "Gallery of USAF Weapons," *Air Force Magazine,* May 1991.

Zakheim, Dov S., "Top Guns," Rating Weapons Systems in the Gulf War, *Policy Review.* Summer 1991.

Zimmerman, Peter D., "The Case of the Missing Air Force," *Los Angeles Times,* Jan. 22, 1991.

Zimmerman, Stan, "Gulf War Strengthens Navy Hand in Budget Wars," *Navy News & Undersea Technology*, Aug. 13, 1990.

Zoglin, Richard, "What Is Left of Kuwait?" *Time,* March 4, 1991.

Zuckerman, Mortimer B., "The Real Issue In the Gulf War," *US News & World Report,* Feb. 18, 1991.

Index

Note: *Page numbers in italics indicate illustrative material.*

About AFA and AEF ...

Air Force Association

The Air Force Association (AFA) is an independent veterans' organization whose objective is to promote greater understanding of aerospace and national defense issues. Among the ways AFA disseminates information are publication of AIR FORCE Magazine, sponsorship of a series of national symposia, and through educational outreach programs of its affiliate, the Aerospace Education Foundation. AFA is a grass-roots organization. Total membership is nearly 200,000 of whom more than 38,000 are Life Members. There are 328 AFA chapters in the United States and twenty-three overseas. The Association has 240 Industrial Associates, and its chapters have established ties locally with more than 2,700 businesses in the Community Partner program. The Air Force Association was incorporated in the District of Columbia on February 6, 1946.

The Aerospace Education Foundation

On May 1, 1956, the Air Force Association established the Aerospace Education Foundation (AEF). The Foundation was established as a nonprofit organization in order to formulate and administer AFA's educational outreach programs. AEF is supported through tax-deductible contributions. Over the past thirty-six years, the Foundation has made progress in educating AFA's members and the public about the critical role aerospace development plays in the modern world. By doing so, the Foundation promotes a greater understanding of technological advancements and aerospace education. AEF's scholarship programs also encourage higher education in the technological career fields. The Foundation sponsors symposia, roundtables, workshops, contests, and many other programs in order to highlight the full range of educational interest of AFA and to help meet the growing need for scientific and technological expertise.